Unbearable Lightness

Unbearable Lightness

A STORY OF LOSS AND GAIN

PORTIA DE ROSSI

**SIMON &
SCHUSTER**

London · New York · Sydney · Toronto

A CBS COMPANY

First published in Great Britain in 2010 by Simon & Schuster UK Ltd
This edition published in Great Britain in 2011 by Simon & Schuster UK Ltd
A CBS COMPANY

3 5 7 9 10 8 6 4 2

Simon & Schuster UK Ltd
1st Floor
222 Gray's Inn Road
London
WC1X 8HB

www.simonandschuster.co.uk

Simon & Schuster Australia
Sydney

Photograph credits:
pp. 265 and 267 © Davis Factor/D R Photo Management;
p. 269 © Albert Sanchez/CORBIS OUTLINE;
p. 271 © Lisa Rose/jpistudios.com.

A CIP catalogue copy for this book is
available from the British Library.

ISBN: 978-0-85720-411-0

Designed by Dana Sloan
Printed and bound by CPI Group (UK) Ltd, Croydon, CR0 4YY

To Ellen, for showing me what beauty is

Unbearable Lightness

PROLOGUE

E DOESN'T WAIT until I'm awake. He comes into my unconscious to find me, to pull me out. He seizes my logical mind and disables it with fear. I awake already panic-stricken, afraid I won't answer the voice correctly, the loud, clear voice that reverberates in my head like an alarm that can't be turned off.

What did you eat last night?

Since we first met when I was twelve he's been with me, at me, barking orders. A drill sergeant of a voice that is pushing me forward, marching ahead, keeping time. When the voice isn't giving orders, it's counting. Like a metronome, it is predictable. I can hear the tick of another missed beat and in the silence between beats I anxiously await the next tick; like the constant noise of an intermittently dripping faucet, it keeps counting in the silences when I want to be still. It tells me to never miss a beat. It tells me that I will get fat again if I do.

The voice and the ticks are always very loud in the darkness of the early morning. The silences that I can't fill with answers are even louder. God, what did I eat? Why can't I remember?

I breathe deeply in an attempt to calm my heartbeat back to its resting pulse. As I do, my nostrils are filled with stale cigarette smoke that hung around from the night before like a party guest who'd passed out on the living room sofa after everybody else went home. The digital clock reads 4:06, nine minutes before my alarm was set to wake me. I need to use the restroom, but I can't get out of bed until I can remember what I ate.

My pupils dilate to adjust to the darkness as if searching for an answer in my bedroom. It's not coming. The fact that it's not coming makes me afraid. As I search for the answer, I perform my routine check. Breasts, ribs, stomach, hip bones. I grab roughly at these parts of my body to make sure everything is as I left it, a defensive measure, readying myself for the possible attack from my panic-addled brain. At least I slept. The last few nights I've been too empty and restless, too flighty—like I need to be weighted to my bed and held down before I can surrender to sleep. I've been told that sleep is good for weight loss. It recalibrates your metabolism and shrinks your fat cells. But why it would be better than moving my legs all night as if I were swimming breaststroke I don't really know. Actually, now that I think about it, it must be bullshit. Swimming like someone is chasing me would have to burn more calories than lying motionless like a fat, lazy person. I wonder how long I've been that way. Motionless. I wonder if that will affect my weight loss today.

I feel my heartbeat, one, two, three—it's quickening. I start breathing deeply to stop from panicking, IN one two, OUT three four . . .

Start counting
60
30
10 =
100

I start over. I need to factor in the calories burned. Yesterday I got out of bed and walked directly to the treadmill and ran at 7.0 for 60 minutes for a total of negative 600 calories. I ate 60 calories of oatmeal with Splenda and butter spray and black coffee with one vanilla-flavored tablet. I didn't eat anything at all at work. And at lunch I walked on the treadmill in my dressing room for the hour. Shit. I had only walked. The fan I had rigged on the treadmill to blow air directly into my face so my makeup wouldn't be ruined had broken. That's not true, actually. Because I'm so lazy and disorganized, I'd allowed the battery to run down so the plastic blades spun at the speed of a seaside Ferris wheel. I need that fan because my makeup artist is holding me on virtual probation at work. While I am able to calm down the flyaway hairs that spring up on my head after a rigorous workout, the mascara residue that deposits under my eyes tells the story of my activities during my lunch break. She had asked me to stop working out at lunch. I like Sarah and I don't want to make her job more difficult, but quitting my lunchtime workout isn't an option. So I bought a fan and some rope and put together a rig that, when powered by fully charged batteries, simulates a head-on gale-force wind and keeps me out of trouble.

As I sit up in bed staring into the darkness, my feet making small circles to start my daily calorie burn, I feel depressed and defeated. I know what I ate last night. I know what I did. All of my hard work has been undone. And I'm the one who undid it. I start moving my fingers and thumbs to relieve the anxiety of not beginning my morning workout because I'm stuck here again having to answer the voice in my head.

It's time to face last night. It was yogurt night, when I get my yogurt ready for the week. It's a dangerous night because there's always a chance of disaster when I allow myself to handle a lot of food at one time. But I had no indication that I was going to be in danger. I had eaten my 60-calorie portion of tuna normally, using chopsticks and allowing each bite of canned fish to be only the height and width of the tips of the chopsticks themselves. After dinner, I smoked cigarettes to allow myself the time I needed to digest the tuna properly and to feel the sensation of fullness. I went to the kitchen feeling no anxiety as I took out the tools I needed to perform the weekly operation: the kitchen scale, eight small plastic containers, one blue mixing bowl, Splenda, my measuring spoon, and my fork. I took the plain yogurt out of the fridge and, using the kitchen scale, divided it among the plastic containers adding one half teaspoon of Splenda to each portion. When I was satisfied that each portion weighed exactly two ounces, I then strategically hid the containers in the top section of the freezer behind ice-crusted plastic bags of old frozen vegetables so the yogurt wouldn't be the first thing I saw when I opened the freezer door.

Nothing abnormal so far.

With that, I went back to the sofa and allowed some time to pass. I knew that the thirty minutes it takes for the yogurt to reach the perfect consistency of a Dairy Queen wasn't up, and that checking in on it was an abnormality, but that's exactly what I did. I walked into the kitchen, I opened the freezer, and I looked at it. And I didn't just look at the portion I was supposed to eat. I looked at all of it.

I slammed the freezer door shut and went back to the living room. I sat on the dark green vinyl sofa facing the kitchen and smoked four cigarettes in a row to try to take away the urge for that icy-cold sweetness, because only when I stopped wanting it would I allow myself to have it. I didn't take my eyes off the freezer the whole time I sat smoking, just in case my mind had tricked me into thinking I was smoking when I was actually at that freezer bingeing. Staring at the door was the only way I could be certain that I wasn't opening it. By now the thirty minutes had definitely passed and it was time to eat my portion. I knew the best thing for me in that moment would be to abstain altogether, because eating one portion was the equivalent of an alcoholic being challenged to have one drink. But my overriding fear was that the pendulum would swing to the other extreme if I skipped a night. I've learned that overindulging the next day to make up for the 100 calories in the "minus" column from the day before is a certainty.

I took out my one allotted portion at 8:05 and mashed it with a fork until it reached the perfect consistency. But instead of sitting on the sofa savoring every taste in my white bowl with green flowers, using the fork to bring it to my mouth, I ate the yogurt from the plastic container over the kitchen sink with a teaspoon. I ate it fast. The deviation from the routine, the substitution of the tools, the speediness with which I ate silenced the drill sergeant and created an opening that invited in the thoughts I'm most afraid of—thoughts created by an evil force disguising itself as logic, poised to manipulate me with common sense. *Reward yourself. You ate nothing at lunch. Normal people eat four times this amount and still lose weight. It's only yogurt. Do it. You deserve it.*

Before I knew it, I was on the kitchen floor cradling the plastic Tupperware containing Tuesday's portion in the palm of my left hand, my right hand thumb and index finger stabbing into the icy crust. I ran my numb, yogurt-covered fingers across my lips and sucked them clean before diving into the container for more. As my fingers traveled back and forth from the container to my mouth, I didn't have a thought in my head. The repetition of the action lulled the relentless chatter into quiet meditation. I didn't want this trancelike state to end, and so when the first container was done, I got up off the floor and grabbed Wednesday's yogurt before my brain could process that it was still only Monday. By the time I came back to my senses, I had eaten six ounces of yogurt.

The alarm on my bedside table starts beeping. It's 4:15 a.m. It's time for my morning workout. I have exactly one hour to run and do sit-ups and leg lifts before I get in the car to drive forty-five minutes to the set for my 6:00 a.m. makeup call. I don't have any dialogue today. I just need to stand around with the supercilious smirk of a slick, high-powered attorney while Ally McBeal runs around me in circles, working herself into a lather of nerves. But even if I'd had actual acting to think about, my only goal today is to be comfortable in my wardrobe. God, I feel like shit. No matter how hard I run this morning, nothing can take away the damage done. As I slip out of bed and do deep lunges across the floor to the bathroom, I promise myself to cut my calorie intake in half to 150 for the day and to take twenty laxatives. That should do something to help. But it's not the weight gain from the six ounces of yogurt that worries me. It's the loss of self-control. It's the fear that maybe I've lost it for good. I start sobbing now as I lunge my way across the floor and I wonder how many calories I'm burning by sobbing. Sobbing and lunging—it's got to be at least 30 calories. It crosses my mind to vocalize my thoughts of self-loathing, because speaking the thoughts that fuel the sobs would have to burn more calories than just thinking the thoughts and so I say, "You're nothing. You're average. You're an ordinary, average, fat piece of shit. You have no self-control. You're a stupid, fat, disgusting dyke. You ugly, stupid, bitch!" As I reach the bathroom and wipe away the last of my tears, I'm alarmed by the silence; the voice has stopped.

When it's quiet in my head like this, that's when the voice doesn't need to tell me how pathetic I am. I know it in the deepest part of me. When it's quiet like this, that's when I truly hate myself.

PART ONE

1

M Y HUSBAND left me.

Two months ago, he just left. He had gathered evidence during the trial known as couples' therapy (it was revealed to me during those sessions that not every woman's idea of a fun night out was making out with another woman on a dance floor; I was shocked), judged me an unfit partner, and handed down to me the sentence of complete sexual confusion to be served in isolation. I watched breathlessly as he reversed out of our driveway in his old VW van packed with souvenirs of our life together: the van that had taken me camping along the California coastline, that had driven me to Stockton to get my Maltese puppy, Bean, and that had waited patiently for me outside casting offices in LA. As he cranked the gearshift into first and took off sputtering down the street, I ran after him with childlike desperation, panicked that my secret, true nature had driven him away. And with it, the comfort and ease of a normal life.

In a way, I loved him. But I loved the roles that we both played a lot more. I had assigned him the role of my protector. He was the shield that protected me from the harsh film industry and the shield the prevented me from having to face my real desires. Standing by his side in the role of his wife, I could run away from myself. But as his van drove away from our California bungalow with its white picket fence, it became clearer with the increasing distance between me and the back of that van that I was, for the first time in my life, free to explore those real desires. The shield had been ripped from me, and standing in the middle of a suburban street in Santa Monica with new skin and gasping for air, I realized that as his van turned the corner, so would I. It was time to face the fact that I was gay.

I had met my husband Mel on the set of my first American movie, *The Woman in the Moon,* three years earlier. During the arduous filming schedule of the lackluster indie movie, which had brought me from Australia to the Arizona desert, I entertained myself by creating a contest between him and a girl grip whose name I forget now, mentally listing the pros and cons of each of the two contestants to determine who was going to be my sexual partner. The unwitting contestants both had soft lips and were interesting choices for me. Mel was my onscreen lover and his rival was part of the camera crew that captured our passion on film. Of these two people I had met and made out with, Mel was the winner. The fact that I chose him over the girl grip was surprising to me because, although I didn't show up to the movie a full-fledged lesbian, I was definitely heading in that direction. During my one year of law school prior to this movie, I'd had an entanglement with a very disturbed but brilliant girl that I guess you could call "romantic" if it hadn't been so clumsy. By this point, I knew that the thought of being with a woman was exciting and liberating, and the thought of being with a man was depressing and stifling. In my mind, being with a woman was like being with your best friend, forever young, whereas being with a man felt like I would be trapped in adolescence with acne and a bad attitude. So it was surprising to me when I felt a rush of sexual attraction to Mel. (It was surprising to him, too, when I showed my attraction by breaking into his Holiday Inn hotel room, pummeling his chest and face and stomach while yelling "I'm gay," and then having sex with him.) And not only was I attracted to him, I could actually imagine living with him and his black Lab, Shadow, in LA. The mere thought that maybe I was capable of living a "normal" life with a man made me so excited that at the airport lounge waiting for my connector flight that would take me to Sydney, Australia, via Los Angeles, I drew up another list of pros and cons, this time for getting off the plane in LA.

Pros: 1. Acting. 2. Mel.
Cons:

Almost immediately after arriving in LA, however, the rush of sexual attraction evaporated into the thin air of my wishful thinking. By the end of our first year together, despite my desire to be attracted to him, my latent fear of my real sexuality was simmering and about to boil. I was almost positive I was gay. So I married him. The fact that I got shingles the minute we returned from city hall didn't deter me from my quest to appear normal, and so my husband and I attempted a happily married life in an apartment complex in Santa Monica that had closely resembled the television show *Melrose Place*.

There was a girl who lived next door. She introduced herself to me as Kali, "K-A-L-I but pronounced Collie, like the dog. She was the goddess of the destruction of illusion." Kali. A quick-witted artist with elegant tattoos and a killer vocab that made you feel like carrying a notepad so you could impress your less cool friends with what you'd learned. Every night she'd be sprawled on the floor of her studio apartment sketching voluptuous figures in charcoal, her thick burgundy hair spilling onto the paper. Every night I'd excuse myself from watching TV with my husband to go outside to smoke. I'd find myself positioning the plastic lawn chair to line up with the one-inch crack where her window treatments didn't quite stretch all the way to the wooden frame so I could watch her. I would smoke and fantasize about being in there with her, but due to my being married and the fact she was straight and only flirted with me for sport, all we ever had together was a Vita and Virginia–type romance—a conservative exploration of hypothetical love in handwritten notes. She would often draw sketches of me and slide them underneath our door. Kali's drawings were so precious to me that I locked them away in the heart-shaped box my husband had given me one Valentine's Day. This was a contentious issue between Mel and me, which culminated in him demanding that I throw them away in the kitchen trash can while he watched. A seemingly endless succession of thick, wet tears dripped into my lap as potato peels slowly covered ink renditions of my face, my arms, my legs.

During my evening ritual of smoking outside and watching her, I was in heaven. Until invariably I was dragged back to earth forty minutes later by a loud, deep voice asking, "Are you smoking another cigarette?" Mel and Kali. Melancholy.

Strangely enough, none of this seemed strange to me. In fact, playing the role of heterosexual while fantasizing about being a homosexual had been my reality since I was a child. At age eight I would invite my school friends over on the weekends and convince them to play a game I called "husband and wife." It was a simple game that went like this: I, in the role of husband, would come home from a grueling day at the office and my wife would greet me at the door with a martini and slippers. She would cook dinner on the bedside table. I would mime reading the paper. Occasionally, if I had the energy to remove my clothes from the closet, I'd make her remove hers to stand inside the closet's long-hanging section to take a make-believe shower. The game didn't have much of a sexual component to it; we were married, so the sex was insinuated. But I carried the role-play right up until the end where I judged my friend on her skills as a wife by timing her as she single-handedly cleaned up the mess we'd made playing the game in my room. Although I was aware of that manipulation (I could never believe they fell for that!), I think my intentions behind the game were quite innocent. I wanted to playact a grown-up relationship just like other kids would playact being a doctor.

It was the beginning of a recurring theme until the day my husband left me: I was pretending to be in a heterosexual relationship while exploring a gay one. My husband leaving put an end to the flirtation between Kali and me, as I realized I was no longer playacting. I couldn't pretend to be in love with my next-door neighbor anymore, I had to find a relationship with someone who could simultaneously make me grow up and keep me forever young. I continued therapy, painted the kitchen walls, and fantasized about my future life: I would bring water lilies home to her every day in summer, I would wrap my arms around her waist as she chopped vegetables, I would fall asleep holding her hand . . .

OOD NEWS!" It was early to be calling my mother. It was 2:00 p.m. in Los Angeles, which would be only 7:00 a.m. in Australia, but I couldn't wait a second longer.

"Hang on a minute, darling. I'll just get my robe on and go to the other phone." I stood breathlessly next to my car in the parking lot of Fox Studios, my cell phone plastered to my ear. I was too excited to get in my car and drive.

"Okay, darl. What's going on? Did you get a job?"

"Ma. I'm going to be on *Ally McBeal*! I'm their new cast member!" I waited for the enormity of what I was saying to compute, but as the show hadn't yet reached Australia, I was forced to say this: "Ma, I'm going to be famous!" Both of us fell into an awe-filled silence. I was excited, wondering what my brand-new life would be like, but with the excitement came a little fear. I was gay. I knew that being openly gay wasn't an option, but what if they—the press, the public, my employers—found out? As the silence grew I couldn't help but wonder how I was going to pull this off. I could sense by the length of the silence that my mother was thinking the same thing, since the subject of my being gay had featured heavily in all of our recent conversations since my breakup with Mel six months prior. Although I had come out to my mother at age sixteen after she found *The Joy of Lesbian Sex* under my bed, I had thwarted my own attempts to convince my mother that

I was a lesbian by being with Mel, despite the fact that my dalliance with heterosexuality was actually the "phase" she referred to when talking about my lesbianism. However, after months of hour-long phone conversations, she finally accepted that I'd married Mel to try to bury my homosexual tendencies, and she was forced to take my sexuality seriously. Her feelings about it were a source of conflict to her and of confusion to me. She would be supportive to the point where she would talk to me about dating girls, but still she encouraged me to be secretive with everyone else, especially people who had the power to advance my career. She told me not to tell anyone, that it was "nobody's business," including close family members. She convinced me that because they were from another generation and from small towns, "They just wouldn't understand." So I didn't talk to anyone about it. I didn't want to upset anybody. I had upset myself enough as it was. And at least I could talk to her.

After several moments of processing and a few exclamations of pride, my mother gently said, "You'd better be careful, darling."

"Don't be crazy, Ma! I'm not even dating anyone. No one will ever know."

And with that, my excitement about my impending fame dropped substantially. Well and truly enough to allow me to drive. I got in the car but instead of going straight home, I drove down Santa Monica Boulevard to a popular lesbian coffee shop called Little Frieda's. I sat outside and savored every sip of coffee and every moment of being at a lesbian coffee shop, because after this, I knew I would never allow myself to go there again. The feeling that came with getting *the* job, the feeling that I had been chosen, was better than limply sitting outside at a lesbian coffee shop too afraid to glance at the other patrons much less approach them. I was not ready live my life as a gay woman. I had a career to establish. Being a regular cast member on a hit TV show was what I had been working toward. Famous actresses were special people. At last I had a chance to be special.

My quest to be special had begun in childhood. My aunt and uncle had lifelong family friends, the Goffs, and the Goffs had three daughters. The eldest, Linda, was a lawyer. The middle one, Amanda, was a physiotherapist. And the youngest, Allison, was a model. Despite the obvious accomplishments of her sisters, Allison received the lion's share of my family's interest, admiration, and praise. There wasn't a week that went by that my mother didn't point out "pretty Allison" in a catalogue that would be left in our mailbox to announce a spring sale or a winter bargain. Although I was quite a smart kid and received A grades, I needed something that would be exciting to people. I needed to be the girl my mother pointed to in a catalogue. So I decided to become a model.

I wasn't that pretty, nor was I particularly tall. I was okay looking, but I certainly wasn't good-looking enough to have one of those annoying stories that supermodels tell on talk shows about how the boys teased them at school and called them "horse face" and "chicken legs" because they were so skinny and "plain." When I was eight, Anthony Nankervis used to call me "Lizzie," which was short for "Lizard Eyes" because, as he brought to my attention daily in a singsongy chant, my eyes turned into slits when I smiled. Instead of deflecting the insult like any other eight-year-old would have done with a retort about his body odor, I took him to a mirror in the playground to explain to me what he meant. To the soundtrack of bouncing balls and playground squeals, I alternately smiled and frowned and to my horror, I discovered he was right. When I smiled, my eyes disappeared behind two fatty mounds of flesh. The memory of Anthony and me standing in front of that mirror, both of us horrified by my fatty, slitty eyes, is still quite painful. Being called a lizard is not something that ages into a compliment, not like having the legs of chicken.

If her parents had allowed her to pursue modeling, my friend Charlotte Duke would've been that girl with the annoying talk show story. Not only was she teased for being tall and skinny, her nickname was MX Missiles because she had unusually large breasts for her age. She had short, sandy hair, and freckles covered her face, and when she got head-hunted for an editorial modeling job (which her mother wouldn't allow her to take), I couldn't have been more shocked. She was so ordinary in my opinion. She never wore makeup or put hot rollers in her hair. She didn't care about fashion or models or magazines. At twelve, what I thought was beautiful was the cast of *Dynasty* and anyone who guest starred on *The Love Boat*, and I looked more like any of them than Charlotte Duke did. With Breck Girl hair and my face covered in makeup, I thought I could pass as pretty. What I lacked in looks and physique I made up for in determination. I took a series of Polaroid pictures of myself in various outfits, including an Indian-style headdress, in the front yard of our suburban house, and sent them to the modeling agencies in the big city, an hour from where we lived.

But I wouldn't just hit the Melbourne modeling scene unprepared. I'd already been to deportment school, as my mother thought having ladylike manners and learning about makeup was part of a well-rounded education. For me, it was one step closer to becoming a model. I finished first in the class at a runway show/graduation ceremony that took place in the daytime in a dinner-only restaurant, but with the win came my first flush of insecurity. There was a girl called Michelle who was a very close runner-up. We were locked in a dead heat and received the exact same scores for Correct Posture, Makeup Application, Photographic Modeling, and Social Etiquette, but due to my ability to walk better in high heels, I took the Catwalk Modeling category and took center stage to receive my trophy. (Actually, I stood on the carpet between two tables already set for dinner and received a sheet of paper.) But the fact that another girl had been close to taking my crown made my mother and me equally nervous and had a huge impact on both of us. I know this is true for me because I can still remember every physical detail of that girl, and for my mother because whenever my child-hood accomplishments are discussed she says, "Do you remember that girl in deportment school who nearly beat you?"

Two weeks after sending the photos off to various modeling agencies, I received a call from the Modeling World. A new agency by the name of Team Models had seen me in my Indian headdress and were impressed enough to request a meeting. This was slightly problematic because after my father's death three years earlier, my mother had taken a full-time job at a doctor's office and she couldn't just take time off to drive me to appointments. Although she enjoyed the idea of me modeling almost as much as I did, she told me that I had school and to be realistic. So I did what any twelve-year-old would do. I screamed and cried and told her that she was ruining my life. I threw a tantrum so violent and relentless that my mother was forced to take a sick day and chauffeur me to the meeting. As it was my foray into the working world, I felt I had to appear independent and in control, so I instructed my mother to wait in the car while I went in to "wow" them. I'd rehearsed just how I was going to do this several times in the two weeks since I'd sent the photos and waited for the call. My plan was this: I would walk through the lobby and would pause in the doorway of the agency, my hands on either side of the frame, and once I got the bookers' attention, I would simply announce my name, "Amanda Rogers." They would show me to a chair, tell me that I was the face they were looking for, and welcome me to the Team Modeling family. And honestly, that's not too far off from what actually happened. Except for "the face" line. And, thank God, no one saw me posing like a fool in a doorway. But even then I knew that it wasn't my looks that got me a place in the agency, it was my gift of gab. I talked them into it. I told them that I would be the youngest model on their books and that I would make them the most money. I told them that my look was both commercial and editorial. I told them that I was dedicated to modeling and would be professional and always available. They were no doubt amused by the bravado of this twelve-year-old, and because of that they decided to give me a shot. I collected my empty gray and pink Team portfolio and walked like a model back to the car where my mother was patiently waiting. "Good news," I told her when I got into the passenger seat. "I'm going to be a model." And from that day on, "good news" was the phrase I would use to tell my mother when I booked a modeling job, a TV show, or a feature. And "good news" remains the phrase that my mother is always the happiest to hear.

3

DURING THE week before I started work on *Ally McBeal*, my excitement about my new job continued to be overshadowed by my fear of public scrutiny. Perhaps it was because I was so judgmental of other actors when they were less than brilliant on talk shows or when their answers to red carpet questions didn't convey the information in a succinct, perfectly witty quip designed to politely yet definitively wrap up the probing interviewer. I've always had a gut-wrenching feeling of embarrassment for people when they say stupid things. And now I was going to be held up to the same scrutiny. Would I be smart enough? Would I have the perfect comeback to Letterman's subtle jab? Would I be able to convey intelligence and yet be fun and flirty with Leno? And how was I going to answer anybody's questions when my answers couldn't be truthful? Truthful answers to any of those red carpet questions would kill my career in an instant. "I'm not a fan of *Ally McBeal*. I've only seen one episode and I didn't really like it." Or "I actually don't follow fashion and I prefer engineer's boots to Jimmy Choos" wouldn't be a friendly introduction to the world, and I'm sure Joan Rivers wouldn't have appreciated it either.

The more I thought about it, the more I realized that David Kelley had made a mistake by casting me as the new hot lawyer on a show about hot lawyers and their romantic entanglements. When I met Mr. Kelley to discuss a possible role on *The Practice*, a show I had watched and liked, something I did—like flicking my hair off my shoulder or the way I crossed my legs—made him say, "I see you more for *Ally*." And with that I was Photoshopped into a poster of the cast, squeezed into the show's trademark unisex bathroom. He had made a mistake for sure. Apart from not being that fun and flirty leading-lady type that I knew the character had to be, I just wasn't good-looking enough for the role. I was okay at certain angles, but my profile was ugly (I knew this from years of modeling), and my face was very large and round. Plus the character itself was a stretch. Playing a commanding, intimidating professional brimming with self-confidence was going to be a challenge. While I would eagerly accept such an acting challenge for a movie, the thought that I had to play this powerful woman who was so vastly different from myself year after year on a television show was daunting. How was I going to stop my head from tilting in deference to the person I was talking to like I did in real life? How was I going to always remember to stand with my weight evenly balanced on two high-heeled legs when I usually slouch over my left hip in boots? Because I would need to fight every natural instinct to act out the character, I decided it would be immensely helpful if I could change my natural instincts. I would teach myself to stand straight and listen with my head straight. I would practice sounding self-assured and confident. I would stop sounding Australian and always sound like an American when I spoke. It was too late to get out of it, so I had to change myself significantly in order to get into it.

I needed to shed my old self and step into this new role. And not only did I have to become the role of Nelle Porter, I also had to play the role of a celebrity. But what did celebrities do? Did they go to parties, get spray-tanned, become philanthropic? Did they get their hair and makeup done when they went to the supermarket? Did they go to the supermarket at all? Becoming a celebrity felt like a promotion to me. The problem with thinking that being a famous actress was an upgrade from being just an actress was that I wasn't given a new job description. As an actress, I learned my lines, interpreted and performed them. But there was no actual profession that went along with being a celebrity. After observing Elizabeth Hurley's meteoric rise from actress to celebrity, I knew, however, that becoming a celebrity had a lot to do with clothes. As I didn't read fashion magazines or care which celebrity wore the same gown more elegantly than her counterpart, how was I going become the fashionable celebrity that the new cast member on *Ally McBeal* was expected to be? I was given this promotion but then left alone to guess how to do the job.

Either that or I could ask an expert.

When Kali wasn't painting, she was absorbing fashion. I say "absorbing" because watching her hunched over a *Vogue* magazine, her arms protectively wrapped around it, her body still and focus intent as she traced the outline of clothing with her eyes, you'd swear she was recharging her life source. You couldn't talk to Kali when she began to read the new issue of *W* or even talk to anyone else within her earshot. One summer, a houseguest of Mel and mine saw a plastic-wrapped *Vogue* on the stoop next door, unwrapped it, and was discovered by Kali reading it in the courtyard. After finding out that this thief who had robbed her of the great pleasure of being the first and only one to handle her subscriber's copy was a friend from my modeling days in Australia, Kali stood in our living room in a state of shock quietly repeating, "Who would do something like that?" Mel and I were forced to take sides: My husband, who leapt at the chance to argue with Kali, told her she was overreacting and took the model-friend's side. This argument was one of many that created the state of melancholy in which I lived, as there was a lot of tension between Mel and Kali. Naturally, I took Kali's side. Since she was a creative genius, whatever inspired her was obviously important. It didn't matter that I didn't care for fashion magazines.

With only one week before I had to begin work, I called Kali in a panic. Kali told me not to worry about buying new clothes and becoming someone else. She told me that they hired me for my uniqueness. She told me to be myself.

"A lesbian?"

Kali agreed to meet me at Banana Republic that afternoon.

Dressed in a vintage Iggy Pop T-shirt, faded black denim jeans, and a pair of perfectly worn black leather engineers' boots, I walked across the outdoor mall in the heat of a Pasadena summer toward Kali, who was waiting for me in the store. She was going to help me put together a new, casual, everyday look that I could wear to work. I chose Banana Republic, because I figured that I could find clothes there that would help me smooth out the sharp edges and make me look more like an acceptable member of society. Or at least less like an outcast.

I saw Kali among the racks of white and beige dressed in a uniquely cool vintage dress that made her stand out in the store designed to help you blend in. My face must have conveyed the anxiety in my head because Kali just skipped the "hello"s and hugged me, wrapping her arms around my waist, each hand clasping shirts on hangers that dug into my back.

"Thanks for doing this, Kals."

"It'll be fun. I don't know if you need me, though, Pickle. You have a great sense of style."

"Yeah, well, I don't see too many photos of leading ladies in ripped black jeans and engineers' boots."

I became self-conscious of my black clothing. No one else in the store was wearing heavy black boots or a black T-shirt. They were wearing summer prints and skirts.

"You could use some lighter colors for summer. Do you need skirts?" Kali was looking me up and down like I was more of a project than a friend.

"I guess so. I don't know. Do I?"

She smiled at me sweetly and handed me the two shirts she was holding.

"Why don't you start with these and I'll find you some pants. Do you like Capri pants?"

As I wasn't certain that I knew what they were, I shrugged my shoulders and took the shirts. I found a dressing room with a full-length mirror and tried on the shirts. I tried the white one and then I tried the other white one.

As I waited in the dressing room for Kali to bring Capri pants in a color palette that would make me more palatable, I looked at my body. I looked at my big thighs, the fat around my knees. I looked at my hips and how they formed a triangle where my butt hit the top of my legs. It wasn't the first time I was critical of my body. I'd spent my life trying to change it, but I was overcome with the feeling that it would continue to beat me—that I could never win the game of successfully changing its shape. I thought about the time when I was eighteen and got stoned and stared at my reflection in a sliding glass door, sobbing, "I will always look like this." Or when I met the voice when I was twelve and a modeling client asked me to turn around so she could see my butt. She asked me to take down my pants, turn around, and face the wall so she could see my ass. I faced the wall with my pants around my ankles for what seemed like a long time before she asked me to turn back around to face her. "I'm surprised your butt is so saggy for such a young girl," she said in a friendly, inquisitive tone. "Do you work out?"

You need to work out. That was the first thing the voice said to me. It was a very deep, male voice that was so loud and clear I wondered if the other rejected models in the elevator with me could hear it. It continued to ring like a shock wave long after it had delivered the message. And standing in front of the mirror in Banana Republic, I was ashamed to think that at twenty-four, it had to keep giving me the same message.

"What size are you?" Kali's innocent question sent me into a mild panic. Not because I thought I was fat other than the parts that needed reshaping, I just didn't know how sizes ran in the States. In Australia, the perfect size to be was a size 10. But in the States, what was the equivalent to a 10? I'd only ever shopped at thrift stores or at Urban Outfitters with their "one size fits all" clothing since coming to the States, or I wore the same old jeans and T-shirts I'd always had.

"What size should I be?"

"What do you mean?" She looked at me with an inviting smile on her face, like we were about to play a game. She had no idea that her answer to my question was going to change my life.

"What size are models?"

"Well, a sample size is usually a six." Kali knew a lot of things like this.

"Then I'm a six." As it turned out, I actually was a 6. Mostly. The Capri pants that were a size 6 were too tight, but I bought them anyway as incentive to lose a few pounds. It didn't occur to me to go up to the next, more comfortable size because as far as I was concerned, a size 8 didn't exist.

As I left the store with my new buttoned-down wardrobe I felt immobilized with anxiety. I sat down with Kali on a concrete bench in the outdoor shopping mall, bags strewn around my feet, feeling overwhelmed. I had a few days' worth of acceptable clothes, but what would happen after that? I would have to keep shopping for this new personality or else people would figure out who I really was, and if that happened, I would lose my career. Nobody would hire a lesbian to play a leading role. Ellen DeGeneres's TV show had just been unceremoniously canceled after her decision to come out, and there had never been any openly lesbian "leading lady" actresses—ever. In the three years I'd lived in LA, I'd realized that in Hollywood, there were really only two kinds of actresses: leading ladies and character actresses. The character actresses wait around all day in a toilet-sized trailer for their one scene, and they get to eat from the craft service table for free, while the leading ladies get the story lines, the pop-out trailers, and dinners with studio executives at The Ivy. Oh, and the money. No one I could think of in the history of acting had ever been a leading lady and a known homosexual, and being revealed as such a person would mean sudden career death. Of that I had no doubt whatsoever. After I explained this to Kali in order to convince her how stupid her suggestion to "just be myself" was, I was able to collect my new things and head to the shoe store for some high heels—something to wear with my size 6 clothes. As I walked across the mall wondering if the way I walked made me look obviously lesbian, my mind switched to thinking about how much weight I'd have to lose to fit comfortably into those Capri pants. And so I gave myself a goal. I would wear those pants on my first day of work.

The diet was a very simple one. It was the same diet that I had gone on six to eight times a year since I did it to get ready for my first fashion show. Instead of eating 1,000 calories a day, which seemed to be the recommended weight-loss calorie consumption for women, I ate 1,000 kilojoules. I was Australian, after all, and turning it metric was only right. It was a pun with numbers that I thought was funny. As 1,000 kilojoules was approximately 300 calories, I embarked on my 300-calorie diet with the goal of a one-pound weight loss per day and I would do it for seven days. I knew how it would work because I'd done it so many times before. The first three days I'd lose a pound each day, and then days four and five I'd see no movement on the scale, then day six I would lose a satisfying three pounds, and the last day I'd round it off with a one-pound weight loss to total seven pounds. It was a no-fail diet, and losing weight just before starting my new job seemed like the professional thing to do. Not only would it make me look fit and healthy, but because being thinner always made me feel more attractive, psychologically it would help me to feel confident and ready for whatever acting challenge I'd be given. And then of course, there was the imminent wardrobe fitting. If I could lose weight it would make the costume designer's job easier, since she could pick up any sample size for me and know that I'd fit into it. Losing weight was the silent agreement I'd made with the producers, and I was ready to keep up my end of the deal.

4

AS I pulled into my parking space out front of a sound stage on Kelley Land, aka Manhattan Beach Studios, I was dizzy with excitement and nerves. It was my first day at work on the set of *Ally McBeal*. I got out of the car, smoothed out the wrinkles in my comfortably fitting Capri pants, and looked around. It was a very austere and sterile lot. It had been built recently and accommodated David Kelley's production company, and it appeared that the final touches that would make it look habitable still needed to be done. The studio lots I had worked on in Hollywood and in Burbank were bustling with people walking in and out of a café or from a newsstand manned by a colorful employee who knew every actor and producer who went there for *Variety* or the *LA Times*. But there were no people at Manhattan Beach Studios, only cars. There was no commissary, no park where you could read a novel at lunch under a tree. In fact there were no plants or trees. The buildings were huge, monolithic peach rectangles with no overhangs for shade, so the sun bounced off the clean white pavement and onto the windowless structures making the whole lot look like every corner was lit by a spotlight. In Kelley Land there wasn't a shadow in which to hide. It looked like headquarters for a research and development company where scientific tests were conducted under the intense scrutiny of plant managers, unseen by the outside world. Either that or a minimum-security prison.

I walked out of the late-morning summer heat and into the hallway of the air-conditioned building looking for the dressing room with my name on the door. The first door read Peter MacNicol, next was Greg Germann, and then there it was: Portia de Rossi. I had arrived. It was the nicest dressing room I'd ever had. There was a deep green sofa and matching chair, a desk with a desk chair, and a bathroom with a shower. Everything was squeaky clean and new. No actor had ever been here before, it was a sterile environment, and that was comforting and yet also somehow disquieting. No actor had rehearsed her dialogue, paced the room in anticipation of a scene, or smoked cigarettes out of boredom or nerves in this dressing room. There were no memories or stale cigarette smoke trapped in these walls. It was just going to be an alternately anxious and bored Portia de Rossi wanting to smoke but unable to smoke, looking at her flawed reflection in the full-length closet door mirrors.

I threw my bag on the sofa and checked my watch. It was 10:30. I was early. At 11:00 I had a wardrobe fitting and then at 12:00 I would begin makeup and hair. The reason for wanting to be early was less about first-day jitters than it was about my appearance. Despite being told as a child model to show up to shoots with a clean face and clean hair, I have never turned up to a job with a freshly scrubbed face or just-hopped-out-of-the-shower hair. I just got better at concealing it. I loved concealer. The magic oily stick of beige makeup was as essential to me as oxygen. I could have half my face covered with the stuff and still look like I was clean and naturally flawless. Of course, this careful application of concealer was painstaking and time consuming (trying to cover up shameful secrets always is), and it was for this reason I arrived a full half hour early. Naturally, before leaving home, I'd made the first pass over my red, blotchy skin, dark circles, blemishes, and scars of blemishes, but the drive across town was a long one, and I had anticipated that I would need to patch the areas where the heat had melted away my artistry. After I was satisfied that I'd done all I could to be the attractive, new actress that the wardrobe girls were no doubt expecting to meet, I headed over to the wardrobe room. It was in another building quite far from my dressing room and I roamed around in search of it for what seemed like an eternity. Finally, I was intercepted by a production assistant and escorted the rest of the way.

The PA wore shorts and sneakers. She looked flustered and told me that she'd been frantically looking for me. She told me that she was scheduled to be waiting for me at my parking space at 10:45. The more she talked (who feels confident enough about their legs to show them off without the help of high heels?) the more stupid I felt for arriving so early and for leaving my dressing room before a PA came to get me. *Damn it. All I had to do on my first day was appear to be professional, to know what I'm doing, and I have already given myself away.* By the time I got to the wardrobe rooms, I had a knot in my gut. I was dying for a cigarette. What was a lesbian doing here on this show playing an ice-cold attorney in the courtroom who would, no doubt, be hot in the bedroom in an upcoming episode? Would I fit into a size 6 suit?

I hovered at the doorway of the costume designer's office, waiting for her to acknowledge me as she sat at her desk. When she turned to find me standing at the door, I could see that she was on the phone.

"Come in," she mouthed, gesturing for me to enter. I walked across the threshold and into the rooms that would be the main stage for the drama my life was about to become—a drama in which I wrote, directed, produced, and played all parts: my very own one-woman show. I stood in the middle of the room since racks of clothing flanked the walls and took up most of the space, leaving only a small, carpeted square in the center like a tiny stage, but instead of facing an audience, it faced a large, full-length mirror.

"Hi. I'm Portia." I extended my hand and smiled at her as she hung up the phone and walked toward me from her desk.

"It's nice to meet you in person. I'm Vera. Welcome to the show."

Vera and I had met over the phone when she asked for my measurements.

"Thirty-four, twenty-four, thirty-five."

That sounded better than the truth, which started at around 32 and probably ended up around 38. I stopped measuring after my first interview with my modeling agents at age twelve when they told me to call them with my bust, waist, and hip measurements when I got home.

"Thirty-two, twenty-seven, thirty-seven," I had told the Team Modeling booker.

"Are you sure?" A long silence followed, then my next instruction. "Well, just tell people you're thirty-four, twenty-four, thirty-five, ok? We'll put those measurements on your card."

Now I stood center-stage in the *Ally McBeal* fitting room in front of the mirror, dressed in a pinstriped suit with a nipped-in waist and a large, rounded lapel. All the suits I had tried so far had fit. I was relieved. After all my anxiety preceding the fitting, I felt relaxed. I admired my reflection in the mirror. The suit I was wearing was my favorite for no other reason than it was a size 4. I was almost giddy with excitement. For my first episode of *Ally McBeal*, I would wear a size 4.

"Ugh. Take that off. That's horrible."

As I began to reluctantly take off the size 4 suit, Vera walked to her desk and picked up a large folder. I could see that the script inside had colored tabs and notes all down the margins.

"I think your character would only wear monochromatic suits. Conservative. Do you think there would be a hint of sexiness to her—like, say, a slit in the leg of a pencil skirt?"

"Umm. Sure." I thought Nelle should have some sexiness and I guessed a pencil skirt was really the only way to make a business suit sexy. I was worried, though, that my hips looked big in pencil skirts.

"What do you think she'd wear on weekends?"

I attempted to sound like I had given the character's costumes a great deal of thought, but it was immediately obvious to me that Vera's exploration of my character was far more extensive than my own. To my surprise, her preparedness was the only unnerving part of the whole fitting. I was so busy trying to fit into the size 6 suit, to be the perfect-looking addition to TV's hottest legal show, I'd forgotten to think about the clothes as an expression of the character I was about to portray, potentially for years. She closed her folder and walked back to her desk.

"Well, we've got a pretty good start. Let's just go with what we have for this week and we'll figure the rest out later."

I put my Capri pants back on, thanked Vera, and headed out. I left the fitting and was escorted by the PA to the makeup trailer in a state of mild shock. I was amazed that I could ever walk out of a fitting feeling ashamed for something other than my imperfect body. Still, I had passed my first big test of fitting in, and in the case of clothes, fitting into a sample size, and I was on to my second. My body had passed the test, next was my face.

As I shook the hand of the makeup artist, Sarah, and looked her in the eyes, I registered her pupils dilating to begin their scan across my face. Could she see imperfections? Discoloration? Makeup?

"Are you wearing makeup?" The question was straightforward, but her tone was slightly incredulous. Enough to make me feel very embarrassed.

"No." When attacked, defend by lying.

"Sit down. Let's get started. Is there anything I should know before I start?"

"No. You're the expert. I'm sure it'll be great."

The truth was, I wasn't so sure. Practically every time I sat in a makeup chair, I'd look worse at the end than I did before we started. But I had never really learned what it was that made me look bad, plus even if I had, I didn't feel it was my place to tell a makeup artist how to do her job, much less the head of the makeup department for *Ally McBeal*. As I was shuffled back and forth between the two chairs due to the hair and makeup artists alternately being needed on set (God, what was going on in there in the scene before mine? What was I about to face?), I applied a similar philosophy of trusting the experts in the hair department to do their job. After we collectively decided that Nelle Porter should wear her hair in a bun, how my hair was pulled back and all other decisions were my hairstylist's business. After all, I was the new girl. I didn't want to make a scene or stand out, I just wanted to fit in. I wanted everyone I met to think of me as quiet and professional. I wanted the headline to be "how the new character melted seamlessly into the ensemble cast." And now that I'd left Portia on the floors of the hair, makeup, and wardrobe rooms, it was time for Nelle Porter to meet the cast.

5

Everyone. I'd like to introduce the newest member of Cage and
Fish. Please welcome Nelle Porter.

ELAINE

(to Ally and Georgia)

Just so we're clear, we hate her, right?

ALLY AND GEORGIA

(nodding in agreement)

Uh huh.

"Cut. Back to one."

I stood on the stairs of the law office set staring out into the crowd.
There they were. Ally, Billy, Georgia, Elaine, Fish—assembled on the
floor of the office foyer, looking up at me standing midway down the
staircase preparing to deliver a speech about how I was going to breathe
new life into the firm and shake things up around the place. I hadn't
even met them yet. I just stood on the staircase smiling awkwardly at
each cast member as they tentatively smiled and waved, sizing me up
just as their characters were directed to do in the script. I was meeting
the lawyers as Nelle Porter for the first time, and I was meeting the cast
as Portia de Rossi in the same way, from the same step, and we were
all carefully and awkwardly smiling and waving. How ironic that my

character was supposed to be intimidating to these people, and yet I was too scared to hold a script to check my lines because I knew the shaking piece of paper would give me away—the trembling hands that were supposed to encase nerves of steel, the hands that belonged to "Sub-zero Nelle," the self-assured woman whose only purpose in the show was to be the antithesis to insecure Ally. I worried about meeting them. I worried that I would say something that would show them that I wasn't going to be the outstanding addition to the cast that they'd been told by the show's producers I would be. What if they could immediately see that I wasn't exceptional and special, that I was merely an average girl?

I knew I was average. I had learned this fact on my first day of Geelong Grammar School. In Grovedale, the suburb of Geelong where I grew up, we had the biggest and most beautiful house in the neighborhood—a brand-new two-story AV Jennings home with a swimming pool. My father was a well-respected community organizer, the founder of the Grovedale Rotary Club, and there was talk of him running for mayor. But on my first day at my new school, when I saw one kid being dropped off in a helicopter and others arriving in BMWs and Jaguars, it became obvious to me that I was not like them. They owned things my family couldn't afford. And while I had felt jealousy before, seeing that boy get out of a helicopter elicited a brand-new, uncomfortable feeling. Jealousy for me had been rooted in the belief that what I was jealous of was attainable, but this was different. I felt intimidated. I felt less than, not equal, and on a completely different, un-relatable level. Throughout the day I heard stories from the students of summer vacations spent yachting around the Caribbean while I had spent my summer pretending to be an Olympic gymnast in the cul-de-sac. I was embarrassed to think that I had been strutting around town like a spoiled little rich girl when I wasn't rich at all.

"Why didn't you tell me we were poor?" I fired at my mother with uncharacteristic anger when I got into the car. (I have since learned that anger is my first response to embarrassment.) My mother was clearly hurt by my question, and as we drove home in her Mazda 626, she stared at the road between her hands clenched at 10 and 2 on the steering wheel, and explained to me with tears in her eyes that she'd tried very hard to make sure our lives continued as if dad were still alive.

"But we've always been poor!" She couldn't possibly know how poor we were. She probably didn't even know what a yacht was.

When I saw my brother later that night, I attacked him. I was especially angry with my brother, since he had attended the school for two years prior to my arrival. Surely he could've told me the truth.

"We're not poor, stupid. We're average."

Average. It was the worst, most disgusting word in the English language. Nothing meaningful or worthwhile ever came from that word. In my twelve-year-old mind, there was no point in living if you were average. An average person doesn't cure cancer, win Olympic medals, or become a movie star. What kind of a boring, uninspired life was I going to live if I was thought of as "average" in any category? My brother could not have levied a greater insult than calling me average with the exception of "normal," "ordinary," and "mediocre." These were words that I hated just as much as the word "average," and I knew they were lined up right around the corner ready to attach themselves to me like a name badge unless I did something exceptional and gave myself a better label, starting with my unexceptional, common-sounding name. My name was average. I knew this because I wasn't the only one who had it. When I was eight, I was a track and field star. My race was the 200 meters. At the regional track and field meet, there was a girl in my heat with the same name—Amanda Rogers—who was my only real competition. I simply couldn't see the point of running the race. Where's the glory in beating the girl with the same name? Why make a name for myself when somebody else already had it? Amanda Rogers in first, followed by Amanda Rogers in second?

I needed to give myself a better label. Model. Law student. Actress. No one was average at my new school. They were rich. I needed to be exceptional just to fit in.

The thought of being in the middle of the pack had always worried me. From my first awareness of competition—that someone could win and another person could lose—the pressure to excel in everything I attempted was immense. I had to win, get an A, and take home the prize. Even when I took first prize, topped the class, won the race, I never really won anything. I was merely avoiding the embarrassment of losing. When ability is matched by expectations, then anything less that an exceptional result was laziness. And laziness in my opinion was shameful.

But I wasn't naturally inclined to excel in all the tasks I was given as a child. For example, I was never good at math. Even basic addition eluded me. I learned my multiplication table at school because we used to have "heads up" competitions in front of the class. The teacher would invite two students to come to the blackboard and would then proceed to ask them various multiplication questions such as "six times seven" or "five times three." I drilled the answers into my brain. All day long this little eight-year-old would be silently playing the game of teacher and student; the teacher firing questions with machine-gun rapidity, the student, armed with preparation, deftly deflecting every bullet. I made it through the third grade undefeated. But I wasn't a math champion for long. By age fourteen I was bawling over my physics homework.

Devastation was my usual reaction to things I couldn't comprehend. It would start with mild anxiety if the answer wasn't at the ready, and would progress to full-blown terror, physically manifesting in sweating, yelling, crying, hitting myself on the head, and chanting, "I don't understand" until I was exhausted and on the verge of collapse. In order to prepare myself for a less than perfect result, I would occasionally give myself the opposite of a pep talk by writing hundreds of times in a journal, "I will not get honors," as I awaited the results of a ballet exam, for example. I'm not sure if this ritual actually helped me to accept the less than perfect grade I was preparing myself for, because I always did get honors. Dancing six days a week for two hours a day, plus hours of practice at home will get anyone honors, much less a nine-year-old whose only competition had just learned to point her toe. The ballet school I attended was a small side business of a onetime professional dancer who rented out a church hall to teach young kids the basics of dance in a suburb of a mid-sized town. Nobody took it seriously. I treated it like it was the Australian Ballet.

I don't know where this pressure came from. I can't blame my parents because it has always felt internal. Like any other parent, my mother celebrated the A grades and the less-than-A grades she felt there was no need tell anybody about. But not acknowledging the effort that ended in a less than perfect result impacted me as a child. If I didn't win, then we wouldn't tell anyone that I had even competed to save us the embarrassment of acknowledging that someone else was better. Keeping the secret made me think that losing was something to be ashamed of, and that unless I was sure I was going to be the champion, there was no point in trying. And there was certainly no point to just having fun.

FISH

Can I have your attention please? Everybody. I really have splendid news. I would like to introduce to you all, Nelle Porter. As of today she'll be joining us as a new attorney. She is going to be an outstanding addition, and I trust that you'll all help make her feel as welcome as I know she is. Nelle Porter.

NELLE

Thank you. Thank you. It's a tough decision to change jobs, but I'm excited. I'm grateful to Richard and to Paul for the offer and also Ally . . . my brief chat with her . . . well, I knew coming here it would be fun.

6

COULDN'T LIGHT a cigarette fast enough. In fact, even though I was scared that someone would catch me, I greedily inhaled a lungful of smoke before my car had driven off the lot. My first day had definitely been challenging, and not having a hiding place in which to smoke made it even worse. I hadn't eaten all day either. But my need for food wasn't from hunger as much as it was the need to fill a hole in my gut. Since I didn't have to go to work the next couple of days, my brother Michael and I decided to meet at our favorite restaurant to celebrate my first day. When my husband left me, my brother moved in to my place. I loved that he lived with me. The living arrangement was to keep both of us company after my husband ran off with his wife. My husband ran off with his wife, so we kept each other company and we liked to go out for margaritas and Mexican food to commiserate. Or to celebrate. And after the day I'd had, I wasn't sure which of those things I would be doing tonight. Naturally, he'd think we were celebrating and I wouldn't let him think otherwise. He already thought I was a bit of a drama queen as it was.

"How did it go, Sissy?" He called me Sissy when he was happy to see me and the feeling was reciprocated. If I'd had a cute way of turning "brother" into something to express my love, I would've done it then, too. I just called him "brother." Since moving to LA, he'd had to deal with a lot. He had married his longtime girlfriend, Renee, just before leaving Australia and the two newlyweds moved into an apartment in the same *Melrose Place*–style complex that was home to me and Mel. In the evenings, the four of us were inseparable, but during the day, when my brother and I were at work, Renee and Mel formed partnerships. They were professional partners in my husband's cappuccino business and in his carpentry business. The fact that Renee would wear skimpy, lacy underwear clearly visible underneath her oversized, gaping overalls should have indicated to my brother and me that a personal partnership was also forming, but when Mel left me and Renee suddenly sabotaged her marriage to my brother to be with Mel, Brother and I were left idiotically scratching our heads in disbelief.

My brother's first year in Los Angeles was tough. Apart from his wife falling in love with my husband, he had a great deal of drama in his new job as a manager of a biomedical engineering company. We had both come to the United States to pursue our dreams of a bigger, more challenging life. Either that or we were both really influenced by our father's love of America after he came back from a business trip with stories of wide freeways and snowy mountains, fancy cars and Disneyland. In any case, the fact we both ended up here together was a blessing.

"It was great, Brother. The scene went well, the place is great, and the people are really nice."

"That's great. Table for two on the patio, please."

"Certainly, sir, right this way."

The Mexican restaurant was a dark, seedy place with greasy food and an outdoor patio where I could smoke. I started smoking when I was fourteen for two very good reasons: to win over the cool girl at school with the shaved head and to suppress my appetite—a tip taught to me by my modeling colleagues. While I never really became friends with the cool girl, I did learn that the more I smoked, the less I'd eat, which is particularly important when you sit down to dinner at a Mexican restaurant. So despite its average food, the fact that this restaurant was the closest one to our house with an outdoor patio made it my favorite.

As I smoked and talked and allowed the tension of my day to melt into my margarita, I made the decision to eat nachos. The blend of cheese and sour cream with the crispiness of the corn chips and creaminess of guacamole will always turn a sour mood into a happy one. A peace came over me when I ate food like that. Like life had no other purpose than pure enjoyment. I had nowhere to go and nothing to accomplish. For that moment, I could put life on hold and believe I was perfect the way I was. I was focused in the present—in the moment—and the moment was bliss on a corn chip.

I hadn't eaten any bad food since the day at Banana Republic when I decided to get professional, and I really felt like I needed to reward myself for all the hard work that went into getting into that size 6 suit. Besides, I'd made too much of a big deal out of it, anyway. The suits were very conservative and would easily hide a pound or two. I didn't need to be rail thin to wear them. So I didn't feel bad when I ordered an additional meal of enchiladas. I simply wouldn't eat the following day.

"So that idiot in lab went over my head today and told Chris . . ." As he talked about his lab geeks and his psychotic boss, I wondered how he'd take the news that I was gay. I hadn't told him yet because it was too soon after my marriage to Mel and I was afraid he wouldn't believe me. Of the few people I'd told, most didn't believe me for some reason. Some thought it was a phase, some thought I was just saying it to be different, to get attention. It's a particularly bad reaction because sharing that deep secret with someone takes a lot of courage, and disbelief feels like ridicule. Like two little girls together is something silly not to be taken seriously. I simply couldn't risk my brother reacting that way. He was all I had.

I kept ordering margaritas and eating enchiladas, and when I was done with mine, I got to work on his. After the main course was over, I went back to the appetizers we'd been served at the beginning of the evening and ate the last of the corn chips with the puddle of salsa that was left in the stone bowl. I was amused at the thought that an appetizer was supposed to stimulate appetite and I silently congratulated ours for doing its job.

As my brother and I finished up our conversation, our watered-down drinks, the last drag of a cigarette, I knew I'd done some damage. There was a dull ache in my gut and a layer of fat on the roof of my mouth that proved it. It's a weird sensation knowing that you've just altered your course. In a fleeting moment of arrogance, in one self-congratulatory thought, I decided I was good enough, that I could stop right there. My quest for perfection, for discipline, for greatness, was over. I'd reached my goal. I had nothing more to do. I'd completed one day of work, worn the suit with the character in it, and done a good job, and that was enough. As I got up from the table, I looked down at the wreckage. I saw the ugly plastic checkered tablecloth and the flimsy utensils for the first time that night. I saw the cigarette ash on the table, pools of water dripped from the glasses that were cloudy with greasy fingers, lipstick-tipped butts in an overflowing ashtray that wasn't clean to begin with. And then there was the food. Food looks so ugly when it's half-eaten and torn apart. The refried beans smeared on the plate looked like feces, and the browning guacamole and clumps of rice looked like vomit. What disgusted me the most in this grotesque tableau was that the cheese from the enchiladas had a wide greasy ring around it that separated it from the plate. Like a beach separated land from the ocean. I had ingested a beach of grease. I grabbed my keys from underneath a few grains of rice that had spilled over the edge of my plate during this mindless, repetitive act of filling my mouth with food and headed out to the car.

There's a big difference between eating and what I had just done. What I'd done was an act of defiance.

I pulled away from the curb and lined up behind my brother's car that was barely visible through the curtain of exhaust smoke that separated us. The bright red stoplight reflected off the black road and as I sat there on the cold leather seat, I wondered who I was being defiant toward. *You're only hurting yourself,* was the phrase I kept thinking, and while I knew that was true, why did my bingeing feel like someone else was going to be pissed off and hurting, too? Was anyone else really invested in my weight and how I treated my body? All I thought about when I continued to eat after the initial rush of the food wore off, after the taste became familiar, and after my stomach was full was *HA HA! You can't stop me!* But who was I saying that to? As I drove down the road toward home, now separated from my brother by several cars and a lane or two, I wondered if my little act of rebellion was over for now or if it would continue with a stop at 7-Eleven.

I stopped at 7-Eleven on the way home for food. I barely felt any anxiety as I pulled into the parking lot because I think I'd subconsciously planned this stop from my first bite of nachos. As I'd already blown the diet, I figured I might as well keep going—I might as well eat all the things I'd denied myself for the last few weeks. And I had to get it all done in one sitting because if I allowed myself to do this again—to eat all this food—I'd get fat. If this reckless eating continued into the following day, I'd get fat and I'd end up in TV purgatory, kept on the show due to an unbreakable contract, yet disappearing, making only the occasional background cross as my character's life with all the promise of great story lines faded into the blank page from whence it came. Of course, I'd have to throw up after, but that was okay. I would've had to throw up anyway just from the Mexican food. I didn't have work for the next two days so I had time to get rid of the dots above my eyes that were caused by my blood vessels bursting from all the pressure and strain of purging. With that much pressure, something had to burst.

I could either force myself to throw up the food or gain weight from it. Of the two options, I figured that it was better concealing a few red dots on my eyelids than showing up to my second day of work two pounds heavier with my skirt stretching across my thighs. And if I had to throw up anyway, I might as well eat all I could. I might as well eat everything.

Throwing up was something I had taught myself as a child. I learned from the more experienced models I worked with that it was something you could do if you had to eat in front of people, including the clients that book you. Apparently, it was more desirable to look as though your body was naturally stick thin than trying hard to get it that way, so models ate pizza before a fashion show, then threw it up quietly before showtime. That would take a lot of practice, since you'd have to be neat and clean about it. No matter how much I practiced, I was never good at it. Apart from the red dots above my eyes, my eyes and nose watered badly from the heaving efforts. Plus I was so loud. The gagging sounded like really loud coughing and would serve as an alarm to let everyone in the public restroom know what I was doing.

Unlike the other girls, I didn't throw up because I had to eat to impress the client but because I wanted to eat. Nothing was better after a modeling job than food. It was the only thing that took all the bad feelings away. Like an eraser, it allowed me start over, to forget the feelings of insecurity and awkwardness I'd experienced that day. But the comforting ritual of rewarding myself with food started to backfire as the jobs started being booked back to back. Instead of having a week of starving to counteract the weight gained from eating fries, ice cream, and candy, I was given a day or two to get back on track, to be the 34–24–35 model that they'd booked off my card. The client was expecting an image of me that wasn't who I really was. They wanted a self-confident young woman who was naturally thin, beautiful, comfortable in her skin. Who I really was, was an average-looking child staving off puberty with its acne and weight gain just waiting to expose me for the phony I was. So I'd throw up.

After my first day of *Ally*, I needed to start over. I needed to forget the insecurity and awkwardness I felt standing on that staircase, pretending to be the fabulous Nelle Porter. Just hearing the words "outstanding addition" gave me a hole in my stomach that no amount of food seemed to fill.

Go on, eat it, you fat piece of shit. You're pathetic. You can't even handle one day of work without bingeing. You have no self-control. You don't deserve this job.

Driving home from 7-Eleven with a bag full of food, I hated that my brother lived with me. Now I had to eat in the car a block from my house and throw up in the street so he wouldn't know what I was doing. And I had to do it fast because he'd wonder where I was. I started by eating a large bag of Cheetos. The bright orange color would serve as a marker during the purge. It would be a map, almost, telling me how far I'd come and how much further I needed to go. When I saw orange vomit cascading from my mouth and flowing in chunks between the two rigid fingers jammed against my gag reflex, I'd know I'd passed 7-Eleven and then I'd make my way back to the restaurant and back through each course beginning with the corn chips, the enchiladas, and ending with the nachos. As I shoved the jelly doughnut into my mouth, I came up with my lie. Mom called and my cell service was beginning to drop out so I had to pull over to complete the call. That would do. I barely swallowed my last item, the Snickers bar, before I began regurgitating it. I shoved my fingers down my throat and threw up in the plastic bag five times before I was satisfied that I'd gotten most of the food out. I took off my T-shirt from underneath my sweater and wiped my face and hands on it. I found a trash can. I drove home.

As I walked in the front door, I saw my brother on the couch with the phone to his ear.

"Where the hell have you been? Mom's on the phone."

He handed the phone to me.

"Hi, darl! How did it go?" My mother was more excited than I'd ever heard her. I knew that she'd been thinking about me the whole day, just waiting to hear news of the cast, the set, and my new life as a star of a hit TV show.

I took a deep breath. I mentally selected the appropriate pitch to my voice.

"It was really great, Ma. I had the greatest day."

It was a lie, but it should've been the truth. It would've been the truth if not for my debilitating insecurity, and I was certain that insecurity would fade with time once I had proven to myself that I deserved the job. In time, I was sure that I would be happy. After all, anyone else would've been. Most people would kill to have the opportunity that was given to me. How could I possibly complain to anyone that I didn't like it, that loads of money and fame, the most desired things in society, made me feel uncomfortable? While I waited for my genuine enjoyment of it to set in, I would simply lie about how much fun I was having. Complaining to my mom would have just been immature and embarrassing. In fact, anything short of perpetual joy seemed pathetic.

I'd pretended to enjoy modeling also, so I'd had practice in pretending. It was my goal to be known as a model because I wanted to be the envy of my seventh-grade peers and be thought of as beautiful and worldly. But being called a model and actually having to model were two different things entirely and caused me to experience very different feelings. At the very beginning of my modeling career, I needed test shots by a well-known photographer whom my new agents had chosen for me, and filling a modeling portfolio cost money that we didn't really have. I was told that I was lucky that I had caught the photographer's eye and should jump at the chance to have my pictures taken by him. His fee was a whopping $1,400 for three different looks. Prints would cost extra. So I struck a deal with my mother. If she bankrolled my test shots and drove me to Melbourne, I'd pay her back all the start-up money with my earnings from my first few jobs. She agreed, and my modeling career began.

In preparation for the test shots, my mother had rolled my hair in rag curls the night before, and the lumpy twisted rags felt like steel rods between the pillow and my head and made it impossible to sleep. This method of curling the hair was really unpredictable because often one section refused to curl at all and so the "naturally curly, I can't help it, I just woke up this way" look became the "I hate my straight, limp hair and so does my mother, who spent all night curling it in rags" look. On top of that, the rags had stray threads of cotton that would snag in my hair, and prying them out gave other sections an Afro-like frizz. I knew I had done the wrong thing by curling my hair the minute I walked in the door. The hairstylist grabbed my hairsprayed ringlets and proceeded to lecture me on how I should go to every job with clean, unstyled hair. As a twelve-year-old it never occurred to me I may have insulted him by doing my own hair. I was just avoiding what I thought would be an instant cancelation of the shoot if the photographer saw that I had just ordinary, limp, straight hair and, as a consequence, wasn't worthy of his time. I felt like I'd bullshitted my way into making the modeling agency take me in the first place and that my hair was going to expose me for the fake I really was. Luckily, my hair and makeup were done before the photographer arrived, so my real identity, with my ugly hair and my red, blotchy skin, remained undiscovered.

The photographer was a sluggish, heavy-set man whose droopy eyes accidentally registered me as he was glancing around the studio look-ing for something of interest—like a light or an assistant. After several hours of ordering and eating lunch, tweaking lights, and touching up my makeup, I began the actual modeling part of the photo shoot tired and wilted, and spent several more hours in that sweltering hot studio shooting the three different looks. For $1,400 I got a close-up wear-ing a jean jacket and a beret, a ridiculous jumping-up-and-down photo on a mini trampoline wearing a Mickey Mouse T-shirt, and a more grown-up look in a skintight black dress with a black plastic trash bag on my head scrunched into an abstract shape. The latter, I was told, was high-fashion, avant-garde.

Although the photos turned out to be something that I showed anyone who cared to look at them, the experience of taking them was horrible. No matter which pose I struck for him, he had a correction, each more embarrassing to me than the last. "Don't jut your hip out like that, stand normally. Chin down, relax your mouth, open your eyes." He yelled his orders at me all day, demanding that I change what I was doing, chipping away at my joy and confidence with each command. By the end of the shoot, I had stopped attempting to inject my personality into the pictures. Instead I was like a scared puppy that sees its master and automatically rolls over because it knows that's the one thing it can do to avoid a beating. I left the shoot feeling tired, anxious, and insecure, but because my mother had paid for it and taken another day off work to act as my chauffeur/chaperone, I felt I couldn't tell her the truth of how the photo shoot made me feel. So I lied and told her that I was excited about my new career.

On the way back to Geelong from the big city, we stopped at McDonald's. I held her hand as we stood in the "order here" line among other twelve-year-olds and their mothers. I stuffed myself with cheeseburgers, French fries, and a vanilla milk shake. And for the first time since the start of my career as a model, I was happy. Stopping at McDonald's became a ritual for my mother and me after a go-see or a modeling job. It was a midway point between the big city and the smaller bay city where I lived, and it became the midway point between the person I was and the person I was pretending to be. I sat down to eat as a child, but talked about my exciting day at work like an adult. For that one moment, I let it all go and my mother watched me without judgment or concern. I'd passed the test, and food was my reward. I'd pretended to be an adult, and going back to who I really was, a child excited to be at McDonald's, was my prize for being such a good pretender.

The only problem was that I couldn't stop rewarding myself. Returning to regular school life, I started to gain a little weight. I don't know why exactly, but I just couldn't stop eating. After my first photo shoot, eating seemed to be a huge comfort to me, and so every day after school, my friend Fiona and I would walk to the local supermarket to buy potato chips and candy. I knew I shouldn't be doing it, I knew I should be working out and trying to stay skinny for a potential modeling job that could happen at any moment, but eating just felt so good. My friend was a year older than me, and she told me that when I got to thirteen, my body would start changing, that I would hit puberty and get my period and get fat. Because she was older and knew more than I did, and because she had definitely gotten fatter since turning thirteen, I had no reason to doubt her, and so the inevitability of my weight gain made me think depriving myself of eating candy was futile. If it was going to happen anyway, I might as well make myself feel less anxious about it by soothing my nerves with a bag of potato chips. But I knew it was wrong. I knew my mother couldn't see me doing it. She'd just lent me thousands of dollars to get my modeling portfolio with the proviso that I would model my way out of debt. No one would hire me in this condition. I weighed 120 pounds!

After four long weeks, I received a call from the Modeling World. My agency was hosting a runway show in Melbourne with a local designer so they both could show off their wares to the fashion industry. They asked me to walk in the show, which would take place in a nightclub, and the event was only five days away. I felt no excitement, just panic. I dreaded the fashion show and I hated myself for getting so fat. I was nervous about being on a catwalk in front of the fashion industry anyway, much less modeling clothes that might show them all the reasons not to hire me—my big hips, my bulky calves, my fat stomach. To be perfectly honest, after my experience with the test shots, I would've been happy if I'd never gotten hired to model. I had the glamorous pictures to prove that I was pretty, and a story to tell of what it was like to be a model while never having to admit how terribly insecure modeling made me feel. Proving that I could do it if I wanted to but not actually having to keep proving it over and over again would've been perfect.

The only thing between me and this plan was my ego with its inflexible stance on failure. The embarrassment of failure was too much for me to bear. I'd already told everyone that I was a model, I'd convinced an agency that I had what it took to be a success, and, of course, I couldn't disappoint my mother. The only thing standing in the way of devastating embarrassment and success and admiration was a Cadbury Caramello Bar. There was no other option but to starve myself for the five days and hope that I could at least lose the five additional pounds I'd gained in the last two weeks.

Not eating is pretty easy when you have a gun to your head. I just needed those five pounds off for the fashion show, and then after that I'd eat salads and I'd never again eat junk food. After this stupid, extreme diet, I was going to work out every day and never have to starve myself again to get ready for a job. It was all about being ready, being prepared. As I had discovered, 90 percent of my nerves and feelings of insecurity came from being underprepared—whether I hadn't studied enough for a test or trained enough for ballet exam—most of my feelings of terror would go away when I felt I knew the answer to every conceivable question. Modeling would be no different. If the question was, "Will you look good in this tiny bathing suit at any angle?" then my answer would be, "Yes." It was that simple.

My mother, a dieter from way back, approved of this quick-fix plan not only to get me ready for the show but also to shut me up. Unfortunately, when I was nervous, I'd cry a lot. I'd wail and howl and stomp around the house moaning about how stupid I was and how I was doomed for a life of failure and mediocrity. My plan to starve myself, although not the healthiest plan, was a one-time Band-Aid that was better than the wailing, and so she reluctantly taught me a couple of her dieting tricks. Mostly they consisted of caffeinated beverages without milk, Ryvita crackers with beets and steamed vegetables. Oil, butter, dressings—everything that made food taste good—were out. Dry was in.

And so I embarked on my first diet, wanting desperately to succeed as a good dieter and to get this situation behind me.

Over the next five days, I consumed a total of 2,000 calories and had lost the five pounds. Thanks to my self-discipline and determination, I was a success. I felt like I could accomplish anything. I was proud of myself, and my mother was proud of me, too. We drove up to Melbourne for the fashion show with confidence and maybe even a little excitement. I was ready. I was twelve years old and about to start my career.

I arrived to pandemonium. Due to our hitting some traffic in the hour-long journey from Geelong and the fact that we were left alone to find our way to the backstage area, I was slightly late for the show.

"The girl that just walked in hasn't been through makeup and hair," yelled a man with a clipboard. I was yanked by the forearm from my mother and guided over to an empty stool. From that point on, I was a product on an assembly line. My head was doused with cold water and blown dry, the round brushes tearing at the knots in my hair while I was simultaneously poked in the face with a coarse brush that at certain angles felt like hundreds of fine dressmaking pins. Bright, ugly, unflattering colors were slapped on my face with the brushstrokes a house painter would use to apply primer. I sat in silence looking at my reflection as it became uglier, unable to even introduce myself because of the guilt I felt that my lateness had caused this panic. Nobody had asked me for my name anyway. There were models to the left and right of me in varying stages of completion, none of whom even glanced my way until the makeup artist exclaimed in a shrill voice, "What am I supposed to do with these eyebrows?" And that made the model next to me turn to look at them.

"Whoa. They're some crazy eyebrows!" the male model said to me in a big, stupid way that made me angry rather than ashamed.

"They're exactly like my father's eyebrows and he's dead." That shut him up. I started thinking about my dad and wondered how he would feel about me modeling. Although I felt really bad about using him to justify having big, bushy eyebrows, it wouldn't be the last time I did it to stop people from talking about them. Until I realized you could pluck them. Other than that one interaction with the model, I didn't actually talk to any of the other Team models until after the show when we were directed by the bookers to mingle with the crowd. As I was awkwardly standing alone at a high-top table trying to look so-phisticated by sipping sparkling water, I overheard one of the girls say, "Apparently there's a girl here who's only twelve," and I blurted out in excitement, "That's me! I'm twelve!" as only a twelve-year-old could. After that, word spread and other models talked to me in the conde-scending way adults talk to children. I was hardly a child and they were only a few years older than me, so I didn't appreciate it. But the most upsetting thing about meeting them was that I realized how beautiful all of them were. Stripped of their crazy fashion show makeup I could see their big eyes, set far apart and cradled by their perfect cheekbones that the rest of their face hung from in perfect proportion. Their hair, thrown up messily yet beautifully in a hair tie, and their loose, easy clothes spoke of their attitude toward their beauty—it was effortless and unconscious. It didn't require their critical eye reflected in a mirror to craft it; it just was there. They were so much more beautiful than me that I was in awe of them. I felt so ashamed of the dress and heels I'd bought for the occasion, and so stupid to have reapplied makeup after removing the show makeup. But the thing that gave me the pit in my stomach was the fact that I knew I needed it. Underneath the caked-on foundation was red blotchy skin, and if I didn't wear eyeliner, my eyes looked too small for the roundness of my face. I was different from all those girls, and I had to be careful not to let anyone see it.

The show itself was pretty uneventful. I had to model only one unrevealing outfit—culottes and a T-shirt with built-in shoulder pads. I was sent down the runway with a male model who strutted around like he was line dancing, holding me by the wrist and twirling me around like I was a prize he'd won at the state fair. I felt stupid that I'd made such a big deal about the show. After I'd stood around practically in silence for over an hour, overhearing conversations that intimidated me because I couldn't understand what anyone was talking about, I was finally allowed to go home. I felt relieved that the night was over. I got into my mother's car, took my heels off, and curled my cold feet underneath me. I sat facing her as she drove, talking to her all the way like she was my best friend. I ate a whole bag of mint candies that my mother had put in the car for me as a reward for getting through my first fashion show and for successfully losing all that weight. I ate them greedily and steadily until there were none left. As we pulled into our driveway an hour later at midnight, exhausted and full of sugar, it crossed my mind that eating all those candies might have caused me to gain a pound. As I walked barefoot to the back door, my belly distended in my skintight dress, I devised a plan to stop the sugar from turning into fat. Tomorrow was sports practice at school, and I made a promise to run ten extra laps around the hockey field to make up for it. And that wasn't the only promise I made that night that I didn't keep. I promised myself I wouldn't binge again.

7

EY, PORTIA. How were your days off?" I walked into the wardrobe fitting room passing Jane Krakowski as she was leaving.

"Great, thanks." I was aware as I spoke that I hadn't talked in awhile. It felt unnatural and my voice sounded raspy and constricted with phlegm, the telltale sounds of a chain-smoker. I cleared my throat, embarrassed.

"See you in there." She said it in a way that sounded like we were both in trouble, like we were about to walk into a detention room at school. I couldn't help but smile when I saw Jane. Her facial expressions were infectious, like she was keeping a naughty secret that could crack her up at any moment. Apart from Jane, I hadn't really gotten a sense of the cast yet. They all seemed pretty quiet and professional, more like corporate businesspeople than the actors I had known in the past. The cast of my first movie, *Sirens*, interacted with each other in a much more playful manner than I'd observed with the cast of *Ally*. During *Sirens*, we'd eat lunch together and listen to Hugh Grant's hilarious stories or Sam Neil's dry explanation of what it was like to be a supporting actor to a dinosaur in *Jurassic Park*. But maybe I would eat lunch with them today and hear their stories. Maybe I'd even tell them some of Hugh's stories. They were much funnier than mine.

As I said my hellos to the folks in the fitting rooms, it occurred to me that in a great ironic twist, I could possibly be perceived by the cast as a threat. Any new cast member threatens to take away airtime from the ensemble cast members, their story lines and attention. No television actor really embraces the idea of a new cast member, with perhaps the exception of the overworked titular character. I didn't feel as though the cast was threatened by me, however. I felt that they were threatened by the change that my presence signified, that it prompted them to ask themselves, "If this could happen, then what's next?" While everyone was very pleasant to me, I got the sense that they were all just wondering why I was there. They were celebrities on a hit television show, and I'd only had small parts in three movies and two very short-lived sitcoms to my credit. I guess we were all wondering why I was there.

I was in the wardrobe rooms to check-fit my outfit for Day Two. I was nervous to try on the size 6 suit the tailor had taken in after my first fitting three days prior. After bingeing and purging I feared that I'd gained weight. I always tended to gain a pound after a binge and purge even if it was just bloat. I struggled to zip up the skirt in front of the costume designer, her assistant, and the tailor, who all witnessed the effort.

"It fits," I said to the crowd, as I stood straight with my legs pressed together, careful not to show them that it would likely bunch up at the slightest movement. Even though I had to wear the skirt for the last scene that day, I was too ashamed to admit that it was too tight.

"Is it comfortable?" the costume designer, Vera, asked, squinting as if seeing better would help her sense my discomfort.

"Yeah. It should be fine."

"I think I take in too much," the tailor told Vera in a thick, unrecognizable accent. "I take out a little."

I didn't say anything. I just took off the skirt and handed it to the tailor, allowing her to believe that it was her fault that the skirt didn't fit. I slipped into my new beige Banana Republic pants, walked outside, and headed into makeup, all the while fighting the desperate urge for a cigarette.

• • • •

"Hi, Portia. How were your days off?" Peter MacNicol was sitting in the makeup chair next to the empty chair that was waiting for me. He looked tired and I could tell that he was slightly envious that I'd had days off when he was working twelve-hour days all week.

"Great, thanks." It occurred to me that the more important the character, the fewer the days off. I hoped I would never be asked that question again.

I stared into the mirror at the red dots on my eyelids. Despite my efforts to conceal them, they were so pronounced I could see them clearly in the mirror from several feet away. To my amazement, my makeup artist didn't comment. It was almost worse that she didn't, as it suggested to me that maybe she knew how I got them and didn't need to ask. She began my makeup by thickly applying foundation with a wide, flat brush. After several minutes of silence, Peter got up from the chair next to mine.

"See you in there."

The makeup trailer wobbled as he walked down the steps.

"Yeah. See you in there."

"Cut!" the director yelled loudly to the cameraman and the actors, which was then echoed by several ADs stationed all over the set. I heard the word *cut* about ten times after each take to release the background or let the people who were at craft service go back to making noise as they fixed themselves coffee or a snack. We were all waiting this time, however, for the first AD to ask the cameraman to check the gate, which meant that the cast and crew could break for lunch. The scene was a "walk and talk" that took place in the hallway next to the courtroom. It was a short scene where I met up with Ally and asked her to have drinks with me at bar at the end of the day, explaining, "I would like to talk to a woman's woman" before making a decision to join the law firm of Cage and Fish. I did well, even though it made me nervous as it reminded me of a scene I did in the movie *Scream 2*, in which my character, a nasty sorority girl, walked up to the entire assembly of the movie's stars, and for some reason, had to say, "In a six degrees of Kevin Bacon sort of way." I kept screwing it up. Take after take I would wrongly say, "In a six degrees of separation sort of way." I was panic-stricken before each take and the panic made my head spin with fear and my mind go blank. I literally saw white light as I incorrectly repeated the same line over and over again. In this scene where I bullied Ally into meeting me for a drink, despite my urge to say, "I'd like to talk to a woman first," I got the line out without any cause for panic. I was very nervous, though, as I was lauding it over Ally, intimidating her. In between takes I felt just as nervous, feeling as though I should fill in the silence with small talk, even though no one was really doing much talking. I, like the crew, was breathlessly waiting to be released for lunch, only I didn't need to eat. I just needed to be released from the stress of being looked at, being judged. Was I good enough?

"Check the gate."

The cameraman shone a penlight into the camera to check for dust on the film. "Clear."

"Gate's good. That's lunch. One hour."

I walked from the set to the dressing rooms with Calista and Peter.

"Where do you guys normally eat lunch?" The minute I said it, I felt stupid, and like a nerdy schoolgirl who was attempting to force an invitation to be part of the cool kids' group. There was a slight gap between my asking and their answering that reinforced my feeling of stupidity.

"I tend to nap during lunch." Peter spoke sweetly but in a way that informed me that there would never be an exception to this routine.

"I have a phone interview." Calista made a slight face that suggested that in another time before she became the poster child for America's changing views on skirt length and feminism, she would've gladly swapped stories over lunch with another actor. The face she made was enough to make me think she really did wish things were different. I knew in that second that I liked her. But I also knew that I would never really get to know her.

"How are you liking it so far?" She looked directly into my eyes.

I inhaled and nodded my head up and down a few times. I wanted to tell her that it felt strange, that I felt out of place, that I was scared of not delivering. I wanted to tell her that I felt pressure to look good, to be fashionable, to be someone other than who I was. I wanted to say that I felt isolated and that maybe I kind of hated the show. But I didn't. In the four years of working on that show I never did say any of that to her.

"I love it."

"Great! See you back in there."

As I walked through the door with my name on it and into my dressing room, I heard my name being called from the hallway. It was Courtney Thorne-Smith in sweatpants walking toward the makeup trailer.

"You break for lunch?"

"Yeah. What are you up to?" Maybe I could have lunch with Courtney. I hadn't had any real scenes with her yet and I wanted to get to know her. I used to watch *Melrose Place*.

"That's weird. They just called me into makeup. Everyone's at lunch?"

"Yeah. You wanna grab lunch with me?"

She looked at me in a way that suggested that she felt sorry for me. I guess you could call it condescending, but there was a glint in her eye that told me that she too thought what she was about to tell me was strange.

"We don't really eat lunch together here."

"Oh. Cool. Okay." I stared down at the carpet, embarrassed, as I began to close the dressing room door. "See you later, then."

I looked at my bag that was sitting on the new green chair opposite the full-length mirror. I had an hour. I grabbed my cigarettes, stuffed them underneath my shirt, and started walking out of the building. I walked away from the windowless monolithic peach rectangles that housed the stages and away from the offices, stacked one on top of the other, David Kelley's office sitting on top of them all. In the far corner of Manhattan Beach Studios, out of sight of anyone and in between the chain-link fence and the loading docks, I embarked on what would become my lunchtime ritual. I hid from the people who made me feel awkward, stupid, or like a schoolgirl. I hid from producers, directors, and people who evaluated me. I hid from the voice that became very loud in front of that full-length mirror in the dressing room that was supposed to make me feel comfortable. And I chain-smoked.

8

FELT NERVOUS. As I walked through the house with wet hair to make myself tea I heard the television broadcasting my thoughts. "What will she be wearing? Who will win for best comedy?" The Emmys was a thing that I'd only seen on TV; I'd never actually helped provide the content that made it a show. *Ally McBeal* was nominated, Calista and Jane were nominated, and I was a debutante about to be introduced for the first time to the public who could potentially love me or hate me. My brother, thinking he was being supportive, had turned on all the TVs in the house for the preshow. I knew at some point my nerves would get the better of me and I'd lose my nonchalant attitude toward it and would tell him to shut it off. But I was trying on a different personality, one that was excited to walk the red carpet and show people who I was because I thought I was perfectly fabulous. This personality was not a bit worried or nervous that I'd say something stupid or be wearing the wrong thing. As I made my tea and listened to what was left of the segment after the kettle had sputtered, boiled, and whistled, I was completely unaffected by the shrill voices of the entertainment news reporters and the judgment of fashion commentators. I liked this new personality. It was calming, mature, balanced. I wondered how long I could keep it.

I found that if I sat still for too long, my insecurity seized the opportunity to take control of my mind. Especially if the chair I was sitting on was positioned in front of a mirror. It's not that I hated the way I looked, it's just that I worried that I wouldn't look good enough. That I wouldn't be transformed from the girl who often forgot to shave her legs and rarely got a facial into Portia de Rossi, Hollywood actress and new cast member of the hottest show on television. In an attempt to avoid looking at my face as my hair was blown-dry, I looked down at the notes in my hands. My hands; my big, ugly, red hands that had only recently seen a manicure because that was what my cast mates did on weekends to ready themselves for the week ahead. I did whatever they did because they knew things I didn't. Although I hated going to a nail salon, I wasn't going to ignore the people around me who were more successful than me and who had figured all this out. I really hated my hands. My hands were manly. They belonged to a working-class boy who helped his dad around the farm. In my ugly hands were the pieces of paper that would act as my safety net, my little bit of reassurance, proof that if I studied them, I could ace the ensuing exam on that bright red carpet. On sheets of lined, reinforced paper I'd written:

How did you get the role on *Ally McBeal*?

I met with David Kelley for a role on The Practice, *but he saw me more for Ally, and within a couple of weeks, I was sent a script that featured my character, and that became the first episode of the new season.*

Describe your character.

Nelle Porter is a very driven, ambitious woman who has sacrificed her private life for her career. She's seemingly ruthless and insensitive, but deep down she wants love and happiness like everyone else. She's so cold her nickname is "Sub-zero."

Were you a fan of the show?

Yes. I love the show and I'm so proud to be a part of it. It's like a dream come true.

What is everyone on the show like? Have they welcomed you
to the cast?

*The whole cast is great. Everyone is lovely and has been really friendly
and welcoming toward me. I feel very lucky to be working with such a
talented and nice group of people.*

What is in store for Nelle Porter this season?

Well, you'll have to watch and see . . .

As I memorized my scripted responses to hypothetical questions
in the kitchen chair that could barely fit in the bathroom of my one-
bathroom house, I wondered if anyone else out there sitting in hair
and makeup was doing this. Did any other actor rehearse "off the cuff"
responses to red carpet questions? Did they rehearse their talk show
stories as they sat in foils at the hairdresser's? When you're under spot-
lights and nervous, it has to help to have a script to fall back on. The
fact that my character always knows what to say is one of the reasons
I love acting. If I could be given a script to answer the hard questions
seamlessly, I wouldn't be so nervous that I might say the wrong thing.
Sitting in front of the mirror and learning my answers, a feeling of self-
hatred and shame came over me as I remembered a conversation with
Greg Germann a couple of weeks earlier. On set and in between takes, in
an attempt to be friendly, Greg had asked me what he no doubt thought
was a simple question, but it was a question that silenced me with fear.

"Do you have a boyfriend?"

When I froze and was unable to answer this seemingly easy question, Greg raised his eyebrows and in a joking, incredulous tone asked,
"Are you gay?"

The question took me off guard. I wasn't prepared. If only I'd had
a script of perfect witty responses, I could've flicked through the bril-
liantly written pages in my brain and found the right one. But without
the script, all I could think to say was, "I don't know."

I hated seeing him at work after that. I worried about that conversation every day.

I arrived at the Shrine Auditorium alone after getting into the car an hour earlier and chain-smoking the entire way. The last twenty minutes had been spent circling the venue, waiting in line as the celebrities, in order of importance, were given the drop-off spots closest to the red carpet. My driver told me all of this as we were waiting, which suggested to me that despite my silver dress and diamonds dripping from my neck and ears, he instinctively knew I was a nobody, even though my clothes suggested otherwise.

When I eventually got out of the car at the mouth of the red carpet, I felt assaulted by the heat. For the first time, it occurred to me that it was the middle of the day, the hottest part of the day, and all these people were in gowns and diamonds pretending it was evening. It looked ridiculous to see a sea of sequins and tulle and satin at 3:30 in the afternoon on a hot summer day. Of course, it was just another costume, and these were actors. The red carpet was full of people. There were hundreds of people all jammed on a carpet, some trying to hurry through to the entrance of the Shrine, some lingering, trying to be noticed by photographers. And then there were the publicists, the people in drab black "stagehand" outfits swimming upstream to grab a client by the hand and hurl him or her in front of the firing squad, the section at the beginning of the carpet with photographers, all screaming and sweating, in rows ten deep. The noise coming from this section was aggressive, and it came in surges depending on who walked near them. The photographers yelled the name of the actor to get her attention and then a few minutes later the fans in the bleachers did the same. There was definitely a lot of yelling and sweating, posing and cheering for such a glamorous and important event. I didn't know why, but it seemed different on TV. It seemed like the actors simply walked to the entrance and happened to be shot by photographers, quietly and respectfully as they breezed past. The fans, in my fantasy, would fall silent as the celebrities passed by, awed by their proximity to these precious creatures, like people do at the railing of a zoo enclosure. This seemed more like a sports event.

The Fox publicist found me patiently waiting at the start of the carpet after beads of sweat had formed all over my face and body. This was my introduction. This was my turning point. After today, everyone would know who I was and have an opinion about everything I did. And with my hair in ringlets and my individual eyelashes glued onto the corners of my eyes, scripted answers and a silver Calvin Klein dress, I was ready to face the firing squad. She took me to the start of the photographers' section of the carpet. As I'd just watched several women get their picture taken, I wasn't terribly nervous. I knew I'd stand in four different spots as the photographers yelled out my name and jostled for the best picture. I approached the line of fire as the publicist stated my name and place of business. "Portia de Rossi–*Ally McBeal*." As I stood there, smiling, hip jutting out in a casual but elegant pose, I was alarmed by the silence. Not one of these people with machines for faces had called my name or asked me to spin around. No one was asking me who I was wearing. I instantly felt like this unenthusiastic response was my fault, like I should do something to make the picture better, more interesting. I felt sorry for these people whose bosses expected something more than just a girl in a silver dress. They expected a star with personality. They wanted to see the reason for adding a cast member to an already successful show. At the end of the stills photography section I saw a news crew whose reporter was handing out plastic fans. In a desperate attempt to justify the photographers' time, the jewelry designer's generosity, the publicist's uphill battle to get me noticed after swimming upstream to come fetch me, and to not make David Kelley look like he made a mistake by casting an ordinary girl with no personality, I grabbed a fan and dramatically posed with it high in the air–like Marilyn Monroe with her dress blowing up, but different. The photographers liked it. They were taking pictures. Some of them were even yelling, "Over here!" so I'd turn more toward them while holding the pose.

I was officially a hypocrite. I wanted to blend in and disappear yet be noticed doing it.

Before I knew it, I was answering questions into a microphone.

"What is the one beauty item you can't live without?"

Shit. I didn't know the answer to that one. I mean, "concealer" was the truthful answer, but what was the right answer?

"Lip gloss."

I hate lip gloss. I hate anything on my lips, but it sounded right. It sounded pretty and feminine and like something boys would find attractive; big, goopy lips, moist and inviting. Next . . .

"What is your must-have fashion item for the season?"

Shit. I didn't know fashion at all. I didn't read magazines and I wasn't really interested. I wished Kali were there; she would've known the answer to that question. In fact, a few months ago she'd wanted Chanel ballet flats . . .

"Chanel ballet flats."

My answer took a little long in coming, and the interviewer could sense it wasn't going to get any easier, so I was dismissed from the interview with a "Thanks for stopping to talk to us." I was surprised by the questions I was asked. Most of the interviewers didn't care about my character or the show. All anyone wanted to know was who I was wearing and what my beauty tips were and how I stayed in shape. As I walked away from the news crews, I heard the last reporter ask my publicist, "What's her name?" The reporter didn't discreetly whisper the question to my publicist in an attempt to save me from having hurt feelings, she yelled it. She had just been interviewing me like I was important enough to tell the public my thoughts about the increasing number of actresses who wore their hair down to the Emmys and yet she had no idea who I was. The answer came over raucous screams announcing Lara Flynn Boyle's arrival so she asked again as if she wondered if she'd heard correctly. "*What's* her name?"

I was embarrassed and a little afraid. I was often embarrassed to tell people my name because I had made it up. I had a deep fear of someone discovering the truth, that this exotic name wasn't mine—that I'd borrowed it like I had borrowed the dress and the diamonds, that it was a little too fabulous for me to own and at some point I was going to have to give it back. Portia de Rossi. A fabulous name. A name that belonged to a celebrity.

I made it up when I was fifteen. I was illegally in a nightclub when the club's manager took me into his VIP room to award me with a coveted all-access, never-wait-in-line medallion. I knew I couldn't give him my real identity for fear that he would discover my age and never again allow me back in the club. I was flustered coming up with a name on the spot, but I knew I had to do it. Not only was he offering me a key chain medallion to flaunt, a sliver tag announcing to the world that I was in with the "in-crowd," he was offering me a job. I could be a hostess for the club, and all I had to do was show up twice a week. All that—if I could come up with a name other than Amanda Rogers, the name that belonged to the fifteen-year-old kid that stood before them. I could be a VIP if I could come up with the right name.

I hated my birth name. Amanda Rogers. It was so ordinary, so perfectly average. It had "a man" in it, which annoyed me because every time I'd hear someone refer to a man, I would turn my head, waiting for the "duh." I'd toyed with changing it the way most kids do. When I became a model, my modeling agents suggested I change it, as reinventing oneself was pretty common practice in the modeling world in the eighties. Sophie became Tobsha, and Angelique became Rochelle. What Amanda could become was something I was still fantasizing about until I heard one manager in the VIP lair say to another, "What's her name?" as he hovered over a book of entries with a black fountain pen.

"Portia . . . de . . . Rossi." The words came out slowly but with certainty. I really wanted that medallion.

"How do you spell that?"

I wrote the name in the air with my index finger behind my back to see whether a small *d* or a big *D* would look better. I got Portia from *The Merchant of Venice,* and de Rossi from watching the credits of a movie. The last name stuck in my mind among a million names that flew by. In a sea of a million unimportant names, I saw de Rossi. I put it all together in that room, got my medallion, a job, and walked out in shock. I had changed my identity. Just like that.

As I walked into the Shrine Auditorium where the Emmys were about to take place, I freaked out about how caught off-guard I'd been, how unprepared I was for the biggest test of my life—the test that required me to show them all why I was special and chosen. I made a mental note to buy fashion magazines and start caring about beauty items and perfume and exercising. I needed to find answers to these questions if I were going to feel confident next time. It was time Portia de Rossi earned her name.

9

AS I drove to work, my thoughts kept returning to my wardrobe. For Day One of the scripted days in this episode, I wore the black pencil skirt and long jacket. That would be okay because the waistband on the skirt was a little roomy, unlike the jeans I was currently wearing, which were cutting into my flesh and making my stomach fold over the top of them. I took my right hand off the steering wheel and grabbed my stomach fat—first just under the belly button and then I worked my way over the sides in repetitive grabbing motions. For fun I did it in time with the music. In a way it felt like a workout or a kind of dance of self-hatred. The fat extended all the way around to my back—not enough for a handful, but enough to take a firm hold of between my thumb and forefinger. As I looked down at my cavernous belly button I couldn't help but wonder if I was getting away with it. Did I still look like the girl they had hired? Did people notice? Obviously, my costume designer was aware of my weight gain over my first month on the show as she watched the weekly struggle of trying to pull up a skirt over my hips or straining to clasp the waistband. If pretending not to notice is the kind thing to do, then she was very kind to me. She always blamed the zipper for getting stuck because it was cheap or not properly sewn into the item of clothing even if she had to call her assistant in to hold the top of the zip as she put some muscle into trying to move it.

Did people look at me and think, "She's let herself go?" Did my actress rivals look at me and smirk, satisfied that my weight gain rendered me powerless to steal roles, scenes, or lines? As I pulled into my parking space, I couldn't help but wonder if maybe it was not just increasing familiarity but my nonthreatening physique that was the reason everyone had seemed a lot more comfortable around me lately. My presence no longer prompted them to ask themselves, "If this happened, then what's next?" as another actress, Lucy Liu, had joined the cast and answered that question. I was no longer the new girl, and I had proven to them that I wasn't a threat to their status on the show. With the weight gain, I wasn't exactly the hot blond bombshell that Cage and Fish talked about almost daily in their dialogue to each other. I cringed to read their lines and how they would talk about my character as being "hot" and "untouchable." While I wanted to be considered attractive, it made me uncomfortable to be thought of as being sexually desirable to men. But mainly the dialogue made me uncomfortable because I knew that reality didn't match up to the character David Kelley had written.

"Hey, Porshe. Haven't seen you in awhile. How were your days off?" Jane passed me in the hall on her way to set.

"Great, thanks."

"See you out there."

I walked into my dressing room and threw my bag down on the sofa.

There was a sharp knock on my dressing room door.

"Good morning, Portia. Makeup is ready for you."

"Be right there."

I walked around the desk to look in the mirror. The fat that I'd felt on my way there didn't really show under my sweater. At least not when I was standing. I lifted my sweater so I could see my bare stomach and the fat that I remembered feeling. But I didn't see fat. My stomach was flat. I stared into the eyes reflected in the mirror. They were smiling at me as if to say, "Oh, Porshe, what the hell are you worried about?"

For a brief moment, I felt relief. But it didn't last long. As I opened the wardrobe and looked at its contents, a wave of panic passed through my body; a hot, rolling rush of panic beginning in my stomach and ending at my head. Hanging on the bar were ten, maybe fifteen, sets of bras and panties. They were the kind of bras and panties that are intended to be seen, not the plainer flesh-toned kind that I was used to finding on the rack. Attached to the first pair was a note:

"For next episode. Please try on at your convenience. Thanks, V."

Shit. Shit! The next episode was eight days away. There was a knock at the door. I jumped out of my skin.

"Portia. Can you go to makeup, please? We're going to get to your scene in less than an hour."

"Alright! I'm coming!" As usual, the people who deserved it the least get the brunt of my anger. The person who deserved my anger the most was my fat, lazy, self. I had been in complete denial. I'd decided that rather than get off my fat, lazy ass and accept responsibility for my job, rather than seizing this amazing opportunity and using every scene as a showcase for my talent, I'd just sit around drinking beer and eating Mexican food. I stormed out of my dressing room and walked toward the makeup trailer, the voice in my head berating me.

You can't eat again until that scene. You need to work out. You're such an idiot for thinking you could get away with bingeing on Mexican food and not working out when this kind of thing could've happened at any time.

For a brief moment, I was aware that Peter MacNicol had passed me in the hallway. I'm sure he said hello, but it was too late to reply. The underwear scene probably had something to do with him. Our romance had been heating up and I bet there was some kind of love scene in the next episode. Maybe that's all it was. Maybe it would be a shot of me lying down on a bed in my underwear, or a waist-high shot of me unbuttoning a shirt to expose the top part of one of those pretty, lacy brassieres hanging in my closet.

"Hey!" My makeup artist gave me a hug and with a guttural laugh she said, "Did you read the next episode? You're doing a striptease, girl!"

I pulled the script from her hands and with a cold, emotionless expression I looked at what she'd been reading. I didn't want to give her any more enjoyment at my discomfort than she was already having. Of course, I didn't know if enjoyment was what she was experiencing for sure, but given the way we talked about our weight struggles almost every day, I couldn't imagine that she wasn't enjoying my discomfort a little, if just in that way that people are grateful they aren't dealt the same fate. The "better you than me" comment that is always delivered with a weird laugh makes it seem like they're ready to pull up a ringside seat for the ensuing spectacle. The script read: Nelle waits in her office for Cage. Cage enters. Nelle begins to remove her clothing. Cage is flustered. Nelle, in underwear, walks toward him. He runs out of the office and down the hall. At that moment, I would've done anything to run out of the makeup trailer, to my car, and out of this ugly studio with its square buildings and its one-way windows. I would go home and pack my suitcases and take my car to the airport, get on a plane, go back to Melbourne, Australia, and just start the whole damn thing over. Start my whole damn life over. I'd go to law school, a studious, serious girl who wasn't bopping around from photo shoots to lectures, having earned a place there after attending the local high school where I was the richest and smartest girl in the class. I would never have modeled, and so I'd think I was attractive just as I was, and I'd live in this blissful ignorance with my mother and father, because maybe for some reason he'd still be alive, too, and he wouldn't need me to go out and prove I was pretty and special, because he'd know that I was pretty and special, and he'd tell me that anyone who thought I wasn't the prettiest and smartest girl they'd ever known was stupid. Or jealous. Or both.

"Wow. That's really exciting. That's great for my character." When attacked, defend by lying.

I sat in the makeup chair staring at my reflected image as it was transformed from a hopeful twenty-four-year-old to a beaten down, emotionally bankrupt forty-year-old; the thick foundation covered my pores, suffocating my skin, the heavy eye shadow creating a big, deep crease in my eyelids, the red lipstick drawing the eye to my thin, pursed lips. Until now, it had looked to me like the mask of a character. No matter how scared or insecure I was, there was always a glint in my eyes underneath the thick eyeliner that reminded me that this was just a character, that I was young and exciting and had a life away from this world where there were no trees and no one to talk to. But sitting in the makeup chair at that moment, watching the transformation, the lines were blurred. It seemed like less work to create the defensive, cold character. It seemed like we were just putting some makeup onto my face. We were just defining my eye, giving color to my pale lips, covering up my imperfections. The fat was back, too. The fat that I'd felt in the car, spilling over the waistband of my jeans, was visible through my sweater, and I knew that everyone in the trailer was looking at it, wondering how I was going to get it off in eight days. But no one was wondering more than me.

I joined a gym. It was close to the studio, so if I had a break during the day I could just hop in the car and onto a treadmill. That was part of how I got the weight off. The other part was just not eating, which is a highly underrated strategy as zero meals a day works just as well for weight loss as six small ones. The only problem was I was so hungry and weak I limped to the finish line, no longer caring how I was going to stand in my underwear, or which angle would most flatter my body. I stopped caring to the extent that after the rehearsal, my hunger wrestled with my common sense and like a diva I demanded that a PA go to a Starbucks and bring me back a bran muffin. But if that kind of behavior is ever justified, it was at that moment when the script called for an extreme situation and I was just expected to comply. There was no question in David Kelley's mind as to whether I would do that scene. He demanded that I do it, and so I made my demands in retaliation. "Let's see the new blonde in her underwear!" Well then, I said, "Get me a muffin!" Actually, *demanded* is the wrong word. I asked. But it was so unusual for me to ask for anything, it replays in my mind as being a little harsher than it was. It was very common for actors to ask PAs to get them food or to mail a package or to put gas in their cars, but I always felt quite disgusted by it. I always felt that actors were just testing the limits of what someone would do for them just to see if they'd do it. I hate entitlement. But more than that, I hate that someone else in the same position as me feels entitled when I just feel lucky as hell.

I ate it before I shot the scene. I ate that muffin with its salt and calories and wheat and butter and all of the other bloating ingredients.

I hated everything about the underwear scene. I hated that in just a few episodes, I'd gone from playing a high-powered attorney to a woman desperately trying to get her boss to sleep with her. I hated that I'd have to play a love-interest character from now on, and I especially hated what I wore. I chose black lingerie with tiny red and pink hearts sewn onto it. It was ridiculously uncharacteristic for Nelle, who would have worn a more conservative style, perhaps something in navy blue—small, lacy, and revealing yet dignified, and worn with an air of supreme confidence in the goods the underwear displayed. The lingerie I chose was trashy with a stripper vibe. If ever I was to take care of my own needs before worrying about acting, it was in choosing the most flattering underwear. Here was my thinking: I would wear the largest, fullest cut with the most distracting colors to deemphasize my hips and thighs as much as possible. I would pad up my bra to offset the roundness of my stomach and look more proportional from head to toe. I chose a dress that I could remove in one easy motion so I wouldn't have to bend over and risk rolls of fat creasing on top of each other as I removed a tight skirt or a difficult blouse. I chose the highest of heels, because we all know that the taller you are, the more weight you can carry, and I wore my hair down, shaken all around, in an effort to lift the viewer's eye north of my abdomen and away from my thighs.

I shot the scene and awaited the verdict. I didn't have to wait long as it aired within a few weeks. Of course, when shooting a scene like that, some of the feedback is immediate. The energy of the crew changes, and no matter how professional you are, you still feel exposed, cheapened, paid to show your body. Or at least that's how I felt. And in that scene I was no longer a brilliant attorney who could make the firm more money than it had ever seen. I was stripped of that ability and the respect that comes with it when I stripped down to my heart-covered bra and panties. I was just another blond actress playing a vulnerable woman who has sex with her boss, in the costume of an efficient, crafty attorney. I was just an actress playing a lawyer, which, after dropping out of law school, was the only kind of lawyer I'd ever be. I don't know why I thought I'd be any more respected for simply pretending to be that which I didn't have the stamina to become.

By the time the episode aired, my life had changed. For many reasons, I'd decided to move out of the place in Santa Monica that I shared with my brother; the place that I'd shared with my husband. I moved away from the life I'd known since coming to Los Angeles and into an apartment in Hancock Park. I was on my own. Kali had moved back to Pasadena anyway, and my other friend, Ann, a girl who made difficult, emotional conversations easy, had moved to New York. Ann is the friend that everyone wishes they could have. She pries the truth out of you in a nurturing way and then stays around to clean up the tears. Ann's departure was one of the reasons I moved. But mainly I moved away because of paparazzi. Granted, there was only one photographer who had found my house, but the pictures of me sitting on my front steps, hair in curlers and smoking a cigarette, made me feel ambushed, watched, hunted almost. That one photographer made me feel like any of my private moments could be captured at any given time—unseen, unknown. I felt like I had a peeping Tom and every time I did something that I wouldn't want anyone else to see, my thoughts escalated into paranoid panic—not only over the present moment, but over those that predated the smoking picture. Retroactive paranoia.

There was nothing fun about seeing my picture in the *Star*. It served as a warning that I'd better watch myself or I could embarrass my family. I'd better watch myself or I could ruin my career. The photo of me smoking upset my mother. She'd much prefer it if people didn't think I did that, and now there was proof. Was there proof of my homosexuality yet? (Did I even have proof of it yet?) I wondered if the paparazzo was crouched behind the fence, overhearing my side of phone conversations with Ann when I would sit outside and smoke and talk to her about my therapy sessions. I talked to Ann about therapy and other important life-changing things. Ann had recommended I go to therapy and had also recommended the therapist. Ann listened to my panic and my confusion and to most of my dramatic statements like, "If I get into a relationship, if I even try, then people will find out I'm gay!" She replied, "What's so bad about that?" Which was ridiculous, of course. Everything was bad about that.

The episode with the scene of me in my underwear aired in New York three hours before it would air in LA. So I told Ann to watch it and call me immediately.

"Hey."

"What did you think?"

"I thought the show was great. You weren't in it as much this week."

"Ann! What did you think of the scene? How do you think I looked?"

"Great."

"What do you mean, 'great'?"

"Sexy. You know, great."

"Did I look thin?"

"I thought you looked like a normal, healthy woman."

Normal. Healthy. Woman.

My mother told me a long time ago that "healthy" was a euphemism for "fat." She'd say to me, "Don't you just hate it when you see someone at the supermarket and they tell you, 'You look healthy'? They clearly are just trying to tell you that they think you look fat." She'd tell me how she'd handle the backhanded compliment by smiling and pretending she was receiving a genuine compliment all the while ignoring their attempt to be insulting. After all, it's in the way an insult is received that makes it an insult. You can't really give offense unless someone takes it.

All of the words Ann used were euphemisms for fat. *Normal* just meant that I was fat. Since when did anyone ever go to the doctor's and feel good about being in the weight range that's considered normal? A normal size for women in this country is a size 12. Models aren't "normal." Actresses aren't "normal." She may as well have told me that I'd just embarrassed myself in front of 15 million people. If she didn't want me to think that, she would've used words like "overworked" instead of "healthy," and "girl" instead of "woman." How could the image of a woman, with her big voluptuous hips and round thighs and big, heavy breasts be applied to me if I was the skinny, straight-up-and-down, shapeless girl I was starving myself to be?

Message received loud and clear, friend.

You can't give offense unless somebody takes it.

10

BOUGHT A treadmill and put it in my dressing room. That way I was able to run during my lunch break on the set. I also bought another treadmill and put it the guest bedroom in my new apartment. With two treadmills, I didn't have an excuse not to work out. Because I had started to bring my Maltese dog, Bean, to the set with me, it was hard to get to the gym after work, and having a treadmill in my dressing room allowed me to run for the entire lunch hour instead of taking time out of my workout to drive to the gym and park. Although I hadn't had exercise equipment in my dressing rooms prior to *Ally McBeal*, I didn't invent the concept. Many of the cast members had them.

I got a nutritionist. Her name was Suzanne. I met her during a routine checkup at my gynecologist's office. She worked out of a small office in the back a couple of days a week and helped women change their diets to decrease their weight and increase their fertility. My doctor introduced her to me after I'd complained about my inability to maintain my weight. I told him that there were weeks when I'd gain and lose seven pounds from one Sunday to the next. After doing tests for thyroid disease and other medical problems that might have explained my weight fluctuation, he decided that the fault lay with me, that I didn't know how to eat. I agreed with him and hired Suzanne to be my nutritionist.

I loved the thought of having a nutritionist. It made me feel professional, like I was considering all aspects of my work in a thoughtful and serious way. Before my first session with Suzanne, I made the decision to do everything she said. Like a faithful disciple, I would follow her program without question the way a top athlete would drink raw eggs if his coach told him to. This was the kind of private, customized counseling I needed to be a working actress. Like a top athlete, I needed this kind of performance-enhancing guidance. I needed a coach. But mainly, I loved having a nutritionist because Courtney Thorne-Smith had one.

"Hi! Come on in. Mind the mess." Suzanne was a tall, thin woman with a sharpness to her movements. She dressed blandly and conservatively and was almost sparrowlike with long, thin arms and bony hands that would dart back and forth. I wondered why a woman like that, who was naturally thin, would be drawn to nutrition. I knew there were reasons to be interested in food other than weight loss, but I couldn't imagine those reasons being compelling enough to make nutrition your life. Instead of seeing her at the gynecologist's office where we met, I met with Suzanne at her home in Brentwood. When we'd first met she was wearing a white lab coat, and although the meeting was brief, from behind a desk she seemed officious, judgmental, bossy. But a layer of expertise and officiousness was immediately removed just by stripping her of her white coat and placing her in a different setting, in her home with her child's toys strewn about, her family in photographs looking at me. They were conservative-looking folk, poised to judge me for being so much fatter than she was. Then again, I felt they were judging her for being so messy. The fact that she was a black sheep made me feel a lot better.

"So from what the doctor tells me you have trouble maintaining your weight and knowing what to eat. Please know that you are one of millions of people who struggle with this, which is why people like me have a job!" Suzanne was no longer a skinny bird poised to judge me. She was caring and concerned. It was off-putting.

"Tell me why you think you can't maintain a healthy weight." She looked at me with kindness and openness, but there was a fragility to her that I found disarming, perhaps because I recognized a similar vulnerability in myself. Did she starve and binge and purge, too?

"Well . . ." I was surprisingly nervous. I really hadn't planned on opening up to someone about my eating habits, and all of a sudden it seemed like no one else's business. It seemed too personal. It seemed strange and a little idiotic to talk about food, like I was a five-year-old sitting cross-legged in a classroom learning about the five food groups.

"I don't know. I guess I just never knew of a really good diet that I can do every day so my weight doesn't fluctuate."

"Well, Portia. I'm not going to teach you a diet, I'm going to teach you a way of life. We'll talk about what you like to eat, and then I'll devise an eating plan that will be healthy and help you lose weight."

Sounds like a diet to me.

She talked and I listened. She had a lot to say about the kinds of calories one should eat, the value of lean protein, the dangers of too many carbohydrates, the difference between white and brown carbohydrates, and the importance of choosing the "right" fruits without a high sugar content.

"I like bananas. What about bananas?" Bananas were a staple in my "in-between" dieting phase. After starving myself by only eating 300 calories a day, I would often eat a slice of dry wheat bread with mashed banana.

"Well, Portia. Bananas are the most popular fruit, probably because they're the most dense and caloric of the fruits, so you'll have to be careful not to have them too often."

That explained why my "in-between" diet packed on the pounds. Bananas. Of course, the only fruit I liked was the only fruit this big fat country likes. I'm so typical.

"What are your eating habits now?"

"Now? Well, unless I'm getting ready for something, like a photo shoot or a scene like I just did on *Ally* where I had to be in my underwear, I guess I eat pretty normally. But you know, with the occasional binge."

"What do you mean by 'getting ready'? What do you do to 'get ready' for a photo shoot?" She leaned in slightly toward me. What I was saying seemed to intrigue her. I was wrong in thinking that maybe she starved, too.

"I eat three hundred calories a day for a week." I was shocked to see that her eyes widened with disbelief as she registered the information. It made me angry. She was judging me.

After a pause, she asked, "What do you eat to make up the three hundred calories?"

"Dry bread, mainly. Crackers. Pickles. Mustard. Black coffee."

"What happens when you're done with the photo shoot?" She asked like she didn't know the answer. It annoyed me.

"I binge, I guess. I eat all the foods I didn't eat while I was dieting, and then sometimes I eat too much and well, you know . . ."

Should I continue? Should I tell this conservative woman who already looked slightly shocked by my eating habits that I vomited? She's looking at me with anticipation and encouraged me to continue with a slight nod of her head. "I throw up."

I could see that she was uncomfortable, but I felt compelled to continue. "If I feel like I haven't thrown it all up, I'll take twenty laxatives to make sure it's all gone." Why would dieting and throwing up be so surprising to her? Really, as a nutritionist, she should have heard all that before. It made me wonder if she was qualified to help me. Maybe she helped really fat people take off a little weight, not someone like me who really needed to be taught the "way of life" that she was pitching. It made me mad because I didn't want to talk about myself and feel judged, I just wanted to learn about the five food groups like a five-year-old and take home a weekly eating plan.

I knew that I was being overly dramatic and that maybe she didn't need to know about the purging, but her reaction to my eating habits embarrassed me and that's what happens when I'm embarrassed. I get mad and I punish. And in response to my aggression, she leaned back in her chair and held a book up to her face, like a shield in between us.

"Have you seen one of these?" She waved it around. "It's a calorie counter. It'll help you figure out which are the healthy foods you can enjoy so that you'll never have to feel like you need to do those kinds of things again." Her eyes and her voice lowered as she lowered the book, her defenses. "Portia, it's really important that you understand food and stop this unhealthy cycle of yo-yo dieting."

Yo-yo is an inaccurate way to describe weight fluctuation. It is not the term anyone would use to describe the highs and lows that were the basis of my self-esteem. Yo-yo sounds frivolous, childish, disrespectful. Yo-yo sounds like a thing outside of yourself that you can just decide to put away and not pick up anymore. It suggests that there are end points, predetermined stopping points where the highs and lows end, because the string of a yo-yo is a certain length that never changes. My "bottom" would always be 140 pounds, my "high" 115. But it isn't like that. There's nothing predetermined about gaining and losing weight. Every day of my life I woke up not knowing if it would be a day on the path to a new bottom, a new big number that I'd never before seen on the scale, or if I would have a good day, a day that set me on the way to success and happiness and complete self-satisfaction. Since I was a twelve-year-old girl taking pictures in my front yard to submit to modeling agencies, I'd never known a day where my weight wasn't the determining factor for my self-esteem. My weight was my mood, and the more effort I put into starving myself to get it to an acceptable level, the more satisfaction I would feel as the restriction and the denial built into an incredible sense of accomplishment.

After introducing me to the calorie counter, Suzanne was all business. As well as teaching me how to count calories, she taught me to weigh my food. She told me that portion size was very important and to ensure I was getting the right portions, I had to buy a kitchen scale. She told me what to put on that scale for which meals. She told me that I should eat six small protein-enriched meals a day. She told me to keep a journal of what I ate.

Chicken, turkey, orange roughy, tuna, egg whites, oatmeal, blueberries, nonfat plain yogurt, steamed vegetables, brown rice, wheat bread, bran muffins, nuts—all weighed and documented—were my stable of foods I was allowed to eat. Most other things were not part of the program.

As I left her house that day I felt an overwhelming sense of relief. I had heard that in order to know how to overcome difficulties, you needed the "tools" to do it. Suzanne had given me a program with tools. A no-fail system of calorie counting, weighing, and adding up my daily intake so there would be no guesswork to my weight loss. Now that I had my curriculum in the form of my "allowed" foods, homework assignments in the form of a diary, and weekly exams when Suzanne would evaluate how I'd performed, I could be a good student.

11

WAS OFFERED the cover of *Shape*. *Shape* is a health and fitness magazine that depicts lean, physically strong women. Its articles explain the secret to killer abs and each month it unveils the no-fail diet. On the cover it displays a fit woman, a celebrity if they can get one, who promises to tell you her strategy for weight-loss success. They take pictures of their cover girls in skimpy outfits, like a bikini or spandex shorts, and then interview them about how they achieved optimum "health." I knew why they picked me. It wasn't for my lithe body or killer abs, and they certainly didn't see the underwear scene before offering it to me. I was simply the new girl on the hot TV show. I doubted anyone making the decision had even seen me on the show. Of course, I panicked and gave a million reasons why I shouldn't do it, but my publicist and manager thought it was a great opportunity. A cover is a cover.

It was hard to argue with my publicist and manager. My publicist and manager knew better than I did. The cover of *Shape* complemented the clean-living, fresh-faced image they were trying hard to create. They had subtly written a character for me to play in public, gently coercing me to play the role of an ingénue, fresh but glamorous and with an ounce of naïveté. They guided me into the character by favoring romantic dresses over sexy dresses for red carpet events and to most questions about the show or my life, they smiled with approval when I answered that my journey from law student to Hollywood actress was "a dream come true." It seemed effortless and surprising: a Cinderella story. I understood their reasoning. I needed an image to sell; the truth of who I was needed to remain a secret and Portia, the young, heterosexual, self-confident Australian actress needed to emerge. Besides, most of the successful, leading-lady actresses had graduated from this rite of passage. However, the ingénue was a difficult role for me to play—more difficult in fact than a commanding, self-assured attorney. Even if I ignored the fact that I was gay, at twenty-five I was too old, too cynical. I played the ingénue once in *Sirens* when I was twenty, and even then I felt more like Dorothy Parker than the character of Giddy, the gullible artist's model.

I didn't know how to play that character for the *Shape* interview. With neither health nor fitness being of interest to me, I didn't know what to talk about. How could I possibly explain my weight maintenance when it was attributed to starving and bingeing?

SHAPE: *Portia, tell us how you stay in shape?*

PORTIA: *I eat three hundred calories a day for as many days as I can before a photo shoot. The rest of the time I binge and purge.*

SHAPE: *What's your favorite workout?*

PORTIA: *I'm afraid to work out at all because I'm worried that muscle definition makes people look bigger. I hate the look of fit, muscular women. I prefer the long, waiflike look of models who are most likely just as sick as I am.*

Suzanne had stopped me from crash dieting. It was a cycle of loss and gain, she explained, that once started, could never be stopped. It was true. After shooting the scene in my underwear I had gained a lot of weight. Reluctantly and fearfully, I put my new diet into practice for the week leading up to shooting the cover of *Shape*. I was extremely nervous that because I'd not starved myself the way I usually did before a shoot, my body wasn't really in good enough shape to grace the *Shape* cover. Walking into my trailer that was sitting atop a hill at the location they'd chosen for the shoot, I felt unprepared and anxious. I had weighed in at 125 pounds that morning—not a number on the scale I was used to seeing the morning of a photo shoot, much less a cover shoot wearing a bikini. I had already eaten, too, another abnormality before a shoot. I had eaten my individually packaged oatmeal sachet with antioxidant blueberries and Splenda, a sugar substitute that Suzanne said was so healthy she gave it to her baby. Although I knew that I was being a good student and following the only program that had a chance of actually working for me, the guilt and unworthiness I felt by not starving myself in preparation for the shoot were unbearable. I was embarrassed to shake the hands of the picture editor and the executive editor of *Shape*. I was ashamed that even though I had a gym membership, I rarely used it. Although I'd never really liked the "fit" look, I wished that I could drop my robe to reveal muscular arms and legs and a defined abdomen and waist. I was dreading dropping my robe and showing them the exact opposite of what I knew they were expecting to see. During the shoot, and in a fit of insecurity, I asked one of the photographer's assistants, an unattractive guy who looked sandy and sunburned, like he'd spent the morning surfing, how my body compared to the other girls who'd modeled for the cover. I'd been watching him all morning, not because he was interesting, but because he looked so bored, so uninspired by working on photo shoots, or perhaps this shoot in particular. He was the perfect person to ask because I knew he'd answer with complete honesty. He wouldn't care if he hurt a girl's feelings. His expression changed the second I asked the question, as if the question were like a plug inserted into his brain that reanimated him and sent energy flooding to his face. With a big, dumb smile he responded slowly, giving more weight to each word than was necessary to make the point. "We photograph some women with really sick bodies."

I got what I asked for. Honesty. I knew my body couldn't compare to the other girls; I just needed to confirm it. This dumb guy said what all the other guys out there were thinking. And if I were going to have a career, I would need to impress men just like this one. If I couldn't be the *Maxim* girl with big breasts and a tiny waist, I could be model-like. Unattainable. I could be elegant. Graceful. Thin.

I would just have to get myself one of those sick bodies.

"Morning, dear. How was your photo shoot?" Vera, the costume designer, looked exhausted and like she really didn't care to hear the answer. I was the fourth actor she'd seen that morning. But because she was very polite, she added, "What did you do again?"

"I did the cover of *Shape*."

"*Shape*? What's that?"

I told her that it was a fitness magazine and as I told her how important it was to me because I was passionate about exercise, I sounded like the well-versed liar I had been trained to be. My agent and manager would've been proud.

As I slipped into a navy skirt, I thought about my plans for the summer. I created a picture in my mind of me lying by a pool overlooking the Caribbean ocean, the most beautiful girl on the lounge next to mine. In my mind, the girl turned her head and smiled a sleepy smile, her eyes full of love for me. I had an uncanny ability to escape the present moment and into my fantasy world whenever I wanted to. I especially liked to think about other things during a wardrobe fitting. It made the inevitable comments about how the tailor can let the waist out a little, "just to make the skirt more comfortable," somewhat bearable, knowing that I could choose a happier moment in another place and time. But I was going to be in the Caribbean with the girl of my dreams, so my daydream was borne more from excitement and a little wishful thinking than it was from a place of complete fantasy. Only a few more weeks of wardrobe fittings and my fantasy would be a reality. I held my breath and sucked in my stomach as the zipper closed the gap to the waist. I felt the pinch of the waistband and held my breath again, this time for the conversation between the costumer and tailor that would inevitably ensue.

Go to hell.

As I stood in the fitting room, I almost laughed out loud as I remembered the first words I spoke to Sacha, the girl I was going to be with over summer in St. Barths. It was my first day of Melbourne Girls Grammar School and a stunning black girl who I later knew as Sacha, had left the group in the corner of the quadrangle to talk to me, the new girl. Sacha looked as if I'd slapped her across the face. I didn't know why. "Go to hell," was the only thing I could say. She had strutted up to me with no prompting or subtle invitation and said to me, "You have such pretty hair you should wear it down. Take it out, I want to see it."

The All Girls Grammar School was extremely strict and had a policy about hair, among many other things. The uniform had to be worn with a blazer when off campus, the socks had to always be pulled up to the knees, and the hair must always be neatly pulled back off the face. So you see, she was definitely just having a go at me. She was trying to get me in trouble—or worse. She was trying to get me to pull my hair out of my rubber band and shake it all around like a shampoo commercial so that the pack of girls she was standing with who dared her to come tell me to let my hair down could laugh their asses off at the new girl. I knew girls like that—mean girls. Besides, I was an easy target. I was a model who recently changed her name from Amanda Rogers to Portia de Rossi, so I was prepared for that kind of bullshit. So you see? "Go to hell" was the preemptive strike needed at the time and really the only thing I could say. I can't really remember what happened after that, or how Sacha and I became friends, but we did. Over a period of weeks, we became inseparable. We would spend weekends at her parents' home, staying up all night watching MTV and eating loaves of white bread, butter, and apricot jam. We borrowed each other's clothes. We went out to nightclubs together and flirted with men. For years we were good friends, best friends. Until one day, long after we'd left school, I fell in love with her.

I fell in love with her the day I left home to audition for the movie *Sirens*. I was nineteen years old when I left law school and flew to Sydney to audition for a career I didn't even think I wanted. I had spent my life studying to go to law school, and with one phone call from my modeling agency asking if I'd like to do a movie, I was prepared to ditch law and become an actress. By the time I disembarked and collected my baggage at the terminal, I had fallen in love with Sacha. She was no longer just a friend; she was the reason I had to get the movie. If I was successful, I could win her, seduce her with money and power just as Martina Navratilova and Melissa Etheridge had won their previously heterosexual girlfriends. By their actions, these powerful, famous lesbians told the world that straight women were more desirable than gay ones and if you were rich and powerful enough, you could snag one of your own.

Sacha was not a lesbian. But then, neither was I. I just liked to sleep with women.

My girlfriend had to be heterosexual because I didn't want to be a lesbian. If she was heterosexual, then it suggested that I was also heterosexual. Also, I was scared of lesbians. In fact, I would cross the street if I saw one coming toward me. One time I didn't cross the street and I ended up sleeping with a lesbian because I felt sorry for her. She had just lost her girlfriend in a car accident and I was devastated for her. Nothing sounded worse to me than losing your girlfriend; that the one precious connection that you had made in your whole life was gone, wasted, lost in a car wreck. It sounded so much worse to me than a wife losing her husband—it was worse than anything. I found this woman to be quite unattractive. She was overweight and had a shaved head and facial piercings. But I had to sleep with her. It was only polite.

My girlfriend would have to be someone I already knew, someone I could trust. The last thing on earth I needed at the end of my first season on *Ally McBeal* was to be outed by some girl who just wanted to date me because I was on TV, who just wanted to sleep with me so that she could tell people that I was gay. The career that I once didn't think I wanted was now something that I couldn't live without, and a rumor that I was gay would be enough to end it. As it turned out, I loved acting. During the filming of *Sirens* I discovered that while in character with the camera rolling, I couldn't do anything wrong, that there wasn't a right way to deliver a line, merely a different interpretation. I loved interpreting meaning from words. My happiest moments of learning in school or in college were spent deciphering poetry, reciting John Donne or Shakespeare using inflection with my voice to convey my interpretation of the poem's meaning. I discovered while filming *Sirens* that acting was transformative. I discovered that you could be someone other than who you were and get attention for it, be applauded for it. And all of that was very appealing to me—especially the part about being someone else.

I had planned this vacation for us years before I could afford it, when I began to travel and thoughts of an island and Sacha and I together living on it, if only for a short time, kept me company. Over the years, each time I was away from home, I would write her long, romantic letters that explained my feelings, what our lives would be like together, and how I would take care of her. When I lived in London to complete postproduction after *Sirens* and then hung around to try to find a reason not to go back to law school—like a play in the West End or another movie—I would go down to the coffee shop in the morning to begin writing, and I'd finish the letter in the evening, sitting alone at the corner table of the local pub just off King's Road in

Chelsea, close to where I lived. Writing to her, I was no longer lonely. I had someone waiting for me across the world in Australia. I could tolerate anything as long as I had a notepad and a pen and could pour my heart out to her in these letters. In airport lounges, thoughts of her would engulf my senses to the point where I'd almost miss planes, and in Los Angeles, thoughts of her would numb the pain of losing a job, of hearing no after an audition. My fantasy life with Sacha was as helpful to me as it was adjustable. For when I was in a relationship with Mel, or had a crush on Kali, Sacha would again revert to being just my best friend. Sacha also had relationships of her own, long-term, serious heterosexual relationships. Because of that, I never sent her any of the letters that I had written. But she knew how I felt about her. I'd told her that I loved her after long drunken evenings of partying and making out with her on nightclub dance floors. I knew that given the chance to move to Los Angeles and be with me, she would no longer want to be tied down by these demanding, serious boyfriends. So none of that really mattered to me.

Besides, I had a boyfriend, too. His name was Erik.

Erik was Kali's ex-boyfriend. He became my boyfriend when I invited him to be my date at a Hollywood event. Although he didn't see why it was necessary for me to hide the fact that I was a lesbian, he assured me that he would play the role of my boyfriend to the best of his ability, so I made Erik my permanent beard. The fact that he agreed to be my beard proved his affection for me. Hollywood events were something he had no interest in attending, and in fact, as a budding novelist, he had expressed contempt for the whole industry. His idols were Hemingway and Vonnegut, not Cruise and Gibson.

I had adored Erik from our first meeting at Kali's apartment in Santa Monica. He was deeply thoughtful, attractive, and intelligent. If I could have, I would've slept with him just to show him how much I adored him, but on the one occasion when he crashed in my bed and sex had crossed my mind, the smell of him took the thoughts away. He didn't smell bad. He just smelled male. All men do.

Although Erik quickly learned his role, our first public outing as a couple was nerve-racking. I had never walked a red carpet with anyone before and his attitude toward the media was not helping to quell my nerves. To Erik, a television camera was an opportunity to be a wiseass. (He had told me that if he were to ever appear on *Letterman*, he'd give a shout-out to all the black people in the audience.) As usual, I'd left nothing to chance. I had memorized answers, this time to the right questions: What was I wearing? What are my workout tips? What is my must-have beauty item? In the rented stretch limousine on our way from my apartment to the event on Rodeo Drive in Beverly Hills, Erik and I rehearsed answers to possible questions the two of us might be asked.

"So, if they ask something like, 'How long have you been dating?' just say something vague like, 'just a few months.' "

"I think it's funnier if I say that we just fucked for the first time on the ride over here."

"Erik! This is serious! Don't be a dick."

It was all very funny to Erik. There was nothing on the line for him. He wasn't gay and trying to appear straight. He could attend the event like a spectator, listen to Bocelli, observe this weird Hollywood charade, and drink wine and eat food without concern of getting fat. He wasn't going to have to face the press and pretend that all this was real; he just had to say one easy thing or nothing at all.

"Please say nothing at all."

He shot me an unnerving wink from underneath his mop of blond hair as he got out of the limo, straightened his jacket, and stood with his back to me like a statue, offering his arm like the gentleman escort role I had asked him to play. Despite the fact that he was a smart-ass in my ear all the way down the red carpet, he managed to obscure his disdain from the photographers, and my little plan worked. I was asked if he was my boyfriend and I decided that by answering coyly ("We're just friends"), I would pique their interest more than by announcing that we were dating. Plus it carried the added benefit of being the truth. Because of him the event felt less like work. As someone who wasn't particularly smitten with the world in which I lived, he gave me perspective on my job as an actress, served up with a drink and observations that made me laugh. The women at work assumed he was my boyfriend, and I did everything in my power to keep that assumption alive.

I had a boyfriend called Erik. He was smart and handsome and tall, and he was mine. Except Erik had a girlfriend. Erik left me for a woman who would have sex with him because he didn't smell strange to her. He left me because I was never his to leave. It was a devastating breakup.

12

"COME ON in, Portia. How have you been doing this week?" Suzanne was holding an unwashed dinner plate in her hand as she opened the door. I assumed she'd noticed this dirty plate on her walk from wherever she was, through the living room and to the front door. She was surprisingly messy for such a thin woman. I said hello to her, but in my mind I was thinking how funny it was that I would equate thinness with cleanliness. That observation triggered a memory of being in art class when I was asked to describe how Kandinsky painted and to explain why I didn't like him. "He paints like a fat person," was all I could think to say at the time, as his painting was messy, nonlinear, disorganized, as opposed to Mondrian, a painter who worked in the same period and used colors sparingly, modestly, and who stayed within the lines. He was orderly, clean, and thin.

By the time I left art class in my head and joined Suzanne, I was on the couch. I was beginning to trust her despite my initial fears and wanted to talk to her about my past. From my first session, I had become more aware of the abnormalities of my eating habits as a kid, and it felt good to talk about it out loud. I had considered going back to the therapist who had helped my husband and me realize that our relationship was doomed to failure, but food and eating seemed to be more of a nutritionist's area of expertise than a couples' therapist's, so I told Suzanne everything. I no longer cared whether she was shocked.

I told her that from the age of twelve, starving and bingeing and purging had been the only way to reach my goal weight. That starving was easy because there was always an end in sight. Junk food was around the bend just after the photo shoot or the round of go-sees. But by the age of fifteen, I needed to devise a plan to not only lose weight but to maintain my weight loss. At the end of the school year, I'd convinced my mother that the strict girls' grammar school I attended was "getting in the way of my education" and that I needed to take a year off to model, make some money, and then enroll in a more progressive private school the following year. The fact that I needed to lose weight was nothing new. Ever since I'd begun modeling, I'd always needed to "get ready" for a photo shoot. Me losing weight before a job was like an athlete training for a competition. But if I was going to take a year off school to model, I had to figure out a more permanent solution to the weight problem. I couldn't starve and binge and purge like I had always done. By the time I was fifteen, the purging and the laxatives had become part of my everyday life, and although I wasn't concerned about the possible damage it could cause to the interior of my body, it was a drag to have to spend so much time in the bathroom. Plus, there was only one bathroom in my house.

I told Suzanne that I had asked my mother to help me. Every time I was booked for a job that I had to drop pounds quickly for, I'd beg her to help me the next time so I'd never again be in the predicament of having to starve before a job. I'd say, "Please don't let me eat chocolate." And, "If you see me eating too much of anything, just remind me what I go through every time." This request bothered my mother because, like an addict, when I was in the throes of eating, I could get quite angry and yell at her if she commented on my habit. "You don't want to eat that," was the most common thing she'd say as I was stuffing a chocolate-covered cookie in my mouth. She was wrong. At that moment, eating that cookie was all I wanted to do and I told her so in many different ways over the course of that little experiment. In sober moments, I'd apologize for my hurtful words and plead with her to continue to help me. I told her to hide the cookies. Then when I found them underneath the living room sofa, I'd angrily eat them, saying that all she cared about was how thin I was. That she didn't really care about me. That all she cared about was my modeling career.

"That sounds like a difficult situation for both you and your mother."

"It was."

Using my mother's watchful eye as a deterrent to bingeing was probably the worst thing I could have done. While I'd always binged, it had never disappointed my mother as much as it did during this time. It had worried her greatly that I had left school to model, and if I wasn't thin enough to book jobs, then leaving school didn't serve any purpose. Since I'd asked her to help me maintain my weight, we were in it together. We had a problem that we could overcome together. The list of taboo foods got a lot bigger, too. In the past, while I may've hidden the occasional chocolate candy bar, now eating any food that wasn't diet food sent the message that I was not helping myself. That I'd given up. It was simply heartbreaking to see the disappointment on her face as I sat the plate down on the dinner table piled high with the same food she'd once encouraged me to eat to make me big and strong. It disappointed me, too. Because a simple meal that my brother, mother, and grandmother would eat was never something I could eat. Models don't eat mashed potatoes with butter. And as my mother kept pointing out, I was the one who wanted to be a model.

So I stopped eating in front of her. In front of her, I'd eat steamed vegetables. In the back alleys of restaurants, sitting in between two Dumpsters, I'd eat anything I liked. If my mother wasn't home and lack of pocket money forced me to make do with the food that was in the kitchen pantry, I'd keep one eye on my grandmother as she sat in the living room and hastily get to work on half a loaf of bread and butter with apricot jam. I'd then walk to the supermarket with a butter knife, buy bread, butter, and apricot jam, throw away the few slices of bread to make it look like the untouched original loaf, then use the knife to remove the portions of the butter and jam to make it look like everything was just how I found them. Or I should say, just as she left them.

My mother thought there might be a medical solution to the weight problem in the form of a prescribed appetite suppressant. A drug called Duromine was well known in Australia. It is phentermine, the *phen* in Fen-phen, and was similarly heralded for its effectiveness in weight control. I was prescribed Duromine after a physical examination by a doctor and started taking the drug.

I lost weight. I lost weight and was thin—bony, even. I was ready for any modeling job without concern and was the envy of my school peers. The only problem with the drug was that I couldn't sleep. If I took it every morning with a cup of tea, I felt jittery all day long, speedy almost, and that feeling of restlessness and anxiety stayed with me throughout the day and continued into the night. I could take it daily for only a couple of weeks before I felt like I needed a break from it. Instead of being the answer to helping me with consistent, steady dieting, the Duromine became like a yo-yo in itself. It became another wagon to fall off. It was yet another way to disappoint myself with my lack of willpower, of toughing it out. I just couldn't hack it, just like I couldn't hack dieting. I'd stop taking it, claiming that it affected my studies and my overall health, but secretly I missed eating. I missed the comfort that tasting and chewing and swallowing gave me. I missed the warmth in my belly and the feeling of wholeness; I was incomplete on Duromine, and on food, I was whole.

I realized during the sessions with Suzanne that it almost didn't matter who I was talking to, it was good to talk. And while I talked, she listened. She gave me my program for the week, gave me some helpful tips for the upcoming holidays, and sent me back into the world with my homework.

13

I SURVIVED SEASON TWO OF *ALLY MCBEAL!*

HAT WAS the slogan on a T-shirt that was given out to the cast and crew by a cast member. I survived season two—but barely. Since beginning the show I had felt a constant indescribable pressure, a lurking threat of being fired, even though there was no evidence to suggest that I was displeasing the executive producer. While it was a good place to work and people were generally respectful, there was an eerie stillness and a certain kind of silence to the set that felt like a breezeless summer day, and while there were no insects, there were no birds chirping either. During the last four weeks of the season, every night after wrap, I would get into my car, smile and wave good night to hair and makeup, and like clockwork, I would burst into tears once I made the right turn from Manhattan Beach Studios onto Rosecrans Boulevard. And I would sob, not just cry. I made loud wailing noises that sounded more like "ahhhhhh" than the kind of crying I'd done over other things. In fact, I sounded like Lucille Ball as Lucy Ricardo when she would cry loudly, embarrassing Ricky to the point where he'd do anything she wanted just to shut her up. No one could hear my wailing, however. I wasn't doing it for effect. I was doing it to soothe myself, to comfort myself. And I didn't know why I was crying either. I would cry just as loudly if I'd spent the day performing a wordy two-page closing argument to a jury as if I'd been propped up on a chair in the background of the law office with no dialogue at all.

With the end of the season came the holidays. I had booked the trip with Sacha to St. Barths. While I was excited to realize my dreams of being with her, there was no doubt that I was nervous to see it through. I was worried that by embarking on a romantic journey with Sacha, the journey could come to an end, taking my romantic fantasies with it; the daydreams that lulled me to sleep smiling, the fantasies that filled otherwise empty hours, and the soothing thoughts that took pain and loneliness away would all go with it. These thoughts gave me both anxiety and hope toward the end of the season. Finally, for better or worse, our romance would become a reality.

In St. Barths, however, reality was shocking. It ruined romance like an annoying little brother. It was a pestering ever-present element in our conversations, especially as the conversations featured her boyfriend, Matt, to whom she was considering getting married. Our precious time alone in that tropical paradise was not filled with longing glances and passionate lovemaking, but rather it was spent with our heads stuck in our respective books and in arguments. A conversation about the book I was reading, in fact, ended all arguing, as reality punched me in the face and knocked illusion out cold.

"What's that book you're reading?"

"Ellen DeGeneres's mother, Betty, wrote it. She tells her story about what it's like to have a gay daughter."

"Who's Ellen DeGeneres?"

Her having a fiancé in Australia didn't deter my quest to make Sacha my girlfriend, but not knowing who Ellen was two years after she made international headlines for coming out on her show suggested to me that being gay wasn't even on Sacha's radar, despite her willingness to make out with me on a dance floor from time to time. From that moment on, I knew that I was alone without my imaginary life to keep me company. So I swallowed my disillusionment in the form of cream sauces, piña coladas, and pastries, served up to me by the private chef I'd hired to help me seduce Sacha into a life of lesbianism. Now the chef's role was to reward me for my hard work on *Ally* for the season. I ate my way into relaxation in St. Barths. And I got really fat.

The fact that I got fat was unfortunate as I was scheduled to shoot the cover of *Rolling Stone Australia* two weeks after my vacation ended. I went back home to Melbourne to my mother feeling more like a deserter than the war hero I had dreamed of. I thought I'd be paraded around Camberwell, the town where my mother lived, as the American TV star triumphantly returning. To be honest, there was still some parading, some walking up to the Camberwell shops with my mother to talk to the shopkeepers about my adventures overseas, but it felt wrong. The pounds were evidence of the pressure. Heaviness overshadowed the levity of talking about what I wore to the Emmys or what Calista was like as a person. People could sense my depression and discomfort, and that really ruined the fun for everyone. So my mother dutifully hid her chocolate-covered cookies, and I starved and cried and went back and forth to the gym I used to go to for aerobics classes back in the eighties.

ROLLING STONE AUSTRALIA. ISSUE 566, OCTOBER 1999

> *There are two rumours about Portia de Rossi . . . So which rumour would she like to address first?*
>
> *"Oooh, I love this," the 26-year-old says in her peculiar LA via Melbourne accent. "It's just like truth or dare!"*
>
> *OK, the first rumour is about the hair. We know it's real. We know she's a natural blonde because her mum has shown us the baby photos. Even as a four-year-old her white-blond hair was worn long and girly. So that's that out of the way . . . The second rumour is that De Rossi was spotted in clubs around Melbourne recently cosying up to other girls. So does that mean she's bisexual? A lesbian? A long, delighted squeal*

comes down the telephone line. "Ooooh, how fun! I love that question!"
she says, shouting now . . .

"Let's just say every celebrity gets that rumour and now I feel like
I've joined the club. Hooray!"

Hooray indeed. Not only were they "on to me," a phrase that my
mother would use when my secrets were being pried out of their vault
and into pop culture, but the photo shoot exposed another terrible
secret, possibly worse than being gay. It told the world, or at least the
people of Australia, that I was fat. I tried as hard as I could to get the
weight off, but whittling down from 140 pounds in two weeks proved
to be too much of a feat even for this crash dieter. If only Sacha had
fallen in love with me, none of this would've happened. Now I was on
the cover of a magazine, fat and looking like a hooker in a chainmail
boob tube and leather hot pants. Over the previous six months, I was
told that I had ranked highly in the polls featured in men's magazines
as being "hot," mainly because of the icy, untouchable nature of my
character. Nothing was more of a foil for my real, gay self than to appear on the cover of men's magazines as a sexy, man-eating young
actress. Another difficult role to play, I was discovering who I was while
desperately trying to convey the image of the woman I wasn't.

> *When Portia de Rossi looked at the clothes we'd chosen for this*
> *month's cover shoot—leather hot pants, chainmail boob-tube, handcuffs,*
> *G-string, she only had one thing to say: "Oh fuck!" Several cigarettes*
> *later and a few soothing words from her mum and her aunt Gwen*
> *(also at the shoot), she was happily admiring herself in the sexy clob-*
> *ber. "Mama, do you think it's too kinky?" she asked. "No," her mum*
> *replied. "You look very pretty."*

After the photo shoot, I went to the airport. I had to fly back to Los
Angeles to meet with executives from L'Oréal to discuss being their new

spokesperson for a hair product. I knew that people thought I had nice hair. I knew it was special because I was often told that it was the reason for my success. The fact that I played the title role in the Geelong Grammar School production of *Alice in Wonderland,* for example, was because of my hair, according to all the girls at school. Occasionally, on modeling jobs I was singled out to be featured in a campaign because of my hair, and on *Ally McBeal* toward the end of my first season, my hair acted out more drama than my character did. It went to court to showcase how women use sexuality to get ahead in the workplace, it indicated when my character's walls were up, and it even performed a few stunts, notably when John Cage "wired" my hair to remotely shake loose from its restrictive bun when he wanted me to "let my hair down." So the fact that my hair had garnered some attention from people who sell hair products wasn't surprising to me. In fact, it was the only thing that had made sense for quite a while. The fact that I didn't like my thick, unmanageable hair was irrelevant.

I didn't write letters to Sacha in the airport terminal. I ate. There was nothing left to say, no fantasies I could act out on paper of how we would be happy together in a tropical paradise, so I ate. I ate English muffins with butter and jam. I ate potato chips and cookies and gulped down Coke. I threw up. I left the first-class lounge to shop for food in the terminal. I ate McDonald's burgers, vanilla milk shakes, and fries. I threw up again. Then I got on the plane.

"Can I get you a drink, Ms. de Rossi?" The American stewardess had a lipsticky mouth and overpronounced the syllables, as Americans tended to do. It was strange to hear the American accent after being in Australia. It reminded me that I had an accent, too. It reminded me that Australian-born Amanda Rogers was now American-seeming Portia de Rossi. If magazines didn't say otherwise, I could definitely pass as a Yank. My dad had called Americans Yanks. I thought it was funny when I was a little kid. He'd also sung me to sleep with a passionate, out-of-tune rendition of "The House of the Rising Sun."

"Baileys Irish Cream, if you have it." Of course I knew they had it, it just sounded more polite, more whimsical. I was aware that the stewardess would think that an after-dinner cream liqueur would be a ridiculous drink to order before dinner, and I needed her to know that I knew it was ridiculous, too, so I said: "I've been looking forward to some Baileys. I always have it on planes." That made it better.

When I refused dinner and asked for my sixth Baileys, the stewardess got weird again. Of course, she served it to me; I was a first-class passenger after all, but I could detect concern in her pour, more than just the concern that comes with pouring liquid into a narrow-rimmed glass on a moving vehicle that is subject to bouts of turbulence. She was judging me. She looked disgusted. She was worried for me. She had reason to be worried, I guess. I had spent a lot of the plane ride quietly crying, as I often do because I hate hovering between one place and another. "Neither here nor there" was an expression my grandmother would use to describe confusion and displacement, and it is a disturbing place to be. This state of hovering during the fourteen-hour journey was once filled with fantasy scenarios of being Sacha's obsession or having a beautiful body on the cover of a major magazine. Now I had no choice but to fill the time by bringing a glass of thick, creamy liquid back and forth to my lips. I was neither in LA nor in Melbourne, neither straight nor gay, neither famous nor unknown, neither fat nor thin, neither a success nor a failure. My Discman played the soundtrack for my inner dialogue—rare recordings of Nirvana and so here we were, Kurt Cobain and I, displaced, misunderstood, unloved, and "neither here nor there"—he being neither dead nor alive, both in his life and in his death. It occurred to me as I listened to lyrics like "and if you killed yourself, it would make you happy" that if I were at the end of my life, I wouldn't have to keep running the race. If I were really old and close to dying, I wouldn't have to do another season, another magazine cover. I could be remembered as a successful working actor, a celebrity, even. I had been given the challenge of life and beaten it. The pressure I had put on myself to excel in everything I did made life look like a never-ending steeplechase. The thought that I had fifty more years of striving and jumping over hurdles and being the one to beat in the race was enough to make me order another drink.

After my seventh Baileys I threw up. I made myself throw up, but it took a long time to do it, and because I was drunk, it was sloppy. I've never liked airplane toilets. They've always disgusted me, so the unclean, smelly toilet made me nauseous and the nausea made me think there was more food and liquid in my gut to get rid of. A lot of dry heaving and coughing followed. My fingernails had cut the back of my throat where my gag reflex was and I was throwing up saliva, maybe bile, and a trace of blood. Several times, I heard knocking on the door. I ignored it. It didn't bother me at all, actually. I deserved to be on this plane and in this bathroom just like they did. By the time I had unlocked the door, there was a guy in a uniform waiting for me. He looked officious and slightly angry, which made me angry. There are other toilets on the plane, for God's sake.

"There's some concern that you're not feeling well. Is there anything I can do to help you, Ms. de Rossi?"

"No. I'm fine." The purging session had given me a colossal headache. So I added, "Maybe some aspirin."

As I walked down the aisle, I noticed a contraption in the way. It was in the aisle blocking access to my seat. It was silver, and looked like a cylinder on poles with wheels attached. The stewardess stood next to it and as if reading my mind she replied, "Oxygen. I think it'll make you feel better."

Something shifted. As I looked into the face of the stewardess, I no longer saw expressions of judgment and disgust. I saw concern. The once angry, officious-looking man in the uniform returned from getting aspirin for my headache and gave it to me with a smile. I looked at my two uniformed nurses, and their caring, nurturing expressions, and quietly sat in my seat and attached the oxygen mask to my face.

When I woke up to the plane preparing for landing in Los Angeles, the silver contraption, and my headache, were gone. I was in Los Angeles.

My name is Portia de Rossi. I'm an American actress about to embark on my second season of a hit TV show. I am here and not there. I am here.

14

HERE ARE a few places in Los Angeles where art meets up with commerce for a drink and the Four Seasons bar is one of them.

As I walked in from the lobby, I saw little plays being acted out at nearly all the tables—the actor, writer, or director presenting himself as something to invest in, the producer or executive sizing them up before deciding to purchase or pass. Sometimes, like a chaperone, the manager or agent will be present at one of these sales meetings. The manager tends to lubricate things with friendly, ice-breaking conversation. Also, the manager orders lunch or drinks for the table and plugs the awkward silences by asking after the producer's kids. Most times, their kids play soccer together. Or attend the same school. Hollywood is a club. And with the help of a couple of referrals, I got to fill out my application.

I walked through the bar to the assortment of floral lounge chairs that would serve as the site for my success or failure. I was meeting with the L'Oréal executives. I was a potential new product. I approached them in the dress and heels I'd agonized over wearing for a week. Did the dress convey respect and excitement and downplay desperation? Or did it somehow expose the truth: that my self-esteem hinged on their decision? Was it too low-cut or too high-cut? Was it too tight? Did it display my wares in an attempt to arouse interest in a cheap, throw-in-everything-you've-got way? I led with my hair by running my hand across the nape of my neck to scoop up the thick blond "product" and dumped it over one shoulder for inspection: cheap, but effective.

"Hi. I'm Portia."

Handshakes all round. They looked interested. They looked like they liked what they saw. I prayed that it would go well. I prayed they would pick me.

I really needed that campaign. My ego needed it. During the course of my first season on the show, I felt like I was blending into the background. The initial thrill of writing for the new character, Nelle Porter, had given way to the thrill of writing for an even newer new character, Ling Woo. I really couldn't believe what happened. Instead of introducing one cold, calculating woman, David Kelley had split one character and given it to two people. He'd given us half a character each. If Nelle was given one cutting comment, Ling would take the other. Nelle would romance one boss at the law firm of Cage and Fish, Ling would sleep with the other. As always I had to wonder if it was something I had done wrong. Maybe I wasn't vicious enough? Maybe my vulnerability shone through the austere exterior? Maybe I wasn't sexy enough for the kind of nasty-in-a-good-way attorney he had in mind? Maybe I was just nasty in the bad way because no matter how hard I tried I didn't give off a flirty, sexual vibe. I'd signed up to play an intelligent professional, not a sex kitten. And when I'd tried to break through the icy veneer to find the sex kitten, I tended to just look like a kitten: vulnerable, fragile, in fear of abandonment, and needing to be held.

Maybe I looked too fat in my underwear.

The L'Oréal campaign would fix all this. A beauty campaign would be an opportunity for me to restore my dignity, my uniqueness. Apart from gracing the cover of *Vogue*, I couldn't imagine anything in the world more glamorous than a beauty campaign. A beauty campaign had the power to validate. Like becoming a model, it was a way to convince people beyond a doubt that you were, in fact, attractive. Selling shampoo serves up an answer to a question that's vague and subjective.

It tells you what beauty is, that the face selling this product is a beautiful face.

There's nothing like external validation. I craved it. It's why I went to law school. The theory of objectivism claims that there are certain things that most people in society can agree upon. A model is pretty. A lawyer is smart. Our society is based upon objectivism. It's how we make rules and why we obey them. That was perhaps the only thing I learned in law school. I was too busy modeling to go to class.

The L'Oréal bigwig was a pleasant, smiling man and he ordered a Heineken from the server. I could tell he was the bigwig, because no one else who sat in a floral lounge chair would have had the gall to order alcohol in a meeting. It bothered me slightly that he did that. It seemed like meeting with me wasn't terribly important. That he didn't need to impress me, win me away from Garnier or any other competitive hair care brands that might be offering me a similar deal. But what bothered me most about the Heineken was the thing he said as he picked up the icy green bottle and pointed to it with the index finger from his other hand.

"No more of this for you, Portia."

Now, I liked beer. I especially liked Heineken, and I didn't like that anyone would say something like that to me. If he'd been a doctor who was explaining my impending liver failure while demonstrating what caused it at a bar, or if I was that Olympic gymnast I'd pretended to be in summer as a kid, who was celebrating her last night before going to a foreign country to compete for gold, I might have been okay with such a statement. At least, I would've understood it. But why did he not want me to drink beer? Could it be because alcohol is fattening? Aging? Makes you stupid if you get drunk? I didn't understand. But what I did understand from that comment was that I had just been offered the job of being the new face of L'Oréal.

A fitting followed a week after the meeting, and with it all the excitement and beer drinking that came with celebrating my new, prestigious job. The fitting for the commercial took place at the Four Seasons again, and I figured the hotel served as a kind of L'Oréal office base away from the home office in New York. The executives took their meetings in the bar, conferred in a conference room, slept in their individual suites, and lavished their new star with a room full of beautiful clothes to try in the presidential suite. My manager came with me to the fitting and both of us were excited.

After the initial meetings and greetings of the stylist and her assistants and tailors, I wandered into the main room of the presidential suite wide-eyed and my mouth agape. All the furniture had been removed and the walls were lined with racks and racks of clothing. Hundreds of suits hung on the racks and on every rack, on the north, south, and west walls, was the same gray suit.

"Great. I was just looking for a gray suit! Now I know where they all are."

The mood in the room was quiet and not jovial, so I put my smart-ass personality to rest and took out the pleasant, compliant, easygoing one I've been using at work since the day I started. I knew this kind of client, the kind where every little detail mattered; I'd modeled for them for years. I'd just never worked for this giant of a company at this level. My experience with clients who tested every little detail in a think tank of consumers who'd been randomly collected from shopping malls was limited to the smaller companies in Australia. And nothing says, "You're in the big leagues" like two hundred near-identical suits in the presidential suite of the Four Seasons in Beverly Hills.

I looked at a gray suit with a short jacket and a pencil skirt with a side slit. Then I looked at a gray suit with a pencil skirt and a short jacket with a slightly different lapel than the one I'd looked at five minutes prior that had a pointier, larger lapel and a skirt that was slit on the opposite side. Some of the fabrics were a different weight than others with a different ratio of cotton to wool. It was clear to me that my opinion or preference of suits didn't matter at all, and so I went into the dressing room and tried on jackets and skirts as they were handed to me.

Undressing in front of my manager was embarrassing. I didn't feel quite thin enough to be standing around barefoot in my G-string, but I didn't want to tell her to leave the room. After all, the only reason for her to be here was to help me navigate through the sea of suits, and I knew she'd have much preferred to be somewhere else with another of her bigger, more famous clients. She was a busy woman whose time was important, so I couldn't have her wait in the living room. Besides, there was no furniture anywhere else in the hotel suite. Comfort had been cleared away for productivity. And the skirts that were passed in and out of that dressing room from the stylist's assistant to the stylist to the tailor and then back to the stylist's assistant to be hung back up on the rack of suits that didn't fit looked like a production line in a factory–an unproductive factory. So far, not one of the suits had fit. The skirts either didn't zip up in the back, or if they had Lycra or another synthetic fabric helping them to stretch, the skirt did that telltale bunching that looks like ripples on a lakeshore between two gently rolling hills that were my thighs. They didn't fit. None of them. I tried on suit after suit until it was obvious to the stylist and the tailor that the fitting should take place skirt by skirt. It was pointless to try the jacket if the skirt was so small it couldn't be zipped up in the back.

They were all a size 4. My modeling card measurements–34, 24, 35–had put me at a size 4. And it seemed like the more expensive the suit, the tighter it was. A size 4 in Prada was a size 2 in the type of clothes I'd wear for *Ally*. I could've argued that the European sizing was different. I could've made a case for myself, but none of that was important when I couldn't zip up the fifteenth skirt in a row. None of what I could've said would be important.

You can put on a brave face for only so long. I put one on for about three hours before it cracked. After three hours I fell silent. There was nothing to say. We all knew what was going on. I was unprofessional.

I didn't deserve the campaign. My manager had slid down into her chair with her hand on the side of her face, exhausted, no longer willing to go to battle for me. The stylist, who had lacked a personality in the beginning, found one toward the fourth hour of the fitting, and it wasn't pleasant to be around. She'd stopped addressing me directly. Everything she said in front of me was to her assistant or tailor: "Go get the Dolce skirt. Let's see if she can fit into that." Or "What if you let the skirt out as much as you can. She might be able to get away with it."

She stopped cold as the door of the suite was knocked upon and opened simultaneously. It was the L'Oréal executives come to see what was taking so long. They had been in the conference room taking meetings but had been expecting to see some pictures of Portia de Rossi in several gray suits. We were supposed to have given them Polaroids of all the options by now. We had given them none.

"Hi."

I didn't bother to smile or go to them in the hallway. My manager didn't even get up.

"What's going on in here?" The female executive had a smiley yet accusatory voice. The kind of pissed-off yet polite voice one would expect from Hillary Clinton if she had the sneaking suspicion that someone was trying to pull the wool over her eyes.

There was an awful silence. It was a silence full of thwarted hopes, a stale-air kind of silence.

The explanation they were seeking was summed up with a simple statement from the stylist that everyone seemed to understand.

"Nobody told me she was a size eight."

Like a dead man to the galley, I walked with my manager to the Four Seasons parking garage. When I'd driven in that morning, I'd been given the option to self-park or to valet park and, quite honestly, I didn't know which one was the cool thing to do. I thought maybe it said more about the type of person I was if I did away with all the ceremony of a valet. It said that I was self-sufficient, that I could see through artifice, that I wasn't falling for it. I was happy about that now because the vast gray parking structure was empty of people, except for my manager and me, the emptiness echoing the clicking of our heels as we walked through it. It occurred to me as I was walking miles to my car (valet parkers got all the good spaces) that the parking garage held up the rest of the building and was its true nature, that all the floral lounge chairs and Hollywood dealings were like costumes and a character to an actor; another kind of empty shell that needed a good stylist and a purpose. I'd been given another fitting two days from now, a time and address scratched on a piece of paper. That would give the stylist time to find bigger sizes. The second fitting would take place in the rented space of the stylist in a not-so-good part of Hollywood. That's what you get for drinking beer.

My manager walked me as far as the elevators, but that was as far as she'd go. We'd come down the stairs, tried to find my car around that area, and then started walking because I thought that maybe my car was at the other end. I have no sense of direction. If I haven't been to a place before, I'll get lost. In the car, if I haven't traveled the exact route, I'll get lost and almost force myself to go the wrong way to prove that I knew it was the wrong way. I deliberately go the wrong way so I can predict the outcome with confidence.

At the elevators, as she was trying to leave me and get back to her pretty Jaguar and her pretty office with the ocean breeze, I showed her the big gray empty space inside me. I didn't mean to; it's just what happens if I disappoint someone I'm trying to impress. The crying seemed to come abruptly and from my stomach and as I cried, it folded in half and bent over and couldn't be straightened back up. My head was somewhere past my knees and my heels could no longer balance the weight of my head and torso—all of it making heaving, sobbing motions and so I sank to the cold gray concrete. I was on the ground. It was a brief moment, but for that moment I was on the floor of the bottom floor of the Four Seasons: from the presidential suite to the floor of the bottom floor in four hours. My manager yanked me up by the arm with the super-human strength that comes with embarrassment, the way a mother yanks up a child who's thrown a tantrum in a department store.

"I can't do this, Joan. I'm too fat. They don't want me. They want someone else. I think we should get out of it. I don't want to do this anymore. Joan, I'm too fat. They told me that Heather Locklear was a size zero and Andie MacDowell was a two!"

She looked around to make sure no one could see us. She made sure none of her producer friends whose kids play soccer were anywhere around to see this spectacle and then she said:

"Honey. You have big legs."

I stopped crying. I was shocked into stopping. I'd never heard that before in all my years of modeling. I was hoping for some bullshit reassurance about how the stylist should have had more sizes and how women my height shouldn't be a size 2. Instead I was told the truth.

Yes. Of course, I have big legs. I have big thighs that make all the skirts tight no matter how much I weigh. Everything makes sense now. In fact, Anthony Nankervis, the boy who told me I had slitty, lizard eyes also told me I had footballer's legs. I don't know how I could've forgotten that.

With a dismissive hand gesture to punctuate her point, she said it again. She announced it with certainty, the way that any fact would be stated, requiring no qualification and inviting no rebuttal.

"Just face it, honey. You have big legs."

. . .

"What part of your body do you like?"

The Jenny Craig counselor is talking to a jovial woman at the two o'clock spot in the group circle. She is a very fat woman with dull brown hair.

"My hair?" Laughter all round.

"Well, that's not exactly a body part, now is it, Jan."

The circle has about twelve people in it, and I am at six o'clock. While Jan consults her list of several of her body parts that she likes, I look at the blank sheet in front of me and try to think of one of my own. Hands? No. I hate my hands.

"I like my hands," says Jan, looking down at her fatty, pasty hands. I wonder how she can like her hands because even if she thought that her right hand was graceful and slender, her wedding band on her left hand, barely visible through the mounds of flesh suffocating it, tells the story of the big fat body attached to it. As she waves them around to help her mouth make a point, I wonder who put that band on her finger with a promise of being true to her through thick and thin. I wonder if that promise is diminished now, relative to the sliver of band now visible: a once-thick gold band now seemingly thin: a seemingly happy bride now thick with disappointment. But I guess if you only looked at her right hand and heard her laughter, you might still think she was happy. And maybe her husband's fat, too.

Three o'clock likes her eyes. That would've been an obvious one for me because my eyes can't gain weight, but I don't like my eyes. They're too small and close together. Four o'clock likes her calves. They're strong and lean apparently, although I can't see them through her pant leg so I'll have to take her word for it. My calves are my least favorite *part of my body because after years of treating my local ballet class like it was the Australian Ballet Company, they are enormous. You can't see them, so you'll have to take my word for it. Five o'clock likes her arms. Really?*

"Portia?"

"Has everyone met Portia? She's a newcomer to the group and is the youngest Jenny Craig member we've ever had. Tell us your favorite body part, Portia."

My workbook is blank. My mind is blank and yet racing through thoughts. I am fifteen years old and 130 pounds in a room filled with people twice my weight and age and yet I can't think of a thing. My feet have crooked toes, my ankles are too thin, my calves are too thick, my knees are dimply, my thighs are too big, my ass is droopy, my hips are too wide, my stomach is round and has rolls, my rib cage . . . ? No. My ribs stick too far out at the bottom and that makes my whole torso look wide. My breasts are tiny and disproportionate to the rest of my body . . .

"Portia?"

"Umm. I don't know."

What about my arms? My back? My shoulders? My wrists? Wrists. No, my wrists are too small for my forearms and my hands, and so because of my wrists, my hands and arms look bigger.

"There's nothing I like."

The room falls silent. We were all laughing a second ago and complimenting three o'clock on her mauve eyes that looked like Elizabeth Taylor's and now we're all silent, all around the clock. All the fat people sitting from twelve right back around to eleven are looking at me at six o'clock. I know that look. It's the look of the thoughts that run through your mind when you're looking at a smart-ass. I was the joke to them— the kind that makes you not want to laugh.

"Come on, dear. There must be something that you like?"

There was an ounce of anger to her tone. My lack of an answer probably looked like unwillingness to play along, but in truth I was still running through all my parts trying to find something to say.

"Well, if you don't think you have any good body parts, then I guess we're all in trouble!"

That was the kind of joke that makes people laugh.

PART TWO

15

AWOKE TO a strange silence and shafts of light stabbing into the room from the corners of the blinds. The light carried millions of tiny dust particles, which I guess were always there yet only now visible because of the soupy, thick air with its beams of light illuminating them. I was eerily calm when I awoke. I was aware that I had cried myself to sleep over the L'Oréal incident; my eye sockets felt misshapen and water-logged, as though they could barely keep my sore, dry eyes in my head. But it felt like I had cried for the last time. That I was never going to cry myself to sleep like that again. Despite the heaviness of my head, with its headache and sinus pressure, there was a levity to it, a lightness to it, like everything inside of it that made the world I lived in a place of peace or a place of torture, was weightless—quiet, floating. I felt over-taken by a sense of peace, by the feeling that today was truly a new day.

I got out of bed and immediately started stretching. An odd thing for me to do, but I wanted to feel my body. I wanted to "check in" with it, acknowledge it. As I stretched, there was a certain love I gave to it, an appreciation for its muscles straining and contracting. I liked the way it felt as I touched my toes and straightened my back. I felt like I was sud-denly self-contained. Like the answers lay within me. Like my life was about to be lived within the confines of my body and would answer only to it. I didn't give a shit what anyone thought of me.

As I stretched my arms out to the sides, I ran my fingers through the beams of light, cloudy with the dust that swirled around my bedroom. I saw the beauty of my messy bedroom and inhaled the summer air. All the clothes I'd tried on and discarded on the floor before going to my L'Oréal fitting were looking up at me, wondering what they had done wrong. Despite the mess and the dust, it smelled sweet and I felt myself smiling as I inhaled. I liked that smell. It was the smell of the imported Italian talc in the yellow plastic bottle that I had bought to pamper myself but only now enjoyed as talc and not a status symbol. As I walked barefoot on the painted concrete floor of my bedroom toward the bathroom scale I felt confident that what I was about to see would make me happy for the rest of the day. I felt empty and light and I didn't care what number the scale told me I was, today I was not going to define myself by it. Today I knew that despite what it said, it was unimportant. Today I would start my new life.

I had the answer to my problems.

I would always be prepared.

I was about to make everything easier.

The scale confirmed what I'd suspected. It read 130. The weight I had always returned to no matter the effort to get beneath it. In the past, this number had invariably plummeted me into despair. It reminded me that no matter what I did, I could never win—that my body with its bones and its guts and its blood weighed in at what it felt comfortable being as a living organism with its own needs. It hated me and thought I was stupid for attempting to change it with my tortuous rituals of forcing regurgitation and starving it of food. It always had the upper hand, the last word. And the last word was 130.

Today being the first day of my brand-new life, with its sunshine and its soupy air, 130 was a beautiful weight. It was my weight. It was Portia, a straight-A student who earned a place at the most prestigious law school in Australia, who had an exciting modeling career and the courage to try her hand at acting in a foreign country. It was the weight of the girl who was a successful actress, who made money, who was independent. For the first time in my life, I didn't view my body as the enemy. Today it was my friend, my partner in all the success I'd accomplished. As it stepped off the scale and over the pile of discarded clothes, onto the wooden floorboards and toward the food journal on the coffee table, it expressed its strength and joy by lunging, deep and controlled, thighs burning, stomach taut. And with an outstretched arm the hand flicked through the pages of lists of food items and calories and wrote in big, curly pen strokes something the journal had never before seen: my weight.

130

I was hungry and yet unusually unafraid of being hungry. I went to the fridge and then the pantry and proceeded to line up all the possible breakfast foods on the counter. Sitting on the counter in a row, equally spaced and looking like *The Price Is Right* game show items, were the foods Suzanne, my nutritionist, had given me to eat. The breakfast options of oatmeal, egg whites (you can buy them in a jar, you know), bran muffins, wheat toast, and yogurt were all looking at me and available, but Suzanne had preferred me to eat oatmeal and egg whites because the combination of the two gave good amounts of carbohydrates and protein and because the two-part process of cooking and eating, she believed, made you feel as though you were eating a big, satisfying meal. I made the decision to eat egg whites and oatmeal. I read the calorie contents of the single-serving prepackaged oatmeal sachet: 100 calories. I wondered what 100 calories meant to my body, what it would do with it. Would it use it just to drive to work today or could it drive to work, sit through hair and makeup, and act out a scene all on 100 calories? Would it gently prompt my mind to produce feelings of hunger when it was done burning the calories or would it ask for more food before it was done using the energy from the food I'd given it? If the body was so clever and knew what it needed for health and survival, how come obese people got hungry? The body should use the stored fat to sustain itself to prevent diabetes or heart failure. If it was so clever, it should take over the mind of a self-destructive obese person and send out brain signals of nausea instead of hunger. I came to the conclusion that no matter what my body said it needed, I could no longer trust it. I couldn't rely on my body to tell me what I needed. From now on, I was in control. I was its captain and would make all the decisions.

I decided that I didn't need the full 100-calorie oatmeal packet. It was clearly a common measurement for a normal common portion of food that ordinary people would eat. Obviously, it wasn't a portion that was meant for a person who was dieting. If the average person who wasn't going to lose weight ate a 100-calorie packet for breakfast, then I should eat less. I immediately felt so stupid that I hadn't seen that before. Of course you couldn't lose weight if you relied on Quaker to allot your portion; I had to take control of it. I calculated the grams of food that would deliver an 80-calorie serving on the kitchen scale, and after being careful to give myself the exact amount of oats, I poured it into a bowl. I added hot water and a sprinkling of Splenda. I ate it slowly, tasting every morsel of oatmeal and its claggy syrup. Then, instead of randomly pouring a generous dollop of egg whites from the jar into a hot pan coated in oil, I got out the measuring cup. I measured half a cup of egg whites and poured it into a pan coated with Pam—a no-calorie substitute for oil. I added a sprinkling of Mrs. Dash and salt. Next step was coffee. A mindless consumption of calories in the past would now be another thing ingested that needed measuring. How many additional calories I could spare in my coffee would be determined by the rest of my meal; if I was particularly hungry and needed a large portion of egg whites with my oatmeal, for example, I would take my coffee black, but if I came in under my allotted calorie consumption for the morning, I could measure out a tablespoon of Mocha Mix, a nondairy creamer, to add to it. In the past I would just randomly pour calories into a cup, not caring that a generous pouring of Mocha Mix could run 50 calories. Fifty calories. That was more than a third of my actual food for the morning. After drinking the coffee and eating the egg whites and the oatmeal, I had never felt more satisfied. I was full. I was clever. I had halved my morning calorie intake. I planned on re-adjusting my whole program. I would take my diary everywhere I went and record each calorie that went into my mouth. Suzanne had taught me to weigh, calculate, and document like a mathematician solving an equation, and with my new education I was ready to solve the weight problem.

Suzanne had set my calorie intake for optimum weight loss at 1,400 calories a day. I reset it to 1,000.

Problem solved.

16

WELL, HELLO there. I'm a big fan of your show. What a delight to meet you."

A middle-aged gray-haired man sat behind the desk of the Granville Towers lobby and practically sang his greeting to me in a gently lilting Southern accent. He seemed genuinely excited to meet me, and his happy demeanor was contagious. I shook his hand and smiled an involuntarily broad smile and I realized that I hadn't really smiled in awhile, that his sparkly nature was in stark contrast to my dullness. Everything about the Granville made me happy. Situated at Sunset and Crescent Heights, the location was perfect, and the building was historic and beautiful. A true example of 1920s architecture, the penthouse apartment that I was about to see had the potential to saddle me with a mortgage. It was time to buy a home, to invest in my life in Los Angeles. I needed a place of my own and a penthouse apartment in an Old Hollywood building on Sunset Boulevard sounded like a place an actress should live.

As I waited in the lobby for the real estate agent to arrive, the doorman, who introduced himself as Jeff, got up from his station and walked around the desk, talking excitedly as if I was the only visitor he'd had in months.

"Mickey Rourke lived here. He just moved out, oh . . . what . . . it'd be a couple of months now. He had three little dogs, Chihuahuas I believe." It annoyed me that people find celebrity so impressive that they have to talk about it. What annoyed me more was that I was impressed. Somehow the building was instantly more valuable to me just because a celebrity had lived in it.

"I'll show you his apartment if you like, but don't tell the agent—I'll get in trouble." Jeff spoke from the corner of his mouth in an exaggerated whisper even though there was no one else in the lobby to overhear. It was dramatic and I would usually have found it annoying, but I liked the fact that he'd invited me to share a secret with him. It felt warm, welcoming.

"It's on the ground floor, but I like it more than the penthouse you're going to see because it has the beautiful coffered ceilings, you know."

On our way see Mickey Rourke's apartment, Jeff told me of other celebrities who had lived at the Granville: Brendan Fraser, David Bowie, and Amy Locane. Michael Michele, an actress on *ER*, was a current resident.

"You know, the place was built in 1929 and it was called the Voltaire. It was a hotel back then, but sometime after that it was made into apartments and apparently, though there's no real proof of this, Marilyn Monroe lived here with Joe DiMaggio."

Jeff wore a jacket and tie. In fact, everything about him was old-fashioned. He seemed to be part of the history he so loved to talk about, as if he lived in a black-and-white movie. If he weren't so enamored with movie stars, I could also picture him living in the South before the Civil War. I could see him as a gentleman on a plantation in Georgia in his hunter green library dwarfed by ceiling-high shelves filled with leather-bound books. But Jeff clearly loved Hollywood, and he loved his job. He was the doorman, the gatekeeper of the Granville Towers, and his excitement over me made me feel as though I could be one of his movie star stories, just as Mickey Rourke and his dogs and his ceilings will forever be one of his stories.

The penthouse apartment wasn't spectacular. It didn't have the molding on the baseboards or the high coffered ceiling that Mickey's had. It wasn't particularly spacious, and the views, although beautiful from the east window, were blocked on the north side by the Virgin Megastore building at Sunset 5, the shopping complex next door to the Granville. In fact, from the first floor of the apartment, looking out the floor-to-ceiling windows on the north side created the optical illusion of a scorching desert. The yellow paint on the Sunset 5 building looked like sand and the heat that spewed out from the air conditioning vents on the roof created that warped-air look of a heat wave. After seeing the small galley kitchen and the modest bedroom and living room, we took the staircase next to the public elevator that led to the attic above the penthouse apartment, while the real estate agent explained to me the resale potential if I connected the penthouse apartment to the attic with an interior staircase. I hadn't planned on renovating, but when I saw the view from the spacious high-ceilinged attic I no longer had a choice. I had never been so excited in my life. On the north wall were thirty or so large windows in rows of three, pitched in an A-frame, and beyond the windows, instead of the desert that I saw from the floor below, was the vast industrial roof of the Sunset 5. Clouds of smoke billowed from the metal chimneys and swirled in the wind, occasionally clearing to show the enormous steel tubes in a cross-section of right angles looking like the indecipherable circuit boards my brother as a kid used to spend hours soldering wires onto to make LEDs light up. The space was currently being used as a studio for the portrait photographer who owned the unit, and the tungsten lights and paper backdrops clamped onto C-stands made the apartment even more loftlike. I felt as though I had been transported to an artist's loft in a city like Philadelphia, which was much more exciting to me than where I actually was. Where I was, was predictable. But the apartment made me think there was more to life than being an actress on a David Kelley show. It made me remember who I used to be and where I had wanted to live if I had stayed in law school in Melbourne: in a nongentrified artist neighborhood off Brunswick Street, the place that made me happier than any other place on earth. For on Brunswick Street I was gay. I wore motorcycle boots, had slightly dreadlocked hair, and wrapped leather around my wrists. I drank beer at the Provincial and ate penne Amatriciana at Mario's and saw indie bands with my best friend, Bill.

"I'll take it."

I left my new apartment with its own industrial city and flew past Jeff, the doorman, in a hurry. I had to get back to my sublet in Hancock Park in time to make dinner. Since lowering my calorie intake to exactly 1,000 calories a day, I discovered that the best time to eat dinner was at exactly six o'clock to give my body a head start in burning the calories. If I ate at six, I still had five or six hours to move around before I lay still for six hours. If I ate any later than that, I worried that overnight the unused calories would turn to fat. I discovered that although I didn't want to lower my calorie intake to under 1,000, as anything lower would be the equivalent of crash dieting, I could speed up the weight loss by increasing the amount of exercise and eating at the right times. Occasionally, if I felt particularly energetic, I could squeeze in a quick workout before bed and if I didn't actually get on the treadmill, I would do sit-ups and leg lifts on the floor next to my bed.

When I got home, I prepared four ounces of lean ground turkey and a spattering of ketchup, cooked with Pam and lightly sprayed with I Can't Believe It's Not Butter spray. As annoying as the name of the product was, every time I doused my food with the stuff I would silently congratulate the marketing team behind the brand. For yes, I too, couldn't believe it wasn't butter. More than that, I couldn't believe something that delicious didn't have any calories. I sprayed it on everything. It tasted great with my morning oatmeal, mixed into my tuna at lunch, and was a perfect partner for my ground turkey with

ketchup at dinner. It even tasted delicious as an ingredient of a dessert
I concocted: Jell-O, Splenda, and I Can't Believe It's Not Butter spray
all mixed together. At 10 calories per serving, it satisfied my sweet tooth
and was my favorite new recipe that I had created. I had never thought
of myself as a chef before, but I was quite impressed with my cooking.
I was impressed that I had the ability to take foods that weren't usually
paired and put them together for a delicious, low-calorie meal.

I picked up the phone before deciding which number to dial. Kali?
Erik? Would either of them care about my new apartment? I had originally wanted to live with Erik. I wanted to buy an apartment that was
big enough so I could have Erik as my roommate. But the thought of
what the pantry in the kitchen would look like stopped me from pursu-
ing it. Erik would buy food. All kinds of food would assault me as I
opened the cupboard to reach in for a can of tuna. And I would have to
prepare myself mentally every time I opened the refrigerator, as maybe
one of those foods would tempt me enough to trigger a binge. On
Sundays he might invite friends over to watch a game, eat pizza, and I
would be left alone cleaning up the kitchen with the tortuous decision
of whether to eat the remaining slice or throw it in the trash. Even if I
threw it in the trash I couldn't be certain that the thought of eating it
wouldn't keep me up all night, worried that I would retrieve it and eat
the cold discarded piece despite the fact that it smelled of cigarette ash
and beer. I would certainly get up out of bed and eat it. Then, knowing
that I'd blown it, I'd have to keep going. I'd eat every bit of his food,
his potato chips, and his leftover Chinese food, his breakfast cereal,
and those chocolate cookies he eats when he needs to be comforted.
My kitchen would be a dangerous temptress—and she would constantly
flirt with the fat slob inside.

*In my new apartment my fridge will be sparse. My cupboard will be bare.
My house will be safe.*

I picked up the phone to dial Ann in New York. I couldn't help but
feel like a conversation with her would feel more like the second round

of a boxing match than a celebration of my new apartment. Since the underwear episode on the show, Ann and I had barely spoken. Upon further evaluation of her comment about my looking like a normal woman in my underwear, I was quite sure she wasn't aware that she was insulting me. However, I was sure she was careful not to compliment me, either. She had expressed her opinions about not emphasizing looks and weight and had tried to get me to read feminist literature like Naomi Wolf's *The Beauty Myth*. No, Ann didn't mean anything by it. Nevertheless, I couldn't let a comment like that slip by again without retaliation. My gloves were on, ready to strike if Ann was being insensitive.

"AC. PdR"

"PdR!"

For some reason, when Ann and I first became friends, I had to call her by her full name, Ann Catrina, when I was referring to her. Then I had to say her full name to her face. Eventually it got so tedious to call her Ann Catrina, I shortened it to AC. She reciprocated by calling me PdR. So now we have that.

I excitedly told her about my new place while pouring my fourth Diet Coke; a low-calorie substitute for the wine I used to drink with dinner. Not drinking was yet another healthy change I had made since taking nutrition and fitness seriously. I told her about what had happened in St. Barths with Sacha. She said she was glad because she seemed to think there was a great gay girl out there who could really love me. That if I kept chasing Sacha as she was busy chasing men, I would miss this wonderful, proud-to-be-gay girl as I ran right by. What she couldn't quite tell me was how this self-confident, happy gay woman was going to meet a closeted Portia and be perfectly okay with going back into the closet to be her secret girlfriend. Where would I meet her? Would it occur at a supermarket when our shopping carts accidentally collided and we telepathically exchanged the information that we were gay, available, and interested? Ann Catrina needed to understand that there wasn't a solution to this problem. To shut her up, I told her the most disturbing information:

"There's a morality clause in the L'Oréal contract."

"A . . . what now?"

"It states that if I'm caught doing something that damages the image of the company, I'll have to pay all the money back. I'll have to pay back the advance, everything."

My agent and manager had called me to go over the contract just before the fitting. Remembering how I sat in the car with the cell phone to my ear, having to pull over in order to calm myself, I felt as sick telling Ann about it as I had when it was told to me. The clause cited examples like public drunkenness, arrests, et cetera, but I knew that it would include homosexuality. The wording of the contract was vague, and I was unsure exactly what would constitute a breach of the contract and how "morality" was defined. The whole thing made me sick. I was so scared about the morality clause I didn't want to even talk about it. I just wanted her to stop talking about how easy it would be for me to live my life openly. I just wanted her to shut up about it.

Before she could ask any questions or try to reason with me, I told her about my nutritionist.

"She has you on one thousand calories a day?"

"Yes. Well, no. I modified the diet a little. She told me to eat fourteen hundred for weight loss, but I wasn't really losing weight so I got rid of some extra calories here and there."

"She thinks you need to lose weight?"

"Yes. Oh. I don't know. We haven't really talked about that."

"What do you talk about, then?"

"Eating healthily. You know. Not gaining and losing all the time like I've been doing."

The more I talked, the more concern I could hear in her voice. Which annoyed me. She didn't understand the pressures of being an actress, of showing up to a photo shoot where the wardrobe was nothing but handcuffs and a strip of chainmail. She didn't know what it was like to try to find a dress for the Golden Globes and having only one good option because it was the only sample size dress that fit your portly body. She didn't know what it was like to hear that you have a normal-looking body after starving for weeks to get a thin-looking one, hoping that your friends would admire it. "Normal" isn't an adjective you wish to hear after putting that much effort into making sure it was spectacular.

"Ann. I gotta go."

"Go pour yourself a glass of wine and relax about it all. You've always looked great, PdR. There's nothing to worry about."

Right. Like I was going to drink wine two days before the L'Oréal shoot.

"Okay, AC. See you later."

"Oh! Before you go, can I stay with you in a couple of weeks? I'll be in town for a few days. A friend from UCLA just got engaged, so I thought I'd come to LA for the party."

No. No, you can't stay. Even if you come after I shoot L'Oréal, I need to keep going now this diet has started working for me. I need to eat at exactly six o'clock every night, and I can't drink alcohol with you like we used to. I can't go out to dinner anymore. I don't get to take a night or two off where I can eat whatever I want. I'm about to look good for the first time in my life, and for the first time I know I'm never going to gain it back again. So I can't take a few days off. If I eat and drink, I'll gain again. Besides, I don't even have the room anymore. I need to work out on my treadmill at 10:00 at night and 6:00 in the morning in the spare bedroom where you're expecting to stay.

"Yes. Of course you can. When?"

"Around the fifteenth. I'll email you."

I hung up the phone. The fifteenth was twelve days away. So I gave myself a new goal. Over the next twelve days, I would eat 800 calories a day. I needed to give myself a cushion so I could enjoy my time with Ann and not worry about gaining weight. If I lost a little more than I'd originally planned to lose, I would regulate my weight loss again after she left because I knew that weight lost too quickly was sure to return. Suzanne told me that. So I opened my journal and in the top right-hand corner of every dated page for the next twelve days I wrote 800. I would be ready for Ann's visit. I even looked forward to it.

I weighed myself first thing. I was 120 pounds. Actually I was probably a pound more, but my mother once showed me a trick to play on the scale where you set the dial a couple of pounds below the zero, but in a way that isn't very obvious to the logical part of your brain—especially from standing height looking down. If the needle sidles up to the zero, sitting next to it but not quite touching it, your brain is tricked into thinking that the needle needs to start in that position or the reading will be inaccurate. In fact, if you tap your toe on the scale the needle often resets itself to zero anyway, so to me lining up the dial perfectly with the zero was like sitting on a fence. Like I should've picked a side. Shall I choose denial of truth on the side that reads heavier but with the comfort of knowing that in reality I'm lighter, or shall I choose the immediate thrill of weighing in under the real number, to help with incentive?

I hated that zero. The zero is the worst part of the scale because the zero holds all the hope and excitement for what could be. It tells you that you can be anything you want if you work hard; that you make your own destiny. It tells you that every day is a new beginning. But that hadn't been true for me until recently. Because no matter what I did, no matter how much weight I lost, I always seemed to end up in the same place; standing on a scale looking down past my naked protruding belly and round thighs at 130 pounds.

But I was 120. It was the day of the L'Oréal commercial shoot. I should've been happy and yet I felt disturbed. My stomach was protruding very badly. It looked distended, almost. Or as my mother would put it, it looked like a poisoned pup. I hated it when stupid phrases like that popped into my mind. I hated that I had no control over my thoughts. But I especially hated that my stomach looked bloated and yet the rest of my body felt thinner. What was the point of dieting like I'd been doing, if on the most important day, my stomach was sticking out like a sore thumb?

I walked to the shower and punched my stupid stomach as I went. What could have caused this? The night before I ate only 200 calories of tuna with butter spray and mustard. How could I still see so much fat on my stomach? I stood under the shower and watched the water run between my breasts and over my stomach, cascading onto the shower floor from just past my navel because of the shelf that the protrusion of bulging fat had made. I picked up inches of fat with my fingers. It wasn't just bloat, it was fat. It was real fat; not something that I could take away by drinking water and sitting in a sauna. I'd ignorantly thought I wouldn't have any fat at 120 pounds.

I felt sick. I felt like I couldn't face the L'Oréal executives and the stylist again after what had happened last time. My suits were at least bigger, but with my stomach puffed out like this, I didn't know if that would even matter. What if I didn't fit into anything again? I started to cry. Stupid weakling that I am, I had to cry and make my eyes puffy to match my puffy body. I had finished shampooing my head when I realized that I used the wrong shampoo. With all the crying and obsessing about my stomach, I accidentally used cheap shampoo instead of the L'Oréal shampoo I was supposed to use the morning of the commercial. Now I would have red puffy eyes, a fat stomach, and hair that felt like straw to bring to the set. A derisive laugh escaped my throat as I realized that I was the spokesperson for the new shampoo but didn't use the shampoo that I'm selling because subconsciously I didn't believe the famous L'Oréal slogan, "Because I'm worth it."

"Because I'm not worth it." I said it out loud looking at a zit on my chin in the mirror using the same inflection the other L'Oréal girls use to tell the world that they are worth it: the same inflection that I'd use that day. It sounded funny so I kept saying it as I walked around the house.

"Because I'm not worth it," as I looked for pretty underwear that I didn't have among the ugly, stretched-out panties in my drawer. That I didn't think to buy some pretty, new underwear for the shoot was unbelievable to me.

"Because I'm not worth it," I said as I sipped my black coffee, wishing I were thin enough to have creamer in it because the strong black coffee tasted putrid and assaulted my taste buds. I skipped breakfast altogether because I wasn't worth it.

As I picked up my cell phone and walked to the door, I was aware of the time for the first time that morning. I was late. I should've been at the set already, and I didn't even know where I was going. With a surge of adrenaline, I rushed out the door and down the stairs, trying to decipher directions from the map. I was the star of the commercial and I was going to be late. All those people would be waiting for me. The L'Oréal executives, the director, the hairstylist and makeup artist who were both so renowned they had published books and signature product lines—all of them were waiting for me. Maybe that was a good thing. Maybe that's what stars were supposed to do. They're supposed to display their power by making other people wait for them. As I caught one red light after another, I had a choice to be in a frenzy of anxiety or relax into a character that keeps people waiting—like an R&B diva or a rock star. The lyrics of "Pennyroyal Tea" came to my mind. "I'm on my time with everyone." It was easier to play that character than to care.

17

WHEN ANN arrived I was still not at my goal weight. Although I had worked hard and I was ready to eat and drink with her, I still had weight to lose. I was 115 pounds and my goal was 110. I still had big thighs. I still saw round bulging thighs when I looked in the mirror. I didn't know if getting to 110 would take the bulges and the roundness away, but it was worth losing the extra pounds to try to make them straight. I just wanted them to look straight. Still, I needed to at least allow myself to have a drink with Ann Catrina, as it had been a while since I had seen any of my friends and I needed to have a little fun. Besides, I knew that depression caused weight gain because of some kind of chemical in your body that is released if you're unhappy and that can slow down your metabolism. Cortisol? Something like that.

Eating 800 calories a day was difficult. Not because it was too little food but because it was too much. One thousand calories divided perfectly into my daily meals, but no matter how I tried, I couldn't quite get 800 to fit. I removed the egg whites from the breakfast menu, opting to eat a serving midmorning, which left me with just the oatmeal. I had gotten used to eating the reduced portion of the prepackaged single serving of oatmeal and now it weighed in at 60 calories a serving. I added some blueberries, Splenda, and the butter spray so with the teaspoon of Mocha Mix I got my 100-calorie breakfast. I ate 60 calories of egg whites at around ten o'clock. One hundred and fifty calories of tuna with 50 additional calories for tomatoes, pickles, and lettuce was ample for lunch. Three ounces of turkey with butternut squash was around 300 calories and then an additional 40 calories for miscellaneous things—like gum or Crystal Light and coffee throughout the day—brought my total in at around 700. Quite often, if I was working and didn't have time to prepare the egg whites, then the daily total would be somewhere in the low six hundreds.

I fine-tuned my workout regimen. On days when I didn't have to go to the studio, I would begin my workout at exactly 6:00. On days I worked, I got out of bed at 4:15. I ran for forty-five minutes on the treadmill at 6.0 on a 1 incline. I didn't like running uphill. It did something weird to my lower back, but I felt I had to run harder and with my stomach tight to make up for it as most people run on an incline. I did sit-ups after my run. I did exactly 105 sit-ups. I wanted to do 100, but the 5 extra sit-ups allowed for some sloppy ones during my ten sets of ten reps. If I had time, I would do leg lifts: 105 with each leg. In addition to my workouts at home, I went to Mari Windsor Pilates and got a Pilates trainer. A costar had gone there and I'd read about Pilates in magazines so I thought I'd try it. It seemed that most celebrities were doing it, and I felt it was a particularly appropriate body-sculpting workout for me because it was originally designed for dancers and I used to be a dancer. It was slightly intimidating, however, because the other clients there were so thin and toned. It was a new goal to be thinner and more muscular than the other women at the Pilates studio, which ultimately was a good thing, because I have always thrived on healthy competition. After I was confident that I had the best body of all the paying customers, I would set my sights on the trainers.

Round Three: I was in my corner and Ann was in hers. Ann, a featherweight from New York City takes on Portia, the middleweight from sunny Southern California. Ann rang the bell by saying:

"Okay, I understand that you want to lose weight, but you should have some perspective on how much you're losing—like some way of measuring that isn't necessarily a scale. I know for me, there are clothes that are tight when I've gained weight and a little loose when I've lost weight. Certainly you have that, too. Like if you can fit comfortably into your skinny jeans, or if they're just a little loose, you're done losing weight, right?" She took a sip of wine, stroked my dog sitting in her lap, and waited for my response. I could tell that this conversation wasn't easy for her. And while I was quite chuffed that she'd care enough to have it with me, I wished she'd just shut up.

According to her laws, I guess I had no perspective. But what's perspective when you started out fat? Why would I ever want those jeans to be a little loose when they were a 28 waist? I couldn't tell her this, of course, because then we'd have to talk about how now I was on TV and that the "normal" life I lived at my "normal" weight no longer applied. I couldn't sit there and brag about how I was different now because I was on TV. I just wished she understood that without me having to explain it.

I was losing weight, though. I ordered a pair of 26 waist pants that took four weeks to arrive, and they were too big, too big by at least a size, maybe even two. I was really disturbed by this because I thought I'd looked good four weeks ago. God, I did a photo shoot for *Flair* four weeks ago and the magazine hadn't even come out yet. How disgusting that that was what people would think I looked like.

I guess some time had slid by without a response and Ann didn't like silence in a conversation, so she continued:

"I have to tell you something."

Here it comes, I thought. Here comes the part where she tells me I drink too much and right now I'm too drunk to take it well.

"You're too thin."

It was all I could do not to laugh. Really. The laughter was in my torso somewhere waiting to escape, but I stuffed it down because her face was so serious, plus I was enjoying it so much—the thought of being too thin. That's funny: too thin. Just this morning on the set I had to clench my buttocks as I walked through the law office on a full-length lens because if I walked normally the part where my hips meet my thighs bulged out rhythmically with each step: left fat bulge, right fat bulge, left fat bulge, and cue dialogue, "You wanted to see me?" Too thin. She continued talking about my arms being sinewy and veiny and how I looked like an eleven-year-old and that it wasn't attractive, but I just wanted to laugh. Oh, why not just enjoy this surreal moment and laugh? My face was contorting to control it from escaping anyway. I knew my face well enough to know that it's a traitor to my mind. It gives away all my secrets. And so I laughed. I laughed really hard.

"I'm sorry. It's not funny. I don't know why I'm finding it funny. It's not funny. It's just . . . you're so serious!"

"This is serious! You didn't have dinner tonight. And you don't look good, P. I think you've lost perspective."

My laughter died away. Not because what she was saying made sense to me but because I knew it was just an illusion created by my clothes or the way I was sitting.

It's not real. I'm not really thin. Should I show her my stomach and the rolls of fat? Or do I sit here on the floor and keep the pose that's making her think that I am thin so I can enjoy this moment longer?

I never wanted it to go away. I knew the minute I stood, it would be over. Or when I changed out of these magical jeans and into my pajamas. I was jutting out my collarbone subtly and separating my arm from my body to make her not feel stupid or wrong. She was going to realize it tomorrow, but for right now I knew she needed to be right and I needed to hear that I was thin. So I kept posing as a poor, starved waif until she stopped talking.

"Does any of what I'm saying make sense to you?"

What could I do? Answer her honestly? Say, no, AC, none of this makes sense because none of it is true. Even if you think you are telling me the truth, that I'm too thin, it's just your truth, your perspective. It's not society's perspective, the clothing designers' perspective. If it was, then models would have curves and actresses would have round faces and designers would make sample dresses bigger. What did she know? She was at NYU getting her master's in ... something. Business? Besides, I'd never gotten so much attention for having a good body. I had just been featured in *In Style* for having the "Look of the Week." *US Weekly* gave me the "Best Dressed" accolade for the Rick Owens dress I wore to the Fox party. And last week Vera told me that I was her favorite actress to dress. I'd never gotten so many compliments. Everyone told me I looked fantastic.

"P, I'm just concerned, that's all."

"And I appreciate it, but there's nothing to worry about. I ate dinner."

"You didn't have dinner."

I had dinner. I ate grilled vegetables. I did stop eating them, though, because I could tell that they had used a lot of olive oil to cook them. I didn't wear any lip balm because I wanted to make sure I could detect if anything I ate was cooked with oil. I couldn't tell how much oil was used unless I had nothing waxy or oily on my lips. Besides, who knew whether the shea butter in lip balm contained calories that you could accidentally ingest? I had to worry about all the incidental calories, the hidden calories. Oil has a lot of calories and is a hidden ingredient in so many foods.

Oil is really my main problem right now.

"Look." I thrust my wineglass in her face. "I'm drinking alcohol! Plenty of calories in that."

God. I've drunk my weight in wine and she thinks I have a problem?

Ann shifted Bean slightly on her lap and looked around the room. She looked intently into each of the living room's corners as if searching for a way to change the subject. Her eyes settled on the open kitchen door. They remained there and I realized that my kitchen scale and a calorie counter were probably what she was looking at. While it occurred to me that there was a slim chance she actually thought I was too thin, I had decided moments ago that she was just jealous. Who wouldn't be? While I knew I wasn't skinny, it was obvious that I had gained control over my weight, which is a huge feat worthy of jealousy. Everyone wants to be in control of their weight.

"So. How was the L'Oréal shoot?"

"Great . . . really fun, actually. I think it'll be a pretty good commercial. I had to do that classic 'hair shot.' You know, where they fan out your hair? I felt pretty stupid doing that, but it should turn out okay." I took a sip of my wine. I wanted to tell her that I fit into my clothes and that most of them were even too big, but I couldn't. Usually, that would be the kind of thing we'd talk about, but after her rant about my being too thin, I had to keep quiet about the one thing that made me really happy. I wanted to tell her that they kept testing me by telling a PA to ask me if I wanted to eat or drink anything, like lunch or coffee, and I passed the test. I didn't eat all day and everyone was really impressed because they kept talking about it and asking me over and over again if I wanted food. I wanted to tell her that I got back at that bitch of a stylist for announcing to the L'Oréal executives that I was a size 8, by being too thin for her precious clothes. I wanted to describe the tailor's facial expression when she had to rush to take in the skirts that she once said didn't have "enough in the seam" to take out. But I couldn't. So I told her that I had fun and everyone was really nice. It was the kind of answer I'd give in an interview.

Just as I began to feel sorry for myself for having to lie to everyone, including my best friend, I remembered something that I thought she'd find funny.

"Well, there was one thing that was pretty funny. At one point the makeup guy and his assistant started talking about whether I could do makeup as well as the hair products—if I had good enough facial features . . ."

"That's great," she interrupted. "L'Oréal wants you to sell makeup as well?"

"No. No. They don't. My God, Ann—it was hilarious. They went through every part of my face—in front of me—tearing each feature apart like, 'What about lips?' And then the assistant would say, 'Well, she has lovely lips, but her teeth are a little crooked and not that white.' And then they got to my eyes. They almost agreed on mascara because I have really thick eyelashes until one of them mentioned that my eyes were too small."

I already knew that I had small eyes. *Us Weekly* told me. Thank God for that because before the article I thought my eyes were fairly normal and I treated them as such. Without their proper diagnosis, I couldn't apply the correct antidote to disguise this flaw. It was a piece on beauty and how the reader, if she identified with a particular flaw that could be seen on a celebrity, could deemphasize the problem. I had, "small, close-together eyes." I took their advice and have since applied dark swooping upward lines at the corners to lessen the appearance of the smallness and roundness of my close-together, beady little eyes.

"Anyway. It was pretty funny."

"That doesn't sound funny to me."

By the furrow in her brow, I could tell that unless I left the room I would be listening to another lecture—this time about how the L'Oréal executives aren't the experts and how I'm perfect the way I am. I would have had to nod my head and pretend to agree with her even though we both knew that I wasn't perfect and that L'Oréal clearly are the experts.

"I'm so sorry, AC, but I gotta go to bed because I have to get up early. You got everything you need? You good?"

"Yeah. I'll go to bed in a minute. And I won't see you before I leave, I guess, but I'm here if you want to talk. Call me anytime, okay?"

"Okay. Good night." I bent down and hugged her. I adored AC. She had only ever wanted the best for me. Unfortunately, she didn't understand that what was best for me before getting the show and what was best for me now were two different things.

I glanced at the treadmill as I passed the guest bedroom door on my way to the bathroom. *Get on the treadmill.* I couldn't even imagine how many calories were in those three glasses of wine. The voice in my head told me that I was lazy, that I didn't deserve a day off, but there was nothing I could do about it and so I brushed my teeth and slipped into bed.

Lying in bed was always the worst time of the day. If I hadn't done all that I could do to help myself, I imagined what the insides of my body were doing. As I lay motionless and waiting for sleep, I stared at the ceiling and imagined molecular energy like the scientific renditions I'd seen in science class as a kid, shaped like hectagons and forming blocks of fat in my body—honeycomb parasites attaching to my thighs. Or I'd see fat in a cooling frying pan and imagined the once vital liquid energy slowly coagulating into cold, white fat, coating the red walls in my body like a virus. The unused calories in my body caused me anxiety because I was just lying there, passively allowing the fat to happen, just as I had passively allowed myself to keep ballooning to 130 pounds. But did I have the energy to get out of bed and do sit-ups? The wine had made me lazy. I had the anxiety, but I was too lethargic to relieve myself of it by working out. I could've thrown up. But if I threw up the wine, Ann might have heard and then she'd never get off my case. If I threw up, then she'd feel validated and I'd feel stupid because that's not what I did anymore. I was healthy now. I had the willpower not to crash diet and then binge and purge. I had solved that problem.

I got out of bed and onto the floor to start my sit-ups. I couldn't think that I had solved the problem of my weight fluctuating if I just lay in bed allowing the sugar in the wine to turn into fat. As I began my crunches, I heard Ann getting ready for bed. I could hear her checking her messages on her cell phone and I could vaguely make out a man's voice on the other end. As she turned out the light and got into the bed that I'd moved against the wall to make way for the treadmill, I couldn't help but wish I were her. I wished I were a student living in New York, dating and going to parties. I wished I could travel to another city and stay over at a friend's house without worrying about what I was going to eat. I wished I could just eat because I was hungry. I wished my life wasn't about how I looked especially because how I looked was my least favorite part of myself. I wished I had a life where I could meet someone I could marry.

18

What did you eat last night?

I awoke to this question in a room that was still slightly unfamiliar even though I had lived in the new apartment for over a month. As I calmed myself by running through the list of foods I'd eaten the day before, I noticed a crack on the bedroom ceiling where it met the wall and was beginning to run toward the window that faced the yellow desert that was the wall of the Sunset 5. Not only was the bedroom still slightly unfamiliar to me, but the whole downstairs level also, as I only ate and slept on the first floor, spending most of my waking hours upstairs in the attic. My treadmill was upstairs in the attic and it was beckoning me as it always did after I had completed my mental calculations of calories in and out. The treadmill was really the only thing up there and was perfectly centered in the attic, between the wall of windows that showcased the industrial city that was the roof of the Sunset 5 and the east windows through which I could see all the way downtown. The wall opposite the smokestacks acted as a bulletin board where I had taped pieces of paper. Because the walls would soon be replastered and repainted, they were not precious; they had no value other than as a place to put my thoughts. Mostly the pieces of paper were exaggerated to-do lists. I say "exaggerated" because they said things that were more like goals that I wanted to achieve than things that needed to be done. The largest piece of paper with the boldest writing stated, I WILL BE 105 POUNDS BY CHRISTMAS. Another stated, I WILL STAR IN A BIG-BUDGET MOVIE NEXT SUMMER.

Starring in a movie had only recently become important to me, as Lucy Liu had just gotten *Charlie's Angels*. Suddenly being a cast member on *Ally McBeal* didn't seem to be enough anymore. Everyone at work was reading movie scripts and going on auditions. I often recited my audition lines while I was on the treadmill. I recited them out loud, loudly, over the noisy whirring and the thud of my footfall as I jogged at a 5.5/1 incline. I also put a TV up there with a VCR so I could run and watch movies, which was so much better than sitting to watch them. I had discovered that I could do a lot on the treadmill. I could read books and scripts and knit on the treadmill.

As I began my morning workout, I looked over at the cards on the left of the to-do list which ran down the length of the wall.

111
110
109
108
107
106
105

I was 111 pounds. Each time I lost a pound I took the card off the wall. It helped keep me focused and it helped me to remember that once I'd achieved the new lower weight and the card stating my previous weight was gone, that I could never weigh that much again; that the old weight was gone. It was no longer who I was. It was getting more difficult to lose weight as I got thinner, so I needed all the incentive and motivation I could muster. Putting my weight on the wall was a clever thing to do as it always needed to be in the forefront of my mind, otherwise I might've forgotten and walked on the treadmill instead of run, sat instead of paced. I once saw a loft where a famous writer lived, and all over the wall was his research for the novel he was writing. He described the book to me as his life's work, his magnum opus. I felt like controlling my weight was my magnum opus, the most important product of my brain and was worthy of devoting a wall to its success.

I liked doing my morning workout in the attic even though I lived next to a Crunch gym. When I first moved into the apartment I went to Crunch often, but I discovered that I didn't like showing my body to the other patrons who were no doubt looking at me as critically as I was looking at them. I hated the thought of them recognizing me and telling their friends that Nelle Porter had a round stomach or that when I walked on the treadmill the tops of my thighs bulged out from side to side. What I hated most about going next door to Crunch was the possibility of paparazzi finding me on the way home after a workout, when I looked bloated and my sweatpants were clinging to my thighs. So instead of subjecting myself to the worry of being seen by people and cameras, I preferred to use my treadmill in the attic or to run up and down the stairs next to the elevator for exercise. Sometimes, if I felt particularly energetic, I would time myself as I ran the six flights that connected all the floors of my apartment building. I would run up and down, all the way from the penthouse to the ground floor and back. I could do this mostly unseen by the other tenants, as most of them were lazy and only ever took the elevator.

As I ran on the treadmill in my attic, however, I occasionally felt paranoid. Although it wasn't very likely, I sometimes felt that it was possible that a photographer was taking pictures of me from the industrial roof, that through the smoke he could get clear shots of Portia running on the treadmill in a big empty room. Or he would take video of me lunging from one side of the room to the other, as I had decided I would lunge instead of walk, since lunging would maximize the number of calories I could burn and help tone my legs at the same time. What made the possibility of paparazzi finding me in my loft even more frightening was that I wore only my underwear when I was at home because I liked to stay as cold as possible to burn calories and because, since I was always running when I was home, if I wore workout gear I'd just have more laundry to do. It terrified me to think of that tabloid picture: Portia in just her underwear, running and lunging, a wall of numbers and weight loss goals behind her.

My paranoid thoughts were interrupted by the shrill sound of Bean's bark. Although I would've loved to ignore her and finish my workout, I knew she needed to be taken out. I had only been running for forty-five minutes and I had to leave for work very soon. Reluctantly, I got off the treadmill and went back downstairs to clothe myself and collect her. Having to travel between floors in my underwear using the exterior public staircase was interesting. I had planned on renovating shortly after owning the apartment, connecting the floors and making it more my taste, but I couldn't find the time to search for the perfect architect and designer in between working and working out. I kind of liked it separated, too. I liked that I was hard to find in this secret room that no one, not even a housekeeper, knew existed. I could hide in the attic. And while I didn't like the beige carpet and the previous owner's bed frame and cheap dining table on the first floor, I couldn't be judged for my apartment's decor since it wasn't mine, it wasn't my taste. It was liberating, actually, to live in a space that I owned yet it didn't announce my personality. I could still be anything I liked. I didn't have to live with my previous conclusions of who I was reflected all around me in furnishings and paintings, fabric and stainless steel appliances. I lived in a blank canvas, albeit an old and sullied blank canvas, upon which one day I could create a tasteful masterpiece. While I waited to create my space, however, I had barely any furniture. I had no chairs and no sofa, no coffee table. The only indication that someone lived there was my large collection of antique mannequins that were propped up around the living room. While I had always enjoyed them as an expression of the female form, the mannequins became useful as sometimes

I measured them and compared my body measurements. I had just started measuring my body parts as a more accurate indication of my weight loss. Mannequins represented the ideal form. By comparing myself to the mannequins, I could take an honest look at how I measured up to that ideal. But mostly I just liked to look at their thin, hard limbs.

As I pulled out of the parking garage of my apartment, I checked the time. It was 9:02. It took a long time to drive to work from anywhere in Los Angeles, since Manhattan Beach was far from the city. I didn't get to finish my workout, as Bean took an inordinately long time to go to the bathroom on the lawn of the garden terrace on the second floor. While I could have left her there on her own and come back to collect her on my way down to the parking garage, I decided to wait with her, however impatiently. Although the garden was walled and looked quite safe, I couldn't risk losing her. She was my best friend.

I seemed to catch every traffic light on Crescent Heights Boulevard. As I sat and waited, staring at the big red light that was preventing me from moving, I began to feel lightheaded. My palms were sweaty. I was feeling nervous and anxious and yet I couldn't attribute these feelings to being late for work—I'd given myself plenty of time for the long drive. I realized that I felt anxious solely because I wasn't moving. When the light finally turned green, my stomach continued to feel fluttery, my palms still slipping slightly on the steering wheel, my sweaty hands unable to grip it firmly. Sitting behind the steering wheel, pinned to the seat with a tight strap, I felt as though the cabin were closing in on me; the faux-suede roof was barely tall enough for the loose knot of thick hair that was held on top of my head by a chopstick. As I turned my head to the right to check on Bean who had jumped from the passenger seat and into the back, the chopstick scraped against the window; a sound that shot through my nerves, filling my mouth with saliva that tasted like metal. I tried to shake it off. I shook my hands and pumped my arms. I made circles with the foot on my left leg. I lit a cigarette to counteract the metallic taste and to calm my nerves, but the wisps of blue smoke curling up into the windshield looked poisonous, which cigarette smoke sometimes did to me when I was in confined spaces and forced to look at what I was actually inhaling. It looked very blue trapped between steering wheel and the windshield before turning white and making its way through the front, turning clear as it reached Bean in the back. I painstakingly extinguished the cigarette, careful to be sure that it was completely out, and I wondered when I was going to use up the calories I'd eaten for breakfast as I hadn't had time to do my full one-hour run. As I followed the last wisp of smoke from the ashtray as it meandered upward and collided with the passenger window, I saw a beautiful tree-lined street on my right named Commodore Sloat. The name struck me as being very odd as it sounded more like a street name you'd come across in London than where I was, south of Wilshire in Los Angeles. I checked the time: 9:20. It occurred to me in a flash of excitement that I had time to get out of the car and away from this anxious feeling of being trapped, stale, and inactive. I would take a quick run up and down that street.

"Good morning, Portia." Vera smiled as I walked into the fitting room. She smiled and shook her head. "Could you get any thinner? Look at you! Every time I see you, you just keep looking better and better. I hate you!" Vera laughed and wheeled in a rack of clothing. I started to undress in front of her and stood proudly in only a G-string and platform shoes. I felt liberated. I felt free because I no longer had to worry about how I looked, or whether the clothes would fit, or if I deserved to be on a hit TV show. I didn't have to worry what people were saying about me. Anyone who looked at me could see that I was professional.

The first suit was too big, as were the second and the third. My mind didn't wander to a happier time and place like it usually did during a fitting. I simply couldn't have been happier than I was in the present moment.

"Can you get twos and fours for the Skinny Minnie from now on," Vera called out to her assistant. "And maybe get her some shorter skirts. Let's show off those long legs of hers."

Skinny Minnie. As stupid as that name was, I felt delighted that someone would attach it to me. She handed me sweaters rather than jackets because, as she explained, the jackets she pulled for me would all be too big. To my amazement and delight, everything was too big. We set a time for another fitting the following day.

She shook her head again. "I wish I had a tenth of your discipline."

"Well, I had help. I have a great nutritionist." I looked at Vera's body. She was chubby. I'd never noticed before. "You don't need to lose weight. You look great."

Conversations about weight are practically scripted. There are only a couple of things to say in response to a woman complaining about her weight, and the response I just gave Vera was probably the most popular.

"I need to lose twenty pounds—at least! Seriously, will you tell me how you did it? Like, what do you eat? What's, like, your average day?"

She admired me. She really looked as though she was a little in awe. She thought I could teach her how to be disciplined, which was ridiculous. You can't teach someone self-control any more than you can teach them common sense.

"I'd love to, but it's really tailor-made to what my body responds best to. I really don't think it would work for you."

I wouldn't have ever told her my secrets. This was mine. I was successful at the one thing almost everyone wants to be good at, dieting. Besides, I couldn't tell anyone what I ate. I could just imagine her face when I told her that if she wanted to achieve this level of success then she'd have to eat two-thirds of an oatmeal sachet for breakfast, tuna with butter spray for lunch, a spoonful of ground turkey with butter spray for dinner, and for a treat, Jell-O mixed with butter spray.

"Okay then, Skinny Minnie. Fine. You're done losing weight now though, right? 'Cause you look perfect—but any more and you'll be too thin."

"Yep. Hard part's over. It's all about maintaining it now."

I wasn't done losing weight. Although I thought I looked good, I knew I could look even better. When I turned sideways to a mirror, I could see that the front of my thighs were shaped like a banana from my knee to my hips. At 105 pounds, my goal weight, they would look straight. I still had six more pounds to go.

"Gotta go to work. They need me on set. See you tomorrow." I left the wardrobe rooms feeling elated. I didn't even need to smoke a cigarette. As I walked to the set, I felt calm and in control.

"Morning, Portia." Peter greeted me as I walked into the unisex bathroom set where my one half-page scene would take place. I didn't have any dialogue. I seemed to be used less and less, which was annoying because I'd never looked more camera-ready. I'd never looked more like an actress should look.

"Hi. Good morning. How's it going here?"

"You know. Same old stuff. I'm in court again this episode." He rolled his eyes. He was always in court.

"Better you than me." I said it, but I didn't mean it. I was extremely jealous that David Kelley gave Peter his clever cross-examinations, his brilliant closing arguments. I thought that I had proven my chops as an attorney the previous season, and yet I was relegated to the odd scene in the background of the law office. I had even lost my status as the sexy, untouchable love interest that had me revealing myself in my underwear. It seemed ironic that since I had spent hours a day sculpting my body, preparing myself for scenes that I used to be unprepared for, I no longer had the scenes.

Although I was acting in the scene with him, it felt like I was watching Peter perform, just as the crew was watching him perform. He walked into the unisex bathroom, saw me in the character of Nelle, yelped, and walked back out. In every take he was hilarious. I did nothing. I just had to stand still and in a very specific spot so the mirrors in the unisex set didn't reflect my face into the lens. I was told that if the camera saw me, I would ruin the joke.

After I finished my one scene that morning, I met my brother for lunch at Koo Koo Roo. I usually ate lunch alone, preferring to eat my canned tuna and butter spray in the privacy of my dressing room. I had made a makeshift kitchen in the shower of my bathroom where I stocked spices and bottles of Bragg Liquid Aminos, canned tuna, and Jell-O. I also kept all the tools I needed—a can opener, chopsticks, and bowls. One bowl, however, I had to take back and forth with me because I used it to help me measure portions. It was a cheap Chinese-looking footed bowl with fake pottery wheel rings on the inside, and the first ring served as a marker to show me how much tuna I should eat. If for some reason, when I was mixing my portion of tuna with the seasoning and butter spray it went over the first ring, I tended to throw it away and start over. Usually, if it went over the first ring when I was mixing it meant I was too anxious to eat and I was hurrying out of sheer greed. As I ate approximately a third of a can of tuna per meal, there were three chances to get it right.

I didn't like to eat out or with other people, but I hadn't seen my brother in a while and so I made an exception. He had been asking me to celebrate with him for some time as he had quit working for the biomedical product company and started his own helicopter company, Los Angeles Helicopters. I chose the venue. Koo Koo Roo was the only restaurant I would go to, as they seemed to use very little oil or fat. When I walked in, my brother was already sitting down, a plate full of food in front of him.

"Sorry, Sissy." He gestured to his food. "I have a meeting at two o'clock." He reached into my bag where he knew he'd find a silky white head to pet. "Hi, Beany." He whispered his hello to my dog who illegally went everywhere with me in that bag.

"Don't worry about it," I told him. "Clearly Mr. Bigshot Pilot is too important to wait for his sister."

My brother is a pilot and I am an actress, I thought. Two kids from Australia and here we are in LA, both living our dreams.

"I'll go order."

I was secretly very relieved that he had gotten his lunch before me. Ordering the four-ounce turkey dinner at Koo Koo Roo in Manhattan Beach could be tricky. Only the one in Hancock Park near my old apartment weighed my turkey under the four-ounce portion because they knew I liked it that way. At other locations, like this one, the people behind the counters argued that I would have to pay the same price for the full four ounces so I might as well have the full four ounces. It was a tiring argument for me and a confusing one for them as they thought I was presenting them with some kind of riddle. I liked the restaurant chain, but because the one closest to my home was difficult for me to frequent, I tended to eat there less. I couldn't go to the Koo Koo Roo on Santa Monica near my home because it was in the middle of boys' town, the gay part of town, and I was terrified that if I were seen there, people would know I was gay. Although sometimes I thought that was ridiculous, mostly I thought staying away was the right thing to do. After all, everyone in there was gay, so why wouldn't I also be gay? Would I be the only heterosexual in the whole place looking for turkey? Would the customers look at me with surprise and concern, having had a rare sighting of a heterosexual who has clearly lost her way, and offer to give me directions to get back to the straight side of town? Or would they quietly snigger and congratulate themselves for having a finely tuned gaydar, for knowing that I was gay all along, as they stood in line to place their orders?

I sat down with my plate of turkey—all four ounces of it despite asking for three—and immediately began feeding Bean from the plate. She loved turkey and she helped keep my portions down. She loved Koo Koo Roo as much as I did. I was so busy feeding Bean, it wasn't until my brother spoke that I realized that he had been watching me in silence for quite some time.

"You gonna eat any of that yourself?" I looked up at my brother and was surprised to see that he looked almost angry. His arms were folded tightly across his chest. His lips looked thinner than usual and his eyes seemed shallow, like he'd put an invisible shield behind them that blocked out the kindness in his soul that he'd shown me only moments before.

"You're giving your lunch to your dog, Porshe." Now my brother sounded angry. He never called me anything but Sissy unless he was pissed.

"Chill out, would ya? What's wrong with you?" Now I was getting pissed. "I don't eat all four ounces of it because it has too many calories, okay?"

"And how many calories do you eat?"

"Fourteen hundred a day, like everyone else." I hated lying. I found myself doing so much of it lately. I couldn't tell anyone the truth anymore.

"Bullshit. You can't be eating that much. You look really thin."

It was all I could do not to smile. What with Vera calling me Skinny Minnie and now this, I had had a really great day.

"That's not a compliment, idiot."

Damn. I must have smirked.

"I know." I knew he didn't mean it as a compliment because of the tone of his voice, but how could anyone ever take "you look really thin" as anything but a compliment?

"Okay—I'll gain a little weight. Jesus." When attacked, defend by lying. "It's not deliberate. I've just been working too hard lately." I was watching him become more relieved, but there was obviously something more that he needed to hear.

"I know I'm too skinny."

That did it. He looked happier, his lips fuller, his eyes not so cold. His arms fell to his side.

"Don't you have a meeting?" I asked him.

He nodded.

"Okay then. Bugger off." I kissed his cheek and smiled.

He reached into my bag to pet Bean. He started to leave but then turned back toward me.

"Just because you work with someone who's skinny, doesn't mean you have to be skinny, too."

19

SAT ON Suzanne's couch. Seeing Suzanne had become a pretty exciting ritual for me as I got to show her how well this little student was doing with her homework. I had certainly lost weight on her program, even though I had to lie about how many calories I was eating. I never went back to 1,400 calories a day because I didn't need to. After Ann's visit, I actually never went back to 1,000. There was no point in increasing my daily calorie intake when 600 to 700 was working so well for me. My weight loss had slowed down slightly since going under 110 pounds, and that was even more reason to stick with the lower calorie consumption.

"How many calories are you eating, Portia?"

"Fourteen hundred." I answered her with a slightly incredulous tone in my voice, hoping that the tone would convince her that I was telling the truth.

"Can I see your diary?"

I reached into my bag for the journal, careful to pull out the right one. There were two journals in my bag at all times, the real one and the one for Suzanne. Not only did the real one show my actual calorie consumption, it had notes and messages in it as incentive for me to stay on track. I used the same motivating techniques in my diary as I did when I was a kid striving for high honors in my ballet exams, but whereas I wrote, "You will not get honors" on a sheet of paper for the ballet exams, now I wrote "You are nothing," on every page of my diary. I don't know why, but that statement filled me with fear and then the desire to be "something." I always used the thoughts of being nothing and going nowhere to help me achieve goals. When I was a teenager studying to get into law school, I would repeatedly listen to a Sonic Youth song called "Song for Karen" about Karen Carpenter, who died from anorexia. In the song, the phrase that Kim Gordon repeats, "You aren't never going anywhere. I ain't never going anywhere" was like a mantra for me and pushed me to study longer, to try harder.

But I knew my motivating techniques weren't conventional and I couldn't share them with Suzanne. Especially because in my diary I referred to my homosexuality, which was something she didn't know about. I could imagine how horrified Suzanne would be if by accident I pulled out the real diary and she saw YOU ARE A FAT UGLY DYKE written all over it. She probably thought she'd never even met a lesbian. It made me smile just thinking about the expression on her face if she'd known there was one in her living room.

I handed her the fake journal. It was very time-consuming having to make up the "proper" amount of food with its weight and calories. Thank God for the calorie counter. But the most annoying thing was putting variation in my pretend diet. I had to pretend to be interested in a wide variety of foods, which I wasn't. Most people aren't. My mother ate practically the same thing every day. In fact, I only ate seven things: turkey, lettuce, tuna, oatmeal, blueberries, egg whites, and yogurt; eight if you included Jell-O. She looked over it as I sat opposite her feeling like a schoolkid who cheated on a test. Only when she handed it back to me was I aware that I had been holding my breath.

"What does your exercise program look like, Portia?"

"You didn't tell me to write it down." Even though I had wanted to brag to her about the amount of exercise I did, I didn't write it down. At least not in the fake diary I made especially for her.

"No. I'm just curious. What kind of exercise do you do?"

"I run, mainly. Pilates, sometimes. But running, I guess." I told her about the amount of time I spent on the treadmill and that I'd found a way to run on it for my entire lunch break at work without ruining my makeup. I told her about my long drive to work and how I liked to break it up with a run. I knew she'd be proud of me. It must be heartbreaking for a nutritionist if her clients are too lazy to increase their exercise to help her do her job. I bet they'd blame her, too, if they didn't lose weight.

"I found this nice, tree-lined block just south of Wilshire where I can run because sitting for too long kills me."

"What do you think will happen if you sit for too long?"

"I'll get fat, Suzanne! Diet is only half of it, you know."

She looked concerned. The look didn't surprise me because she always looked concerned when I spoke. I had decided that that was just how she looked all the time. I learned to ignore it.

"Portia, can I ask, do you get your period regularly?" She looked slightly embarrassed at having to ask the question.

"Sure, I guess." I'd never really thought about it. Because I wasn't scared of getting pregnant, I didn't really pay attention to it. I thought back over the last couple of months and realized that I couldn't remember having it.

"No, actually. Now I think about it, I can't remember the last time I had it."

She nodded her head repeatedly, but the movement was so small it was almost imperceptible. If I hadn't have been looking directly at her, I wouldn't have seen it. But her silence commanded my attention. I found myself breathlessly waiting for her next word, yet I didn't know why.

"Portia, have you ever seen anyone . . . like . . . a counselor . . . who could help you deal with your weight issues?"

I was confused. Wasn't she helping me deal with my weight issues?

"You mean, in the past?"

"Yes. Did your mother have you see anyone when you were a teenager?"

I went to Jenny Craig and Gloria Marshall. I guessed I could tell her about that.

"When I was fifteen—the year off school to model—I went to a couple of weight-loss centers."

I told her that after the Fen-phen-type drug didn't work, my mother and I decided to consult the dieting professionals. Jenny Craig was first, with its eating plan and meals in cans purchasable at the counter after each group session with fat women in chairs sitting in a circle. I didn't lose weight. I gained it. I stopped eating the canned food and became too busy with homework to attend the scheduled meetings. But my mother and I discovered Gloria Marshall, with its flexible schedule and gymlike atmosphere and so I joined that as well.

The Gloria Marshall center closest to my house was two train stops and a short walk away and I could go there any time I liked. I would pack loose-fitting clothing into my bag and stop by on my way home from a modeling go-see. I would change, weigh in, and get to work, kneeling on one knee while placing the length of my thigh on a wooden trundle machine that looked more like a wheel used for spinning wool than workout equipment. While my thigh was being pummeled by the wooden spinning wheel, the radio would play "A Horse with No Name." Always. There was no exception. The song made me very depressed that the man was a nomad with no attachment, no home. I didn't think he was free and had chosen to forgo all the other ways humans make themselves feel falsely purposeful and safe. I thought he was lost. And that his survival depended on the horse and that he could care for the horse but not have attachment to it scared me and made me feel empty. But I've always read too much into songs. When I was eight years old, the song that would play to call us in from the playground at the end of afternoon recess was, "Those were the days, my friend, we thought they'd never end," and every day I became instantly nostalgic for the moment that had just ended, knowing that I'd never be eight again, that I'd soon be burdened with knowing more than I did at that moment when I had two loving parents and no responsibility.

I was received by the patrons of Gloria Marshall in a similar way to those at Jenny Craig, with disdain, only the Gloria Marshall counselor used me as an example of how effective their program was so the ladies regarded me with hope and a little awe. They didn't know that 128 pounds, the "target" weight to which most of them were aspiring, was my starting weight. When I became the model Gloria Marshall client, I hadn't even started the program.

It was clear by the look on Suzanne's face that what she was hearing wasn't normal to her. I had never before thought of myself as abnormal in my approach to food and weight. As a young teenager I was surrounded by models who would drink only watermelon juice for two days before a shoot, or eat a big dinner, do cocaine, and go wild on the dance floor of a nightclub to burn the calories from the food. But I didn't need to be a model to surround myself with diet-obsessed unhealthy people. School was full of them. Suzanne's shock made me think she lived in another world, an unrealistic world where teenage girls were happy with their bodies just the way God made them and nourished them with the home-cooked meals their mothers made so they could grow up to pursue a career knowing that what a girl accomplished was of far greater importance than how she looked. And maybe that world did exist, although I have never even briefly visited, much less lived in it. There was a moment in the session with Suzanne when I thought about law school, how everyone seemed to place value only on grades, not looks, and how I had carried over from high school the idea that somehow my personality would help my grades. That if I mooted with sarcasm and wit, I would win the mock trial by being the most entertaining. I also thought that hair, makeup, and wardrobe would win quite a few points. I thought that if I rolled into a lecture on Rollerblades flush from a modeling job, I could be the teacher's pet, that I'd get more attention, more private tutoring. None of that happened for me. Instead I felt vacuous, frivolous, a dumb blonde who didn't belong. There was nothing cute about an obnoxious girl flitting around from modeling jobs to lectures on Rollerblades. I became deeply ashamed just thinking about it.

It felt strange, all of a sudden: sitting there, exposed and abnormal. I'd said too much. After all, Suzanne was just a nutritionist. I had come to learn what to eat and how to stay on track with my diet, not to spill my guts about my childhood and my insecurities. I realized at that moment what she was referring to when she asked if I'd seen a counselor at the beginning of the session. And in the silence following my rambling, I could see by her smug expression that I had confirmed to her that I was in the wrong place.

"Portia. I want you to be healthy and happy, but I don't know if I'm helping you achieve that. I don't think I'm qualified to help you."

I looked down past my manly hands that were sitting on my lap to a stain on the carpet.

Of course you can't help me. I'm losing weight on my own.

The fact that I had to write a pretend journal should've been an indication to me that I knew more than she did on the subject of weight loss.

I looked at her and smiled sweetly.

She went on to tell me that I had issues that were best handled by a specialist. She told me she would research eating disorder therapists. Then she asked for my mother's phone number in Australia.

20

WITHOUT HAVING an assistant go to the Beverly Center to run my errands for me, I was forced to pull into the parking structure of the dreadful shopping mall on my way home from work to take care of a couple of items myself. I had been contemplating whether to get an assistant, but it was hard to justify such a self-aggrandizing hire. I could certainly afford one, but I wondered how that would look to my friends and family. How would it look to my co-stars when most of them didn't have one even though they worked a lot more than me? As my character seemed to be appearing in fewer and fewer scenes as the weeks and episodes rolled on, Nelle Porter required hardly any of my time at all, which gave me all the time in the world to shop.

I hated going shopping. I always tended to feel lonely, even with Bean in a bag by my side. I hated being surrounded by people and yet having no one to help me make a purchase other than the person trying to sell it to me. I hated feeling the desperation of sales assistants and knowing that the commission from my purchase could make or break their day. I also hated people looking at me, I hated children screaming, I hated loud, distracting music, I hated the pet stores with the sick tiny puppies in hot glass cages, and I hated who I was. I discovered how pathetic I was in a store. I defined myself by the items I chose. I could find what I was looking for in black and in pink, and for twenty minutes I would try to decide if I wanted the black one or the pink one. I would think that I was more of a "black" person but that getting it in black was too ordinary. It made me wish that I were a "pink" person when I'm not a "pink" person. This kind of thinking was amplified in a clothing store because invariably I would be overwhelmed by everything I was not only to discover that who I was didn't even have a place in the store. That in all of Barneys, there wasn't a tank top or a pair of cargo pants that let me know that I was a welcome member of their society; that they have covered the fashion needs of the upwardly mobile young women who can afford to shop there while sending a message to me that I was not welcome. I didn't belong there. It told me that their young women wore short skirts and heels and delicate tops with small straps and elegant, tiny necklaces. Their young women were delicate, with soft manners and good bone structure because these young women had inherited the delicate, tall, thin gene from their beautiful mothers who, twenty years prior, were seduced into making offspring by their wealthy, powerful fathers. The Barney's clientele had no need for tanks with thick straps, boots, and cargo pants. "Go to the Gap with the average, ordinary, people" is the message the store was sending. "You'll find something for yourself there."

As I boarded the escalator and rode down into the bowels of the Beverly Center shopping mall, I became paranoid that my activities might be recorded by the paparazzi. It wasn't that I feared being caught doing something wrong, it was that I feared being caught doing something so ordinary. I hated paparazzi. Paparazzi made me feel like I was a criminal under investigation for insurance fraud, stalked by photographers who were hired to provide the evidence. Paparazzi are the ultimate hunters. They are patient, prepared, and precise. There's a wordless exchange that occurs between the hunter and the hunted. They tell you that while you may have gotten away with your life this time, they'll take away your life next time. They'll ruin the illusion that is your fake life—the life that you show to the world while keeping all the secrets of your real life hidden. The photographers and you both know that it's only a matter of time; that with persistence they will expose you for the fraud you are. They told me with one glance that they knew I was gay, that I was fat under the flattering shirt I was wearing, that I was Amanda Rogers, a no one from nowhere. Having an assistant would lessen the chance of being caught as I tended to play the "maybe I can get away with it" game. I would let my guard down, feeling stupid for having an over-inflated ego and thinking that people cared about me enough to take my photo, only to discover that indeed they did.

As far as I could tell, there were no paparazzi at the Beverly Center. After buying a black exercise mat and nude underwear, I headed back to the car. I decided that because I hadn't eaten for many hours and my calorie count was fairly low that day, I would allow myself to have a piece of Extra chewing gum. I always allowed myself to have the gum, but at 5 calories a stick, I had to add it to my daily calorie allowance because it was these kinds of unrecorded calories that could build up and cause you to gain weight. I put my seat belt on, reached into my bag for a piece of gum, and put it in my mouth. The sweetness and coolness of it filled my body with a current of ecstasy, and a rush of syrupy water flooded my mouth and my belly. After what seemed like only seconds of chewing, the initial surge was over and I could almost feel my endorphins screaming for survival as they slowly faded back into the blackness of my empty body. Worse than feeling depressed that the rush was over was the feeling of ravenous hunger ripping through my head and my gut. It was a pain that I had never experienced. As if under hypnosis, I reached into my bag again. Robotically, I unwrapped the gum and fed a piece into my mouth. I fed another piece into my mouth. I spat the wad of chewed gum into the ashtray and fed one more piece into my mouth. And then I shoved the pieces into my mouth two at a time. I spat them out. I repeated the frenzied feeding, chewing, and spitting. And then it was done. There were no more sticks of Winterfresh gum left. I slowly came back into my mind only to realize that I'd just consumed 60 calories. I sat in the car unable to turn the key, terrified by what had happened. There was no reason for it, no upsetting situation that had sometimes triggered me to binge in the past, nor was it a conscious decision to blow my intake for the day. It was a normal day, pleasant even. Without an indication, how would I know when this might happen again? What if it happened once a day? How the hell was I not in control of the only thing I thought was possible to control in my life?

I had been abducted. I was not in control. Now I would live in this state of constant anxiety that I would be overtaken by this vacancy of mind. I would hover there, in this place of helplessness and uncertainty, waiting to be abducted again.

A surge of fear and anger rushed through my body, and I ripped off my seat belt and got out of the car. In the crowded parking structure of the Beverly Center, I started running. If I couldn't control the intake, I could control what happened next. I could eliminate it. I could run it off. I started sprinting. I ran as fast as I could to the concrete wall at the end of the parking structure, slapped the wall with my hand like a swimmer at the end of a lap, and like a swimmer I used the energy to turn back in the direction I came with ferocious speed, getting faster and faster with each pump of my arms and legs. When I ran past my car, I could hear my dog barking, her barking getting fainter as I sprinted to the other end of the parking structure, dodging the occasional car that pulled out of a space, and slapped the opposite wall, catapulting myself off the wall in the other direction to repeat the exercise. I was aware of loud screeching noises as cars passed me, their tires making that sound as they struggled to grip onto the slick concrete through the turns, some of them bulging into the oncoming lane to avoid running into me as I sprinted from end to end. But I couldn't worry about that. I had to stay focused and keep running. I could eliminate half of these calories if I kept running.

"Stop running!"

A young man holding the arm of an elderly woman on a ventilator yelled at me as he crossed my path and attempted to put her in a medical van. He was angry. Maybe my running made him angry because seeing someone freely express their desires by doing whatever took their fancy made him feel trapped, tethered to the ventilator as if he himself depended upon it for life and not the old woman. Although I thought he was very rude to yell at me so loudly, there was something about the tone in his voice that startled me and made me slow down. Once I slowed down it was hard to get the speed back in my sprint.

I became aware of my footwear, too, and wondered how I could have reached that speed in five-inch rubber platforms. They were my work shoes, my "off-camera" shoes. They were purchased, as the name "off-camera" suggests, for use on the set of *Ally McBeal* when the camera couldn't see my character's feet, but I had given them a leading role. For although they were plain and from Payless, they made my legs look thin. Because their height gave my body the perfect proportion, they were the last things I took off before bed and the first things I put on in the morning. I'd started not to wear any other shoes, even to workout or hike, and I never walked barefoot in my house anymore for fear of passing a reflection of myself in a window. But to be able to sprint in them . . . that's something that I didn't think I could do.

I hated that stupid nurse for breaking my concentration. How dare he interrupt me as I was trying to fix this awful situation I found myself in. It was hard to understand the importance of something like this unless you were desperately trying to lose weight, but I couldn't say that to anyone for fear of it sounding trivial. No one knew that my whole career hinged on its success.

I got in the car to drive home. I was angry and riddled with anxiety. If I waited too long to finish burning off the calories consumed by chewing the gum, the calories might turn into fat. At the red lights, I took my hands off the steering wheel and pumped my arms furiously while holding my stomach tight. I alternated putting my left foot and my right foot on the brake so as to bend and straighten my legs an equal number of repetitions. I sang loudly the whole way home while thrashing my head around. I was not a huge fan of Monster Magnet, but there was one song I played repeatedly in the car because it helped me expend energy while driving. I couldn't get home fast enough. I turned onto Crescent Heights from Beverly and started thinking about a strategy to burn the excess calories. I would park, take the elevator to my apartment, drop Bean off, change into workout gear, and go next door to the gym. No. I would park, drop Bean off in the garden, run up the six flights of stairs, take the elevator back to the garden floor, get Bean, run back up, and then get on the treadmill at home.

I got myself and Bean out of the car as quickly as I could and started running with her to the garden floor. I hurriedly put Bean outside in the walled garden and took off up the stairs. She would be okay there for a minute. It was an enclosed garden and she needed to stretch her legs. I took the stairs two at a time so I could feel the burn on my thighs. When I reached the fifth floor, I went back to running one stair at a time, but fast, so it felt like I was running in place. I admired my coordination and athleticism. Running that fast up stairs is tricky, especially in platform wedges. I liked wearing the shoes for these tasks, though. I felt as though they burned more calories because I was forced to be aware of protecting my ankles from spraining. Perfect balance was required to land each step with my weight spread evenly on the balls of my feet between my big toe and my little toe, and perfect balance, as I had learned at Pilates, requires energy. And after putting 60 unwanted calories into my body, I had energy to spare.

When I reached the top of the seventh floor and there were no more stairs to climb, I faced a decision. Would I take the stairs back down to the second floor to get Bean? Or would I take the elevator down and run up the whole staircase one more time? Going down stair by stair couldn't really do much to burn calories, and it seemed that it would be smarter to take the elevator down and run back up in the time that I had to burn it off before it settled on my stomach and thighs. I got into the elevator, hoping Bean would forgive me for leaving her out there alone for another five minutes, but I had no choice. In the quiet space inside the elevator, I started to comprehend what had just happened to me. I'd binged without reason. I had lost control. I'd lost control and I could do it again without warning. If I lost control again, I could get fat again. I would have to start this thing over again. I would fail at the one thing I knew I was good at.

I went all the way down. I was at the bottom floor and I ran fast, two stairs at a time, past Bean, past exhaustion, past the memory of what happened in the parking structure of the Beverly Center. I took my hands off the rail and just used my legs to propel me two at a time up the tubelike staircase, with its forgotten wallpaper and its unappreciated carpet. I reached the top, hit the elevator button, and furiously ran in place, crying now as I figured that crying has to burn more calories than not crying. The elevator door opened and I rushed in. I realized after I was in the elevator that a man had been exiting. Could that have been my only neighbor? I'd never met him. The doors closed and my crying seemed to get louder perhaps due to the confined space or the fact that I had stopped jumping up and down for fear that the jumping would cause the rickety old elevator to break down.

I shook my hands and twisted my torso from side to side. I thought about the fact that I had to eat again soon. It was getting dark outside probably, and I liked to eat dinner before it got dark so I could digest my food before I went to bed. If I just ate egg whites, just pure protein, I'd probably be okay. But I should do it soon. I should run again and go make food.

I started back up the stairs, a little more tired now, and took them one at a time. It was still better than sitting on my sofa, worrying. I started a breathing exercise. Inhale four stairs, exhale four stairs, inhale four stairs, exhale four stairs. It helped me keep the pace I needed to reach the top of the seventh floor in two minutes. I started noticing how long it took to get from the bottom to the top on my second trip up the stairs and I could still do it in the same time as it took when I first started. Since I was obviously not as tired as I thought I was, I decided to do it again. Dinner could wait five more minutes. This time in the elevator, I visualized the food entries in my notebook and calculated my calories for the day. My heart leapt out of my chest not because it was straining to pump oxygen to my overworked body but with panic. My notebook was still in the car! My bag was still in the car! Where were my keys? Did I leave them in my bag?

When the elevator hit the bottom floor I ran past Jeff, the doorman, and into the parking garage in search of my bag. As I opened the heavy steel door of the parking structure I saw my black Porsche, the driver's door wide open. I was embarrassed running to get my things and close it, but there was no need for my embarrassment because no one was around. I felt stupid anyway. I felt stupid because I was sure someone saw that I'd forgotten to close my car door. Everyone in the building knew whose car that was and now someone who lived near me knew that I was "scatty." Scatty was the word my second-grade teacher used to describe me to my mother. "Amanda is a bright girl, and has potential to be a good student, but has trouble focusing in class and is scatty." I was scatty, unfocused, forgetful. I was the kind of girl who would drop out of law school to pursue acting, the kind of girl who would leave her car door open with her keys in the ignition and her purse on the seat. The kind of girl that couldn't maintain her weight.

I could see through the barred windows of the above-ground parking structure that it was dark outside, and although it would be harder to run up the stairs with my heavy bag, I knew it was my last chance before I had to start preparing food. I started back up the stairs again, two by two again, this time using my bag as a weight to add difficulty to the climb and to make balancing on my platform shoes harder. I held the bag with both arms out from my chest and climbed the stairwell with its ugly lighting and stained wallpaper. I climbed slower this time but because of the weight I could feel the burn and so as I got to the top I decided to repeat the whole exercise one last time. It was the only time I had used a weight to aid in burning the calories, and if I did it one more time I felt pretty confident that I could forget that the little mishap with the gum had ever happened.

I arrived at my front door. It had beckoned me at the end of the climb all six times in the last thirty minutes and now, because of my hard work and determination, I got to walk through it. I got to be home. I could finally rest. I turned the lights on in my cold apartment without furniture and threw my bag on the floor. Under the glare of the bare bulb hanging from the ceiling, I saw all the little round stains on the carpet where Bean had previously gone to the bathroom. It wasn't her fault, and I was just about to pull up that carpet anyway. She was a good dog. It's just that sometimes I didn't have time to take her out.

Shit! I had forgotten Bean.

I ran out the door, and down the stairs frantically hoping that I would find her where I left her thirty minutes ago in the garden on the second floor. Bean! My sweet little friend was alone and in danger of being stolen or of getting out onto the busy street and I was the idiot who left her there. God! I hated myself! As I ran down the hallway to the glass door that led to the garden I saw my little Bean. I saw a little white face with big black eyes, scared and shivering from cold and fear, squished onto the glass of the door as if trying to push through it to be in the safety and warmth of the hallway on the other side. I scooped her up and held her close to my chest as I slid down the hallway wall and onto the floor with relief. She was my baby and I had left her. My obsession with weight loss had made me neglectful of the things I cared about. I looked in her big, trusting eyes and stroked her silky white head and said:

"Beany. I'm so sorry. I'll never do that again. I love you so much." I noticed for the first time in weeks that her eye stain had gotten really bad. There were mats in her fur.

"Come on. Let's go home."

Clutching Bean and with tears streaming down my cheeks, I was again faced with the choice of taking the stairs to my penthouse apartment or the elevator. I found myself in a small crowd of people who were waiting for the elevator, some of whom had acknowledged me by asking, "Are you okay?" I knew the elevator would be more comfortable for Bean and I really should've been thinking just about her. She needed to feel calm and safe, not jolted around as I ran up stairs. But it might be quicker to take the stairs and what Bean really needed was to eat and feel safely tucked away in her bed at home, and so I started the journey up the seven flights of stairs. I watched her head bob up and down with each stair and I felt so bad, but it would be over soon.

As I reached my apartment door, left wide open, I remembered that my purchase from the Beverly Center was still in the trunk of my car. A black exercise mat lay in the trunk of my car. How typical of me to buy exercise equipment and never use it. How typically disorganized of me to forget that I bought it so I could begin my workouts with my trainer at home. She would be here first thing in the morning.

It was clear I needed an assistant. I was overwhelmed with all the things that needed to be done. I needed an assistant to help me remember Bean, that she needed to be groomed, walked, and taken downstairs so she wouldn't go to the bathroom on my rug. I needed an assistant to go to the convenience store and to remind me of my workouts. But mainly I needed an assistant to go to the Beverly Center so that this would never happen again.

21

THE NOISE of the escalators as they took people to the gym was a strange one. It was dull and barely there, like the hum of a refrigerator. It was a backdrop to the screaming of the coffee grinder coming from within Buzz Coffee and the music that would blurt out of the Virgin Megastore as its glass doors spat out another customer or sucked one in. But the escalators were beckoning me, politely but relentlessly inviting me to the gym as I sat and waited to interview an assistant. Now that my body was thinner, I wondered if I wouldn't mind the other women in the gym seeing it. Maybe I could ignore their critical looks long enough to work at defining my muscles now that they're not buried underneath layers of fat? As I waited for her to arrive, I watched the escalators go up and down regardless of whether there are people on them or not. They took people to the gym and then they took nobody to the gym. The movie theater was on the second floor also, and I was trying to spot the people who were going to the midday movie, wondering whether the blackness of the theater would fill the void or exasperate it. I would never see a movie on a Tuesday afternoon. Everyone knows workdays are for working.

By the time Carolyn arrived I had come up with a few immediate reasons for needing her, although sitting motionless and watching people go to the gym had made me quietly anxious. I had begun to move my legs up and down to get rid of some of that anxiety, but I found that most of it was thrust at Carolyn, as I began telling her what I needed even before she had time to settle into one of the uncomfortable iron chairs that circled the bolted-down outdoor table. She responded immediately by whipping out her notebook and pen and seemingly matched my anxiety by writing hurriedly and responding to every grocery list item with "What else?" I'm not sure we really made eye contact until the frenzied listing and recording of the to dos was over.

"I need for you to go to a Ralphs to get the yogurt because only Ralphs carries the brand that I eat." "What else?" "I need you to take Bean to the groomer's." "What else?" "I need you to schedule Pilates." "What else?" "I need you to oversee the renovation of my apartment." "What else?" "I need you to go hiking with me because I hate being alone." "What else?"

I'm gay and I need you to be okay with that. What else? I need you to make me okay with that. What else? I need you to keep all my secrets and not tell anyone that I'm a phony.

"That all?"

She signed a confidentiality agreement drafted by my business manager, who knew of no real reason why I should need one, and became my assistant.

"I like to work out. Do you?"

"Yes. I do."

When Carolyn and I finally sat back and breathed each other in, we were already committed. I noticed a few striking things about her. Carolyn was colorless. She had depth to her hair because it wasn't white, yet it had no color. She had a pale, colorless face. She had thin, bony hands that were also colorless except for a thin blue vein that meandered its way from the end of her wrist across the back of her hand to the start of her little finger. Her bony hands matched her thin, bony frame. Among all the round people on the escalators and at Buzz Coffee, Carolyn struck me as straight. I wasn't envious of Carolyn's weight, but instead appreciated it. I appreciated that someone other than me cared about weight loss, and as I instinctively knew that weight loss wasn't a new thing to her, I appreciated that she cared about weight-loss maintenance. And so from that moment on, Carolyn and I would be united in our goal to maintain. With her help, I would maintain my hair color, my nail length, my dog's whiteness, and my car's cleanliness. I would maintain my clothes and my friendships by politely remembering to send apology notes to Kali or Erik explaining how my work schedule conflicted with their dinner parties. And because Carolyn would bring me food and schedule my workouts with my trainers, I would easily maintain my weight.

I returned home after my meeting with Carolyn and was immediately struck by the cold that had crept into my apartment through a crack in the window. I usually left the window slightly open because I liked the idea of fresh air. Actually, it was more than just the air I was wanting. It was the sounds of traffic on Sunset Boulevard, the noise of the industrial air conditioner on top of the Sunset 5. I could sit in my dining room to face another meal alone and yet feel connected to the world around me. I could imagine the actresses rushing to auditions reciting their lines as they waited for the light to turn green at the intersection of Sunset and Crescent Heights. Thinking about actresses driving around to auditions prompted me remember my favorite quote from Mae West when she was asked if she had any advice to give young actresses in Hollywood. "Take Fountain," she said exhaling the smoke from her cigarette. There was so much traffic outside my apartment on Sunset, I wished more actresses took her advice.

I walked into the kitchen to prepare my meal. I would eat 50 calories of egg whites. I found that alternating the egg whites and the tuna for lunch helped with weight loss, as egg whites would cut my lunchtime calorie intake in half. I had been eating egg whites instead of tuna a lot more lately for this reason. Plus, I liked to cook. I never really enjoyed it before, but it was very satisfying preparing a meal, cooking and eating it. I felt quite obsessed with food. It was all I ever really thought about. I was worried that my passion for it would lead to my failure to abstain from overindulging, but I took comfort in the knowledge that people who love to cook are quite often obsessed with food. Cooking was a hobby, an artistic expression, and for me, the ultimate control of what I put in my body. I washed the small mustard plate with the black swirl pattern that I used for egg whites. I washed all the dishes before I ate from them to make sure they were clean. Occasionally the dishes felt greasy when I took them out of the dishwasher and I wanted to ensure that I wasn't ingesting any residual grease or oil that might be on them.

Dishes and utensils were very important. I couldn't just eat from any dish. Each dish had meaning. Each dish helped me in my quest to achieve the perfect body. If I felt anxious about eating, my anxiety was always instantly allayed when I saw my little white bowl with the green flowers, as it had a faint hairline crack that helped me to figure out portions. I had to see the crack at the bottom of the bowl at all times, plus the crack is particularly helpful when I didn't want foods to touch. I also ate every meal with my second favorite tool—chopsticks. Chopsticks were useful for obvious reasons. I'm not Asian, nor am I coordinated. They were unnatural and awkward for me and as a result, the food fell through the little obtuse triangles making me eat slower. If I ate slowly, I didn't eat as much.

I sat down at the dining table to my mustard-colored plate of egg whites. Then I got up and closed the window. The wind had kicked up making it colder, and now the sounds of Sunset Boulevard, once sooth-ing and connecting me to the world at large, were intrusive and grating on my nerves. Horns blasting and muscle cars accelerating reminded me of all the impatience, pretension, and aggression in society that lay beneath my penthouse loft apartment. I was very safe in there with my scale and my schedule. I closed the window, but I turned the air con-ditioner down to sixty degrees. I hadn't really proven my theory, but it just made sense that if you were shivering and trying to stay warm, your body was burning excess calories. It had to. As I hadn't yet begun to eat the egg whites, it occurred to me that maybe my body was burning fat, not calories, as I probably used up the 100 calories from breakfast on my morning Pilates workout. I liked that thought. Although I didn't have to lose more weight, I definitely had a little more fat to burn. My thighs were still big. My stomach still had about an inch of fat on it and, as it was summer during Christmas in Australia, I wanted my stomach to be flat and perfect when I went home. If it wasn't flat, then all that effort would've been in vain. When I went to Australia for Christmas, I wanted my mother to see a determined girl, a girl in control of her life, and a fat stomach doesn't exactly convey that message. A fat stomach said that no matter how hard I tried, it got the better of me. I failed. I couldn't finish the job.

I decided not to eat the egg whites. I didn't need them. As they slid off the plate and into the trash, I felt a surge of adrenaline. I felt invincible, powerful. Not eating them was incredibly difficult and by not eating them I had just proven to myself that I was stronger than my basic instincts, that I could deny them. I wouldn't give in to the desire to eat, because after all, isn't that what fat people do? They give in to desire? They know they shouldn't eat the brownie, but they just can't help themselves. For the first time in my life, I felt like I was helping myself. Although I didn't want to lose any more weight, I certainly couldn't gain any back, especially before Christmas. I wanted to go back to Australia, the hero my mother wanted me to be. I wanted to show my mom that I'd finally conquered the demon. I'd wrestled the beast that threatened our sanity, our relationship, and our self-worth, and I conquered it. We would no longer go to a photo shoot with a sick, sinking feeling in our guts hoping that I was good enough to pass; pass as thin, pass as pretty, pass as a model, pass as a TV actress, pass as worthy of getting attention. Now when I got attention, I knew I deserved it. I'd worked very hard for it.

The kind of attention I had been getting from the press was widespread—from high-end fashion magazines to supermarket rags. I was almost always included in big, splashy tabloid stories about "stars in their dieting hell!" Paparazzi were everywhere I went all of a sudden and I knew the only reason for that was because I was thin. They had been including me in these cover stories about thin actresses and almost every week was another story. Society is obsessed with being thin and a handful of actresses, me included, were showing them that with hard work, it was an achievable goal.

Some of them said that I was anorexic. It wasn't true. At 100 pounds I was way too heavy to be anorexic.

I'd achieved 100 two days earlier. It was a crazy feeling of elation. I wanted to take pictures of my naked body to document it but decided against it just in case I hadn't reached my lowest weight. I didn't want to look at pictures in the future knowing that the image I saw in them wasn't how I'd really looked. I didn't want to have to remind myself that I was actually thinner than the picture showed.

I wanted to document my success because I secretly knew that I couldn't keep this up forever. I knew that one day I'd be looking at those pictures talking about my thinness in the past tense. I just knew that the fat, lazy, overeating piece of shit with her period and her sweat glands and her body odor lurked under the surface of this clean, pristine machine of a girl that I was currently.

With the three hours between lunch and my snack of Jell-O, I had planned to check out a local ballet class in a little courtyard off Sunset. I had seen the studio the previous week when I walked into the courtyard to smoke a cigarette where the Sunset Boulevard traffic couldn't see me. Through the window, I could see that the instructor was an old Russian man with a cane that he banged on the floor in time with the music. I could see his mouth opening wide and his neck straining as he instructed his students: fat, sloppy, middle-aged women in full makeup and tights. I could see an old woman in black on the piano belting out the music, keeping time, playing a two-handed chord to accompany a tondue and a plié. I wanted to go talk to him about joining the class. It would be a good way to exercise and socialize. But mainly I wanted to join it because it would remind me of a time when I was happy, when life was simple and uncomplicated. I could be eight years old again: a skinny, happy girl in a leotard, joking with her best friend behind the instructor's back, our friendship pure and untarnished by sexual desire. It would remind me of a time when I was the best. And I would definitely be the best—and the thinnest.

Look at that inch of fat.

I changed my mind about going to the ballet school when I changed my clothes. When I was naked I could see fat on my stomach and I couldn't imagine showing it to people through a leotard. I knew that I was thinner than the ladies in the class—I was thinner than most people—but also had imperfections, and I just didn't want to reveal them to the other women. It was so bizarre to me to think that these women were extending their big fat legs in the air and prancing around half naked when most of them wouldn't be caught dead in a bathing suit at their next-door neighbor's pool. Or maybe they didn't care. Maybe I was the only one who cared. In any case, going to ballet class would be something I could do when I no longer had to worry about feeling the fat fold over at the junction of where my hips met my thighs in an arabesque. I'd go when I knew that if hypercritical paparazzi found me in the little glass box of a studio, I would be prepared. I would know that they couldn't get a shot of the fat that sat just above my hip bones. I'd go when I knew that the worst the press could say was that I was too thin.

As I lunged my way across the floor to my treadmill to run down the time to my next meal, I wondered if you could really ever be thin enough to be too thin. Even if the tabloid headlines pretended to be disapproving of a girl who was supposedly "too thin," I could always detect envy in the text—that in the tone of the article, there was always the underlying element of awe. And I knew the readers were reading it jealously, wishing that they could be just like us—determined, controlled, not needing anything or anyone to feel special or successful; we'd created our own ultimate success. We had won the battle that the whole world was fighting.

22

WOULD YOU like anything to drink, Ms. de Rossi?"

The airline stewardess spoke softly as if to conserve energy, no doubt gearing up for the ensuing fourteen-hour flight to Melbourne. She already looked tired and we hadn't even taken off yet. She looked old, too. And fat.

"Water, please." I was extremely proud of myself that I was no longer a gross, disgusting pig of a bulimic, downing Baileys Irish Cream and throwing it up in an airplane toilet. I was so glad that I wasn't doing that.

I waved away the mixed nuts that accompanied the water (I asked for water, and yet they assumed I meant water and nuts?), leaned back in my chair, and took out my food journal. There would be no tears on the plane today. I would return home to Melbourne in triumph. I opened the journal and wrote the date, December 19, 1999, and underneath, in big curly writing I wrote something that impressed even me—and I was the one who accomplished it.

95

On December 19, I hit 95 pounds. It was poetic, really, that the day I returned home was the exact day I accomplished this amazing feat. Ninety-five pounds gave me the cushion that I needed to go home for Christmas and eat and drink with my family. Ninety-five pounds would impress them. It might also slightly concern some of them, no doubt, as I had recently become aware that there are certain body parts that looked a little strange. I was okay with that, though. They needed to know that my life wasn't a never-ending Hollywood party; that my money wasn't just given to me, that I had to work hard for all of it. I had been worried that my friends and family might feel jealous of my success. As long as I worked really hard and made sacrifices that were obvious to other people, I wouldn't feel guilty that I made more money than my brother or had a more exciting life than my Australian friends could ever dream of having. Mostly though, they seemed to be more interested in Hollywood at large than they were in my success. I was tired of telling stories about the celebrities I'd met. I'd started to feel like my mother had sent me out as a spy or an undercover reporter to mingle with the special people and bring back the news of what it was that made them special when all I really wanted was for her to think that I was special. Sometimes, if I found a celebrity to be abrasive or rude, she'd disagree with me, citing a tabloid story about the kind acts they did or the fact that other people seemed to like them. She'd always laugh and agree when I told her how ridiculous it was that because of a tabloid she thought she knew better than I did, but her comments came with a subliminal warning: the written word is a powerful thing. The perception of who you are is more important than who are. You are what other people think of you.

The aging stewardess came back, eyes cast downward at her notepad while surfing the tide of turbulence like a pro.

"Can I take your lunch order?"

Something happened to me when flying. I felt that either the calories were impossible to quantify and so that meant that the food had no energy or matter so I could eat everything, or because the calories were impossible to quantify, I could eat nothing at all. Another factor was time. If y equaled 300 calories consumed over a 24-hour period, then what was x if I left Los Angeles at 10:00 p.m. and after fourteen hours of travel I arrived in Melbourne at 6:00 a.m. two days later? How many calories and how many days should I account for? Eating nothing was really my only option.

"I'm not eating lunch today. I had a big meal already."

Why I had to tell her about having a big meal I don't know. I hate it when I do things like that.

When the stewardess came around to deliver the meals, she asked again if I wanted anything, perhaps thinking that the smell of hot beef would send me into a frenzy of regret that it wasn't going to be plopped down in front of me. I reassured her that no, I really didn't want anything. I could resist dead rotting cow on a plastic plate.

After lunch the stewardess rolled a silver tray of cookies and ice cream down the isle.

"Dessert, sir? Would you like some dessert today, ma'am? Dessert, sir?"

She made her way through the seated strangers up the aisle to where I was sitting. She stood in front of me with her cart full of sugar and lard and instead of simply asking me if I would like dessert, she decided to inject some personality into it.

"I'm sure you don't, but . . ." Her sentence trailed off. She had an apologetic look on her face like she was sorry for me that I didn't get to partake in this joyous activity, that being an actress precluded me from all the fun that cookies and ice cream bring. Her droopy eyes seemed to say, "I'm sorry you can't have this. Actresses don't eat cookies." Maybe she was sure I didn't want a cookie just because I'd not eaten any lunch. Then again, what if I had skipped lunch just so I could eat the cookie? How could she have known what I wanted?

By the time dinner came around, I was asleep. Actually, I pretended to be asleep. I didn't want anyone to know that I didn't eat anything during the fourteen-hour flight. Something like that could leak into a tabloid. And while I enjoyed the speculation that I was too thin, I didn't want them thinking I was sick. I wanted people to admire my tenacity and self-control, not to feel sorry for me for starving myself into the shape of an actress.

The long, sleepless night of listening to the drone of the engines was punctuated by the stewardess asking if I'd like to have anything to eat with a cute smile and a "How about now?" in half-hour intervals, which finally trickled down to a raised eyebrow and a quick glance every two or three hours. As breakfast was being served and I asked for black coffee, she could no longer contain herself. I could see that she was gearing up to say something and I thought it would be along the lines of how in her twenty-year career as a mile-high waitress, she'd never before seen a person refuse food. I had clearly made an impression on her and that was something I really didn't want to do. I didn't want her telling anyone that the Australian actress on *Ally McBeal,* the "thin one" (I could just hear it now, "No, not Calista, the other one!") didn't eat and is therefore sick. But to my surprise, her expression changed as she leaned in slightly to speak to me. Her face went from a tired, concerned expression to a hint of a smile. Her droopy eyes became animated.

"You're being so good!"

Yes, lady. I'm always this good.

"Oh! No. I'd love to eat, believe me, but I have this slight stomach virus and you know how awkward that could get on a plane!"

She laughed. Why does everyone think toilets and what goes on in them are funny?

"Well, I hope you feel better." She refilled my coffee cup and I wondered if someone with stomach flu would drink black coffee. I wondered if I'd blown my cover. I pulled out my diary and wrote an entry. I told it that I had eaten nothing and if I weighed more than 100 pounds in Australia it was because of water retention. That's what happens with plane travel. It was good to write it down to remind myself, and the explanation could come in handy if I found myself in a panic in my mother's bathroom on her old pink and black scale.

To say that I hit the ground running isn't an overstatement. When I got off the plane, I began a slow, steady jog through the terminal. There was nothing wrong with that, I thought, as I could just as easily be running to make a connecting flight as exercising my body, limp from sitting for fourteen exercise-less hours. I ran to the airport bathroom to begin my ritual of trying to look fabulous for my mother. I always tried to make a good impression with my hair, makeup, and wardrobe for my mother, as I knew that seeing me looking great always made her happy. But this time was even more special because this time I was skinny. I had the thinnest body I'd ever had to show off to her and so I didn't feel as though I needed the extra-special hair and makeup to counteract my ordinary, girl-next-door body. The package had to say "star" and now my body was helping me deliver that message. After I changed out of my loose clothing and into my skinny jeans and a tight tank, I headed home.

"Mama!" I got out of the cab and ran into my mother's arms, leaving my luggage in the trunk for the cab driver to deal with.

"Bubbles!" My mother dubbed me that when I was a little kid. She still calls me that sometimes. I really like it.

"Darling." She pulled away from the hug and looked me up and down. "You're too thin!" She blurted it out in a way that seemed un-controlled yet premeditated, like her nervousness had built with hours of rehearsal and had culminated in an explosive delivery.

Clearly, she had been lying in wait for me. She was ready for me, armed with evidence. A month ago, Suzanne had called her and tipped her off to my weight loss. According to my mother, Suzanne said my weight loss was extreme and that due to her lack of being qualified in the field of eating disorders, she was racked with guilt and feeling re-sponsible that she had helped cause me to have one. I told my mother that if Suzanne admitted that she was not qualified in the field of eating disorders, how could she possibly diagnose them? It was my mother's lack of common sense that irritated me at that moment standing before her in the driveway, because I knew that she couldn't possibly be concerned by how I looked, only by what she'd heard. Even if I convinced her that Suzanne was wrong, then she would eat up those goddamn tabloid stories about how I was starving myself. She was just waiting for me to arrive so she could levy the insult after a cursory up-and-down glance, a feel of my back when she hugged me, a quick confirmation that the tabloid journalists had once again got it right. This was not the reaction I was hoping for. I wanted her to hug me and look me up and down and tell me that I looked great. I wanted her to tell me that it was obvious that I was working hard, that I had finally got it together after all the years of hell my weight had put the two of us through. Instead she looked horrified.

"Miss?" The cab driver was waiting for me to collect my luggage or pay him or something.

"Sorry. Here." My mother put a bright yellow plastic, Australian fifty-dollar bill in his hand and waved her thank-you at him as he pulled away. She turned to face me as a tram rattled down the busy main road just past the iron gate of our driveway. Several cars sped past in both directions, and the noise and speed of the background made my mother's stillness and silence in the foreground quite surreal. She became aware that she was looking at me strangely and for too long and so she averted her gaze; she wanted to look at me and yet she knew that she shouldn't, as if she were passing a roadside accident. She stood there in silence looking like a little child, her arms dangling limply by her side.

It was clear to me then that she was very worried. I was no longer irritated or angry or disappointed. I was shocked. Did I look emaciated? There had been times when I looked in the mirror and thought I was too thin, but most times all I could see were the inches I still had to lose. If I still had fat on my thighs and hips, surely there was nothing to be concerned about. But her reaction did make me wonder because worry was something that I had rarely felt from her. While I was sure she had a lot of it while raising two kids as a single parent, she never wanted my brother and me to see it. When our dad died and left us in chaos, she rebuilt order with a stiff upper lip. She told me that I was smart and that she had nothing to worry about with me. I made sure I didn't do anything to make her worry. When I was a teenager and all my friends were smoking pot and sneaking out of their bedroom windows to go to nightclubs, I told her that I tried pot, hated it, and in which club she could find me. I was never the kid that gave her trouble. I was the mature and independent one who aced the test and won the race. I was the entertainer, the one who made things exciting with my modeling jobs and my acting and my overseas adventures.

Now, at twenty-five years old, I had made her worry. I took a deep breath, and my eyes welled up with tears. I hated seeing her so uncomfortable, not knowing where to look or what to say, and yet simultaneously, it felt good. I had traveled thousands of miles in search of the opposite reaction, yet I suddenly felt myself preferring the one I'd received. Her concern felt warm, comforting. It seemed as though she was afraid of losing something very precious, and that something was me. Because I'd always been so strong and independent, her concern about me prior to this moment mainly seemed to be about the things I could produce, like a modeling job or a beauty contract. I felt so happy I wondered if I had deliberately lost this much weight in search of that reaction. All of a sudden, I felt worthy of care. I was the one to worry about. Caring for a weak, sick child required a different kind of love. And in that moment in the driveway, I discovered that that was the kind of love I preferred.

I love you too, Mom.

I didn't say that. I really wanted to, but it was too abstract, too heavy and emotional.

Sometimes it's better to keep things happy and superficial.

She obviously thought the same thing because she straightened up and put a smile back on her face as if the incident had never happened.

"Bubbles, you're home!" She'd been looking forward to my return for weeks, getting her petunias in the garden ready for the holiday. Christmas was a special time for her since my brother and I moved to LA. She wanted to dismiss her worry so she could enjoy her daughter's homecoming.

"Let's go inside and see Gran. She's been looking forward to seeing you for weeks." I walked up the back steps and into the house, putting my bags down on the checkered green linoleum floor of the kitchen. I ran over to the rocking chair in the living room to hug my Gran.

"Now, then." My mother glanced at me and then walked away, as if attempting to downplay the importance of whatever she was about to tell me. Not one for confrontation, she chose an upbeat, clipped voice and delivered her message in a tone that enabled me to choose whether to dismiss it or take it seriously.

"What's all this silly business with being skinny? Stop all this silly rot, all this carrying on and eat normally like everyone else, girl!"

A surge of anger bitter like acid flooded my empty body.

Silly? She calls your hard work "silly?" She doesn't care about you. She thinks you did it for attention. You're exhausting to her. You're pathetic for trying to get sympathy. She's not concerned about you, she's sick of you.

"I'm going for a run."

And with that I exploded out the door. I ran down the busy main street of Camberwell, narrowly avoiding cars as they were pulling out of their driveways. I picked up my pace and charged up the hill, past the old people's home and the church and held my stomach tight and twisted from side to side as I ran down the hill toward the shops at Camberwell junction. If my Pilates instructor likened this movement to wringing water out of a towel, then I was wringing out all the acidic anger from my organs that became flooded with it when my mother dismissively called my hard work silly. I waited for the walk signal at the busy intersection and jogged in place to keep my muscles warm, to keep my brain from thinking I was done with my workout or done with the anger that fueled it, since I could use the anger to propel me forward. I sprinted up the busy shopping street, past people walking in and out of the bakery, past the sidewalk café, dodging dogs tied to outdoor tables. I ran past my favorite bookstore, past deathly still people who were standing and reading blurbs of books that promised to help them, entertain them, teach them who they were. It seemed that all the people shopping on that street turned to look at the fool who was sprinting in jeans and platform heels. But I didn't let their obvious disapproval of my running slow me down. I ran fast, right by all of them. I ran until I couldn't run anymore.

I stopped at the train station opposite the doctor's office where my mother used to work. I stood at the corner of Stanhope Grove and watched the trains as they exploded into the station and heaved their way back out once they'd stopped to deliver people and receive people. I watched a green tram putter up the hill. I watched teenagers walk in and out of McDonald's. I was watching my memories. I sat down on the wooden bench next to the taxicab rank and imagined myself in a navy blue school uniform with permed hair, walking out of the train station and across the street to my mother's work, where I would wait for her to take me home. I smiled at that thought. Why I would wait for an hour for my mother to take me home when home was only one more train stop away was something my adult brain couldn't fathom. Maybe it was because I could use the time to sneak off to McDonald's and eat fries and a vanilla milk shake, pretending I was waiting for someone to disguise my embarrassment of being in there alone when all the other tables were full of kids from other schools. I was a model and so I could never go to McDonald's with my friends. I couldn't go with anyone, not only because I thought models shouldn't eat McDonald's but also because I constantly complained about being overweight.

I could never eat in front of anyone because it would be evidence. It would confirm suspicions that I wasn't helping myself and was unworthy of their sympathy. Only a crazy person would console someone for being distressed about her weight and then take her out for McDonald's fries to cheer her up.

As I sat on the wooden bench I became aware of how much pain I was feeling. I pushed down onto the palms of my hands that had been limply resting on either side of my seated legs, elevating my seat bones away from the bench. That immediately alleviated the pain that was caused by my full weight resting on the hard wooden bench. I briefly wondered if it hurt because I was too heavy, that my seat bones couldn't support the weight of my upper body, but quickly dismissed the thought as crazy. Fat people sit on hard things all the time. The pain of being seated and the exhaustion it took to keep me slightly off the bench made me stand. I needed to stand anyway. Standing burns more calories than sitting, and I had forgotten that rule while I had temporarily lost my mind to nostalgia. But standing there, I found myself stuck. I had run quite far and was a long way from home. If I'd had money I could have taken the train or the tram, but since I left the house without any, walking was my only option. After the long flight with no food at all, running back home was out of the question. I should never have stopped. I was not angry anymore and without any motivation I could now only walk. Losing weight really wasn't enough motivation either. My mother's reaction was confusing and it made me wonder whether I had taken this whole thing too far. As I started the long journey home, I wished I could just walk across the street to find my mother behind the desk in the doctor's waiting room, waiting for me. Then she could take me home.

By the time I arrived back at the house, I had completely forgiven Mom. I had thought about her dismissive attitude toward my weight loss and understood it from many different angles. She grew up in the Marilyn Monroe era and liked women to have curves, so she simply didn't appreciate how I looked. She called my efforts "skinny business and rot" because she no doubt realized that she'd completely over-reacted. But even if she incorrectly thought that I was emaciated and sick, I understood why she downplayed her feelings about it, because it was her worry that she was dismissing, not the supposed sickness. My mother often tried to make light of heavy things. When I was a little girl with a gash on my knee, she'd tell me it was just a scratch. If I felt too sick to go to school, she'd tell me that it was in my head, that I just needed a change of scenery. She'd tell me to go to school and if I still felt sick, I could come home. She was usually right; once I got to school I forgot about being sick. She was usually right to ignore it because ignoring it often did make it go away.

When I returned, my gran told me that Mom had gone to the su-permarket to get groceries. She yelled this information out to me as she was quite deaf and since she had to yell to hear herself, she assumed she needed to yell to be heard.

"Marg said you could meet her there if you wanted anything!"

"Thanks, Gran!" I yelled back at her.

I grabbed a knitted shrug and headed out to the supermarket to find my mother. The sleeves covered up my skinny arms, and with them the evidence that achieving a nice all-over body was an effort. My arms were the only giveaway that my weight should have been something other than it was. If you just saw my waist and my legs, you'd have thought I was in terrific shape. You'd have thought that I was just natu-rally thin. Besides, my legs weren't even skinny. They were very average in size. I had to be extreme just to achieve average-size thighs.

I wore the knitted sleeves in an effort retreat from the front line, to surrender from the battle, to silently apologize to her for explod-ing out of the house in anger. I wanted her to feel proud of me as we shopped together, and she wouldn't have been proud if the other grocery shoppers and shopkeepers had seen my arms. I didn't have to hear that from her, I just knew it. She had bragged about me to everyone in the neighborhood and now I had to live up to the image of me she'd been presenting. Everyone wants to see effortless beauty, ease, and confidence. Every script I read described the female leads as "beautiful yet doesn't know it" or "naturally thin and muscular and doesn't have to work at it." Effortlessness is an attractive thing. And it takes a lot of effort to achieve it. "Never let 'em see you sweat" was a principle I'd adopted, and so actual effort was yet another thing for me to hide from the people I was trying to impress. The list of unacceptable things about me that I had to cover up was getting longer. My arms had just made that list.

When I saw my mother she was taking a jar of peanut butter off a shelf in the condiment aisle. She looked so small from where I was standing that I suddenly didn't want her to see me. I felt like a giant. I felt like I was taller and wider than all the people in there and the grocery aisles themselves. I was a big, fat, gluttonous American in comparison to the petite Australians. The shopping carts were small. The boxes of food on the shelves looked like they belonged to a children's tea set. The jam jars were the size of shot glasses, the "family-sized" bags of chips looked like they contained a single serving. When she saw me standing at the end of the aisle, she smiled and waved me over. She had forgotten about her worry, my reaction, her reaction, and my thinness. It's amazing what sleeves can do.

"Hi, Bubbles! I thought we could get some food for you. I don't know what you like to eat now."

As we walked up and down the aisles, she made food suggestions like, "How about I make you a Ki Si Ming? You used to love that." Or, "Should I get some Tim Tams? You always loved Tim Tams." Tim Tams were the chocolate-covered cookies that she'd had to hide from me if she wanted any for the rest of the family.

"Ma. Just let me do my own thing, okay? I eat differently now."

I had finally understood that I couldn't eat normally like everyone else if I wanted to be an actress. Couldn't she see that? Couldn't she see that I'd finally figured out that I had to sacrifice Tim Tams and casseroles and happy family dinners so I could give her something to brag about? As a child model I learned that success and money came when I refused the casseroles and the Tim Tams, and as an adult actress, the rules were still the same. Why would she suggest I eat all the foods that would make me fat?

I did briefly think about eating the Ki Si Ming because I loved it. But I quickly dismissed the thought. I wouldn't deviate from my regular routine. I wouldn't dare. If I ate the curried rice and stir-fry vegetable dish, I worried that I would gain weight. More than gaining a pound I worried that I would keep gaining pound after pound after that; that if I stopped for a moment, got off the train, maybe I couldn't get back on. If I suspended the belief that dieting was the only way for me to be a success in all aspects of life, then in that small window of time it took to eat Ki Si Ming, my desire not to diet would overtake me again. If I ate the Ki Si Ming, I would have to start over, and I knew how much harder it was to start something than to maintain it. Maybe I just had enough willpower to start it one time and if I stopped I would become very fat? I worried that this time the bingeing to make up for all the things I denied myself would never end.

All I ever thought about was the food that I couldn't eat. Sometimes I even dreamt about it. Dieting is hard. That's why everyone admires someone who is successful at it. I had thought my mother would be proud of my precision and my calculations, my self-control, but I had the sense that she thought I was out of control. As I sat down to a tablespoon of dry turkey and watched my mother and grandmother eat the dish they had always made to welcome me home, I wondered if her thoughts were correct. I wondered if I was out of control. If I couldn't eat a scoop of stir-fry because I was terrified of getting fat, then who was in control?

23

What did you eat last night?

WOKE UP at 5:00 a.m. to a quiet, dark house and rummaged through my suitcase for my gym shorts and sneakers. It was time to go running. I wanted to get my workout out of the way so I could see Sacha and my old friend Bill and spend some time with my brother, who was coming home later that morning. I ran down the same roads as I did the day before and thought about how proud Sacha would be when she saw me. The last time we'd seen each other was in St. Barths when I was fat and struggling—at first with her rejection of my advances toward her, but my struggle with my weight closely followed. Of the two issues, my weight problem was the more painful. Her rejection of me didn't hurt my feelings; rather, it clarified my feelings toward her. I was never in love with her. I was merely in love with the idea of being in a relationship with a woman. Over piña coladas, she'd helped me arrive at the conclusion that my future girlfriend would have to be a gay woman, not a straight one. I knew that once I had made enough money where I no longer had to worry about losing my career, I would find a girlfriend. I needed a lot of money, however, because I had an apartment to renovate. But after that, I would find someone to love.

I ran with money in my shoe this time. I wasn't going to be caught again. Besides, I thought it would be nice to eat breakfast at my favorite outdoor café. As well as money, I brought cigarettes so I could run and look forward to ending my workout with a cup of hot coffee and a cigarette. The workout gear I wore for the run made me invisible. It worked as a kind of disguise. No one looked at a girl running in spandex shorts and tennis shoes even if she was running up and down a busy shopping street. Unlike the day before, I could run past the bookstore and McDonald's without turning a head. It is strange that clothes can make that much of a difference.

I stood at the counter of the café and waited to get the attention of the owner. When he finally saw me, I didn't know whether to acknowledge him with a warm smile that suggested we knew each other or just skip the smile and get my coffee. I decided on the latter as it's always very embarrassing when people don't smile back because they are too busy wondering who you are. I used to go there a lot, and although we'd never officially met, he seemed to recognize me when I was with my mother. She's the friendly one in the family.

"Black coffee, please."

"Coming right up." He turned his back to me to pour the coffee, but when he turned around again with a big smile on his face it was clear that he had remembered me.

"Back from America, are ya?"

"Yep. Back home for Christmas."

"Geez!" He blatantly looked me up and down. "Don't they feed ya in Hollywood?"

I couldn't think of a joke. I didn't know what to say.

"How much is that?"

"For you, love, it's free."

I thanked him and took my coffee outside. I found a spot in a cluster of iron tables and chairs separated from the parking lot by a potted boxwood hedge. A couple was sitting at the next table very close to mine, and as I took out the cigarette to light it, I wondered if I should be polite and ask for their approval or just do it and hope I could get a few drags in before they complained. Doing what I wanted without permission and then dealing with the fallout was the method I'd always used with my brother. If I wanted to wear his favorite sweater, the one that he'd never let me borrow in a million years, I'd just take it and deal with the consequences. I liked to think I had grown up a lot since then, but it occurred to me my lighting that cigarette was the same principle. As it turned out, the couple next to me didn't mind the smoke and so I sat there, inhaling smoke and nicotine and feeling quite elated that I was home in Australia with its easygoing people and its trees and its birds with their raucous singing. I would see Sacha later in the day and . . .

"I thought you might like a good Aussie breakfast! Here's some eggs, love. Put a little meat on your bones!"

The owner of the café shoved a white porcelain plate on the metal table in front of me, interrupting my thoughts. Then he dropped a knife and fork wrapped in a napkin next to the plate. On the plate were two eggs, two big orange eyeballs of yolk staring up at me confrontationally, as if looking for a fight. I was too shocked and speechless to send them back immediately and so I was left looking at the eggs as they looked back at me, challenging me to make them disappear. I looked at the planter box filled with the boxwood hedge and wondered if eggs would somehow dissolve into the soil, or if the dirt was loose enough that I could cover up the evidence, but upon feeling the soil I found that it was too tightly packed and almost to the top of the planter. Besides, even if I could cut them up into millions of pieces, how could I get them in there without people seeing me? The café owner came back out to the patio again to deliver food to another table. He winked at me. "On the house," he said quietly so the other customers couldn't hear. For a brief moment I considered eating them just to save him from hurt feelings as he clearly liked his self-appointed role of a nurturing café owner who derived pleasure from seeing people enjoy his food. But that thought was ridiculous. I wasn't going to break my diet for a man who, only moments before, I'd been scared to acknowledge with a nod for fear he wouldn't remember me. I wasn't going to break my diet for that guy.

Disposing of the eggs into the planter wasn't an option and there was no trash can on the patio, so I was left with either cutting the eggs up into tiny pieces and moving the pieces around on the plate to make it look like I'd eaten some or leaving them whole and coming up with a reason for not wanting them, other than the obvious one, which was that I didn't order them. The longer I was confronted with this unsolicited situation, his so-called generosity, the angrier I became. It was quite disrespectful of him, actually, to feed me like this, as if I were a child. I was an adult capable of making my own decisions about what went into my body. I decided that I wasn't even going to attempt to please him. I was going to leave the eggs exactly as they were delivered to me. Now he could deal with not knowing what to do with the two monstrous, confrontational eyelike yolks. My only dilemma was how to appear normal, and as normal people are greedy and love receiving free things, how would I spin this? Who wouldn't want free food? Who wouldn't want free deliciously fresh eggs with their coffee? I found the perfect answer to this riddle just as he came out to check on me.

"Thank you so much for the eggs, but I'm vegan. I don't eat any animal products."

"Vegan." He said the word like he was hearing it for the first time, repeating it as if to get it right. He shook his head. "God, you Hollywood people are a bunch of weirdos."

I laughed at what I assumed was a joke and got up from the table to end this awkward interaction where I was force-fed and called a skinny weirdo. All I had wanted was to sit peacefully and bask in the joy of being home and instead I was ambushed by this Australian weirdo who thought he knew better than I did about what I needed. I jogged home and arrived just as a cab delivered my brother from the airport to the house where we had spent our teenage years ignoring each other.

"Hey!" I hugged my brother as he was collecting his luggage. "God, you stink."

"So do you."

No I don't. I don't stink anymore. I don't get my period. My hair hardly ever gets greasy and I don't sweat, either.

He looked me up and down. "You look awful, Porshe."

"Yeah, well, so do you."

"I'm not joking. You look like a skeleton."

Usually any comment about my thinness made me happy, but being called a skeleton hurt my feelings. My brother and I were always so jokingly sarcastic with each other, sometimes we took it too far. Usually I would've told him that he was being rude, but I didn't want to bring attention to it. I needed to make the conversation casual so that he would let it go. I had to appease everyone lately.

"It's just 'cause I'm in my running clothes."

"You've been running already? It's so early. Why don't you take a break from it? I think you're thin enough, if that's what you're worried about."

It was strange that all of a sudden it seemed like I had to lie constantly just to be left alone.

"I know I'm too thin. I'm gaining weight. And I wouldn't have gone running if I weren't this jet-lagged. I was going crazy lying there—although your bed is really comfortable."

"What?"

"First come, first served, Brother."

I walked into the house through the back door and found my mother in the kitchen.

"Good morning, Bubbles. Do you want some breakfast?"

Jesus.

"No. That man at the café we go to all the time gave me eggs this morning."

That wasn't a lie.

"Michael's here."

My mother ran to the kitchen door and hugged him.

"Mike's home! Look, Gran," she yelled, "it's Mike!"

"Hi, Ma."

As I slipped through the kitchen and down the hall I heard him say, "Hey, you didn't give her my room, did you?"

My brother's arrival diverted mom's attention away from my breakfast, thank God, and I escaped into my bedroom where I had lived my teenage years listening to records loudly and smoking cigarettes, believing that neither noise nor smoke could penetrate my bedroom door. It continued to act as a magic shield from the demands of my family, for when I emerged from my room, dressed in long sleeves and a full, long skirt, breakfast was over and I was greeted with easy smiles. No one seemed to care if I was running or eating. I was wearing a lot of makeup, too, and I think that helped.

"Porshe, you wanna go shopping?"

"Seriously?" I said incredulously. "Again?"

My brother had an enviable ability to dismiss any thoughts of Christmas gifts for the family until Christmas Eve, and I was always dragged along to help shop for them. Strangely enough, though, he never needed my help. He had an uncanny knack for finding the perfect thing, the most thoughtful gift at the last possible second. I loathed him for it and admired him for it. Most times, I secretly enjoyed the ritual, too, because it ended with a trip to our favorite pub. The ritual had a rhythm to it: I had to start out with being pissed off and pretend to have my own plans. He'd beg me to help him although he didn't need it, and I'd grudgingly agree, telling him he owed me a beer. Then it'd end with him asking me to wrap the gifts, which really did piss me off. That was the way it always went. But to my surprise, today I actually was agitated. I was anxiously wondering how and when I was going to eat. I had been waiting for the moment my mother left the house to weigh and eat my turkey, as I wanted to avoid any possible comments that weighing out a portion of turkey might elicit. Then, after that, I thought I could cook and eat egg whites before going to the Hyatt hotel. I had decided to book the presidential suite of the Hyatt and spend Christmas Eve there with my brother to decorate the Christmas tree and to ready the room for our family Christmas dinner the following day. Getting the hotel suite was a gift that I was giving my family, since cooking Christmas dinner in the small kitchen of my mother's house always seemed to be challenging. But leaving my mother's house for the hotel earlier than I'd planned was worrying. Traveling and dieting was hard enough, but without access to my mother's kitchen all day, I began to fret, wondering when I would next eat.

"Why can't you get your shit together like everyone else? I have plans, too, you know. I wanted to see Sacha today."

"I'm not going to carry a whole bunch of crap from LA in a suitcase. Come on, it'll take an hour."

"No it won't." I grabbed my bag, got in the car, and shrugged off my irritation enough to continue the banter. "You owe me a beer." It sounded fun to say it, but I had no intention of holding him to it. I would never drink my entire day's calories in a beer, even if it is Victoria Bitter.

"Hey, what do you think of this?"

Michael was standing in front of a full-length mirror in Myer, Melbourne's largest department store, wearing a purse.

"Who for?" I barely even looked at it. I really didn't care at that point. I hated shopping—especially department store shopping, and I'd been with him in that store for hours. He'd bought about ten gifts so I'd thought we were done.

"It's for me. I need something to carry my work stuff in."

That made me look. My brother, as serious as I'd ever seen him, was checking himself out in the mirror, a thin strap over his right shoulder that connected to a shiny black leather rectangular pouch that was at waist height due to the shortness of the strap. I stared at him, expressionless.

"Guys have bags now! I saw it in *In Flight* magazine on the plane." He turned to me and modeled it a little and by his swagger it was obvious that he thought he looked pretty good.

The ground floor of this department store where we were standing sold shoes and accessories. There was a side that sold men's accessories and a side that sold women's. The two departments were separated with an aisle. While he was certainly standing near a couple of large satchel-type man-bags, he had picked up a bag from the wrong side of the aisle. I waited for him to realize his mistake. After staring at my expressionless face for many moments, he gestured for me to hurry up with my opinion.

"It's a purse."

A look of panic flooded his face as he spun back to face the mirror. He looked at himself and regained his composure, the purse still over his shoulder. He calmly read the tag attached to it.

"Yes," he said simply. "Yes, it is."

We cracked up. We laughed so hard we were snorting. Nearby Christmas shoppers saw us laughing and couldn't help but laugh, too. We left the store and were cracking up all the way to the parking garage, dropping shopping bags as we doubled over. Even after we'd recovered for several minutes, I'd burst out laughing again on our drive to the pub, thinking about my macho helicopter pilot brother wearing a purse. That would set him off again, too, and as I laughed with my brother and drove past red brick Victorian terrace houses and through the eucalyptus-lined streets of my hometown, I felt that I was truly home.

When we arrived at the Great Britain, GB for short, Michael went to the bar and I settled in at a high-top table. I looked around my favorite pub. There was a goldfish above the bar in an old black-and-white TV set and tableaus of mini living rooms, with vintage floor lamps lighting worn sofas and mismatched coffee tables. I never felt more myself as I did in that grungy pub. Bill, an old school friend whom I rarely went anywhere at night without, used to drive me to the GB where we'd meet Sacha and friends from law school. Occasionally I was introduced to girls. Although I was too shy to really do much about it, I loved feeling that excitement of getting dressed to go out thinking that perhaps that night I could meet someone and fall in love. The hope of falling in love was a lot to sacrifice for the sake of my career. Apart from that feeling, I missed being able to relax in public without fear of being noticed, and talking to whomever I chose without worrying about people finding out my big secret.

There was no real reason why I hadn't told my brother that I was gay. Then again, I just didn't really have a reason to tell him. I wasn't dating anyone, and because none of his friends had any idea that I was gay, I wasn't worried that he'd find out from someone other than me. I knew Mom wouldn't tell him. She didn't want anyone to know.

I could hear my brother talking to the bartender about how he just arrived from LA and the old-fashioned cash register make the *ding* sound as it popped open its drawer to swallow up the gold two-dollar coins. I took a drag of my cigarette and found it hard to breathe the smoke back out of my mouth. My throat had constricted with anxiety, trapping the smoke in my lungs. It was time to reveal myself to my brother. I was sure he'd be confused and have a lot of questions, but I had to tell him how alone and misunderstood I've felt. I could no longer keep this secret from him and I just had to hope that he would understand.

He returned with the beers. He put them down on the table. He sat down. He took a sip.

"Brother. There's something I've been meaning to tell you for a long time. Something I've known since I was a kid, really. Well, teenager, I guess. Umm . . ." I took a deep breath and looked at him in his eyes. "I'm gay."

There was an eruption of laughter at the pool table. One man had apparently scratched by sinking the white ball in behind the black to lose the game. The man who won was yelling and walking backward with his arms spread wide, a pool cue in his right hand. He was coming dangerously close to our table. To my surprise, my brother didn't seem to notice and to my even bigger surprise he looked angry. He'd been staring at the table for what seemed like an eternity and for a brief moment I wondered if he'd even heard what I'd said.

"What did you think I would say, Porshe? Why would you think that I'd care about something like that? I'm not some narrow-minded bigot that you'd have to hide this from. I mean, who do you think I am?"

Of all the feelings I thought he would have, betrayal had never crossed my mind. I had betrayed him by hiding the person I really was from him for fear that he would reject me. I had insulted him by insinuating that he harbored thoughts of discrimination and bigotry. His reaction was so surprising to me and it left me feeling ashamed for judging him. And yet I couldn't remember feeling happier. I could tell by his expression that once he got over his anger at me for keeping this secret from him, there was nothing left to talk about. He wasn't confused. He didn't need questions answered. He didn't ask why or how or with whom or whether I thought maybe it might just be a phase. He didn't ask who knew and who didn't know or whether I thought it might ruin my career. I was his sister and he didn't care whether I was straight or gay; it simply didn't matter to him. I'd been worried that he wouldn't believe me, but he didn't even question me. All that mattered to him was that I had been struggling with this tortuous secret without his help.

His phone rang. It was a work call from LA; it wasn't yet Christmas Eve over there—it was just the twenty-third of the month, a day like any other. He took the call and spoke in a tone that was all business. In his voice there was no evidence of anger or betrayal—it was light and friendly without a hint of emotion. He spoke and chugged down his beer.

"You ready?" He didn't even look at my untouched beer.

"Let's go."

As we walked side by side down the Melbourne street in the late-afternoon heat of summer, he put his arm around my shoulder. He understood. He still loved me. We sauntered down the city street listening to the magpies that squarked so loudly we couldn't have heard each other even if we had needed to talk. But we didn't. We just needed to silently acknowledge that we were home, that we were where we came from, that for that moment we didn't need to live in another country just to feel accomplished. We were okay just as we were. Our silence was broken by the remote unlocking the rental car. He uncharacteristically opened my side first, like a gentleman, and just as I was about to thank him for his valor he said:

"You're good at wrapping gifts, aren't you?"

24

CHRISTMAS MORNING, like every other morning since I'd arrived in Melbourne, began in the dark, as jet lag, the discomfort of an unfamiliar bed, and hunger prevented me from sleeping past 4:00 or 5:00 a.m. I lay in the darkness of the master bedroom of my two-bedroom hotel suite and ran through my calorie consumption and calorie burn of the day before. This mental calculation had become a ritual, and it was done with precision and some urgency. Only when I could solve the equation of calories in and calories out could I feel relief and begin my day. There was a scale in the bathroom. I saw it when I arrived the night before. It was digital and measured weight in pounds, unlike other Australian scales, which measured in kilograms. Could I possibly stand on it? Could I weigh myself? I'd been too scared to check my weight since arriving in Australia because of the water retention that can occur during plane travel, and I didn't want to upset myself. But lying in bed Christmas morning, I felt thin. I could feel my hip bones and my ribs. I lay on my side with my legs slightly bent with one knee on top of the other for the ultimate test of weight loss: if the fat on my top thigh didn't touch my bottom thigh, if there was a gap between my thighs even when I was lying down, then my thighs had to be thin. There was a wide gap and I made a mental note to measure that gap with one of those stiff metal tape measures when I got back home. I felt as though I could get on that digital scale and give myself the Christmas present of a good number, a number that would show my hard work; a number that would congratulate me for dieting successfully for eight months.

For eight months, I hadn't gained a pound. I'd stayed the same for a few days at a time, but I hadn't gained. My initial goal weight was 115 pounds. My mistake was that I set a goal weight thinking that 115 pounds would feel different from how it really felt. I thought I would look thinner than I did at that weight. At 115 pounds, although my stomach was flatter and my arms looked good, my thighs were still too big. At 110 pounds, I was happy. I really liked how I looked. I only went under that weight because I needed a cushion in case that uncontrollable urge to binge happened again and it wasn't chewing gum, but ice cream, candy, or potato chips that abducted me.

The only thing I cared about now was not gaining. As long as I never gained, weight loss was no longer that important. But seeing a new low on the scale did give me a high. And the lower the number, the bigger the high.

I walked into the bathroom and used the toilet. I then held my breath as I eased onto the scale, my arms holding me up on the bathroom counter, holding my weight off the scale for as long as it took to gently add weight pound by pound until I could let go of the counter and stand with my arms by my side. In this hotel bathroom, naked and vulnerable, I closed my eyes and prayed. The red digital number in between and just in front of my feet would determine whether I had a happy Christmas or a miserable one. To no one in particular I said out loud, "Please let me be in the nineties. I'll take ninety-five, I'm not greedy, just don't let it be in the hundreds. I'd rather die than be in the hundreds. Please, please, please, please." I started to cry with anxiety, but I quickly calmed myself down as I was worried the jerkiness my body makes when I cry might have caused the number on the scale to shoot up and not come down again. In fact, the more I thought about it, the more I realized that I needed to start over, to ease back on the scale again just to make sure that the number I saw would be the accurate one. As I got off the scale looking straight ahead at my reflection in the mirror, I felt as though I needed to use the bathroom again and I did so hoping that I'd gotten all the excess water out of my body. I eased myself back onto the scale feeling fortunate that I hadn't read the first number, that God had whispered in my ear and told me to get off the scale and use the bathroom so I could avoid the pain that the false read would've given me. I stood now with my hands by my side. I was empty. I was no longer crying. I was ready to receive my Christmas present, the gift of health and self-love that I'd given myself this year. With complete calmness and acceptance, I looked down at my feet.

89

"Merry Christmas, Portia."

"Merry Christmas, Portia." My aunt Gwen and Uncle Len walked through the door of the hotel suite bearing gifts and my uncle's famous Christmas fruit cake. Frank Sinatra was crooning carols in the background, a giant, fully trimmed Christmas tree was the centerpiece of the spacious living room, and my grandmother and mother were sitting on chairs together in front of it, talking. Moments later, my cousins wandered in and the tableau was complete. I silently congratulated myself for providing this lovely experience for my family. This was what I could do with the money that was given to me in exchange for my freedom. I could create a Christmas where they could all relax and enjoy one another without having to worry about anything. I could create the perfect holiday.

The day started out perfect for me, too. I did sit-ups and leg lifts with renewed energy and vigor. I was eighty-nine pounds. It sounded so mysterious and magical I could barely say it out loud. It was special. Who weighed eighty-nine pounds? It was an accomplishment that felt uniquely mine, uniquely special. I went to the gym at 5:30 and ran up and down the hall for thirty minutes, waiting for it to open at six. I was the only one in the gym on Christmas morning, as I was the only one who took health and fitness seriously. In a way, working hard in the gym Christmas morning was the answer to the question I had asked of myself when I began this journey six months prior. This wasn't a passing phase. This was my new way of life. On the day when everyone else slacked off, I worked because being thin was what I liked more than anything else. But something else happened in there, too. I felt lonely. For a brief moment, as I pressed the up arrow on the treadmill until the speed climbed to 7.0, I felt very alone. I heard the thud of my feet as they found the rhythm of the belt and wondered why I had a demanding taskmaster of a voice in my head that could be silenced only if I ran instead of slept, when everyone else in this hotel was waking up gently to a quiet voice that was telling them to stay in bed, that it's only six, it's not time to think just yet.

"Have some champagne, Porshe."

"I don't drink anymore, Ma. You know that."

"Oh, come on. It won't hurt you."

My mother likes tradition and the idea that the family clan will pass on all the same habits and morals and ideas, generation after generation. A tradition in our family was to drink champagne with a pureed strawberry liqueur concoction my cousin made especially for Christmas morning. I felt that I couldn't refuse.

I drank the champagne and my mother instantly looked relieved. I'm not sure if it was the alcohol from the champagne that loosened my tight grip on my diet, but the simple act of drinking a glass of champagne with my family was exhilarating. I was happier in that moment than I had been in eight months. For just that one day, I was going to put the "cushion" theory in play. Seeing my family relax as I drank the champagne encouraged me to continue to drink and eat and be merry.

Next I ate turkey meat and my mother smiled. Then, at my family's urging, I ate potatoes. They relaxed. They laughed. It seemed that my eating potatoes gave them more pleasure than opening gifts, not having to cook, and Christmas Day itself. So I ate some more. I felt invincible at eighty-nine pounds. And I loved that for the first time since I was a small child, I could just be like everyone else. I wasn't a model or an actress who had to eat special food, nor was I an overweight girl who complained about her weight, making everyone else bored and uncomfortable. I was just one of the family at that dining table, partaking in their rituals, their food.

By the time everyone but my brother and my cousin, Megan, had left, however, I was no longer happy or relaxed. I was in shock. I had drunk a glass of champagne. I had eaten turkey roasted in its own fat. I had eaten beans glazed with oil. But what shocked me the most was that I had eaten potatoes. I had eaten two medium-sized roasted potatoes with oil and rosemary and salt. I started to panic. I clenched and unclenched my fists and started circling my wrists in an attempt to take the horror of what was digesting in my gut away from my mind's eye. My body was shaking. I couldn't control the shaking because the panic that was setting in to make it shake felt like itching. Somehow I had to get relief. I raised my arms above my head and shook out my hands as if to expel the energy. My cousin and my brother were still in the living room, sitting by the Christmas tree, but I no longer cared. In front of my cousin and my brother, I started jumping up and down with my arms above my head and shaking my hands to try to get rid of the calories in the potatoes.

"Porshe, what are you doing?" Megan asked me in a tone that suggested she wasn't waiting for an answer. She had something to say to me. She was quite emotional. I could tell because when Australians are emotional, sometimes they can sound bossy.

"I pigged out at lunch and I'm just trying to work some of it off." To downplay the fact that I was jumping up and down and shaking, I

tried to sound nonchalant and used a smiley voice that was on a frequency that sat high above the panic. I smiled and in between bounces
shrugged my shoulders in a "you know how it is" way that I was sure all
women would understand. But I didn't really care if I was understood.
I just had to get rid of all that crap in my stomach. I felt so panicked I
couldn't be still.

"Portia. You ate potatoes, just some potatoes. They're not going to
make you fat, okay? What's the big deal?"

*They will make me fat because it's not just some potatoes that I just ate, it's
the potatoes I know I'm going to eat in the future now I've allowed myself to eat
those. That by eating those potatoes I could get back on the same old yo-yo dieting
pattern and suffer in the way that I'd suffered from age twelve to twenty-five.
Eating those potatoes could cost me my career, money, and my ability to make
money. Eating those potatoes will make me poor. So eating those potatoes will
make me fat. Because without any money or a career, I will definitely end up fat.*

"I'm going for a run." I quickly walked past her and my brother to
the bedroom, changed into gym clothes, and strode past them again
and out the front door. Compared to the earlier laughing and talking
and singing, the suite was eerily quiet. I don't think they spoke to each
other the whole time I was changing. As I jogged down the hall, I re-
played the scene in my mind. I knew I'd end up ruining Christmas no
matter how hard I tried to make it perfect. I knew I'd end up upsetting
the people I love with my selfishness and my lack of thought for others.
I had tried so hard to make everyone happy and yet I just couldn't lie
well enough to do it. Lying was too hard. As I ran out of the elevator
and through the lobby, I could sense that people were staring.

I wasn't like everyone else. I was an actress. I changed my name,
my accent, my nationality. I was gay. It was time to stop even trying to
pretend.

25

I GOT quiet at night on the streets of Camberwell. It was always quiet with Bill unless I was prepared to talk. Sitting on the stoop of the fish and chip shop next to 7-Eleven was something that we liked to do after we'd done everything else. After we drove across town to the less gentrified neighborhood, where the architecture was better but where the people who lived in it were generally poorer, had coffee, drank beer, played pool, saw a band, and drove back across town to the middle-class suburban neighborhood where my mother lived, we'd sit on the stoop of the Camberwell fish and chips shop enjoying the balmy weather and the freedom of not having to look at a clock. There were as many hours as we needed in the middle of the night, if in fact, 2:00 a.m. was considered the middle of it. Usually with these free hours I would tell Bill my troubles, my plans, my desires, but tonight I really didn't have any. I was just sitting there, living. Living was in stark contrast to dreaming about living. Usually I would tell him my plan to make Sacha fall in love with me, the directors I had hopes to meet, why being in Los Angeles was better than being in Australia. When I was bored of talking about myself, I would talk about him, challenge him about why he didn't have a girlfriend, a job, an escape plan from his life. But I was still really just talking about me, talking myself into the reasons why I didn't have a girlfriend, a job that I liked, but mostly, I was trying to find a reason for having had to escape from the place that was my home. To convince myself of my choice, I had to make it a place that everyone should want to escape from. But tonight I really had nothing to say. I wasn't excited about anything. I realized that in stark contrast to Christmases past, I had no drive, no reason to propel me forward. I had nothing to say. And because Bill doesn't really like to talk, Camberwell at 2:00 a.m. was pretty quiet.

Although there were several more days before I had to return to LA, it felt like the holiday was over. The excitement of seeing my family after many months and the thrill of showing off my new body was over. My cousins, my uncles, and my aunts all saw my body. They were all seemingly unimpressed. No one mentioned that I had lost weight or that I looked good or that I was thin. It was baffling to me that they didn't say anything. I didn't even try to hide my arms anymore. I took my sleeves off, put my gym clothes on, and called Sacha. She would be impressed. She would understand the work it had taken to achieve this body. I called her and convinced her to take me to her gym. I told her that she and I were going to work off our indulgences over the holidays. I couldn't wait to see her, to make sure I still had my best friend after what I'd put her through in St. Barths.

I walked past my brother in my gym clothes, my bag slung over my shoulder.

"Where are you going?"

"I'm meeting Sacha at her gym in Prahran."

He looked simultaneously disappointed and determined as he said, "I'll drive you."

I knew I couldn't argue with him. Not when his face looked like that.

My brother pulled into the parking lot at the gym but instead of leaving to go do whatever he'd come into town to do, he parked and shut the engine down.

"Aren't you going to run errands or something?"

"No. I thought I might come in with you."

"To the gym?"

"Yeah."

Shit. I'd told Sacha to meet me at noon. It was only ten. I wanted to give myself a good solid two-hour workout before she arrived.

"Why do you want to go to the gym? I thought you were just dropping me off. You know what me and Sacha are like, we'll be goofing around for hours." Goofing around? Geez.

Now it looked like it was his turn scan his brain for a reason in the form of a rational-sounding lie. But why? What was he doing?

"I thought I might like to see Sacha. I haven't seen her in ages."

Bullshit. Jesus. I wished I'd taken the tram. I didn't know how to get around the fact that Sacha wasn't going to be at the gym for two more hours. As I walked into the almost empty gym with my brother trailing behind me, I decided to cover the lie by acting annoyed at Sacha's lateness. That would do.

"What are you going to do in here? Stand around like a pervert?" He was wearing jeans and boots. He looked like a total weirdo.

"I'm just gonna check it out. Don't worry about me. Do your thing."

I took his direction and stopped worrying about him. I didn't care about the whole Sacha lie either. Once I checked in to the gym I got to work. I did what I came to do. I got on the treadmill and started sprinting for twenty minutes. Then I got on the elliptical. I did twenty minutes and burned 137 calories on that, which I counted as 100. In my mind, twenty minutes on any cardio machine gave me a 100-calorie burn even if the red digital digits said otherwise. I couldn't trust machines. They were all different. By the time I was done with cardio (I felt okay about only doing forty minutes because I'd run for over an hour that morning) and moved to the mats on the floor to begin the glorified sit-ups they call Pilates, I noticed my brother still standing in the corner. I had forgotten him completely.

"Why are you still here?" I had to speak loudly over the whirr of the machines and the yelling of the sports commentators on the TVs.

"Oh. Ahh . . . I dunno. Just do your thing. I'll wait for you." He was acting strangely. He had his head down and was avoiding eye contact, which was so unlike him. He was a helicopter pilot. He loved eye contact. He'd have laughed if he could have seen himself like I did. He really looked creepy standing around in the darkest corner of the gym in jeans and boots. I hoped all the women in there didn't know he was with me.

I did my thing. I finished my forty-minute mat workout (so many reps to be effective!) and moved to the weights. I occasionally did weights to tone my arms and back, and I figured that since I wasn't doing a photo shoot or appearing on camera for a couple of weeks, the muscles would have time to deflate if by accident I somehow pumped them up. I would've hated to look fat because I'd worked out too hard and my muscles added the inches I'd painstakingly taken away.

After I'd worked my bi's, tri's and deltoids, I saw that my brother had found a friend. It was Sacha. My desire to run to her was curbed by the seriousness of the conversation she was having with my policeman of a brother, creepily brooding in the dark corner. I wondered what the hell they could be talking about. Could they be talking about my having come out to him? It seemed unlikely, as I doubted that either of them would betray my confidence. Surely it couldn't be my weight. I knew I was a little thin in places, but not enough to have a serious conversation about it. I started to worry, like perhaps their somber mood had nothing to do with me, and so I went over to them in a hurry. As I approached, I realized they were talking about me because Sacha's mood immediately changed when she realized I was within earshot.

"Peeeee!" She squealed my name and hugged me all at once, leaving me deaf in my right ear. But my brother didn't smile. He stayed the same. He looked at me, this time in the eyes.

"Porshe, can I see you outside?" He turned away from me and walked out of the gym.

The seriousness of his tone made me follow him, leaving Sacha alone, but I got the feeling that she was fine with me following him, too. It was exciting almost. It was so different. My brother had never pulled me away to talk to me seriously about anything before. I couldn't help but be excited because it was so different. I could tell that he wasn't angry, but I couldn't quite figure out what he was feeling and why his feelings were so important that he would pull me away from my best friend whom I hadn't seen for months.

We got all the way to the car before we stopped. The longer we walked, the more concerned I became. By the time he spoke, my stomach was in knots. He leaned on the hood of the car with both hands, his broad back to me, blocking his face from mine. I couldn't see where this was going. I started to get really scared.

"Porshe." When he turned around, I could see that he was crying. I was shocked. He bent over now, his hands on his bent knees, his elbows locked. He was looking at the ground. I was shocked and I couldn't speak. I just had to wait.

He started talking and standing upright at the same time, deliberately but with difficulty.

"I'm just really worried about you. I just can't believe how thin you are."

I couldn't believe what I was hearing. I knew I was thin but not nearly thin enough for this reaction. If I'd worked out in a sweater so he didn't see my arms he wouldn't be reacting like this, but I felt that now wasn't the time to explain that to him. Besides, I'd never been so upset, seeing him cry. I'd never been so upset.

He got himself together a little, enough to look at my face. I was speechless, still, but I could see he wasn't asking me to speak.

I watched as his face started breaking again. His face crumbled into creases. It went red. Tears were falling down his cheeks. He looked at me imploringly although he still wasn't asking anything of me. It confused me.

"Porshe . . ." He cried harder. As he inhaled to say what he was leading up to say, his breath caught, making short staccato sounds. "You're gonna die."

My brother had left shortly after I'd pleaded my case. I told him that I knew what I was doing. When that didn't work, I told him that I would eat, that I would gain weight and stop obsessively working out. He seemed pleased to hear all that so he left me to hang out with Sacha, who, after pointing out a very thin girl in the gym, dropped me home. She didn't say anything about my weight, she just pointed to that girl on the treadmill, exclaiming that she was anorexic and how sad it was, and then she dropped me home.

I had cried a lot with my brother. The tears weren't for me. They came because of him, because I hated seeing him cry like that. The only other time I'd seen him cry was when our dad died and to be honest, I didn't know why my weight made him so sad. And I didn't know why Sacha pointed out the so-called anorexic girl. I knew that I was thinner than usual. I knew that I was underweight, but anorexia was never something that I thought I could have. The girl at the gym didn't have it. Not just anyone could have anorexia. It was a disorder of the highly accomplished, cultured, beautiful. It belonged to models, singers, and Princess Diana.

I had always been secretly in awe of anorexics with their superhuman self-restraint. There is a neatness to it, a perfection. Apart from the fact that I could never be thin enough to be anorexic, I didn't want to be anorexic anyway. I just wanted to excel at dieting.

• • • •

When I arrived home, my mother intercepted me on my way to take a shower and asked me to come to her room. At a glance it was clear to me that my brother had been talking to her about the episode at the gym and it was clear that her nonchalant attitude had been replaced by a very serious one.

"Come in here for a minute, okay? I would really like to talk to you."

I followed her through the living room and into her bedroom. I passed by Gran, who for twenty years had sat in the chair in the corner of the living room, alternating her attention between the TV and her family's lives, all played out in front of her as a source of entertainment. But my grandmother didn't appear disconnected or uncaring, she just seemed like she already knew the end to all the stories. She'd seen all the reruns on TV and in life. She'd seen it all before. We were an episode of *The Golden Girls* in a rerun. Blanche, whose self-worth is based on her looks, has something on her mind but can't communicate it in any way other than by acting out and has been called in to talk to problem-solving Dorothy, who had been given a tip by Rose as she stumbled across the truth, but it was something that Sophia had known all along. Gran gave me a look as I passed her that said, "Oh, yeah! I remember this one. This is the one where you confront your mother about her lack of acceptance of you for being gay and she finally accepts you for who you are. Oh yeah! This is a good one . . ." She couldn't really have known that, of course. My mother and I had decided not to tell her about my sexuality. We had decided that she was too old and knowing that truth about me would be a terrible shock. Something like that could kill her. That the words "I'm gay" might just stop her heart, and she'd topple onto the floor, dead from shock.

My mother stood backlit against the window of her dark bedroom. I could just make out her pink scalp underneath her wisps of gray-blond hair and I wondered for how long gray hair could be dyed. Maybe it became so porous that color would just not take to it anymore. Maybe that's why really old people have gray hair. Until this point I had thought it was because people in their eighties and nineties couldn't be bothered because superficial things like looks didn't matter anymore, but what if the desire to hold on to blond or brown hair was still there but the ability to do it was gone? I wondered if that's what aging felt like. That desire and reality were dueling until the day you die, that nobody ever got to a place of peace. I had always wanted to get old so I didn't have to care anymore, but I began to think that it would be best just to skip the getting older part and just die.

"You're so thin, darling. It's awful."

Yes. I'm thin. I'm exactly what you wanted me to be.

"Well, I guess I can get my Swatch watch now."

The Swatch watch was a carrot my mother used to dangle when I was a teenager if I reached 119 pounds, the magical eight and a half stone. As I had always fluctuated between nine and nine and a half, that number was always just a fantasy, a magical land where perfection lived and all the people who were special enough to get there were covered in Swatch watches. As I struggled to get to that number on the scale, the Swatch watches I wanted were going out of style one by one. First it was the clear one I wanted but was too fat to have, then a yellow one with blue hands, then the black one that passed me by without my earning the right to own it. I really did want my plastic Swatch watch. Even though they didn't make them anymore.

"If you don't eat something, you're going to die!"

My mother squatted down with her hand on the corner of the bed. Her other hand was covering her face as she quietly sobbed. I stood over her, looking down. To my surprise I stood there waiting for something to happen. Where was the rush of emotion that had overtaken me when I saw my brother similarly bent over, sobbing and in pain? Where was that panic I felt that made me search for something soothing to say? Where was the deep regret for making my mother so upset?

To my horror, a smirk involuntarily stretched over my face. My mother was crying and I was smiling. I loved my mother very much. Why was I being so cold?

The answer came to me with certainty and clarity.

I can be gay now. I can be who I am without pretending anymore. I'm forcing her to accept me just the way I am.

I bent down and picked my mother up off the floor. I put my arm around her shoulders and we sat like that on the edge of her bed until she stopped crying. I was waiting for her to stop so I could start in on her. As my mother quietly cried, I planned my attack. I would tell her that I was angry that she didn't accept me for being gay, I was angry that she seemed to care more about how I looked than how I felt or who I was. I was going to tell her to change or she would risk losing me. My comments would hurt her, but it was better for her in the long run. I was going to show her the same tough love she'd shown me.

But I didn't do that. Instead, I burst into tears.

"I'm so sorry that I'm gay, Mama. I'm sorry I'm not what you wanted."

I cried for her disappointment, and for mine. I wasn't the daughter she was proud of, I was the daughter that made her ashamed. And no amount of fame could take take shame away.

"Why are you sorry, darling? You are who you are."

"I know! But you're ashamed of me! You won't even tell our family and they're the people who love me!"

"I just thought that your being gay was nobody's business. It was private."

"Michael's relationships weren't private? You had no problem talking about those! You tell everyone the private things you're proud of!"

My mother swiveled toward me, put her hands on my shoulders, and turned me to face her.

"Listen. I'm a stupid old fool. Alright?" She was looking directly at me. It was like she was seeing me for the first time. "I was scared, okay?

I didn't want you to lose everything you'd worked so hard for. But I was wrong. And I was stupid." She folded me into her arms. "I love you so much."

"I love you, too, Mama."

I felt the weight fall away from me. I lost the weight that I'd been carrying around since I was a teenager. Shame weighs a lot more than flesh and bone.

Within moments we were laughing, talking about how crazy I was to take the weight loss too far. We were saying that all of it was really unnecessary, that I was great just the way I was. We decided that it was time to start dating and "to hell with it." Happiness was everything. "And health," she chimed in. "Without them, what's the point?" We laughed and hugged and agreed that the most important things in life are health and happiness and that they were the only things I had to worry about now. That's all she cared about.

My health and happiness were the only things my mom cared about.

We walked directly to the kitchen arm in arm and we made lunch together. We made fried rice with peas and a teaspoon of oil. We were laughing and talking, we ate it together, and my grandmother watched from the corner of the room in her chair, smiling as the credits rolled. The End.

26

WAS STILL 89 pounds. I liked being 89 pounds. Although the image of my brother crying and my mother breaking down was burned into my memory and I had made promises to them that I would gain weight, January was not a good time to gain weight. I had agreed to shoot the cover of *Angeleno* magazine, a big, glossy fashion/lifestyle rag. I had committed to attending the Australia Day Ball, an annual event held in LA that honored Australians in the film and TV industry. I just couldn't gain any weight until all that was done. What would be the point in sliding backward to the middle of the pack when it was just as easy to take the pictures of me at the finish line, alone in my triumph? My ego wouldn't let me gain any weight. I didn't see the point to it until after the cameras were no longer pointed at me.

As the maintenance took up a lot of time, I barely had time for anything else. Even with Carolyn doing the supermarket rounds to find the brands with the least amount of sodium or the lowest fat content, working out took up most of my day. I decided, however, that I needed a social outlet and I joined that ballet class with the yelling Russian and the fat women in makeup and tights. I figured at 89 pounds I was thin enough to wear a leotard and *développé* my leg into the air. Besides, ballet was a kind of workout, too, if you weren't lazy about it. I met a girl there who liked to count calories and to work out. Melody was thinner than me with a better turnout and a higher extension. She was called on by the yelling Russian to demonstrate good *développés*. I tried to be-friend her as we had a lot in common, but what we shared in common made it difficult to be friends. We were both recluses with rituals. Be-sides, being gay I didn't feel comfortable making new friends. It didn't seem fair after months of presenting myself as a relatable heterosexual to suddenly surprise them with the news that a lesbian had been lurk-ing underneath the whole time, had been in their homes, talking about their sex lives, hugging them and telling them they had good leg exten-sions in ballet class. I stopped going to ballet class anyway. I didn't have the thinnest thighs nor was I the best dancer in the class. It didn't remind me of a time when I was good at something, it made me aware of the sad reality that if I was good as an eight-year-old, then I had got-ten worse. I had peaked at age eight. What was the point in continuing? The old yelling Russian told me that I was too thin and that I needed to gain weight. What was the point?

The *Angeleno* cover shoot was a reward for my hard work. I had trained hard for the event and knowing that I had done the work, all I had to do was relax and enjoy the ride. The ride was a gentle downhill slope with smooth pavement beneath me. The ride was my feet off the pedals, feeling the wind through my hair, smelling the wildflowers as they rushed past me firmly rooted in place. No panic. No doubts. No disgrace. The interview was different. It took place at my favorite res-taurant, The Ivy, which was my favorite because they blanched all their vegetables and never brushed them with oil. I ate my vegetables (with no lip gloss or lip balm—one can never be too careful) and attempted to maneuver gracefully around personal questions as fundamental and important to a person's character as their desires to marry and have chil-dren. Being secretive was exhausting. But the interviewer had a secret, too. She secretly didn't like me while pretending to find me delightful. She suckered me into being a little looser, a little more truthful. What added to my uncharacteristically easy mood was that the interview took place on my birthday, and when the manager at The Ivy presented me with a large slice of birthday cake, I looked at my new journalist friend and said with a wink in my voice, "Like I'm gonna eat that!"

An Australian tabloid picked up the story and on the cover it printed, "Out to Lunch with Portia."

A cover is still a cover.

"Good news!" I stood in my kitchen looking out onto the Sahara desert that was the yellow wall of the Sunset 5 shopping mall and tried to rally excitement for my impending movie. My mother loved to hear of my accomplishments and because of the hell I had put her through over Christmas, I felt that the "good news" of an exciting role in a big studio movie was what she deserved to hear. As I began to describe the film, "It's called *Cletis Tout*," who was cast to star in it, "Richard Dreyfuss plays my father!" and where it would shoot, "In Toronto—you'll have to come visit," my excited, energetic voice was in stark contrast to the exhaustion I was feeling. Landing the role wasn't exciting to me, it was merely the end of the long uphill climb of auditions, callbacks, and negotiations. Getting the role was a relief, like the moment of collapse at the top of a mountain before you begin worrying about how to get down. Like a tourist who travels not to experience foreign places but rather to tell people that she's well traveled—this was how I viewed this excursion to Toronto with its film set and its respected actors. "I'm doing a movie this summer." That was the reason I wanted the movie. As my *Ally McBeal* cast mates had seemingly all succeeded in landing movie roles, I too must do something extraordinary to fit in.

I hung up the phone and felt empty, vacant, directionless. I knew I should celebrate, but I didn't know who to call. I didn't know who would care. I couldn't call my brother because he would want to take me out for Mexican food and margaritas and I couldn't think of an excuse not to go. I couldn't let him see me in person because I didn't want to upset him again. He could think that I was eating more and loosening up on my strict diet from the picture on his TV screen, as everyone looks ten pounds fatter on TV. He could check in with me as Nelle Porter once a week and be pleased with my progress as the wardrobe department had cleverly quilted a disguise of flattering clothing to cover all my flaws: a patch to cover my thin arms, a patch to cover the gap between my thighs. I thought about a glass of wine—heck, champagne!—but knew I couldn't enjoy it without feeling guilty. I was the leading lady in a movie, after all, and Christian Slater was my man. We had chemistry, apparently. A shape-shifting, sexless androgynous girl could have chemistry with anything. My life was just a fantasy with its fantasy lovers and its make-believe conversations with make-believe people in my head. So I was a perfect candidate to fall in love with a make-believe man and consummate our pretend love in a make-believe house. Reality was the difficult part. And the reality at that moment was that it was Friday at 5:00 and I didn't know what to do. So I went to the Pilates studio.

Santa Monica Boulevard, the gay part of town, had an exciting energy. It was the beginning of the weekend, and the restaurant workers were placing candles on the outdoor tables, setting a welcoming scene for their patrons to drink, talk, and unwind from the week of work. As I drove down the boulevard, past the lesbian coffee shop I'd gone to the day I got *Ally McBeal,* hoping no one could see me through my tinted car window, I was once again aware of the emptiness. Losing weight was no longer exciting to me, and maintaining it was hard. I was exhausted most of the time and the ante on exercise seemed to keep going up. Unexpectedly, a voice would sound in my head at the point of my workout where I would usually have quit, telling me to march on, to keep going, that it wasn't enough. It told me I wasn't good enough, I didn't do it long enough, that there was still a long way to go before I could rest.

The drill sergeant voice accompanied me everywhere, recorded all the missed moments when I was sitting but should've been standing, moving around, doing something. It was hard for me to drive anywhere, even to the Pilates studio. I had figured out several different blocks in LA where I could get out of my car and stretch my legs. I wouldn't always run around the block, sometimes I would just walk with a deliberate stride. Sometimes I didn't have the energy to run. I had the urge to get up from being immobile, but I didn't have the energy to make it a useful excursion. The voice that made me get out of my car, that called me a lazy pig for walking instead of running around the block, would get back in the car with me and accompany me all the way to the studio, where it laughed at me for being late to work with no burned calories to show for it.

I pulled into the valet parking lot of the Pilates studio. The parking lot was shared with a restaurant and if you liked to work out when other people were going to dinner, then a valet would take your car. The voice told me to get out of the car as fast as I could and go burn calories. I got out of the car in a hurry and left my keys in the ignition for the valet.

How are you going to pull it off? How could you ever be pretty enough to be a leading lady? You're not even thin. You don't have long, lean limbs. You have ordinary looks and an ordinary body. You can't play a leading lady in a movie. You're gay. What a joke! What happens when people find out you're gay and you've fooled them into thinking you were Christian Slater's love interest? How is that going to work? Give it up, you stupid dyke. How long are you going to pretend you're something you're not? How long do you think people are going to fall for it?

As I reached the top stair and looked down at where I'd left my car, I saw it moving. My car was moving!

"Help!" I screamed. "Somebody's stealing my car!"

I ran down the stairs, my heart beating in my throat. Jesus! Where's my dog? Is she in the car?

"Help! Help me! Somebody's stealing my car!" I got to the bottom step, flung my body around the railing, and ran to my car feeling like there were weights tied to my ankles, like I was running with someone holding me back. Evil was holding me back, allowing my car to be stolen in front of my eyes. And my dog! Oh my God! Bean! I screamed out her name, "BEAN!!!"

The car stopped and a man got out. He was wearing black pants and a blue vest. He held the keys up to me, silently. He looked frightened. We stood there, facing each other, him in his blue vest and me in my platform off-camera shoes and spandex shorts with the elastic waistband that was too loose for my hips. We stared at each other, and now it was my turn to be frightened. I gently took the keys from him and quietly sat down on the warm leather seat. I checked for Bean and she wasn't there. I drove away in silence. No metronome. No marching orders. I drove back down Santa Monica Boulevard and past the lesbian café. Staring into the café, I drove through a red light. I knew that because a man crossing the street at the crosswalk slapped the hood of my car as he narrowly avoided getting hit and then by the time the noise registered, I saw that I was in the middle of an intersection, all alone except for a car rushing at my side. I drove home to my cold, empty apartment and vowed never to go out again.

The number 82 on the scale should've meant something other than what it did to me. All it meant to me was that I was seven pounds lighter than the last time I weighed myself. The number 82 was the reward for my hard work, a nod to my dedication, a flashing red digital recognition of my self-control. It was a way to silence the drill sergeant in my head, and in this subjective world full of conflicting opinions, it was a way to objectively measure my success. Another way to measure my success was to use a tape measure. I had begun measuring the objects and the space surrounding the objects. Like a study of semiotics,

I measured the white and black surrounding the white, the vacuous space that held its object and gave it substance. I measured my big legs with their thighs and the space between my thighs. I measured my footballer's calves and watched as the chunky fat withered away to become a dancer's calves and then a little child's calves, too new and underdeveloped to be labeled anything other than just legs. I measured myself daily after weighing for a more accurate understanding of my progress. Occasionally, I would measure myself visually. I would stand naked in front of a mirror and look at myself. Sometimes I even loved what I saw. Sometimes I saw a boy, maybe twelve years of age, with a straight skinny body and no ugly penis that he would forever be measuring, wondering if he measured up. I sometimes saw a teenage girl with no breasts and no curves that would turn her into a woman with desires and complicate her perfect, sterile life. Sometimes I didn't see a person at all, I just saw the inch of fat on a stomach and thighs that encouraged me to continue to lose weight. I knew I wasn't attractive, and I was very happy about that. I didn't want to be attractive. I didn't want to attract. As long as no one wanted to be let in, I didn't have to shut anyone out. If I could keep people from being interested enough to ask me questions, I didn't have to lie. As long as I could be alone with my secrets, I didn't have to worry about being found out.

At 82 pounds, I wanted to photograph myself. I wanted to document my success. But first I had to silence the drill sergeant that reminded me of that extra inch of fat. First I had to get rid of that.

27

"CHECK THE gate." There was a suspended moment as the cameraman shone a flashlight at the film in the camera.

"Good gate."

"That's lunch. One hour." The scene of the crew and cast broke apart, first at its edges, with the actors strutting off the set and directly to their trailers, then the lights were shut down, the camera track taken apart, and finally the director on a chair on the far edge of the scene, with his script supervisor and ADs in tow, collected his notes and headed toward catering. It was my first day on the set of *Cletis Tout*. I hadn't done any acting yet; my scene was coming up after lunch, but I had been at the set all morning. I had been asked to go to wardrobe for a final fitting and to work with the props guy as my character was a smart-ass, wisecracking potter who was tough on the outside, cold, hard, and glazed over yet fragile and needing to be handled delicately—like her pots.

I went to wardrobe feeling a little insecure, as I had gained weight since my first fitting. I wasn't sure how much weight I'd gained because I'd stopped weighing myself after seeing the number 82 on the scale. I'd given up on the idea of losing that stubborn inch of fat because of what happened to the rest of my body. At 82 pounds, the veins on my arms looked like thick strands of rope attaching my hands to my forearms and my elbows. The unsightliness of it forced me to put ice on my wrists to try to make them disappear, as the hotter it was, the more they protruded. I knew I couldn't show up to a big-budget movie set needing to ice-down my veins in between takes, so I decided to slowly gain some weight. Although I knew I had to look better at a heavier weight, seeing the number on the scale climb back up through the nineties and head toward a hundred pounds was something I couldn't bear.

It was sheer agony, walking into a fitting, not knowing my weight. It was exactly this kind of anxiety—this fear of not knowing if I could fit into clothes—that I had tried to eradicate. I had told the costume designer that my measurements were thirty-four, twenty-four, thirty-five and, ironically, the ideal measurements as told to me by my modeling agency still didn't apply to me. At the time the costumer asked for them, I was 29½, 22¾, 31⅜. And that was a lot more difficult to say over the phone. As I was playing a tough, bohemian artist, my wardrobe started out dark and layered, gradually shedding layers of clothes and softening the color palette as I gradually shed my tough exterior and dulled my witty barbs. It was a typical storyline for a "good" female leading lady character: she starts out hard and ends up soft and the metamorphosis from undesirable insect to awe-inspiring butterfly is reflected in the wardrobe.

My insecurity about my weight gain was unnecessary, as both the black studded leather and the cream silk organza fit me perfectly. I had gained weight before my first fitting, but thankfully, I had maintained since then. I felt enormous relief. I was still in control after all. Standing in front of the mirror, a leading lady in a movie, I made the decision that when I returned to *Ally* for the next season, instead of trying to fit into the off-the-rack sizes, Vera would have to make the wardrobe to fit me. After all, it was actresses taking over the models' jobs of posing on magazine covers that required that actresses fit into the sample size that designers made for models. I wasn't a nameless model expected to fit into any dress. I was an actress. And because I was a very skinny one, like a model, I just happened to be able to fit into any dress.

The hotel where I was staying during filming in Toronto, the Windsor Arms, was a chic boutique hotel with tasteful decor. It was home to all the transients, the U.S. actors who blow through Canada to work a job. The suite was a little dark because there was only one window and that was in the bedroom of the one-bedroom suite. A wall with a door separated the bedroom from the rest of the suite with its dark carpet and mahogany walls, and its black desk, gray sofa, and mahogany coffee table. The bedroom was all white and light because of the window. The light in there compelled me to spend all my time in the bedroom, which really just consisted of a bed, so I spent all my time in bed. I brought my life in two suitcases from Los Angeles to make my long stay comfortable during the five-week movie schedule. In one suitcase was my kitchen scale, ten I Can't Believe It's Not Butter sprays, a large box of Splenda sachets, twenty cans of tuna, forty packets of oatmeal, Mrs. Dash, Extra chewing gum, a carton of Parliament Lights, and my digital bathroom scale. Although I hadn't weighed myself recently and it was very heavy, I had to bring it because if I had the urge to check in with my weight, I couldn't trust that the hotel would have an accurate scale. I also brought chopsticks, a can opener for the tuna, and my blue Chinese footed bowl with the fake pottery rings. I wasn't sure if I would be able to make my frozen yogurt, so I brought my white and green bowl with the hairline crack in case I had access to a freezer and could find the sugar-free, low-calorie yogurt I ate back home. In the other suitcase were my workout clothes, jeans, and T-shirts and a dress for the mandatory "above the line" dinner. I'd always hated the mandatory dinner for a film production, whose guests ran from the top down to where the line was drawn (from the executive producers to the lowest-paid core cast) even when I wasn't watching my weight. I hated having to talk to the producers because, as I was nearly always on the line, I felt like I could lose the job if I wasn't as funny as the other cast members or if the light at the restaurant showed all my imperfections. I hated having to make the attempt to impress just to keep them from changing their minds and sending me home, replacing me with the prettier actress/girlfriend of the leading man, whose relaxed confidence was appealing and whose torso looked great from across the table. On location, I hated ever having to leave the hotel room. Alone in my hotel room was the only place I could relax. And I somehow always felt less lonely when I was completely alone.

I was scheduled to work only one day a week for five weeks, with the rest of my time for myself. So I decided to take up drinking. Apart from the glass of champagne on Christmas Day, I hadn't drunk alcohol for a long time, and I missed it. Instead of eating dinner, I decided to use up my calories with a glass of wine. I felt like I deserved it. I earned it. I worked out hard and ate little, and so a glass of wine at night was a fitting reward. Apart from the wine, I really didn't ingest calories. Because wine didn't contain calorie information on the labels and not all wine had the same amount of calories, I limited myself to one glass a day. But because the calories were unquantifiable I didn't really trust eating anything. Occasionally, if I were working that day, I would start my day with 30 calories of oatmeal with Splenda and butter spray, and maybe have a bite of tuna for lunch, but mostly, I would order pickles from the hotel kitchen and just have pickles and mustard for the day. It wasn't terrific, but having wine was, so it was worth it just for the duration of filming.

"Cut. Back to one." I stood on top of a rooftop building in downtown Toronto gasping for air. "One," my starting position, was all the way down at the other end of the rooftop, and "action" was the cue to sprint from the other end to the front of the building, dive down on my knees, whip out a machine gun, and start shooting. As it was a comedy, the kickback from the machine gun knocked me over onto my back, where I had to wait a beat as the realization that I was in trouble set in, then in a panic hurl myself and my heavy machine gun off my back using my stomach muscles and struggle back onto my feet to make my escape. The rain made it harder. A fine and constant drizzle, not heavy enough to read through a camera lens, made the rooftop slick and dangerous and froze my fingers, destroyed my makeup and hair, and saturated my wardrobe.

Hour after hour of wide shots from the street, aerial shots from a crane, and coverage from the rooftop exhausted me, making it hard for me to keep running. But I had a bigger problem. My joints ached. My joints had occasionally hurt when I was back in LA, after exercise and at night when I lay in bed. But on that rooftop my wrists, knees, and elbows hurt so much it was hard to move them without feeling intense pain, and so I limited their movement to the action that took place within the space of time between "action" and "cut." Any other time I would stand still, not even able to smoke because the motion of lifting the cigarette to my mouth was excruciating for my elbow. Even if I held the cigarette very close to my lips and turned my head to exhale the smoke, the pain in my elbow seemed to localize to the slightest movement. It seemed to scan my body anticipating where the next movement could be and settle there, ready and waiting to strike. The longer the wait between takes, the worse it got. As we started the action sequence in close-up coverage and gradually widened to include the whole building, making my body look like a black ant scurrying on a rooftop, my movements had to be bigger, more exaggerated. And as the camera was on a crane, by the end of the day, I was alone up there on the rooftop, wildly flailing about, without a PA or an umbrella, since there was nowhere for either assistant or umbrella to hide when the camera rolled. Every moment was agony.

I knew I was in trouble when I couldn't make it down a single step of the staircase after wrap had been called. My knees wouldn't bend. They were stiff. The joke that I kept using to the concerned crew, who rushed onto the rooftop when it was clear for them to do so, was that it was so bloody cold I was frozen stiff. It wasn't a funny joke, but I was in too much pain to care. I was taken to the elevator by two men who held me up, the weapons specialist on my left arm and the medic on my right, all the while I was telling them that their help wasn't necessary, that I just needed to get into a warm bath. I don't know why I refused to let the medic examine me. Maybe it was because his viselike grip on my elbow was more painful than walking on my own would've been. I just knew I didn't want him to touch me, I didn't want him to ask me questions, I just wanted to be alone. I knew that if I told him about my elbows and my wrists that he'd send me to a doctor, and I just wanted to finish the movie without any drama. I was already on the verge of making a scene and I didn't want to do that, I just wanted to act out the scenes already scripted.

When I closed the door to my hotel room after the PA had walked me down the long corridor holding my arm (this time by the biceps), I cried. I cried out in pain and then I just quietly cried as a means to console myself. My gentle sobs seemed to say, "It hurts" and a silent tear falling replied, "I know, old thing. I know." I turned the hot water faucet on to fill the tub and crawled into the bedroom to pour a glass of wine. Now that wine was my dinner, I bought my own bottles and hid them under the bed for fear that the mini-bar Nazis would take the corked bottle away even though I asked them to clear the mini-bar and didn't allow them access to my room. I didn't allow the house-keeping team into my room either. I was too afraid they would take away my chopsticks and my dishes by accident, or steal them. When I was on location shooting the movie *Sirens,* a toy mouse that I'd had since before my dad died was lost. I didn't tell anyone that it was lost when the sheets were changed because I was too ashamed to admit to the concierge that I slept with stuffed toys. The housekeepers at this hotel weren't allowed into my room unless I was there watching them. I couldn't bear to lose my white and green dish with the flowers and the hairline crack. I'd already lost my mouse.

By the time I crawled back to the bathtub on three limbs, one hand holding the wineglass, the tub was full. I made another trip to get cigarettes and an ashtray and attempted to slowly remove my clothes. The joints in my fingers joined the cast of painful joints acting out in my body, needing attention and recognition for the important role they had thanklessly performed prior to this moment, and just unbuttoning my jeans was difficult. By the time I slid into the bathtub, the pain ravaged my body. It was like the hot water boiled the acidic fluid that lubricated my joints and the fluid seeped into my bloodstream, attacking the muscles and organs in its path. Everything hurt. I wept and wept. I was aware, however, that being in the bathtub in excruciating pain was the first time I hadn't felt hungry all day. At least the whining, complaining pain in my gut that was like a five-year-old tugging at my shirtsleeve repeating, "I'm hungry," had given over to the real pain in my body. At least I shut that little girl up.

I threw up the wine before I got into bed. I'd always been a bad bulimic but throwing up wine was the only thing that I found easy. Food was really difficult for me to throw up. I tended to give up after a certain point, never knowing if I got it all out. I felt bad about the whole process; the binge made me feel pathetic and out of control and the purging was the punishment. With every heave I hated myself more. I felt the blood vessels in my eyes burst and I knew that for days they would show everyone who cared to look at me that I was a pathetic loser, that I couldn't control myself. But throwing up wine was different. For one, wine wasn't a particularly nourishing thing to drink, and throwing it up is often better for your body than keeping it in. Also, throwing up alcohol is something that almost everyone has done at some point in their life; it wasn't reserved for sick bulimic girls who didn't have enough self-control over something as pathetic as food. Unlike food, at least alcohol is addictive. I threw up the wine because it was easy and because I was aware that asking my liver to break down alcohol when my body was obviously sick enough to cause me so much pain was destructive. I threw up the wine because I'd put my body through enough.

Throughout the night, as I lay in bed rereading Sylvia Plath's *The Bell Jar*, I drank wine and threw it up. I worried that there would be traces of sugar from the wine that would cause me to ingest incidental, unaccounted-for calories, but I just said, "To hell with it!" I'd gotten so loose with the wine anyway. I felt completely out of control and crazy—but in a good way. My loosening up of calories was a healthy, good thing that would enable me to go out for a beer with the director, who I really liked. I could be social again. I just worked out a little harder in the hotel gym and stopped brushing my teeth with toothpaste. It wasn't that I was crazy thinking that I could get fat from accidentally swallowing toothpaste; I was just ensuring that I cut out those incidental calories wherever I could. I ate less chewing gum and I didn't use toothpaste. It was a compromise that worked for me. I really liked wine.

Five days later, we went on location overnight to an out-of-the-way part of town for the next day of filming. I felt a little better, was well rested, and even ate a little more as I realized food worked like Advil, and the more food I had, the less my joints ached. I went back up to 300 calories but kept my wine ritual. I had to finish eating food by 2:00 p.m. so I wouldn't accidentally throw up tuna when I threw up my wine. The place where we went was so remote we had no choice but to stay at a spiritual retreat that didn't serve wine or allow smoking. As I was given a tour of the log cabin they called a facility, I felt nervous and anxious like I was in rehab. I wondered briefly if the production company had sent me to rehab under the pretense of it being the only place close to the location. (Could they know about the wine?) The woman in a turban showed me the spa, which consisted of saunas and a coffin.

"Please let us know if you'd like to use the hyperthermic chamber."

"It looks like a coffin. How does it work?"

"You lie down in the chamber for forty-five minutes and it removes the toxins in your body."

The thought of being in a capsule for forty-five minutes was bad enough, but the fact that it removed all the toxins in your body gave me pause. My body was made up of toxins. I imagined the inside of my body covered in a spider web of toxins that held it all together. Toxins were the thread that bound my stomach to my intestines and the skin to the muscles. The webs in my body were the unabsorbable chemicals, the residue particles strung together from the artificial sweeteners, chemicals from the butter spray, and chemicals from the Jell-O, the alcohol, and the nicotine.

"If I removed all the toxins in my body, there'd be nothing left!" I knew the turban thought that was a joke, even though she didn't think it funny enough to laugh.

I stared at the chamber that would in fact have become my coffin. I imagined a turbaned woman opening the lid and screaming as she looked at my remains. My body would be dehydrated and my blood extracted as the toxin-fighting machine, on a mission to remove every last toxin, couldn't target the invasive toxins without removing all the fluid and the blood. My organs would be eaten up by the machine as it tore apart every last bit of tissue leaving behind a deflated sack of skin—and maybe my eyeballs.

28

WOKE UP with my eyes closed as the dream I awoke from was so disturbing I tried to finish it for several minutes even after I was aware of being fully conscious. In the dream I had found myself standing naked in front of Tom Cruise, who was lying on a bed wearing a raincoat. I was naked and yet the reason for my being naked wasn't completely obvious; the mood wasn't sexual, it was friendly with nothing sinister implied. This bizarre scene took place in a big loft with concrete floors and a high ceiling, which I assumed to be one of his houses. It was the middle of the night, two or three o'clock maybe. The room was brightly lit like a department store or a supermarket, and the bed was in the middle of this enormous room. As I stood naked in front of him, I talked about being gay. I bared my soul in the same manner that I bared my body. I showed him all of me, inside and out. As I did so, instead of becoming lighter by unburdening myself from the secret that weighed me down, instead of losing weight, I became heavier. I felt burdened, heavy and dark, panicked that something dreadful was about to happen despite the kindness and acceptance he was showing me. After I talked for what seemed like hours, I began to make out shadowy figures in the walls that I thought were painted black. As the sun started to rise I could see that the walls behind his bed and to the side were not painted black. The "walls" were floor-to-ceiling windows. To my horror, I could see the silhouettes of what seemed like hundreds of people looking in, and I could see that I was in a street-level glass building in Times Square. I was on *Good Morning America*, and Tom Cruise was conducting an interview.

As I lay awake trying to trick my brain into thinking that I was asleep so I could make it end differently and take away the nervous, sick feeling that carried over from the dream into my reality, I realized that the sick feeling wasn't only from dreaming about being tricked into exposing myself. The sick feeling was also from drinking and throwing up the bottle of wine I'd snuck into the no-alcohol retreat. (I'd stolen a corkscrew from the mini-bar in the hotel in Toronto and added it to my traveling case of tools and utensils.) I'd had a rough night. The pain in my joints increased to the point that I couldn't find a position to sit or lie in to make myself comfortable, even briefly. I alternated between sitting, lying down, and walking in an attempt to relieve the pain, but the only thing that seemed to work at all was wine. So I kept drinking it. I had to keep drinking it, as its numbing effect seemed to wear off when I threw it up. But since forcing myself to throw it up gave me a splitting headache, I began to feel nauseous, and so the throwing-up part of the ritual became involuntary by the time I'd drunk my way down to the middle of the label. In between drinking and throwing up, I ran my wrists under the hot water in the bathroom sink, as the room didn't have a bathtub and hot water seemed to help a little. I felt sorry for myself. I cried a lot. I thought about calling my mother, but I didn't know what to say. I was in the middle of shooting my first big Hollywood movie. I was doing exactly what I was supposed to do. I knew that if I complained to her at all, she would respond in the same way she did when I cried to her about not being able to eat ordinary food with my family. If I were selfish enough to tell her how sad I was and how much pain I was in, I knew she would respond angrily because being angry was easier than being worried, and so she'd say, "Well, I don't know what to tell you. You wanted to be an actress."

And I would say, "Yes, Mama. I wanted to be an actress. I wanted to be a model, and I wanted to be an actress. I wanted to be special, and I wanted people to think I was pretty. What I didn't know was how hard it was going to be to be thin, to be considered pretty, and to be worthy of attention. I've had to work a little bit harder than I first thought, Mama. My journey was a little longer than most girls'. I was born with big legs and small eyes and a round face that's only pretty from one angle." Then I would tell her what I've always wanted to say to her but because we tend not to talk about heavy and emotional things, I've never been able to. "I don't blame you, Mama. I blame Dad."

I blame you, Dad. I blame you for telling me that I was pretty. I blame you for dying before you had time to change your mind. Because of you I make up stories, have fantasy lives, fill in the missing words. You're the blank. You're the "Dear Mum and . . ." letter I had to make up because all the other children at camp had a dad and not a blank where a dad was missing. Being forced to write that letter was the first time I really knew you were missing. And it was a year after you died.

April Fool's Day is a bad day to die for a practical joker. I thought that because you winked only at me, I was the only one that got the joke. Remember when the Easter Bunny came and how you winked at me as you ate the carrot with his bunny teeth marks? We got the jokes, you and I. We were smart and we got the joke.

I didn't sleep at all until morning. I'd seen the shadowy dawn become the light of day, which no doubt set the scene for my horrific dream that was hard to shake even after I opened my eyes.

As I carefully applied concealer to achieve the perfect no-makeup look before going to makeup, I thought about my subconscious and its lack of imagination. It seemed to me that as I became thinner, I became dumber, as even my subconscious failed to conjure up a decent metaphor. One part of the dream stuck with me, however, and that was my casting of Tom Cruise in the role of sneaky interrogator. My mother had always wanted me to marry Tom Cruise. Not just any famous actor, Tom Cruise in particular. He was the living image of the perfect movie star who seemed to separate his private life from his public life—a man of mystery, a private man. Choosing Tom Cruise as an example was perhaps another way of my mother reinforcing that there was a payoff to being private. "There's a reason they call it a private life," I'd often say to interviewers. But there's a fine line between being private and being ashamed.

The day wasn't just any day. It was DAY ELEVEN of filming. Day Eleven was a long bike ride to where the only known photograph of my character's mother was buried in a box under a tree along with the money my character's father had buried after he robbed the bank and before he was incarcerated. The bike ride began with a race for the treasure between a sweet, caring guy and an emotionally bankrupt girl, climaxed when she told him through her tears that she only wanted the picture of her mother, not the money, and ended with the two of them in love. It was a big day. And although I was prepared—I'd learned my lines and could comfortably fit into my wardrobe—I was not ready. I was in agony. And the day hadn't even begun.

"Ride as fast as you can past camera. And go as close to camera as you can, too." The director had to literally cut to the chase to make his day, a term used in movie making that meant that all the shots for all the scenes for that day had to be completed. Today he didn't have a smile in his eyes; he wasn't as full of jokes as usual. Directors can get very stressed about making their days.

"Yes, boss. No problem."

I called the director "boss" because I liked Chris, but I also had no problem lying to him. Because riding the bike fast was a big problem. Nothing hurt my knees more than pushing down on the pedals, especially if I had to lift myself off the seat to get speed. After two takes of riding as fast as I could, I wondered whether or not I would make my day. My ankles, wrists, and elbows hurt almost as much as my knees. My lungs ached with every deep breath. I couldn't believe how unfit I was considering how much I worked out. I'd continued my regular workout routine while in Toronto—an hour on the treadmill at 7.0, 105 sit-ups followed by 105 leg lifts—the only difference being that it wasn't as fun. I no longer had to lose weight and so there was no motivation, no lower number on the scale to look forward to, only a higher number to dread. I had weighed myself that morning. I was 96 pounds and I was never going beneath it. I didn't want to. But what scared me the most was how little I had to eat to avoid gaining the weight back. I ate 300 calories a day and I was just maintaining. I felt trapped, knowing that I would have to continue to be this extreme just to maintain the body I'd starved myself to achieve. It was a realization that was hard to digest.

The next scene was the crying scene. Ironically, I need to be in a happy mood in order to cry; I need to feel pretty self-confident and strong before I can pretend to be insecure and fragile. Usually, crying in a scene makes me feel good, as I get to show off my acting skills. But there was no joy in crying about the death of my father. It was too real, too close to me. I shut down with pain, both physical and emotional. Despite my condition, I managed to cry a little for the scene, but by the end of the day I was crying a lot. I didn't even need to cry anymore, the scene was over; my character was completely over her father's death and on to falling in love with Christian Slater. But I wasn't. I wasn't over my dad leaving me and I wasn't falling in love with anyone. I couldn't stop crying. It was like a flash flood. Its onset and its end were unpredictable and uncontrollable. It just happened, and like a flood, it was devastating.

I was in pain, so I cried. I couldn't move my legs, my wrists, and my fingers, so I cried. I had to be carried into the makeup trailer, so I cried. I was embarrassed, so I cried. I had ruined my career, so I cried. I had ruined my enjoyment of life and wanted to die, so I cried.

I wanted to escape just like my dad had escaped, to fly away, to fade gently into black.

I sat stiffly in the makeup chair to have my makeup removed. It was the first time I'd ever allowed that to happen because I didn't like the makeup artist to see all the flaws I'd concealed before she began her work concealing my flaws—before she made my skin color more even, my eyes bigger, my lips fuller. It was ironic to me that I allowed this end-of-day pampering ritual for the first time on the last day of my career. It was over. I was over.

The lights around the mirror began to bleed into my face. I couldn't quite see my face for the white light around it. I saw two ugly black dots that were my pupils until I couldn't see them anymore either. I felt myself floating away, fading into black. I knew I was passing out, but I could no longer hold on. The last thing I remembered was a hot towel being pressed onto my face. Then I let go.

Out of the blackness came a vision of myself as a little girl spinning around in a tiara and a pinkish-red tutu with a rhinestone-sequined bodice. I'm spinning around and around, doing pirouettes in a church hall. My mother is in the center of the first row. I use her as a spot by focusing only on her, turning my body first before whipping my head around and back to the spot that is my mother's smiling face. With each pirouette, however, instead of being more impressed, she is less impressed. With each spot she is smiling less. The smile turns into a frown and the little girl is no longer wearing a tiara and a tutu but jeans and a black tank top. The little girl has spun into an adult and my mother is no longer there. I search for her in the front row, but she isn't there. Instead I see myself. I realize that the person in the front row, disapproving of me, unhappy with me is not my mother. It's me. I look

disgusted by the image of myself. It is clear by the way my head is par-
tially turned away, my face contorted in a grimace, that I hate myself.
I pirouette again fast, to spin away from the image, too disturbing to
look at any longer. But I keep spinning and gathering momentum, the
centrifugal force won't allow me to stop. I can't stop. Now I can't see
anything. I am tumbling now. I have fallen off my axis. I'm spinning
into the blackness. The spinning suddenly stops.

I have escaped.

29

"MISS DE Rossi? I have Dr. Andrews on the line."

I sat in my dressing room on the set of *Ally McBeal*, lit a cigarette, and breathlessly awaited my test results. I had to get off the treadmill to answer the phone and both the treadmill and the fan I'd rigged to blow air onto my face were straining and noisily whirring. It was quite an effort to get to the phone quickly because sharp movements caused me to feel a lot of pain, sometimes to the point of almost blacking out. I could barely work out anymore, not only because of the pain but because I was too tired. I was tired because I was often too hungry to sleep. When I did sleep I dreamt about food. Last night I had a dream that I took a sip of regular Coke thinking it was diet and the shock of accidentally ingesting real sugar catapulted me back into consciousness. Most times, though, I dreamt about willingly stuffing my face. I dreamt about eating a whole pizza or plate full of French fries. I tended to feel so bad about it when I woke up, I cried. I sobbed as if I'd really done it—it just felt so jarring, so frightening. I thought that I had a problem because I was scared to eat. I was actually scared of food. I no longer trusted myself. I figured I'd lost my willpower.

I felt nervous. Not that I didn't feel anxious all the time, but I felt even worse knowing that what came next was going to change everything.

I can't stay thin. I just wasn't built for it. I wasn't born with thin legs and I can't keep them. For over a year I've managed to maintain my weight, but if I keep up that maintenance to the exclusion of everything else, then I'll have anorexia.

As I sat at the desk and held for the doctor (didn't he call me?), I felt a roll of fat on my stomach. I pinched it with my thumb and forefinger. There was about an inch of fat that went right around to the sides, and yet at 98 pounds, I knew I was grossly underweight. I almost laughed out loud at the irony of it. My rib cage and my hip bones were jutting out, yet there was a roll of fat on my stomach taunting me, letting me know that it had outsmarted me, that it had won. It was ironic also that in order to get rid of that fat, I'd have to have had the energy to do crunches, but without putting caloric energy in my body I didn't have the strength to do them, so now it would just stay there on my stomach in triumph, never to be challenged again. As I sat and waited to hear my results, I felt a little relief knowing that everything was about to change. I couldn't imagine living year after year constantly battling in a fight you could never win. Anorexia is exhausting.

I will listen to what the doctor says and do what he tells me to do.

After collapsing in Toronto, I had no choice but to get help. I blacked out in the makeup chair and my private medical information seemed to be passed around and shared with anyone who cared to ask. My body was no longer under my control. I woke up to the medic taking my blood pressure and ordering blood tests. He called my physician, who called specialists and within days I had undergone a battery of tests. Blood tests, bone density tests; I had to show up with my body to whatever test it was he thought might contribute a puzzle piece to his diagnosis. I couldn't argue. I was under contract and I could barely finish the movie.

But the movie ended two weeks ago and I was still being compliant with the doctors. One doctor turned into four, and so there always seemed to be someone to answer to. They had me cornered. I couldn't escape them even if I wanted to.

But I don't want to. I'm tired. I'm sad all the time, and I'm in pain. I want to give up.

"Hi, Portia?"

"Hi, Dr. Andrews." I waited for some pleasantries to be exchanged but none were forthcoming.

"There are quite a few things I'm seeing from the test results." He took a beat as if to ready himself before delivering a blow. It scared me. I knew there would be something wrong, but his hesitation sent a wave of fear through my body. The wave of adrenaline connected the pain from my ankles to my wrists, and my head began to spin. My head had been feeling like half of its regular weight even when it wasn't spinning. Because of that, I often felt unbalanced. I took a drag of my cigarette. Maybe my head is spinning from the nicotine? I calmed myself.

There is no point in being nervous because I can't affect the outcome. What's done is done.

"Okay. Let's start with your bone density. Uh . . . according to these results it shows that you have osteoporosis."

"Ah . . . how long has it been since you've had your period?"

"A year or more."

"Okay. Your liver enzymes were extremely elevated, which are actually at the levels of cirrhosis."

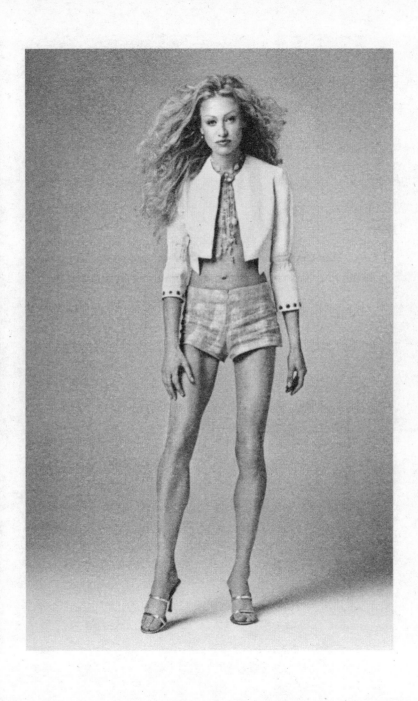

"Okay. Your electrolyte and potassium levels are pretty dangerous. At this rate, they could effect how your organs are functioning."

"Okay. I guess the most important thing that the tests showed is that you have an autoimmune disease called lupus."

I exhaled the smoke in my lungs and extinguished my cigarette in one motion. I limply held the phone and sat staring into the full-length mirror opposite my desk. I saw a round face, thin arms, a bony rib cage, a thick waist, and big, thick legs. It was the same body I had always seen, only smaller. The proportions were the same. If y is exactly half of x, then 2:1 is the ratio of my body parts. My thighs would always be the same in relation to my waist and my arms—it was all the same, but in a smaller version.

Game over. I lose.

The whirring of the treadmill sounded like a vinyl record stuck on a track.

Get on the treadmill.

The bars either side of the belt looked like a cage.

Get on the treadmill.

I don't know what to say to the voice that will shut it up. I'm dying and it still won't be quiet.

"I have lupus! I'm sick!"

You're fat.

"No I'm not!"

The voice was echoing, reverberating. The word *fat* was swirling through my head, sounding the alarms. But above the din of the drill sergeant and the alarms and the ticks of missed beats, a sense of peace overcome me.

I'm sick. I've successfully lowered the bar. I don't have to be a straight-A student or be a movie star to be proud of myself. I just have to live.

I accept myself just as I am. I accept myself.

The voice stops. Apart from laughter coming from the hallway I can't hear anything. It is deathly quiet in my head. And then I said something to the voice I have always wanted to say:

"Go to hell."

EPILOGUE

CAN'T EXPLAIN THE birds to you even if I tried. In the early morning, when the sun's rays peek over the mountain and subtly light up the landscape in a glow that, if audible, would sound like a hum, the birds sing. They sing in a layered symphony, hundreds deep. You really can't believe how beautiful it is. You hear bass notes from across the farm and soprano notes from the tree in front of you all at once, at varying volumes, like a massive choir that stretches across fifty acres of land. I love birds. But not as much as my wife loves them. My wife thinks about them whereas I only notice them once they call for attention. But she looks for them, builds fountains for them, and saves them after they crash into windows. I've seen her save many birds. She holds them gently in the palm of her hand, and she takes them to one of the fountains she's built especially for them and holds their beaks up to the gentle trickle of water to let them drink, to wake them up from their dazed stupor. No matter how much time it takes, she doesn't leave them until they recover. And they mostly always do.

The sound of the big barn doors opening prompts me to begin walking toward the stables. I clutch my coffee mug and walk in bare feet, wearing only my pajama pants and tank to say good morning to my horses.

As I arrive at the barn, Julio, who helps with the horses, is mucking out the stalls, an activity that I would help with were I wearing shoes. I love to muck out stalls.

"Hi, Julio."

"Morning, Portia. Riding today?"

"Yep. A little later."

I love riding horses. I love bathing them and grooming them. I love their strong, muscular bodies, their athleticism, and their kindness. I love the companionship and the trust a rider builds with her horse. I love everything about horses. Horses saved my life.

"Good morning, Mae." The regal head of my big, beautiful Hanoverian horse pokes out from her stall. I wrap my arms around her neck and kiss her muzzle. I bought Mae in 2002 when I was recovering from my eating disorder. Learning how to ride her, learning her language, and being passionate about something other than my weight or looks shifted my focus away from my obsession with being thin long enough to let the doctors and the therapists do their work. I had found love in Mae. I had found a reason to get up in the morning.

"Ellen not up yet?" Ellen usually accompanies me in the mornings to the stables.

"Nah. I'm letting her sleep in."

I crept out of the bedroom this morning and out of the cottage not even grabbing shoes or a sweatshirt as I was trying desperately not to wake her. Ellen works really hard and needs to rest when we're at our farm on the weekends. She especially needed to sleep this morning as she was awake most of the night reading long after I fell asleep. She was awake most of the night reading this book.

After petting Mae, Archie, Femi, Monty, and Diego Garcia, I went back up to the cottage. As I opened the door to the porch I heard the voice that makes my heart the happiest to hear.

"Coff-ee!" Ellen calls out for coffee like a dying man calling out for water as he perishes in the desert. It always makes me laugh.

I walked into the bedroom, plop onto the bed, and wrap my arms around her.

"Baby," she says sleepily, "you were crazy."

"I know."

"So sad. I feel like I was reading about a completely different person."

"I feel like I was writing about a different person."

"You were so sick. What happened to the lupus?"

"It was a misdiagnosis. I just needed to eat. And the cirrhosis and osteoporosis—all of it went away. I was lucky that I didn't do serious damage."

"You poor thing. I wish I could've been there to save you."

"You did save me. You save me every single day."

I kiss her and get up off the bed to make her coffee.

"I'm so proud of you, baby. It'll help a lot of people." As I pour the coffee, she suddenly appears at the doorway of the kitchen, her blond head poking around the door. "Just be sure and tell the people that you're not crazy anymore."

I didn't decide to become anorexic. It snuck up on me disguised as a healthy diet, a professional attitude. Being as thin as possible was a way to make the job of being an actress easier by fitting into a sample size dress, by never worrying that I couldn't zip up my wardrobe from episode to episode, day after day. Just as I didn't decide to become anorexic, I didn't decide to not be anorexic. I didn't decide to become healthy. I decided not to die. I didn't even care to live better than I'd been living, necessarily. I just knew at the moment of hearing my test results that I didn't want to live as a sickly person who would slowly suffer and end up dead. The news that I had seemingly irreversible ill-nesses punctured my obsessive mind and rendered my weight-loss goals meaningless. I lost anorexia. It was too hard to hold on to. By the end I felt as though I was clinging on to anorexia in the same way you would cling to the rooftop of a building, your body dangling precariously over the other side, begging for release. Because it was more exhausting to hang on, and because I had a real reason for the first time in the form of lupus, I let go of dieting. I watched as my biggest accomplishment, my greatest source of self-worth, plummeted to the ground. I had climbed slowly, methodically, all the way to the top only to fall too fast to even see where I had been.

Anorexia was my first love. We met and were instantly attracted to each other. We spent every moment of the day together. Through its eyes, I saw the world differently. It taught me how to feel good about myself, how to improve myself, and how to think. Through it all, it never left my side. It was always there when everyone else had left, and as long as I didn't ignore it, it never left me alone. Losing anorexia was painful—like losing your sense of purpose. I no longer knew what to do without it to consider. Whether the drill sergeant approved or disapproved was no longer a concern because he was no longer there. I let him go with the overwhelming feeling that continuing to fight for him was futile because he was too good for me; he was too perfect, too strict and demanding. Slowly, over several months, maybe even years, the feeling that I wasn't good enough for him dissipated, and I gradually came to feel as though we were just a mismatch, he and I. We never should've been together in the first place. We were too different for each other, and we wanted different things from life. Knowing that, however, didn't make it less painful. Without anorexia, I had nothing. Without it, I was nothing. I wasn't even a failure; I simply felt like I didn't exist.

I was diagnosed with lupus. I had osteoporosis and was showing signs of cirrhosis of the liver. My potassium and electrolyte balance were at critical levels, threatening the function of my organs. I no longer felt lazy, like I was giving up because it was too hard, I felt defeated. I felt as though I simply didn't have a choice. I had to accept that the road I had chosen was the wrong road. It led to sickness and death. I had to allow the voices of the professionals into my closed mind. I had to try to take their road.

As I began the long journey on the road to recovery, there were a couple of detours that I wasn't prepared for. Initially I had thought that once I began to gain back the weight, I would have the strong support base that I'd felt in Australia. I thought I would have loving, concerned people around me to ensure that I was getting healthy. But after I had gained an acceptable amount of weight and looked like a regular person, mostly everyone in my life assumed that the problem was solved. Almost instantly, I felt like no one was listening anymore, no one cared. It felt like caring was only necessary when my life was on the line. As I gained weight I was no longer something to worry about. I truly felt like a pubescent thirteen-year-old, ugly, voiceless; my cute days of being delightful were in the past, and my future accomplishments were too distant to elicit any kind of hope or joy. At that point, if I had still had the axe to grind, if I hadn't got what I wanted from the disorder, some sense of acceptance of my sexuality, I would have relapsed. It would have been very easy for me to start losing weight again to get the attention and the concern that felt like love. It would have felt like a great accomplishment to not just do it once, but twice, proving to myself that I had the willpower I had always suspected was only fleeting.

Gaining weight is a critical time. The anorexic mind doesn't just magically go away when weight is gained—it gets more active. Anorexia becomes bigger and stronger as it struggles to hold on, as it fights for its life. If I hadn't seen my mother break down and accept me for being gay, I would've gotten right back on the path that made me rebel in the first place, because being anorexic did feel a little like rebellion. It felt like a passive-aggressive way of renouncing my mother's control over me. It was definitely a statement that demanded "accept my sexuality or accept my death!" Being sick allows you to check out of life. Getting well again means you have to check back in. It is absolutely crucial that you are ready to check back into life because you feel as though something has changed from the time before you were sick. Whatever it was that made you feel insecure, less than, or pressured to live in a way that was uncomfortable to you has to change before you want to go back there and start life over. And with all the time it takes to have an eating disorder—literally the whole day is consumed by it, both mentally and physically—it's important to find something other than your body image to be passionate about. You have to create a whole new life to check into, and the life I knew was waiting for me was a future relationship and the acceptance of it from my family. I had the key ingredient to want to check back in: I had hope.

For a straight-A student, a model, an actress on a hit TV show, the bar was set very high. I'm the one who set it. I thought that by accomplishing things that were exciting to people, I would receive their admiration and love. I thought that if I accomplished enough, that somehow I would be let off the hook in the future. Like I didn't have to keep striving and achieving because I had done that already, and it would add up to being enough. Anorexia lowered the bar. Instead of having to be a high achiever to receive love, all I had to do was be alive. All I had to do for the caring, nurturing kind of love was lose another pound. All I had to do for acceptance of my sexuality was not eat. Of course, I didn't think I was doing that at the time. I thought I was just trying to stay thin.

Recovery feels like shit. It didn't feel like I was doing something good; it felt like I was giving up. It feels like having to learn how to walk all over again. I felt pathetic. I remember having so little self-esteem that I couldn't talk loudly; I literally couldn't make myself heard because I wanted to disappear. I didn't want to be spoken to or looked at or acknowledged. When someone paid attention to me, I thought they were doing it out of sympathy, kindness, and so it felt condescending. All recovery meant to me was being fat. Unlike the case of an alcoholic or a drug addict, there are no immediate benefits to getting well. My joints might have stopped aching pretty quickly, but after that, I didn't feel better, I felt worse. I experienced all kinds of physical changes that made me feel gross: my period returned, I had gas and was constipated. And then there was the fat that came back. It was truly awful for me. One week I felt lean and perfect, and the next week I was fat. Again. I felt like a failure. I hated every moment of it. I missed my bones so much. I cried at night because I couldn't feel my hip bones and not having them to physically hold onto was like losing a dear friend.

Being anorexic was incredibly difficult. Eating, once I allowed myself to do it, was easy. Being diagnosed with lupus was like a pardon; it granted me the freedom to give up. It felt like an excuse to let go of starvation, and it allowed me to eat again. I could no longer starve or I'd die. Therefore, it was essential to eat. So I did. I ate everything in sight. I ate everything I had wanted to eat for a year but hadn't allowed myself. I started by eating the healthy foods I'd missed: bran muffins, protein bars, granola, and smoothies. But very quickly the list began to include candy, cake, chocolate, and fried food. I felt that if I were going to give up, I might as well give up all the way. The floodgate had opened.

Just because I'd stopped starving didn't mean I didn't still have an eating disorder. My eating disorder felt the same to me. It took up the same space in my head, and driving around the city to find the perfect comfort foods took up as much time as driving around the city to find the tuna with the lowest sodium content. It was still there. It was the other side of the same coin. As it turned out, I wasn't quite ready to rejoin life. I still wanted to disappear, and I chose to disappear behind layers of fat. I still felt unattractive to both sexes, still not really living, merely existing. I was still testing the theory of whether I would be loved and accepted for my mind, my kindness, for everything about me other than what I looked like. I went from one extreme to the other. I went from 82 pounds to 168 pounds in ten months.

At first, after starving for so long, it was difficult to begin eating again even though I knew I had to in order to regain my health. A component in breaking the cycle of starvation was medicine. When the bone-density results showed that I was osteoporotic, I was put on hormone replacement therapy in an attempt to strengthen my bones. I had also quit smoking after hearing the diagnosis and started on a psychotropic medication after having brain scans by a renowned neuro-pharmacologist, Dr. Hamlin Emory. The chemical changes in my body, and I think most importantly, the psychotropic drug quelling the obsessive behavior, helped me to eat again and gain weight.

At the time I walked through the doors of the Monte Nido Eating Disorder Treatment Center, I had gained 27 pounds. It was only four weeks after my diagnosis. I had gone from 98 pounds to 125 pounds in four weeks. Toward the end of my starving phase of my eating disorder, I knew that hovering under 100 pounds didn't feel like my real weight. I was almost certain that the second I began to binge I would immediately catapult back to the weight I'd been before I started starving myself. I knew I would be 130 pounds within weeks. And I was.

I have never felt so ashamed as I did walking into an eating disorder clinic to be treated for anorexia at 125 pounds. I didn't belong there. Even though my treatment was private due to the fact I was terrified that my shameful secret would become public, I was fearful that I might run into people who really had anorexia, who really deserved to be there. I struggled with the feeling of unworthiness throughout my entire treatment. Even though I was paying for it and driving almost daily to Malibu to seek treatment with Carolyn Costin, one of the most well respected and successful counselors in the country, I felt compelled to lie. Every single session I lied to her about my feelings, my eating habits, and my progress. I lied to her because I was embarrassed. I felt like I wasn't worthy of her time when she had girls in her program who were fatally ill when I was so average in size.

I was being treated for anorexia, but due to the fact I was 125 pounds and at a healthy weight for my height, I thought there was no reason for me to be there. I thought that the psychological healing and my relationship to food were not worth talking about. Bulimia and overeating, abuse of laxatives and excessive exercising were not life-or-death illnesses in my mind, and I really didn't share with Carolyn as much as I should have about my dalliances in all of those practices. Despite the fact I thought anything other than anorexia was a second-class eating disorder not worthy of attention, when I was being treated by Carolyn I was severely bulimic. I was grossly overeating. The pendulum had swung the other way, and I was sicker than I had ever been in my life.

Since ending my bout with starvation, I had become addicted to low-calorie, low-carb, weight-loss food. I especially liked low-calorie frozen yogurt and would drive around town all day to different yogurt stores in search of peanut butter–flavored yogurt as all the stores rotated their flavors almost daily. I would drive from east Hollywood to Santa Monica in a day on the search for peanut butter, eating the less tasty flavors along the way. I figured that if I drove all that way, I might as well sample the flavors they offered. I could've called ahead, but then that would leave me with unfilled hours in the day, and as my work on *Ally McBeal* only occupied two or three half days a week, I really didn't know how to fill them.

There was a yogurt store at the Malibu mall and every day before my session with Carolyn, I would stop there. I would order the 12-ounce yogurt regardless of the flavor they were serving and eat it on the floor of the backseat of my car. I was terrified of being photographed eating in my car by paparazzi. Nothing seemed more piggish and gross to me than eating in your car, with the exception of being seen doing it. I had gained so much weight and was so worried that it was noticeable. I figured that all the press would need to do was to get a photograph of me eating to confirm that I had in fact gained a lot of weight. I couldn't think of anything more shameful than my weight gain being obvious enough to talk about. And because the tabloids seemed very interested in my weight loss, I thought for sure they would be just as interested in my weight gain. In fact, during the months when I was at my highest weight, there was a lot of talk about my weight gain. A morning radio show, *Kevin and Bean* on KROQ, commented on the fact that I had "a face like a pie." I distinctly remember this because I listened to them every morning. I remember this because it's not something that you forget.

After eating the yogurt on the floor of the backseat of my car, I took the plastic bag I had asked for in order to carry the yogurt and I threw up into it. At 9 calories an ounce, it was 108 calories that could easily be eradicated. I would then throw the plastic bag into the trash can that I'd strategically parked very close to, and head to my session with Carolyn, feeling very worried that the whole scenario could have been captured on film as Malibu was a hot spot for paparazzi. Without hesitation, when Carolyn asked me if I had binged or purged since my last session, I would reply that no, I hadn't. I hadn't binged or purged or even thought about bingeing or purging. I would tell her how healthy I was and how great I was doing. I don't know why, but it was very important to me to not appear sick to the only person that could help me get better. However, Carolyn had herself recovered from an eating disorder, and combined with her expertise and knowledge gained from treating hundreds of cases, she could see straight through the lies. There is a great deal of shame surrounding an eating disorder, with its abnormal practices and bizarre rituals, and so lying in treatment is common. My stories were only some of many she has had to decode.

My weight gain was horrific to me. I was bulimic again because I didn't want to be fat. I didn't want to be fat, but I couldn't stop eating. I knew that I should work out again to combat the amount of food I put into my body, but because being fat caused me to be depressed, I didn't have the energy. That's the feeling of pulling away from anorexia. The anxiety of feeling fat turns into depression about being fat, and the lethargy and apathy that depression brings make it impossible to get off the sofa. I had found a passion in being thin. It nearly killed me. And while I hated being fat, my new passion was eating.

Carolyn encouraged me to write down the amount of food I ate, and while I mostly lied to her, copying entries from the journals I used to keep for Suzanne, my nutritionist, I decided to send her this email. I had written this entry in November 2000 but only sent it to her in February 2001. It was one of the rare times I wrote down all that I ate in one day. It read:

Apple
Coffee x 2
Half wheat bagel
Whole sesame bagel
Banana
Bowl of pasta with sauce and cheese
Ritz crackers
4 mini-muffins
1 slice bread with tuna
Chocolate—4 mini
2 slices bread with peanut butter
2 cups dried fruit and nuts
bread—2 slices
bowl tortilla soup
half barbeque chicken sandwich
French fries
THREW UP
3 prunes (out of trash can)
mini-muffin
biscotti
coffee bean coffee (vanilla)
rice and beans
chicken taco
quesadilla
crepe and butter

large sugar cookie
ice-blended mocha
baby ruth
white choc crunch bar
pkt famous amos cookies
French vanilla coffee
THREW UP
4 boxes of (cal free) ricola
1 cup of tea with milk
YUP–THAT'LL ABOUT DO IT!!
Pxx (this was back in November)

Carolyn, knowing what I was doing to my body, went to work on my mind. Her therapy included not only discussions about my past, my sexuality, and the feelings I had surrounding food and weight, but we also talked about body image in the larger social sense. We talked about the image of the ideal woman in the form of models who were mostly unhealthy teenage girls. We talked about the idea that women in the postfeminist era, while supposedly strong and commanding and equal to men in every sense, looked weaker and smaller than ever before. We talked about how most women's sense of self-esteem still largely rests on what they look like and how much they weigh despite their other accomplishments. Carolyn photocopied passages of Naomi Wolf's *The Beauty Myth*, and I read them. I remember lying on my bed, reading the badly photocopied text on the pages and saying out loud to no one but my dog, Bean, "Oh my God. I fell for it." I remember feeling ashamed for calling myself a feminist when I had blatantly succumbed to the oppression of the mass media telling me what was beautiful, how to look, and what to weigh. It was a turning point. I had always prided myself on the fact that I was smart, analytical, and someone who didn't "fall for it." By starving myself into society's beauty ideal, I had compromised my success, my independence, and my quality of life. Being overweight was really no different. It was just the "f– you" response to the same pressure. I was still responding to the pressure to comply to the fashion industry's standards of beauty, just in the negative sense. I was still answering to their demands when really I shouldn't have been listening to them at all. The images of stick-thin prepubescent girls never should have had power over me. I should've had my sights set on successful businesswomen and successful female artists, authors, and politicians to emulate. Instead I stupidly and pointlessly just wanted to be considered pretty. I squandered my brain and my talent to squeeze into a size 2 dress while my male counterparts went to work on making money, making policy, making a difference.

I was told that recovering from an eating disorder is hard and not very fun. But apart from honesty, the gift that Carolyn gave me was the knowledge that I would be recovered. Carolyn had herself recovered, and she told me that I wasn't just going to have to learn to manage anorexia and bulimia like an alcoholic managing her drinking. Managing the disorder—thinking about food to any degree other than something nutritious and enjoyable—is, to me, the very definition of disordered eating. I didn't just want to maintain my weight, suppress the urge to purge, and still have a list of foods that were "safe" to eat. I never wanted to think about food and weight ever again. For me, that's the definition of recovered.

After only a few months, and despite Carolyn's urging, I stopped treatment. I didn't stop because I thought I no longer needed her counsel, but because I no longer wanted it. As I was learning that there were no "good" or "bad" foods, just bad eating practices, I listened not to Carolyn but to my eating disorder as it told me that it felt exposed and unsafe. If I stopped weighing my food and myself, like she suggested, its existence was threatened. My eating disorder and I had been to-gether for my entire life, and at that moment, it was easier to continue down the unhealthy path than to pave a new one. In retrospect, had I continued my treatment at this critical point of recovery, I would've discovered that wellness and happiness were closer than I could've imagined. Instead, I resumed the cycle of starving, bingeing, purging, and grossly overeating. And I gained weight.

My weight, the thing that I was convinced was paramount to my success as an actress, wildly fluctuated as I played the character of Nelle Porter. I whittled down to a size 2 from a size 6 and then I be-came almost like a spectator, watching passively as my clothing size went back up from a 2 to a 4, a 4 to a 6. I watched as my biggest fear came to fruition. I was a size 8. I was the size the stylist for the L'Oréal TV commercial had announced to the executives; the size that told them they'd made a mistake in thinking that I was special enough to sell their hair products. I didn't want to be a size 8. It was seeing that number sewn into the labels of my Theory skirts that made me resort to bulimia. But because I was afraid of lupus, mainly I just overate and cried. After reaching the dreaded size 8, I alternated be-tween extreme anxiety about my weight and just giving up caring. Like a binge, I felt if I was going to do a bad thing, I might as well just keep doing it. Size 8 turned into size 10, then a size 12, and in one instance, a size 14. I was so upset and confused that I could ever be a size 14 that I unfairly accused my costume designer of buying a size 14 just to make me feel badly about myself. I lifted my jacket up to expose my bare midriff to a producer to make my case. I told the producer that I wasn't as fat as my costume designer was making me out to be and it simply wasn't fair that she was playing this psychological game with me. I will never forget the look on the producer's face as I cornered her and showed her my stomach, passionately wailing about the size of my skirt and how the costume designer had brought it to me to make me feel insecure.

• • • •

Within a very short time I weighed 168 pounds. More than hating myself, I simply had no sense of myself. It was like I was completely without ego for those months of being at my heaviest. I had reentered life, but it didn't seem like my own life. It seemed like I was passively observing other people's lives. I didn't talk about myself. I was only interested in talking about other people. I had decided that I would very carefully make it known that I was gay to a few gay people around me. I figured that I had completely ruined my career by being fat, so I might as well be gay also. I figured that if I ever worked again, it would be as a "character" actress or playing the best friend to the lead female, so if my homosexuality was rumored around town, it wouldn't really do any further damage to the image I'd already created for myself by being fat. On one very brave occasion I accompanied an acquaintance to a lesbian bar. I stood in the corner at a table facing away from the patrons. I was terrified of being recognized. With a push from my friend I went out onto the dance floor and asked an attractive girl for her phone number. She was attractive not only physically, but there was a sense of freedom about her. The complete opposite of me at the time, she appeared to be both carefree and grounded. We dated for about four months. While I was enjoying being in my first relationship with a woman, my bulimia intensified. I remember after a binge/purge session that lasted hours, she surprised me by dropping over. When she saw the red dots above my eyes and how ill I looked and sounded, she ran to the store to buy ingredients to make chicken soup. As I ate the soup she lovingly made, I felt ashamed. I hated that I had to lie and hide my secrets from my work and from my girlfriend. My paranoia and fear of being exposed—for having an eating disorder and for my sexuality—were excruciating.

There was good reason for my paranoia. A paparazzo had found out that I was gay and made it her mission to out me. She stalked me.

She waited for me every day in front of my building and followed me everywhere, occasionally making eye contact with me and signing to me that she was watching me; that she knew who I was. I had been photographed by paparazzi before, even followed, but this felt like being a deer in a hunter's scope. She and her driver were very aggressive and quite scary. The fear and paranoia led to my relationship's demise as it was impossible for me to leave the house with my girlfriend without feeling intensely anxious and uncomfortable. Not only was I terrified of being exposed as gay, I was scared of being photographed because of what I looked like. I had gained 70 pounds since my last encounter with paparazzi when they were covering stories about anorexic actresses. I didn't want to be in a magazine for being a fat actress.

I met Ellen in 2001 when I weighed 168 pounds. I don't know if I was that weight exactly, but I was heavy enough that the thought that she might have found me attractive or that we could have been a couple never entered my mind. I remember being so excited and overjoyed to be around her that I can still recall the feeling of running after her backstage at a concert we were both attending for Rock the Vote. I caught up to her, sat next to her at a table, and bought her a drink. I remember what she wore: an orange knit sweater, white T-shirt, blue jeans, and white tennis shoes. I remember what we talked about and a joke she made as we were looking down at the mosh pit. I embarrassed myself by laughing too much and too loudly at that joke, but I simply couldn't stop. I thought she was the most amazing person I'd ever met. She was highly intelligent, sharply observant, and funny. She was so beautiful it seemed that light emanated from her bright blue eyes. I had the best night of my life. I felt good about myself around her. I was excited and yet comfortable. At the end of the night, she invited me to come over to her house with the group of friends she'd met up with at the concert. I didn't go. As we'd just met, I thought she was just inviting me to be polite, and I was too shy, too fat, and too insecure to go to her house with her friends. I felt that I had created the perfect memory of being around her that night and I didn't want to ruin it. As it turns out, she had invited those people over only so she would have the excuse of a party to invite me to so she could get to know me better. She was attracted to me. She was attracted to me as a 168-pound woman with a face like a pie. The fact that she got stuck entertaining a whole bunch of people at her house that night because of me is still something we laugh about.

Despite the obvious chemistry at that show in March 2001, Ellen and I didn't reconnect and become a couple until December 2004. Other than the fact that I was overweight, I was also closeted and private about my homosexuality, and so the thought of being with the most famous lesbian in the world didn't cross my mind at that point. I continued working on *Ally McBeal* and taking small steps toward living my life as a gay woman. I had met some lesbians through the girl I'd briefly dated, and I spent time with them, observing them and trying to figure out what it meant to be gay. I soon discovered that I had to figure out what kind of lesbian I was going to be. It was obvious to me almost immediately that I was very different from most other girls. I didn't really fit into either role of "butch" or "femme." I liked wearing makeup and dresses and heels, but I also liked to wear engineer's boots and black tank tops. In the first few months of my coming out to other lesbians, I realized that I was as much a misfit in the gay world as I was in society at large. I was half butch, half femme, neither here nor there. At that point in my life, I didn't understand that playing roles in any relationship is false and will inevitably lead to the relationship's collapse. No one can be any one thing all the time. There is a great deal of lying done while a role is being played in any relationship, homosexual or heterosexual. As I had tried to fit into the sample size clothing, I also tried to fit into a preconceived idea of what it meant to be gay. And any time I try to fit into a mold made by someone else, whether that means sample size clothing or a strict label of "butch" or "femme," I lose myself.

I was a misfit in the lesbian world, I was closeted and scared that I would be outed in the media, so I reverted to being alone. I was still heavy, probably around 150, when 9/11 happened. 9/11 changed my life. I was so deeply disturbed by the realization that I could die without living my life openly and happily that I reached out to a friend who'd wanted me to meet a girl she knew and went on my first date with Francesca. We instantly began a serious and happy relationship that lasted three years. As 9/11 had jolted me into living my life more honestly and fully, my life improved greatly. Although I still struggled with self-acceptance, Francesca was loving and patient and taught me how to be in a relationship. I sold my apartment, and Francesca and I bought a beautiful house in Los Feliz.

When *Ally McBeal* ended, I landed a role in an innovative and exciting new show, *Arrested Development*. I decided to tell my producers and co-stars on *Arrested Development* that I was gay, as I felt that I couldn't be in a serious relationship and hide it from the people I worked with. I felt that trying to do so was very disrespectful to Francesca, even though I was mostly terrified to introduce her as my girlfriend, especially to the show's executive producers, Ron Howard and Brian Grazer. I was truly afraid I could lose my job. But it suddenly seemed pointless to have a girlfriend if I was going to hide her from the rest of my life. Hiding her from the rest of the world was a different story, however.

The paparazzo who had begun stalking me around the time I was beginning to date accomplished her mission to out me when she got photographs of Francesca and me making up after an argument in an alley off Melrose. I had pulled Francesca into the alley after our conversation got a little heated because I didn't want to make a scene and inadvertently out myself to the people walking by on the sidewalk who would surely recognize a couple having an argument. Instead, the photographs went around the world and outed me to everyone who stood in a supermarket checkout line. Because of these photos, I was forced to come out to my aunts and uncles and cousins in Australia before the tabloid hit the stands and hit them over the head with shock. The shock for me was the amount of love and acceptance I received from my extended family, especially my aunt Joan and uncle Stan.

I will be eternally grateful to that paparazzo who I had feared would ruin my life, since she forced me to be honest with my family about being gay. She freed me from a prison in which I had held myself captive my whole life. At my mother's urging, however, I agreed to continue to keep the truth of my sexuality from my grandmother and so began a practice of removing all articles about me from my grandmother's favorite tabloids, something that we continued doing for years. When I finally told my grandmother that I was gay, her reaction was truly amazing. I was back home in Australia to celebrate her hundredth birthday, about a year after Ellen and I had become a couple. My mother and I decided it would be my mother's responsibility to tell Gran that I was gay, since she was going to have to deal with the aftermath if Gran was unhappy about it, which we were almost certain she would be. After Ellen came out on her television show in 1997, Gran stopped watching it, saying that Ellen was "disgusting." My mother, having come to LA for a visit with Ellen and me, was supposed to show Gran pictures of the two of us together: our house and our animals—our life. My mother told me that Gran took the news calmly. But to everyone's surprise, when I sat in front of Gran to yell my hello, she asked me in a yell if I was dating. I yelled at her, "Gran, I'm with Ellen."

"Alan?"

"El-len."

She looked horrified.

"Oh, Porshe. You're not one of those!"

I turned to my mother, panicked. "I thought you showed her pictures and explained everything to her!" My mother swiveled on the sofa to face Gran and yelled, "Gran! I told you Portia was living with Ellen."

"Yes," she yelled back. "As roommates!" She looked perplexed and shook her head. "And all this time I was worried that that lesbian was hitting on my granddaughter!"

Gran closed her eyes for about twenty seconds. There was complete silence. I was holding my breath. It was the longest, quietest twenty seconds of my life.

"Well," she said opening her eyes and holding her arms out for a hug, "I love you just the same." We never talked about my sexuality again, only about how happy my life was with Ellen. From changing the channel in disgust to being Ellen's biggest fan and watching her talk show every day, Gran showed me that people can change, including me, as I was certain that a woman born in 1907 in a small town in rural Australia would never be able to accept me. I had judged her and assumed that she would feel as though I had shamed the family. But I was wrong. In the nursing home where she spent her final few months before passing away at the age of 102, she kept a framed photo of our wedding for all the staff to see on the nightstand next to her bed. She was proud to call Ellen her granddaughter.

By the time I entered into my relationship with Ellen, I had recovered from my eating disorder. Living with Francesca forced me to deal with issues surrounding acceptance of my sexuality, and it also forced me to deal with my relationship to food. I shared a kitchen—and a bathroom. I couldn't binge and purge without a lengthy and embarrassing discussion. I slowly stopped purging and just binged in my car or at work while she wasn't there to see it. The rest of the time I would eat salads with no dressing. I was still fighting a heavier weight over the next two years, but what really became obvious to me was that I was doing something very wrong. I began to understand that every time I restricted my calorie intake, I would binge immediately after. Sometimes I could diet for a week or two without the bingeing and I would lose a few pounds, but then the binge would inevitably follow and I would gain all the weight back, and sometimes a couple of pounds more. I was always on a diet. I was either being "good" or being "bad," but I was always on a diet—even when I was bingeing. I lived my life from day to day by weighing myself and measuring my success or failure solely on weight lost or gained—just as I had done from the time I was twelve. I'd measured my accomplishments and my self-worth on that scale for my entire life, with the same intensity and emotion, from 82 pounds all the way to 168. While I had begun to examine my behavior in treatment, I was forced to continue the self-examination when I was living with Francesca, because simply having to explain my actions to another person made me question them. I finally understood that by being on a perpetual diet, I had practiced a "disordered" form of eating my whole life. I restricted when I was hungry and in need of nutrition and binged when I was so grotesquely full I couldn't be comfortable in any position but lying down. Diets that tell people what to eat or when to eat are the practices in between. And dieting, I discovered, was another form of disordered eating, just as anorexia and bulimia similarly disrupt the natural order of eating. "Ordered" eating is the practice of eating when you are hungry and ceasing to eat when your brain sends the signal that your stomach is full. "Ordered" eating is about eating for enjoyment, for health, and to sustain life. "Ordered" eating is not restricting certain kinds of foods because they are "bad." Obsessing about what and when to eat is not normal, natural, and orderly. Thinking about food to the point of obsession and ignoring your body's signals is a disorder.

Although I had learned about this from Carolyn, my understanding of how it worked was suspended due to my resistance to treatment. At the time of leaving Monte Nido, living without dieting sounded like a utopian philosophical ideal. That is, until I witnessed it at work with Francesca. A naturally thin woman who ate whatever she wanted and never gained or lost a pound was the most fascinating case study for this woman who had spent her life gaining and losing weight. I watched her eat pasta, candy, ice cream, and cheese. I watched her dip her bread in olive oil and wash it down with Coke—real Coke, not diet—while I ate dry salads with no dressing and sipped iced tea. I was dumbfounded that I was eating boring, dry, diet food and maintaining or gaining weight during the course of any given month when she never even thought about what she ate or how her body looked. I was equally amazed as I watched her order food at restaurants and only eat a small portion of her order because she was too full to finish it or skip breakfast or lunch because she got a little too busy and simply forgot to eat. After initially dismissing her eating habits as a result of her just being one of those lucky people who can eat whatever they want and stay thin, it suddenly occurred to me that maybe people who stay thin are the people who eat whatever they want.

I put this theory into practice after an incident between Francesca and me that was fraught with emotion and very revealing. I was sitting in the closet in our master suite crying because I couldn't fit into a pair of pants that I had bought only a month before. They were size 6. I was in despair and when Francesca came to comfort me, I almost accused her of causing my weight gain, saying that she'd let me get fat again and that she didn't care how I felt about myself or that my career depended on my ability to control my weight. After patiently hearing my wailing, she said something that I'll never forget. She said:

"Fine. I'll help you diet. But you'll only gain it back."

It was a simple statement, but the truth of it overwhelmed me. All I had done throughout my life was diet and gain the weight back. Therefore, the only conclusion I could make was that diets don't work. Sitting on the floor of the closet with tears running down my face, I decided that my way wasn't working, that it was time to try something else. From that day on, I decided that I would never diet again.

After that day, instead of watching her eat, I joined in. I ate whatever she ate. We cooked meals together and loaded pasta onto our plates.

We ate ice cream. Because I knew I could eat pasta and ice cream again the very next day if I wanted to, I stopped wanting it in excess. If it were going to be available to me anytime, why eat like it was the last time I'd ever taste it? The fact that I stopped restricting food made it less appealing. The fact that I stopped labeling food as "good" and "bad" made me just see it all as food. Like Carolyn had told me, there was no bad food. There were just bad eating practices. I began eating every single thing I wanted when I wanted it, without guilt, without remorse, without feeling anything other than happy about the taste of the food I had chosen to eat. Initially, I gained a little weight. But over time, I found that I didn't want to eat ice cream every day. Not because of fear of gaining weight, but because it was too cold, or too sweet for my taste buds after a salty pasta. I began tasting food and listening to my internal nutritionist as it told me that I truly wanted to eat a crispy, fresh salad rather than fries. When it told me that fries were what I was craving, it said, "Eat as many as you want knowing that you can always have them again tomorrow." So I'd eat just a few until I was full, or I'd eat the whole damn serving until I couldn't eat anything else on my plate. I stopped overeating. I stopped thinking about food. I ate exactly what I wanted, when I wanted it, without any feelings of guilt or being "good" or "bad."

Within two months of that conversation in the closet, I was maintaining my weight easily at 130 pounds. I was one of those "lucky" people who could eat whatever they wanted and never gain weight. I stopped weighing myself. I simply didn't care about weight anymore because it was always the same, always a comfortable, good weight for my body, and I stopped thinking about food because every single food item was available to me at any moment of the day. There was nothing left to think about.

As I listened to my internal nutritionist, I stopped wanting to eat meat, eggs, and dairy. This was something that carried over from childhood, as I never liked eating chicken breasts or steaks because I was worried about finding veins or fatty tissue. I also didn't like eating processed meat, like chicken nuggets and ground beef, because I was worried that I'd get a mouthful of gristle. I definitely would never eat off a bone because the bones really reminded me of the fact that a living animal that had a heart and a mind and a family had been attached to those bones. I also hated the thought of ingesting the growth hormones that are given to so many animals in recent years to increase their weight and therefore their market value. And it disturbed me that I would drink a cow's milk, which is designed to increase its calf's weight to 400 pounds in as short a time as possible. I have always been a little squeamish at the thought of drinking another mammal's milk. I find it odd that humans are the only species that not only drinks another species's milk, but that we keep doing it as adults.

While I have never felt more healthy and energized, the most important thing that happened to me when I stopped eating animals was a sense of connectedness. When I was suffering with an eating disorder, my life was solely about me. I was living through my ego and didn't care about life around me. I was selfish and angry, and because I didn't care about myself, I also didn't care about littering in the street or polluting the environment. My decision not to eat animals anymore was paramount to my growth as a spiritual person. It made me aware of greed and made me more sensitive to cruelty. It made me feel like I was contributing to making the world better and that I was connected to everything around me. I felt like I was part of the whole by respecting every living thing rather than using it and destroying it by living unconsciously. Healing comes from love. And loving every living thing in turn helps you love yourself.

While I was learning how to eat again (or perhaps for the first time), I cultivated new hobbies that had nothing to do with how I appeared to other people in terms of how I looked or professional accomplishment. My new hobbies required skill, focus, intelligence, and most important, honing and relying upon my own natural instincts. My brother owns a helicopter charter and training business called Los Angeles Helicopters, and I began taking flying lessons with his instructors. Although I didn't get my private pilot's license, I racked up forty hours of flying in a Robinson R22 and moved my focus from weight loss to learning this new and challenging skill. Driving to Long Beach, studying aeronautical physics and learning autorotations took up the time that driving around town to find yogurt had previously occupied.

My passion for riding horses was reignited after spending time with Francesca's mother in England over the holidays. As a small child, I loved horses but after suffering a dislocated shoulder from slipping off a cantering horse, I stopped riding out of fear. Twenty years later, I found myself with the same enthusiasm and excitement for horses that I'd had when I was a child. Over that Christmas in England I would wake up at 6:00 a.m. and head down to the barn hoping to be able to watch Fran-cesca's mother ride dressage and take a lesson on the Welsh cob she kept for interested visitors. When I returned to Los Angeles, I joined a hunter/jumper barn and within a few months bought a horse of my own.

To say that my first horse, Mae, saved my life isn't an overstatement. Just being outdoors all day and breathing in fresh country air and noticing the beauty of the trees as I rode on meandering deer trails through the woods was enough to alter my consciousness, to respect nature and my place within it. The horse was like an extension of myself, a mirror showing me my underlying emotions that I'd become skilled at ignoring. When Mae was afraid, she was telling me that I was afraid. When she refused to jump a fence, she let me know that I was intimidated by the hurdles in my life. She'd speed up when I thought I was telling her to slow down, as she was responding to my internal anxiety not to my voice weakly saying "whoa." Sometimes I couldn't even get her to go. I'd squeeze her sides and she'd just know that I didn't mean it. She'd know that I just wanted to stay still for a while.

• • •

Do I love myself just the way I am? Yes. (Well, I'm working on it!) But that doesn't mean I love my body just the way it is. People who recover from eating disorders can't be expected to have higher standards than the rest of society, most of whom would like to alter a body part or two. I'd still like thighs the size of my calves, but the difference is that I'm no longer willing to compromise my health to achieve that. I'm not even willing to compromise my happiness to achieve it, or for the thought of my thighs to take up valuable space in my mind. It's just not that important. And while there are things I don't like about the look of my body, I'm very grateful to it for what it does. I'm grateful that it doesn't restrict me from doing my job the way I restricted it from doing its job. When I sit quietly and silently thank the universe for all the blessings in my life, I start with Ellen and end with my thighs. I thank my thighs for being strong and allowing me to walk my dogs around my neighborhood and ride my horses. I thank my body for not punishing me for what I put it through and for being a healthy vessel in which I get to experience this amazing world and the beautiful life I am living full of love.

I have recovered from anorexia and bulimia. I am immensely grateful that the disorders, although robbing me of living freely and happily for almost twenty years, aren't continuing to rob me of health. Not everyone who has suffered from eating disorders has the same good fortune. The disorders have left me unscathed both physically and mentally. However, having anorexia has left me with an intense resistance to exercise. As well as being resistant to exercise, I have an intense resistance to counting calories. And reading labels on the backs of jars and cans. And weighing myself.

I hate the word *exercise*. I am allergic to gyms. But I don't think that "formal" exercise in a gym is the only way to achieve a healthy, toned body. I have discovered that enjoyable daily activities that are easy, like walking, can be equally beneficial. I have noticed on my daily walk with my dogs that I rarely see an overweight person walking a dog, whereas I see many overweight people walking on treadmills in a gym. I attribute this not only to the frequency of having to walk your dog, but also the good feeling one has when doing something good for another being. Seeing my dogs' excitement as I walk them around my neighborhood every day makes me happy, and when I'm happy I walk a little taller and a little more briskly. I can only imagine the enjoyment parents must experience when seeing the joy on their kids' faces as they play tag football or shoot hoops with them. I also enjoy being outdoors. I like breathing the cold night air deeply into my lungs as I walk up the hills in my neighborhood and smelling the forest air as I walk on hiking trails after a morning rain. Another way for me to stay fit is to do activities where I can learn a skill, like horse riding or tennis or dancing. I find that if I can concentrate on getting better at something, rather than getting fitter or looking better, I accomplish all three things—the latter two being happy by-products of the original goal. Doing an activity to relax is also important for me. I swim to clear my head rather than count laps and burn calories. Swimming slowly is a form of meditation for me.

I have found ways to increase my heart rate, stretch my muscles, and breathe deeply every day in an enjoyable way that I would never label as exercise. I eat every kind of food that I like, moderating the portions using my appetite and not a calorie counter. I love fat and I love carbohydrates. Nothing fills you up and feels more satisfying than a mashed potato or pasta and olive oil. There are days when I eat a large bag of potato chips for lunch and I feel too full and greasy to eat anything else until dinner. It may not be the healthiest, most balanced day in a lifetime of days, but I more than likely won't repeat it the following day.

To say that you can stay at your natural body weight and be healthy by eating what you want and not working out sounds extremely controversial, and yet people have lived this way for hundreds of years. It seems to me that it's only since around 1970 that the concept of diet and exercise has existed in the way it does now, which is based on exertion and restriction being the key to weight loss, and yet since then, we have seen an increase in obesity in countries that have adopted it. (These are also the countries where the fast-food industry boomed during that time.) The diet industry is making a lot of money selling us fad diets, nonfat foods full of chemicals, gym memberships, and pills while we lose a little of our self-esteem every time we fail another diet or neglect to use the gym membership we could barely afford. Restriction generates yearning. You want what you can't have. There are many ways to explain why the pendulum swing occurs and why restriction almost always leads to bingeing. I was forced to understand this in order to recover from a life-threatening disorder. And in a way, I wrote this memoir to help myself understand how I came to have an eating disorder and how I recovered from it. I really hope that my self-exploration can help not only people who are suffering from anorexia and bulimia, but also the perpetual dieters. You don't have to be emaciated or vomiting to be suffering. All people who live their lives on a diet are suffering.

If you can accept your natural body weight—the weight that is easy for you to maintain, or your "set point"—and not force it to beneath your body's natural, healthy weight, then you can live your life free of dieting, of restriction, of feeling guilty every time you eat a slice of your kid's birthday cake. But the key is to accept your body just as it is. Just as I have had to learn to accept that I have thighs that are a little bigger than I'd like, you may have to accept that your arms are naturally a little thicker or your hips are a little wider. In other words, accept yourself. Love your body the way it is and feel grateful toward it. Most important, in order to find real happiness, you must learn to love yourself for the totality of who you are and not just what you look like.

I made the mistake of thinking that what I look like is more important than who I am—that what I weigh is more important than what I think or what I do. I was ashamed of being gay, and so I only heard the voices that said that being gay is shameful. As I changed, I no longer heard the condemning voices. When my relationship with Ellen became public, I was amazed by how well the news was received. I was still very scared, but I was also very much in love, and love outweighed the fear. I wanted to celebrate our love. I was so proud to call myself her girlfriend that whatever people might have thought about my sexuality wasn't important anymore. I simply didn't hear a single negative comment. I began to see myself as someone who can help others understand diversity rather than feeling like a social outcast. Ellen taught me to not care about other people's opinions. She taught me to be truthful. She taught me to be free. I began to live my life in love and complete acceptance. For the first time I had truly accepted myself.

August 16, 2008

I walk out of the bedroom of the guest apartment where Kellen and Jen, Ellen's and my stylists, have just finished tying the bows of my Lanvin pink ballet flats. The act of getting me into my wedding dress, a fairytale wedding dress designed for me by Zac Posen, is performed slowly and meticulously, with the gravity and respect all ancient rituals demand. My mother, dressed beautifully in a teal dress and jacket that we had bought together at Barneys just days before, is waiting excitedly to see her daughter in a wedding dress, a sight that she could have never imagined experiencing after learning that I was gay. When she sees me, she cries. She tells me that she is proud of me. She tells me that she loves me.

"I love you too, Mom. Now stop crying or you'll start me crying. I can't mess up my makeup."

We never hold ourselves back now. We can get very emotional.

As Molly and Mark put their final touches on my makeup and hair, I recite my vows to my mother for a practice run. I can't wait to tell

Ellen how I feel about her in front of the people who are the closest to us and who support and love us, for richer or for poorer, in sickness and in health, in fame or in obscurity. Among our assembled guests are Wayne Dyer, who is officiating the wedding, Sacha and her husband Matt, the partner she chose over me ten years prior in St. Barths, and my brother and his incredible second wife, Casey.

"This ring means that I choose to spend the rest of my life with you. I promise to love you in the nurturing and selfless way that you love me. I've changed so much since I've known you. Your love has given me the strength to be softer. You've taught me kindness and compassion. You make me better."

I stop reciting and look at my mother. She is proud. She is calm. She is smiling at her healthy daughter who has found a deep profound love with another woman. And not just any woman, Ellen DeGeneres, the woman I used to use as an example of why my public outings with previous girlfriends were nothing to worry about. My mother would say to me, "Now you're in a relationship people will find out that you're gay!" And I would reply, "Relax, Ma. At least I'm not dating Ellen DeGeneres." Ellen DeGeneres was the "worst-case scenario." She would expose me as being gay. She would force me to live a truthful, honest life, to be exactly who I am with no pretense. I thank God for her every day.

I highly recommend inviting the worse-case scenario into your life. I met Ellen when I was 168 pounds and she loved me. She didn't see that I was heavy; she only saw the person inside. My two greatest fears, being fat and being gay, when realized, led to my greatest joy. It's ironic, really, when all I've ever wanted is to be loved for my true self, and yet I tried so hard to present myself as anything other than who I am. And I didn't just one day wake up and be true to myself. Ellen saw a glimpse of my inner being from underneath the flesh and bone, reached in, and pulled me out. I continued reciting my vows to my mother although I was a little nervous about her reaction to what I was about to say. Although I was completely recovered before Ellen and I became a couple, I wanted to remind Ellen of my struggle for self-acceptance and to tell her that because she saw something in me that I hadn't previously seen in myself, my perception of myself changed. She didn't see an average girl, a mediocre girl from a middle-class family who had to win the race and change her name in order to be considered special. She saw a unique and special person. She saw a woman who was worthy of care.

"You treat me better than I've ever treated myself . . ."

As I had expected would happen, my mother interrupts. "But you're all better now, aren't you?" She is extremely concerned about the possibility of my relapsing into the dark and lonely world of an eating disorder.

I look at my reflection in the mirror and I like what I see. I'm not looking at a childhood fantasy of what I should look like on my wedding day or a bride in a wedding dress. I am looking at me. I contemplate the idea of being better and it brings to mind my favorite quote from Wayne Dyer, our friend and the man who is about to marry me to the woman of my dreams. "True nobility isn't about being better than anyone else; it's about being better than you used to be."

"Yes, Ma. I am better."

I am better than I used to be.

ACKNOWLEDGMENTS

I am so incredibly grateful to everyone who made *Unbearable Lightness* possible and who encouraged and supported me along the way.

Peter Borland
Alysha Bullock
Ann Catrina-Kligman
Carolyn Costin
Judith Curr
Ellen DeGeneres
Jonathan Safran Foer
Victor Fresco
Kathy Freston
Mike Hathaway
Judy Hoffland
Nancy Josephson
Alex Kohner
Jeanne Lee
Annick Muller
Harley Neuman
Paul Olsewski
Megan Pachon
Donna Pall
Craig Peralta
Gina Phillips

Sacha Plumbridge
Casey Rogers
Margaret Rogers
Michael Rogers
Patty Romanowski
Kali Sanders
Lisa Sciambra
Nick Simonds
Dana Sloan
Randee St. Nicholas
Megan Stone
Jennifer Rudolph Walsh
Oprah Winfrey
Kevin Yorn

Portia de Rossi is an Australian-born actress best known for her roles in the television series *Ally McBeal*, *Arrested Development* and most recently *Better Off Ted*. She lives in Los Angeles with her wife Ellen DeGeneres.

Kenyon has placed over sixty novels on the *New York Times* bestseller list; in the past three years alone, she has claimed the No.1 spot seventeen times. This extraordinary bestseller continues to top every genre she writes within.

Proclaimed the pre-eminent voice in paranormal fiction by critics, Kenyon has helped pioneer – and define – the current paranormal trend that has captivated the world and continues to blaze new trails that blur traditional genre lines.

With more than 25 million copies of her books in print in over 100 countries, her current series include: The Dark-Hunters, League, Lords of Avalon, Chronicles of Nick, and Belador Code.

Visit Sherrilyn Kenyon's websites:
www.darkhunter.com | www.sherrilynkenyon.co.uk

www.facebook.com/AuthorSherrilynKenyon
www.twitter.com/KenyonSherrilyn

Dianna Love is the *New York Times* bestselling co-author of *Phantom in the Night*, *Whispered Lies*, and *Silent Truth*, as well as the Belador Code series, including *Blood Trinity* and *Alterant*, with Sherrilyn Kenyon. She is a national speaker who started writing while working over a hundred feet in the air, creating marketing projects for Fortune 500 companies. When not plotting out her latest action-adventure, she travels the country on a motorcycle to meet fans and research new locations. She and her husband live near Atlanta, Georgia.

Visit her website www.authordiannalove.com.

THE CURSE

SHERRILYN KENYON

AND

DIANNA LOVE

BOOK 3 IN THE BELADOR SERIES

piatkus

PIATKUS

First published in the US in 2012 by Pocket Star Books
A division of Simon & Schuster, Inc.
First published in Great Britain as a paperback original in 2012 by Piatkus

A CIP catalogue record for this book
is available from the British Library.

ISBN 978-0-7499-5763-6

Printed and bound by CPI Group (UK) Ltd, Croydon, CR0 4YY

Papers used by Piatkus are from well-managed forests
and other responsible sources.

MIX
Paper from
responsible sources
FSC
www.fsc.org
FSC® C104740

Piatkus
An imprint of
Little, Brown Book Group
100 Victoria Embankment
London EC4Y 0DY

An Hachette UK Company
www.hachette.co.uk

www.piatkus.co.uk

We'd like to dedicate this book to Mary Buckham,
who is generous to a fault with her time and expertise

ACKNOWLEDGMENTS

FROM SHERRILYN AND DIANNA

Thank you to our family, friends, and fans. We love you all and couldn't do this without you! You are the best!

A special hug for our husbands, whose endless support means the world to us . . . and we so appreciate the great food! A special thanks go to Cassondra Murray and Mary Buckham for beta reads and terrific feedback, plus being major support at any time, day or night.

A major thank-you to Louise Burke, a publisher whose enthusiasm is only surpassed by her genius, and thank you to our talented editor, Lauren McKenna, who is a joy to work with because of her commitment to publishing a great story. We want to send another high-five to the Pocket Art Department, which has once again outdone themselves on giving us a fabulous cover and for the great banner ads, and we appreciate Robert Gottlieb's outstanding guidance and managing of our projects.

Last, and never least, we want to thank the readers who come out to see us in every city, send encouraging messages that touch our hearts, and read our stories so that we may continue doing what we love. You mean the world to us.

We look forward to hearing from you anytime at authors@beladors.com, or stop by www.SherrilynKenyon.com and www.AuthorDiannaLove.com, and make sure to visit the "Reader Lounge" at Dianna Love's Fan Page on Facebook, where you'll find free Belador items and scavenger hunts.

Cathbad the Druid doth bind Queen Medb
By vow thus struck with blood and blade
Birth afore death and death afore birth
The last shalt rise afore the first

That by fair child of Findabair
Medb queens shalt rule the tower lair
Twenty score years and sixty-six days
Not one more breath shalt they take

Until such time the beast doth rise
Of ancient blood and flame green eyes
And bring to power a queen once more
Immortal to rule as none afore.

—Prophecy of Cathbad the Druid

ONE

A nswer me or accept death," a female demanded.

The smooth texture of her voice was familiar to him, but not the dangerous edge in her tone. Storm floated in a timeless cocoon of peaceful darkness, content to stay here if not for that disturbing ultimatum.

"This is your last chance," she snapped at him, fury powering her words. "I would never have thought you a coward when it came to facing pain, Storm. Speak now or prepare for eternity."

Time. Pain. Death.

Understanding crept into his wavering consciousness. He focused on his body, or lack of one now that he identified this murky sensation as being suspended between life and death. He'd been here once years ago, as a teen.

Threads of awareness pulled together, weaving a tapestry until an image formed of the woman speaking. Kai.

Storm forced his heavy eyelids open to find her. His guardian spirit sat with crossed legs, surrounded by her favorite meadow, where he always met her. He sat in the same position across from her. Acres of wildflowers swayed gently in a soft breeze that swirled with the fresh scent of outdoors. Sunshine blazed overhead, showering golden light across Kai's honey-colored skin and coal-black hair that fell past her waist, sliding over the butter-soft deerskin dress. She sometimes took the form of a shriveled crone. He preferred this younger Kai.

Still fighting his way through a haze of confusion, Storm found comfort in seeing the Southwestern Native blanket she used as a shawl. The colors of a sunset woven in the wrap reminded him of one he owned.

His thoughts bumped into each other, knocking loose a memory here and there. Such as, that this realm was always a sanctuary, a welcoming place.

It didn't feel like that now.

Kai existed only in the spirit world. Storm didn't recall initiating this visit. That was not normal. Something had happened to him, to his physical body.

He wasn't here by choice.

She folded her delicate arms. Worry lingered in her doe-brown eyes. "I have given you all the time I can."

Though simple, her words were weighted with a finality that washed away the last of his mental fog. He asked, "Am I dying?"

"Yes."

"But I have a choice?"

"You do."

"Good."

"Perhaps," she amended.

Less good. "How damaged is my physical body?"

"Your human form is close to expiring. I have fought to prevent your spirit from crossing over for three weeks, but—"

"Three weeks? Am I in a coma?"

"You were, but no longer."

He searched his mind, poking at dark corners to open doors to his past. Nobody *wanted* to die, but he had a strong sense that he had a duty to stay alive, odd as that sounded. Why? "What happened to me?"

"You were attacked, mortally injured. Your spirit burst into my realm, pleading for me to keep you alive, shouting why you *must* return to the human world. It has been a battle to grant your wish to this point."

Images sheared past the inside of his eyes. His body crashing into a brick wall. Bones shattering. Internal organs exploding from the force.

But not in his human form.

He'd been a black jaguar.

Strange. He'd refused to shift into a jaguar for many years. Why now?

A new image surfaced. Glowing green eyes on a woman who sent his senses into overdrive. An Alterant.

Evalle Kincaid.

He'd used his Skinwalker gift to shift into animal form for Evalle. To help her find other Alterants . . . before Sen came to take her . . . to the Tribunal trial. Sen. Liaison to VIPER.

More images. Sen grabbing Evalle. Storm leaping at Sen.

Sen attacking, wielding kinetic power. Slamming Storm into the brick.

A heartbreaking last look at Evalle's horrified face. One brief rush of her emotions across his empathic senses . . . Desperation. Misery. Had the Tribunal locked her away forever?

He had to find her.

One thing at a time. First he had to live.

He nodded, letting Kai know his memory had begun to surface. "Where's my body?"

"Safe and hidden."

"How did you manage that?" He didn't think a guardian spirit could physically move bodies around in the human world.

"I shielded your body from view until I could find help. Then I called upon one you trust. She moved your body to a place where she could tend your wounds. She has kept you alive, but you are not fully healed and now your body is weakening by the hour."

Evalle. She'd be frantic about his dying, but if she was taking care of him, that meant she had walked free from the Tribunal. Finally, something positive. "But I still have the choice to live?"

"You have the choice to go back. Living will depend upon whether your Skinwalker gifts can complete your healing. *If* you choose to return, you must do so now."

"There is no if. I *have* to go back." He paused, to figure out exactly why he absolutely had to return. To fulfill a task—no, a commitment he'd made. "Something . . . about Evalle, right?"

"Yes, you had dreams that the Ashaninka witch doctor who searches for you has followed you to Atlanta and intends to harm her."

That's right. The bitch who'd killed his father back in South America. His last dreams had shown her threatening Evalle.

Everything rushed back to him with a vengeance.

He would *not* let that insane bitch touch Evalle. "Can the witch doctor find my body where it's hidden?"

"No."

Relief shoved his worry aside. With Evalle tending his physical body she would be safe until he returned. She'd been watching over him for three weeks? With her so close he was ready to leap back into his body. He missed her in a way he never thought he'd feel about a woman again.

Missed kissing her. Watching her emotions flare.

He'd do whatever it took to return.

But Kai had said his body was close to expiring.

He asked, "Why haven't I healed in three weeks?"

"You haven't been lucid once in that time so you could draw on your gifts to heal yourself. Taking you to any type of hospital—"

"—would have been dangerous for me," he finished. Because he could have shifted back and forth between human and jaguar form while he had no control over his body.

"Yes. If you had not remained on the edge of crossing over for so long, you would have regained consciousness and started healing by now. As it is, the woman has done all she can. You must return to your body or you will not survive."

"Why didn't you call me back sooner?"

She angled her chin to one side and frowned. Clouds appeared, blotting out the sun and draping her meadow in dark shadows, a sign he'd annoyed Kai.

He held up his hand and humbled his tone. "I meant no insult and certainly no criticism. I just wondered why I spent so much time suspended between life and death when it sounds as though I should have returned days ago."

She relaxed, clearly comprehending his confusion. As the sun shone again, she explained, "You have forgotten our many conversations over these weeks. Every time you started to fade I pleaded, yelled, threatened, anything I could think of to call you back from the edge. Your spirit weakened and slipped further from my hold every day. Had you not answered this time . . . I would not have been able to keep your spirit from disconnecting from your physical body."

His blood chilled at how close he'd been to losing any chance of returning. "Thank you for fighting for me."

She nodded. "I will always be here for you."

"I should get going. Can I return on my own?"

"Not this time. I'll send you, but you must prepare yourself for the pain."

"I'm ready."

"I hope so. And regardless of your physical torment, temper your words. She has been most patient."

Not even pain could make him speak harshly to Evalle. He disregarded the warning and joked, "That's saying something since patience doesn't come naturally to Evalle."

"Evalle?" Kai's soft black eyebrows lifted in question.

"Isn't that who you contacted?"

"You did ask me to go to her first, but I could not find her."

"Then who did—"

Kai's eyes flashed with fear. "You must go *now*, Storm. Your heart is stopping."

In the next seconds everything in the meadow blurred into a wash of color and sound as if someone had flushed the world.

He knew the minute he entered his physical body.

Agony ripped through him.

A fist slammed his chest, with supernatural force behind it. Someone shouted at him. Cursed him. Heat roared across his skin. Nerves caught fire with renewed life, flooding pain everywhere. Perspiration streamed across his face.

His heart beat. Again. The thud echoed in his ears every painful time blood pumped through the battered organ.

He grabbed at his chest, struggling to draw a breath. Blinding pain ripped through his insides. His spine wrenched forward as he curled into a ball of misery. Another cramp tightened his chest muscles, squeezing a guttural moan from his dry throat.

Had he really wanted to return to this? Every nerve in his body screamed.

Finally, slowly, the pain in his chest subsided to a throbbing ache, enough for him to draw a ragged breath and hear someone near him.

A soft voice chanted words that made no sense.

Long moments later, he uncurled until he sagged into the soft bed and let his arms fall to his sides. He licked his dry lips and tried to swallow, but couldn't draw a spit of saliva.

Opening his eyes, he found the answer to the question he'd been trying to ask Kai.

The woman standing next to him was definitely not Evalle Kincaid.

Adrianna Lafontaine's arms stretched out over his chest, hands turned up, eyes closed and lips moving as words danced off her tart-pink lips. Barely five feet tall with silky blond hair and a robust shape packed into that small frame, the Sterling witch turned heads everywhere she went.

But she wasn't Evalle.

He suffered a wave of disappointment almost as crushing as the pain racking his body. Kai had said she'd found someone he trusted. That was a helluva stretch, but he did have to admit he was alive, and safe at the moment, thanks to this witch.

When Adrianna finished her chant, she opened her eyes and looked down at him. "You decided to come back?"

He croaked out something that should have been yes.

She moved off to his left, then returned with a plastic bottle of water, lifting his head to let a few trickles fall into his mouth before she laid him back down. "I've pulled out every trick I know, but I've reached my limit, Storm."

"I know." He tried to look past her to see where he was, but the only light in the chilly, dark room was the faint glow from a lamp near his head. He managed to get out, "Where am I?"

"An underground space in Decatur I *convinced* someone to offer me, then to forget he'd done so once I got you inside."

She meant she'd used a spell or some other ability.

Over the next couple of breaths, he closed his eyes and searched inside himself for the power of his jaguar, relieved when he felt his animal presence stir to life. With a concerted effort, he forced energy to spread through his chest and limbs, flinching every time the energy struck damage. He had no idea how long he'd lain there, focused on healing, until he expelled a long sigh and paused to rest.

He blinked his eyes open, looking around. "Adrianna?"

She stepped into view and gave him another tiny drink of water. That's when he took in the unkempt look of her jeans and sweatshirt. Not her usual fashion statement.

Storm said, "Thank you for all of this."

"You're welcome."

Sterling witches rarely did anything without some form of compensation. He owed her and he paid his debts. "I'll return the favor when you need it."

"I know." Confidence had never been an issue for Adrianna.

"Who knows I'm here?"

"I told no one. I figured you wouldn't want anyone to know where you were since I doubt your guardian would have reached out to a Sterling witch if she'd had another option."

Adrianna made that valid point without any note of

insult in her voice, just stating the facts. Spirits of the light, such as Kai, generally did not interact with witches who dealt in the dark arts. He still had one pressing question. "Do you know what happened at Evalle's Tribunal trial?"

"They released her the next day."

His sore lungs relaxed, expelling the breath he'd been holding. So she was free. "She knows I'm alive, right?"

"I doubt it."

"You didn't tell her?"

"I took a leave from the agency. I've been *here* with you for three weeks."

Storm lifted his hand to hold his forehead. "You should have told Evalle. She'll be worried."

"Let's get this straight." Adrianna put a hand down on the bed when she leaned in close, smoldering blue eyes dark with warning. "I'm Switzerland when it comes to you, Evalle, VIPER and anything else. I have my own set of problems that I've put on hold while I played nurse. Your love life is the least of my concerns. Are we clear?"

Kai's warning to temper his words stopped him from snarling. He didn't see how hard it would've been to just call Evalle and ease her mind, but he wouldn't unload his frustration on Adrianna. "I understand. I appreciate what you've done—"

"I'm sure you do and I want you to remember that when I call in this marker."

Could she be as coldly calculating as she sounded when she'd spent three weeks caring for him?

His empathic senses roared back to life, detecting the

determination of a war strategist. She had a goal of some sort—one that mattered as much to her as his protecting Evalle from the South American witch doctor mattered to him. He was sure of it.

Speaking of Evalle, he asked, "Can you contact her for me?"

"I don't have a cell phone and I'm not about to go hunt down that Alterant."

"Not even to just let her know I'm alive?"

"I told you, I'm not getting involved. And I have *no* desire to be stuck explaining to Evalle why I'm the only one who knows how you're doing or where you've been for almost a month." Adrianna gave a wry chuckle. "Good luck with that."

"Evalle will understand."

"If you really believe that, you're not as bright as I gave you credit for."

The witch might have a point. Evalle did have a volatile temper when it came to Adrianna. Ridiculous really, since Evalle had no reason to suffer jealousy, but a wise man would avoid mentioning that Adrianna had been here with Storm all this time. That might work if not for his Ashaninka ability to detect a lie, which came with a counter side—he suffered serious pain if *he* lied.

A gift that Evalle knew all about.

He was too exhausted to think on that at the moment. He needed to focus on healing fast and regaining his strength so he could get out of this bed. Right now, he'd have a hard time lifting the bottle of water on his own. "I'll find her in a couple of days. What day is it anyhow?"

"Last Thursday in September. Think you'll be fully recovered that fast?"

No, but that wouldn't stop him from sucking it up enough to get behind the wheel of his SUV and track her down. "I'll manage."

"From what I hear, Evalle's not the only woman waiting for you to call her back, Casanova."

"What do you mean?"

"I hear there's a female with a Spanish accent asking around about you."

"What the—where'd you hear that?" He'd told no one, except Evalle, about the Ashaninka witch doctor, but she'd never say a word.

"From a Nightstalker. I heard about her while I was searching for intel for VIPER the week before you got hurt."

"You traded for information on her?" he asked. The old ghoul Nightstalkers could take ten minutes of human form if they shook hands with someone who possessed powers.

"No. The Nightstalker tried to cut a second deal for intel on a woman with *powers* from South America who was interested in a Skinwalker who could shift into a jaguar." Adrianna paused and looked straight at him. "I wasn't aware of any Skinwalkers . . . then."

Adrianna knowing about his jaguar form wasn't a problem, but Storm had kept that information from Sen.

Sen had brought him in as a tracker for VIPER, an agency that protected humans from supernatural threats, but Sen's real purpose had been for Storm to catch Evalle in a lie, to get her booted from the team or locked up. Storm had decided to help Evalle instead.

The question now was whether Sen knew the black jaguar he'd crushed against that brick wall was Storm. *Had he meant to kill me?* A bigger concern shoved forward.

If Sen found out about the witch doctor, he'd have the perfect anonymous weapon for getting rid of Evalle, permanently, and all he'd have to do was point the bitch in Evalle's direction.

And nobody—not even the Tribunal—would be able to prove that Sen had orchestrated the death of an innocent woman.

TWO

Evalle looked up from her menu, expecting to see the tall waitress with blunt-cut, purple hair and tattoos for sleeves . . . not a pissed-off Celtic goddess with the power to destroy everything in sight.

"Hello, Macha." Evalle mustered the calmest voice she could, considering how much trouble she might be in. Macha wanted information Evalle didn't have. Facts about Alterants like her . . . beings who were part Belador and part unknown.

As an ancient race who appeared human, Beladors shared unusual gifts such as kinetic and telepathic powers. Since they all belonged to Macha's pantheon, *they* weren't a concern. It was that *unknown* part of Evalle's blood that labeled her Alterant, an outcast among her own people. *That* bothered Macha.

The Goddess wanted to know what caused an otherwise human-appearing person to shift into a beast with exceptional powers, even beyond those of normal Beladors.

Well, human in appearance, except for glowing green eyes in Evalle's case. The dark sunglasses she wore day and night shielded that little oddity.

Macha arched a graceful, yet deadly, eyebrow at her. A cool September breeze ruffled the goddess's waist-length waves of auburn hair. Her gown shimmered with colors stolen from an aurora borealis. "I have allowed you three weeks."

Evalle had known this day was coming, but not so soon.

Something must have happened to instigate this unwelcome early visit.

She cast a quick glance around the upper deck of Six Feet Under, her favorite restaurant in downtown Atlanta. A few people had given Evalle's dark eyewear a second look when she'd walked in after sundown, but none of this late-Friday-night crowd seemed to notice the gorgeous, glowing female deity.

Macha must be cloaking her appearance and voice.

Think the humans would notice if Macha turned me into a ball of flames? Probably not. They'd just chalk it up to another unexplained incident of spontaneous combustion.

Evalle dug into her pocket for a Bluetooth earpiece she'd found in a parking lot. Clipping on the inactive communication device provided her the perfect cover for conversing with an invisible person. "I know you've been patient—"

Macha's glare returned full force. "What gave you the ridiculous idea that I'm patient? I had you freed from the Tribunal prison based upon your agreement to investigate, and *deliver*, the origin of Alterants. Have you forgotten?"

Let me think about this. No, I generally remember deals made with deities. Sarcasm would only get her toasted. Literally. Evalle explained, "I've been trying to—"

"I know that you have *not* accomplished, such as bringing Tristan in to swear loyalty to me and the

Beladors. You said *that* Alterant would provide significant details about your kind. Where is he?"

"I don't know . . . yet." The night Evalle agreed to the deal with Macha, Evalle had been facing imprisonment for the rest of her life, for crimes she had not committed. Who wouldn't jump to make a deal for freedom at that point? And she'd been sure Tristan would agree, since he and his sister were on the run from VIPER as escaped fugitives. But after three weeks of calling out to him telepathically Evalle hadn't heard so much as a whisper in response.

"Perhaps I was hasty in getting you released."

"No, you weren't." Evalle couldn't afford for Macha to change her mind and end Evalle's hope for true freedom. "The VIPER teams need every able body in Atlanta right now, which is why I haven't had time to hunt down Tristan. You told me I had to fulfill my Belador duties with VIPER. We've all been running constantly because of this outbreak of gang wars."

"Gang wars are a human problem." Macha waved a hand in dismissal at the mention. Belador warriors, who lived secretly among the human population, made up the bulk of VIPER assets. Her derisive tone left no doubt about where Evalle's other commitments fell on the goddess's list of concerns.

"Not this time," Evalle explained. "We've found trolls involved with the gangs." She checked to see if anyone observed her talking, but no one seemed to notice. People flowed around them the way water avoided a rock in a stream.

"Your first priority is your warrior queen when her safety is in question."

That snapped Evalle's attention back to Macha. "Has something happened to Brina?" As goddess of the Beladors, Macha's first concern was Brina, the last living Treoir. Belador powers depended on a living descendant residing on Treoir Island.

"The answer to that should be obvious since you're breathing."

Macha would never be known as the nurturing goddess.

Evalle asked, "But Brina's not under *immediate* threat, right?"

"You don't think so? As of now, you are still the only Alterant who has sworn fealty to me and the Beladors, in spite of the sanctuary I offered to all who will." Macha's tone sharpened, making it clear that she considered the lack of Alterants coming forward to be an insult. "Tristan and his group of *beasts* remain at large, not to mention any other Alterants we haven't located. With so many beasts *and* that traitor O'Meary unaccounted for, of course Brina is under immediate threat."

Evalle flinched at Alterants being called beasts. She hated that term almost as much as she hated the unknown blood that gave her the bright green eyes and the urge to change into a monster when threatened.

As for the Belador warrior queen, Brina should be safe in her warded castle on Treoir, hidden in a mist above the Irish Sea. But Evalle caught the shift in Macha's demeanor, the chill in her tone when she mentioned the Belador traitor, Conlan O'Meary. Evalle frowned. "I don't see how Alterants are connected to the traitor."

Macha's luminous hazel-green eyes turned to flint. Furious energy whipped across Evalle's skin, singeing fine hairs along her arms. "I'll speak slowly so I don't have to repeat myself. The traitor is working with the Medb Coven. *You* claimed the Medb intend to use Alterants to invade Treoir Island and attack Brina. Even you should be able to connect those dots without paper and pen."

Evalle wiped a damp palm on her jeans and bit back a retort. Three weeks ago, she'd been locked in a prison with no hope of escape because she couldn't bring herself to hand over other innocent Alterants and condemn them to the same fate. She owed Macha for her freedom and for giving her a chance to prove Alterants were not mindless animals and deserved to be a recognized race.

She also didn't want to be turned into a charcoal briquette. "I see your point and with a little more time—"

"Neither of us has the luxury of time, especially you. An Alterant has killed one of Dakkar's hunters. He filed a grievance with the Tribunal, demanding justice and compensation."

On a scale of bad news, that slammed the top. Dakkar ran a bounty-hunting operation that VIPER allowed to function as long as Dakkar executed the occasional contract for VIPER. But he could be wrong about fingering an Alterant for the killing since Rías were humans who also shifted to beast state, and the Rías she'd witnessed had slaughtered without thought.

Evalle asked, "Is Dakkar sure an Alterant killed his bounty hunter? Could have been a Rías. Their eyes—"

"Yes, yes, I had a report about Rías eyes appearing human in color instead of bright green like yours, but I doubt the dead bounty hunter was able to report the beast's eye color," Macha finished with dry sarcasm.

Evalle started to point out the differences didn't stop at eye color alone, because she could control her beast when shifted and so could Tristan. But she wasn't allowed to shift, and with the exception of two Rías that Tristan had trained, the other Rías she knew of *were* mindless beasts when they changed form, immediately mauling and killing any humans within reach. To some, all beasts looked alike.

Macha added, "Until you supply information to differentiate the two, a Rías is simply another version of an Alterant."

Evalle had no argument when she couldn't clearly establish the origin of her own kind. "So what happens now with Dakkar?"

"A hearing is scheduled for tomorrow to decide who is responsible to him for compensation and what Dakkar should receive. Deliver me Tristan and his information by the time I return from that meeting or I will withdraw my support for Alterants to become a recognized race."

The goddess disappeared in a flash of blue and pink light.

Evalle hadn't found Tristan in three weeks. What was the chance of finding him by tomorrow?

Even less chance if she didn't get something to eat soon. The smell of fried fish saturated the air and brought on another round of grumbling from her stomach. She lifted a hand to wave over the waitress and order something to go when she felt Belador power blast into her mind.

The telepathic voice of Tzader Burke, Maistir of the North American Belador warriors, yelled, *Calling in Beladors! Gang war going down in Oakland Cemetery.*

The upper deck of Six Feet Under overlooked Oakland Cemetery.

At Tzader's call to arms, Evalle threw cash on the table for her drink and hurried down the stairs, then took off running across Memorial Drive. All Beladors in the area would rush to aid their Maistir, but Tzader was her best friend. She ran hard to protect his back.

She called to Tzader, *I'm coming from across the street. Where're you, Z?*

East end. Potter's Field near Boulevard.

That narrowed down the forty-eight-acre landmark. Oakland was the seventh cemetery in the metropolitan area to be turned into a battleground this week.

Gangs had little respect for the living or the dead, but this level of hostility among so many at one time was unprecedented in Atlanta. Why all these throwdowns now?

And why were trolls all of a sudden infiltrating gangs?

Someone at VIPER had suggested this might be connected to the troll crimes that Belador teams had been investigating in Savannah. That some of those trolls had splintered off to create their own gangs here, but that still didn't explain why they were battling in cemeteries or why every attack involved members of multiple gangs. It didn't make sense.

She found a shadowy spot along the sidewalk where no humans could see her use kinetics. Bending her knees, she vaulted over the shoulder-high brick wall into six acres that had been part of the original cemetery established in 1850. Now she could tap into her Belador speed to cover the half-mile run through a moonless black night.

Tzader added, *This is bad. Must be seventy of them out here . . . something's not right.*

Like what?

There's— His voice cut off and withdrew from her mind as if sucked out.

She ran faster, ignoring the thump of worry pounding her chest at the sudden loss of connection.

She told herself that something had taken Tzader's attention, not his life. Darting between tall marble statues and elegant grave markers, she navigated through pitch dark easily with her natural night vision, which made the world look like daylight rendered in shades of blue-gray, even with sunglasses.

As she watched for any threat, she noticed the lack of normal spirit activity in the burial grounds. Not even an orb. That was just weird.

Her fingers curled, ready for a fight, but she couldn't use her powers, or her dagger that carried a death spell.

Not on humans.

Gunshots cracked the silence, sharp pops, then the *boom, boom, boom* of a higher-caliber weapon.

The acrid smell of blood clung to the wind.

Evalle slowed as she neared the battle. Racing in blind would risk distracting another Belador. Especially if any of them had linked their powers, which multiplied their strength. When linked, Beladors were a near-undefeatable force.

But kill one Belador while they were linked and they all died.

As some of the most powerful warriors among preternatural creatures, Beladors had sworn to defend humans who didn't even know they existed.

Evalle called to Tzader, *I'm here and opening up to link*.

His voice shouted telepathically to all Beladors in the cemetery. *Link now with Evalle to share her night vision.*

Eleven hits of power bombarded her from every direction.

She staggered against the initial linking, then found her footing and stepped into the open space where Beladors fought hand-to-hand with humans. Looked like a hundred in battle.

At least now the Beladors would have the advantage of seeing in the dark.

A twentyish male with facial tattoos of the Ice Blood Posse rocketed out of nowhere, slashing a wicked knife in a quick horizontal arc at her throat.

She bent backward as the blade tip passed below her chin.

The lack of contact threw her attacker off-balance.

Evalle spun forward, planting a foot for support, and kicked the ganger against an oak tree as big around as a fifty-gallon barrel.

His body slammed against the trunk, but he shook his head.

Not dead.

She'd promised Tzader she'd show restraint after putting a gang leader in traction yesterday . . . and that had been *without* tapping her Belador powers. That murdering bastard deserved death for killing a young girl he'd raped and beaten.

Too bad his punishment fell to the legal system or she'd have saved the taxpayers some money.

Shots were fired from her left.

With the cover of darkness, she risked shoving a field of energy up to stop the bullets as she turned toward the shooter. Fortunately, he was too far away to see the bullets bounce off the invisible wall of power. She couldn't use her kinetics to harm a human, but she could protect herself and others, especially if she didn't expose her unusual abilities.

She sent a mild wave of energy across the field, knocking the shooter backward off his feet. His weapon fell loose, then . . . flew up to rest in the nearest tree.

Imagine that.

Two wrestling bodies bumped into her.

She wheeled around, expecting to crack a couple more heads, when one of the men started changing. His head stretched in two hideous directions and his mouth widened, accommodating fangs.

This just turned way worse than a gang war.

She called out to Tzader, *We got a Rías shifting in the open area.*

Tzader called back, *Rías? Not an Alterant?*

Yep. No glowing green eyes. His are natural looking.

Get him away from the humans.

Then another voice came into her mind. *Evalle, Tristan here.*

Tristan called her *now?*

Before she could answer him, Tzader ordered, *Get the beast to chase you. Don't engage him until I tell you.*

Evalle? Tristan said louder in her head.

Power surged through her mind when Tzader started shouting orders telepathically to all the Beladors.

Evalle shook her fist at Tristan's sucky timing, but she had to wait for Tzader to finish before she could shield her mind to communicate with only one person. The safety of her fellow Beladors came first. Nine Beladors had died last year while linked when the Alterant they fought killed one of them. Which is one reason Evalle's freedom was threatened. Those in power questioned whether she might lose control and also harm humans or other beings.

Like the one shifting before her. Unlike the two Rías Tristan had trained, this one showed no signs of restraint.

Which meant it would eat the human it had by the arm.

She ripped the gang member from the beast's grasp and tossed the cursing human thug thirty feet away.

The Rías roared as he finished shifting.

As per Tzader's orders that were still flowing telepathically through her mind, she lifted her hand and slapped the beast with a mild kinetic blast to get his attention.

That worked, aggravating him.

He stumbled back a few feet, shaking his oversize

head, which had two holes for a nose and a mouth big enough to fit a human head in one bite. Fuzzy hair stuck up across his scalp in a Brillo-pad Mohawk. His forehead hung like a canopy over soulless eyes. Thick arms had ripped his multicolored shirt, and three fingers on each hand curled with sharp claws.

Evalle had to get him moving before the other humans saw him. She taunted the beast, "Come on, you ugly dog. You gonna let a woman kick your butt?"

Tzader's orders kept pouring through her mind as he directed the team, then he told her, *Evalle, once the Rías charges you, run toward that patch of trees on the west side of the field.*

Evalle glanced away just long enough to make a mental note of the distance. A good hundred yards away. *Be ready when I get there.*

We will.

Tzader and four Beladors would be waiting to capture this beast . . . unless they were forced to kill it.

The minute Tzader withdrew from her mind, Tristan's voice snapped at Evalle, *You want a tip on the traitor or not?*

The traitor? Could Tristan know where Conlan O'Meary was hiding? That would buy her all kinds of points with Macha.

About time she had some good luck. Keeping an eye on the Rías as the beast's vision cleared and he focused on her, Evalle called back to Tristan, *Where—*

A chain wrapped around her neck and tightened with inhuman power from behind.

The beast howled and rushed her.

THREE

Evalle shut her mind down to everything except surviving. She dug at the thick chain strangling her and focused kinetic energy into her fingers to keep the steel links from crushing her windpipe.

But in two seconds, the Rías in front of her would cut her to pieces with his claws if she didn't block the attack.

Pulling one hand off the chain, she slapped a short blast of energy at the beast.

The chain tightened. Yanked her neck.

Stars shot across her vision. She gagged for air.

But the beast charging her bounced sideways, rolling over the ground.

She stumbled, dragged backward by the bastard trying to kill her. Her vision blurred. She risked splitting her focus for a second to send a quick telepathic burst. *Tzader . . . help!*

No air. She was suffocating. Couldn't force enough energy through her fingers to pull the chain away.

Was the chain charmed? What had ahold of her?

Fighting to stay conscious, she lifted both hands over her shoulders and clapped kinetically at whatever held her from behind, which sure as heck wasn't a human.

Her attacker jerked from the hit of energy and stopped pulling her. His grip loosened.

Blood couldn't circulate fast enough. Her head still felt as if it would explode any minute. She sucked in a hoarse gulp of air before the chain leash towed her backward again. Shuffling quickly, she stayed on her feet.

She stomped her next two steps, releasing blades hidden in the soles of her boots, then shoved a boot straight back, connecting with bone.

Her attacker twisted the chain and growled an unearthly sound, similar to one she'd heard trolls make. Even with Tristan's distraction, no troll should have gotten the jump on her without her feeling his presence first. And she'd never battled a troll so unusually strong.

If every Belador weren't fighting more than one opponent, she'd draw hard on their link for maximum strength and break loose. But that worked best when everyone fought the same opponent and could coordinate their movements.

She wouldn't compromise another Belador's defense by draining power from them when she didn't know what the others faced right now.

The Rías beast in front of her had regained his footing. His body shook with fury when he came at her again.

She blinked at the blurry image and raised arms that trembled from her body shutting down. Defending herself would take her last bit of energy, and she'd still lose.

That left her only one thing she could do—protect her people and her best friend.

She dropped her mental shield briefly and called out

to the Beladors in the cemetery, *Everyone unlink from Evalle . . . now! I'm in mortal danger.*

No! Tzader shouted over her before she closed her mind again, prepared for the Rías to attack.

Her vision grayed. She couldn't think, barely able to focus on three razor-sharp claws whipping toward her throat.

A split second before the Rías made contact, its head exploded, blowing chunks of gross crap all over her.

Who had done that?

The debris from the head bomb must have hit the attacker behind her, who coughed and made spitting noises.

The chain around her neck went slack.

She sucked in a breath and felt unexpected Belador power flood her. Her vision sharpened in time to see Beladors converging on her from all directions. They were focused on her, sending her more energy, but the nearest warrior was over a hundred yards away.

She couldn't waste time waiting for them to get closer and squander the opening they'd given her to escape.

Gasping a deep breath, she gripped the chain, hunched forward quickly and dropped to her knees, jerking her attacker over the top of her body. He landed on his back, then leaped to his feet and turned on her as she stood. Everything from his buzzed black hair, pale skin and beefed-up body to the leather jacket and jeans looked human . . . until his glamour wavered.

All she needed for final confirmation that he wasn't human.

She fisted her hands and sent him a double punch of energy.

His head snapped back with the hit, but he shook it off.

What the…? Was he a troll or not? She'd never known one who could take an energy strike that hard and still stand.

He snarled with a grin, wide mouth stretching with teeth that sharpened to points as a little more of his glamour fell away right before he charged her.

Bad decision.

The last three weeks had sucked, and her frustration level had boiled over with Macha's visit. After holding back all week against human predators, Evalle wanted nothing more than to kick some nasty's butt right now.

She met the troll halfway, whipping her leg in a high arc with a boot aimed at his head.

But he surprised her by moving faster than she could believe, ducking his head, and locking his hands together, then swinging his arms across her body as he raced by.

The blow to her middle knocked her backward and off-balance. Her stomach wanted to heave inside out, but she spun, staying on her feet so he couldn't jump on her back and pin her to the ground.

A troll? Really? Who had trained this thing?

She pitched short, hard kinetic blasts at him that he dodged as she backed up.

The troll's glamour faded more, exposing a slick head

with dark-green-tinted skin cratered like bad acne on one side of his face.

Black and dark green tattoos covered the other half.

He walked toward her, but he had that chain in his hand again, whipping it around faster and faster until the links made a whining sound.

Tzader's voice came into her head. *Wait for—*

She shut her mind down to time her next move.

When the troll released the chain, she waited . . . waited . . . then bent backward at the waist, twisting to the side to avoid the chain as it spun inches above her face. The thick links slapped the ground behind her with a heavy *kathunk*.

The troll had used that only as a distraction.

He kept coming at her and got within two steps of reaching her with his mouth open to bite when she whipped her body from right to left, swiveling at her waist as if she intended to cartwheel away.

He adjusted, thinking she was running.

She didn't run from anyone.

Using the momentum, she scissor-kicked her legs. The blades in her boot soles sliced horizontally across the troll's forehead and beneath both eyes.

Landing on her feet, she swept around and punched the top of his head with her fist, knocking away the frontal lobe and half of his face. The air reeked with stink like a bad sewage drain.

The troll's mouth locked in a silent scream as he fell backward onto the ground.

Tzader ran up to her, yelling, "Are you okay?"

She rubbed her neck and squeezed words out of her raw throat. "Yeah. But is that thing a troll or not?"

He didn't look down at the body, just took a deep breath and shook his head. "You scare the hell out of me some days."

As if the night hadn't been full of enough surprises, her other closest friend, Vladimir Quinn, reached her next. She hadn't seen him in weeks. Two men couldn't look less alike than Tzader and Quinn. Tzader was an ebony Adonis sculpted of lethal edge and cut muscle that stretched his gray T-shirt at the chest, where fair-haired Quinn's deadly air had a certain elegance set off by a black cashmere sport coat and crisp slacks. Only Quinn could look pristine after a battle.

Russian by birth, Quinn spoke with a British accent gained through an Oxford education. Right now that accent held undisguised fear, clearly for her. "How badly did he hurt you, Evalle?"

"I'm good. My throat will be sore for a day or two, but he didn't crush my windpipe." She took in Quinn's narrow face, thinner now than when she'd last seen him. She hadn't seen or heard from him in three weeks, other than a brief e-mail right after her release from VIPER prison, saying he was glad she'd been freed. Tzader had told her only that Quinn had gone away to heal from a particularly bad mind lock he'd performed for an investigation.

Quinn let out a gush of air and ran his hand over his hair. "I had no idea this was going on or I'd have tried to return sooner."

"How long have you been back in town?"

"Just got in. I was on the way from the airport to my hotel when I heard Tzader's call to arms."

She wanted to ask him where he'd been and why he'd disappeared without letting her know before he left, but in her evil mood the questions would sound too much like interrogation.

Speaking of the reason she'd been in a foul mood for weeks, she hadn't heard a word from Storm *either*, not since she'd gotten a vague e-mail that same night Quinn had vanished.

And Tzader wondered why she'd been so pissed off for days?

Storm had partnered with her on several VIPER missions . . . and had stirred up her emotions. She harbored doubts about whether the blunt e-mail she *had* received from Storm had actually been from him.

Maybe sent from Storm's cell phone, but not typed by his hand. She couldn't think about him right now. Not without risk of exposing how every one of the past twenty-two days had been a challenge to get through without giving up hope of ever hearing from him again.

Evalle shoved those thoughts away so she could function. She had another question for Quinn—something that had haunted her since the last time she'd seen him—but *that* would have to wait until a better time, too.

More Beladors crowded around them. Devon Fortier's face popped up nearby. The Cajun was headquartered in Savannah, but Tzader had pulled in as many

Belador assets as possible to supplement VIPER teams in Atlanta when the gang wars erupted.

Devon whistled low and made an *mm-mm* sound. A female operative at VIPER once described his voice as a night wind sneaking through the backwoods of Louisiana. Devon wore his sun-streaked golden hair pulled taut in a ponytail, but a wavy strand had escaped and dangled over his forehead. The perpetual shadow on his cheeks and strong jaw gave him a devil-may-care appeal . . . for a woman who welcomed trouble.

He sent a sly look at Evalle and said, "Another Kincaid massacre. You've been on a tear this week."

"Hey!" She regretted trying to yell at him, swallowed and said, "I didn't do *all* of this." She *had* been taking her frustration out on a few gangers and trolls, but just like tonight's carnage, she'd only inflicted injuries as a result of self-defense. "Is everything under control? Any of ours hurt?"

Devon wiped sweat off the side of his face. "No, our people are good. We had the humans contained when Tzader sent us this way to set up an ambush for the Rías. Most of the gangers ran. I put some Cajun mojo on the others to keep them in La La Land until cleanup gets here to wipe their minds."

Not sure what power or majik Devon possessed, Evalle just nodded, glad the Beladors hadn't been injured while linked to her. "Who killed the Rías?"

"That would be me, my dear," Quinn admitted with a hint of disappointment in his voice. "None of us was going to reach you in time, so I . . ."

"Used your mind lock . . . and blew up his head?" she finished, hating that he'd had to use extreme force for her. Quinn had an unusual ability to mind lock with other beings, and could damage or destroy a mind, but he kept his power under a tight tether and had never before physically exploded a head that she knew of. Plus, he couldn't use deadly force through his mind lock unless he received prior approval or was under mortal threat himself.

"That's a graphic way of stating it," Quinn said. "But basically, yes. Tzader authorized the kill. I tried to stop the beast by taking control of his mind, but he didn't drop fast enough, so I used kinetics to assure he didn't touch you."

Tzader snorted. "Think I remember it more as an order than authorization."

Evalle cocked her head at Tzader. "Thought only Brina, or Macha, could give that approval."

Tzader shifted, lowering his voice. "With the threat hovering over Brina, Macha gave me clearance to give the order if I saw fit." Tzader and Quinn could be over-protective to the point of aggravating, but she appreciated them more than they'd ever know. They were the closest she'd ever come to having brothers, or any family.

She cast a quick glance at the dead Rías and winced. The beast had shifted back into a human form, so now she had to look at a headless, naked human body.

In the face of a threat, Quinn could kill an enemy without hesitation or remorse, but he still suffered when forced to destroy the mind of any living thing, even a dangerous beast. But he would do whatever it took to protect those he cared for, and that's what Evalle kept telling herself—he did care about her.

That's why she'd suffered this sick ball of guilt in the pit of her stomach for the past three weeks.

She hated the seed of doubt that Kizira—a Medb witch priestess Quinn had history with—had planted in Evalle's mind about him. How could she question one of her two best friends in the world?

Her heart knew better than to believe a lying Medb, the most dangerous enemy of the Beladors, but Kizira had produced evidence that Evalle couldn't easily dismiss.

With bodies scattered across the landscape, that conversation with Quinn would have to wait. She told him, "Thanks."

Tzader issued orders, pointing at several Beladors as he did. "You five form a perimeter around this area to keep any other humans from coming in while we wait on additional VIPER assets to arrive for cleanup." He turned to three more, nodding toward the battlefield. "Get a head count of humans and find out if any of them realized what was going on over here. We need ambulances for injuries."

Devon spoke up. "Hate to tell ya, but three humans did see the Rías shift and attack. Two of 'em passed out from shock. Third one pissed himself. I gave him a tap to put him to sleep. We've got those three pulled away from the other humans. Any chance that hot Sterling witch is nearby? She could help us out by altering the memories of a few minds."

"Adrianna's still on leave," Tzader answered. "Supposed to be back tomorrow."

Evalle just realized she hadn't seen the Sterling witch in the past three weeks either. *No loss in my world.* Men acted stupid when Adrianna showed up with her designer clothes, angel-face makeup and red pouty lips, especially now that her bobbed blond hair had grown halfway to her waist practically overnight.

I hope she stays on leave . . . finds a new profession . . . gets kidnapped by aliens . . .

Devon's gaze roamed over the bloody field that darkness thankfully shielded from any curious humans. "Guess that leaves us with calling in Sen."

Of course they'd have to call in Sen, the one person Evalle could go the rest of her life without ever seeing again. She kicked the dead troll. "Thanks." Not meaning it one bit. "This day just gets better all the time."

Her shove caused the troll's head to rock from one side to the other and his arm to slide off his chest. An odd burn scar on the inside of his forearm looked intentional, something like a gang insignia.

Tzader looked down, doing a double take on her lobotomy kill. "What the hell?"

She arched an eyebrow at Tzader. How did *he* get away with cursing? Brina hated foul language. Their warrior queen never left her castle except as a hologram, but she had the ability to reach out kinetically to touch someone if she chose and always seemed to know when a curse slipped out of Evalle's mouth.

"Bloody hell," Quinn muttered.

What was so awful for Mr. Proper to curse, too?

Then Devon jumped in. "That's bad."

She didn't see what they were making a big deal out of. Okay, the top third of the thing's head *was* missing.

Looking from Quinn to Tzader, Evalle said, "What? I know he'll be hard to identify without all of his head, but that couldn't be avoided. And those tats on his face have to mean something."

"They do," Devon confirmed, sighing. "So does that runic *S* burned into his arm. Identifying him isn't the problem."

"If you know who he is, what's the issue?" she asked.

Tzader ran a hand over his bald head, wiping sweat off. "That's not just any troll. It's a Svart troll."

Evalle searched her mind for what she knew of them. "Aren't they some European-based bunch?"

Quinn answered, "Svarts are a black-ops type of mercenary troll who originated in Switzerland. They are the most deadly trolls on earth and hire out to the highest offers. It would require a significant player to even gain their attention."

She'd heard snippets about Svarts, but only trolls with death wishes would tangle with VIPER. Evalle thought out loud, "Who has the kind of jack it would take to send them up against a coalition like VIPER, and why would a Svart troll incur the wrath of the coalition? Atlanta is one of the most powerful VIPER hubs in the world."

Quinn gave her a disheartening smile. "Contracts in our world aren't necessarily about money. Power is far more highly valued than coin. And Svarts don't accept just *any* offer. They choose their contracts judiciously, based upon how powerful their benefactor is and how well they expect to benefit from a successful mission."

She asked, "What kind of extra benefit? Like a bonus?"

"No." Quinn thought for a moment. "Whoever did this is unconcerned about poking around in an area protected by VIPER and the Beladors. I caught up on Belador alerts while on my flight or I wouldn't have understood Tzader's call to arms for a gang battle. All this gang and troll activity makes me wonder if Svarts have been involved all along. If so, those behind the Svart contract would seem to be intentionally engaging VIPER, and quite possibly the Beladors, which means we have a far deadlier problem than just gang battles. We're facing an enemy who wants something they're willing to risk everything for . . . even war."

An icy chill swept over Evalle as she realized what could be brewing. Her gaze dropped to the dead Svart troll. She'd killed their best lead.

Their only lead.

Just wasn't her day. First Macha and now this.

Macha. Conlan. Tristan.

She'd locked Tristan out of her mind, so there went her lead on the traitor, too. She sent out a telepathic call. *Tristan, you there?*

Not a word in return.

FOUR

Evalle rubbed her aching neck, feeling bone-deep tired now that the Beladors had unlinked.

Where could Tristan be?

Was he screwing with her because she hadn't answered?

Overhead lights flashed on, offering bright pockets in the pitch-dark cemetery. With the Beladors unlinked from her, no one else could see without a night-vision setup.

Tzader had just finished sending everyone off in different directions except her, Quinn and Devon when Horace Keefer, a Belador who looked old enough to be retired, showed up.

Horace pulled off his faded blue baseball cap and scratched his grizzled hair before putting the cap back on. His overalls were a bit frayed, but clean. Given his short stature and fuzzy gray beard, Evalle could see him as a leprechaun in a past life, a far more benign 'chaun than the ones VIPER often encountered.

Shaking his head at everything he saw, Horace said, "Ho, boy, this is a mess. Got your call and showed up soon as I could. Where you need me?"

Tzader gave the old guy an understanding smile. "The fighting's all done, but we can use a hand with cleanup."

Always one to jump in and help with anything,

Horace nodded. "I'm on it." He started to walk off and paused, looking down. "What kind of troll is that?"

Evalle said, "A Svart."

"Do tell." Horace shook his head. "Never expected to see one of those, alive or dead. Where's the other one?"

Tzader, Quinn and Evalle exchanged looks, then turned to Devon, who had been working the troll investigations in Savannah for a while.

Devon asked Horace, "What other one?"

The old guy cracked his knuckles during the few seconds it took him to answer. "Don't know, but I heard once that they like to work in no less than teams of two, and most times teams of four."

Nodding as he digested that information, Devon said to Tzader, "I'll put some feelers out when we're through here."

"Do that."

Horace strolled off whistling, always happy.

Evalle envied someone so at peace with life.

Quinn eyed the dead Svart again, shaking his head. "We're lucky to still have you with us, Evalle. Few people live through a Svart attack to talk about it."

That made her feel a little better about giving a lobotomy to their best shot at intel.

"What you talkin' 'bout, Quinn?" Devon could sound as if he'd just walked out of a Louisiana swamp when he didn't want someone to know he'd gone to Tulane University on an academic scholarship. "That Svart didn't have no chance with Evalle goin' through EMS."

She crossed her arms and shifted her feet apart.

"Think you mean *PMS*, and if *I* suffered from that, the body count would be much higher, starting with a smart-mouth Cajun."

Devon chuckled. "Nope, I mean *EMS*. You think about it, you'll figure it out." He strolled off.

When she looked around, she caught Quinn's glance at Tzader, then Quinn's lips twitched as he fought a smile. Based on the knowing glint in Tzader's eyes, he understood Devon's meaning and had just shared it with Quinn.

She growled at them, "What's he talking about?"

Tzader backed away, dismissing himself from the conversation by saying, "Have to call Sen."

"Hope you get a busy signal," Evalle quipped even though Tzader meant a telepathic call.

Quinn muttered something like "Thanks, Z," when he clearly didn't appreciate being left to explain. He cleared his throat and told Evalle, "I believe *EMS*, my dear, is 'Evalle missing Storm.'"

Her skin flushed embarrassingly hot all the way to her ears. She took a step in the direction of Devon, promising, "We're not through tallying the body count."

Quinn put an arm out, stopping her. "If you say a word to Devon now, you'll only confirm his guess. As I understand from Tzader, you've been inquiring as to whether anyone has seen or heard from Storm. Most of the teams will think it's because he was your partner, but a few sharper ones will suspect a more personal interest."

"*Is.*"

"Pardon?"

"*Is* my partner." Evalle refused to believe Storm hadn't survived Sen's kinetic power blast that drove his body against an unyielding wall. But had Sen known the identity of the black jaguar he'd tried to kill? She thought so, even though Storm had said he'd told no one at VIPER that he was part Ashaninka Skinwalker. He'd shifted into his animal form only to help her locate Tristan for a Tribunal hearing to decide her fate.

Then she'd allowed Tristan and his group to walk away. She'd had no choice when she'd ended up standing between Tristan and a human black-ops team determined to rid the world of Alterants.

That decision had almost gotten her killed, then it *had* landed her in a VIPER jail cell.

By the time Evalle had returned home, Storm had disappeared without a hint as to where he'd gone beyond the e-mail she'd received that same night sent from his cell phone, which read:

> *Evalle,*
> *I'll be in touch.*
> *Storm*

That might have been comforting except for one problem. Storm had left his phone in her motorcycle tank bag when he'd shifted into a jaguar. When she'd returned from lockup to retrieve her Suzuki GSX-R motorcycle, everything was there *except* his phone. Until then, no one had ever been able to steal her Gixxer or take anything she'd stowed on it because of a warding that protected her bike. She didn't think Storm had the ability. Who had gotten past the warding? She'd also searched for the clothes Storm had hidden in bushes near the Decatur MARTA subway station.

They were gone, and so was his broken body.

Her soul refused to accept the obvious, the logical, that if he was alive, he'd have contacted her by now. The only other possibility was that he *had* survived and just hadn't gotten in touch.

He wouldn't do that to her.

Quinn broke into her thoughts when he said, "Of course, Storm is *still* your partner. Forgive me for speaking in past tense." He studied her with wise eyes that knew a lot more about relationships between men and women than she did. "And you *are* fond of Storm."

He hadn't asked, only stated that he clearly understood that she had feelings for Storm. True, but what she felt for Storm was complicated, tangled with damaged emotions she waded through every time they were together.

Storm took her flaws in stride and read her too easily at times.

She hadn't realized how much she'd miss him if he went away, until now.

Every day became more unbearable.

Quinn waited silently. He deserved an honest reply, but she wasn't up to sharing something she didn't completely understand, so she said, "I'd just like to know why Storm left and if he plans to return."

"I see." A noncommittal Quinn comment.

Time to change the subject. Her heart hurt too much

to keep talking about Storm. "Thank you for stopping that Rías from killing me, but I'm sorry you had to use your powers that way."

Quinn waved it off as though he blew up heads every day, which he didn't. Just being his usual noble self.

"And," she continued, "sorry I killed our best lead in figuring all this out. You could have read the Svart troll's mind and gotten intel, couldn't you?"

"I'm glad you saved yourself. That was more important than all the intel in the world."

Always thinking of others. This was the Quinn she knew.

The ball of guilt inside her expanded a little more and threatened to choke her. Should she ask him now about what that witch Kizira had said and get it off her chest? Her palms were damp with indecision, but it would have to wait. "You still didn't answer my question about reading the troll's mind."

Quinn shrugged, the movement as refined as his impeccable clothes. "I might have found out something from this Svart, but they are highly trained to prevent being broken during interrogation, and taught to fight to the death. He may have had an iron-tight mind, or there could have been a trap waiting to attack the mind of someone who probed him."

In other words, the Svart might have raped Quinn's mind in return.

In that case, she should be thankful she killed the Svart, because even with the risk of danger to himself, Quinn would have tried to retrieve information.

"None of this makes sense. I thought trolls were more interested in stealing bling than fighting. The ones I've met are generally pretty simple creatures and kill only for food. Think this Svart could have been working with the local trolls we've found in these attacks?"

"Not exactly. Based upon what I read in the briefings about the interrogations, I think the Svart have brainwashed some of the local trolls, who seem to know very little beyond a compulsive urge to fight with gangs in cemeteries."

That would explain the local trolls being in the gang battles, but not the reason for the constant fighting. Evalle brought up the only connection she could see. "Why cemeteries?"

"That's a good question. Perhaps everyone has focused too much on the gang element and *not* the locations." Supporting his elbow with one hand, Quinn tapped his chin as he scanned the activity around them. His gaze settled on Evalle. "Why was the Svart in this particular cemetery and why did he attack you?"

"Have no idea. Maybe I was closest." She ran through recent similar battles in her mind. "This cemetery is larger than the others. Oakland is older and downtown . . . more ghosts . . . history. Who knows?" Swallowing still hurt Evalle's throat. She cupped her neck, glad for chain burn and some bruising as the worst of her injuries, and looked again at the headless human. "Wait. There is one difference here. This *was* the first battle where a Rías shifted."

"Ahh," Quinn said, picking up her train of thought. "Who showed up first? The Rías or the troll?"

"The Rías started shifting, then I taunted him with kinetic hits to draw him away from humans. That's when the chain wrapped around my neck."

"Perhaps the Svart attacked you to stop you from harming the Rías."

"Why would he do that?" She stared at the body of the poor headless guy. He'd probably had no idea he was part beast.

"Perhaps the Svart was searching cemeteries for the Rías."

Could that be? What would a troll want with a Rías when none had even existed—that VIPER knew of—until three weeks ago? Humans had shifted into beasts in a major Rías outbreak, just everyday citizens who'd been clueless that something in their DNA could be triggered by hostility . . . not just any hostility, but a sentient haze filled with supernatural malevolence that had swept across the city.

She snapped her fingers. "The outbreaks three weeks ago happened *after* those predisposed to be Rías entered the fog created by the Medb. That unnatural hostility triggered the Rías to start shifting and attack. This time we had one shift around *us*. Belador power, used in a hostile situation, might have caused it. Maybe the trolls are behind the gang battles—drawing in Belador power to push the Rías to shift."

"But why in cemeteries?"

"I don't know . . . but this guy doesn't have any gang

tats, so maybe he was here by accident or—" A flash of light and a power burst behind her interrupted Evalle's brainstorming.

Quinn muttered, "It appears Sen has arrived."

Oh, joy. She turned as six-feet-seven-inches of perpetual anger stomped up to where she and Quinn stood. Tzader stepped up to join them.

Sen's straight black hair hung down his back in a queue and somewhere along his family lines he'd picked up slanted blue eyes that seemed out of place in his square face. He always had the same type of clothes—dark T-shirt, black jeans and sometimes a jacket or vest.

No one knew much about Sen beyond his being a royal pain in the butt. He served as liaison between VIPER agents and the Tribunal, which ruled the Coalition and also played judge and jury for Coalition members when necessary. Within that capacity, Sen displayed power at times that seemed almost god-level. But Evalle couldn't see a god getting stuck overseeing VIPER, and Sen made it clear to everyone that he had not taken this position by choice.

Who had pushed Sen into a job he didn't want?

Maybe the better question would be why?

Sen glared at the remnants of the battle, then zeroed in on Evalle. "Of all the gang battles in the past month, I constantly have to wipe human minds and dispose of the nonhumans *only* at the ones where you're involved, Alterant. Why is that?"

Ending his phone call, Tzader crossed his arms and angled his body so he stood between Sen and Evalle.

"Got an issue with anything here, or one of my Beladors, take it up with me."

Evalle kept silent for once, rather than spouting off at Sen and making things worse. And right now he couldn't touch her or he'd cross Macha.

But Macha had just drawn a line.

In less than two days, Evalle's protection would be over. Unless she found—and delivered—Tristan before then.

Sen gave Evalle a look that promised the day her deal with Macha fell apart that he'd be waiting for her.

Turning to Tzader, Sen said, "Better find a way to stop these battles soon or the Tribunal may start wondering at the coincidence of an explosion of gang attacks that started *after* the Alterant was turned loose." He lifted a hand over the Svart troll, asking, "Finished with this one?"

Tzader indicated yes.

Sen pointed a finger at the dead troll. The body vanished, then Sen headed off to wipe memories of unconscious or injured humans. Beladors working inside human law enforcement would deal with the poor headless dead guy.

Once Sen moved a good distance away, Quinn spoke softly to Tzader and Evalle. "We need to meet . . . and talk."

Evalle jerked her attention back from Sen. That sounded like Quinn had something important to discuss. Could it be about Kizira? Having Quinn broach the subject first would be a relief, especially if he denied having given Kizira any information on Evalle. "Sure. When do you want to meet?"

"As soon as we leave here," Quinn suggested.

Tzader shook his head. "Brina wants to see me, then I have to brief everyone at VIPER headquarters." He paused, sorting through something in his mind. "Let's meet around midnight."

"If that's the soonest," Quinn said, his face closed down.

Whatever he wanted to discuss obviously bothered him.

We have that in common.

Tzader's phone buzzed, pulling him away again while he answered.

She'd rather talk to Quinn sooner than later, like right after they left here. Before she could suggest she and Quinn grab something to eat, a voice came into her mind.

Evalle, this is your last chance to answer me.

Tristan? She almost shouted his name, but quietly answered, *I'm here. Where are you?*

I'll tell you where to meet me, but if you tell anyone I've contacted you, I'll find out about it and not show.

I won't tell anyone. But how would Tristan know? Until she could answer that question, she'd keep this to herself.

Meet me at the Iron Casket in one hour.

She looked at her watch. That would make it just before eleven, but she didn't have far to go. *I'll be there. Do not leave for any reason, Tristan.*

Don't give me a reason. Then he disappeared from her mind.

She had to get moving. And she *had* to eat. There'd been no time for food, thanks to Macha. With any luck, she'd get to the Iron Casket early and grab a bite while she waited on Tristan, but first she needed to clean the ick off of her from the exploding Rías.

When Tzader finished his call, he said, "Going to be a little later than midnight, more like one. Let's meet at—"

"How about my room at the Ritz downtown," Quinn interjected, giving his room number. "That will allow us adequate privacy."

Tzader's gaze eased from Quinn to Evalle. "Good by me."

Evalle hated putting off talking to Quinn, but with Tristan waiting, she didn't have time right now. "I'll be there by one."

She hoped. Tristan could be slippery and she didn't plan to lose track of him this time. She started picking body goo off her shirt. "Z, you got enough people here for cleanup?"

"Plenty."

"I've got an errand to run."

"Anything I should know about?"

"Nothing I can talk about." She cringed at how that sounded. When Tzader didn't respond, she knew he expected her to expound. "I was talking to Macha right before you called me in."

"Oh?"

She didn't meet his eyes, but she could feel them bearing down on her. Few Beladors spoke *directly* to Macha, Tzader being one of those. Evalle didn't particularly like being in that group, but neither did she have a choice. "I have to do something for her."

When the silence that followed hung too long, Evalle looked up to find Tzader frowning. She held her hands out in a motion of asking him to understand. "You know I'd tell you if I could."

"I know that. I also know how Macha is. Be careful."

"I will, and don't worry if I run a little late." Evalle gave Quinn a smile she had a feeling looked as forced as it felt, but she'd been through a lot with him, and with Tzader. She wouldn't believe that Quinn had betrayed her based solely on the words of a Medb witch. "See you later."

Quinn nodded, too quiet and reserved, even for him.

Time to finally deal with Tristan.

After hiking back down Memorial Drive, Evalle found a water spigot behind a string of restaurants in the block that included Six Feet Under. She cleaned up the best she could, happy not to smell so nasty even if her clothes and hair were now damp. The chilly air felt refreshing on her skin, especially after all that clammy death.

She left her shoulder-length hair loose to dry while she covered the next couple blocks. She found her motorcycle parked where she'd left it on a side street, lit only by a single overhead security light.

Shadows moved and murmured in her wake.

Nightstalkers probably. Ghouls who had once been homeless people before they'd died in natural disasters.

None were trying to get her attention tonight. They just hovered nearby. But when she reached her motorcycle, she felt energy moving toward her. Something nonhuman lurked a few feet away.

Turning, she waited for a Nightstalker to glimmer into view and ask for a deal. But what emerged from the shadows was no ghoul.

Storm was alive.

FIVE

Storm ignored the residual pain lingering in his body and stood with his feet apart, prepared to deal with an angry Alterant.

But seeing Evalle again could heal a dying man . . . which he'd been up until yesterday.

As usual, dark sunglasses protected Evalle's sensitive, glowing-green eyes, but nothing could shield her emotions from him. Like now, when he sensed her turmoil, with no way to ease her anxiety. Not yet.

The first time he'd set eyes on her during a meeting at VIPER, he'd caught her silent distress. Thinking only to help, he'd reached out with gifts bestowed by his tribal ancestors to soothe her . . . and had gotten a biting earful later for his efforts.

She was harder to get close to than a pissed-off hornet, but in those rare moments when he had her in his arms, no other woman equaled her.

"Storm?" she asked tentatively, still standing near her bike. "Where have you been?"

Emotions boiled off of her, slamming him with a chaotic rush of thrill, worry and frustration.

He waited as a noisy beater car passed, leaving the side street silent again in the wake of loud music muffled by the rolled-up windows. Striding forward a few slow steps, he paused close enough to reach out and touch her, but he waited, watching for any signs of hesitation on her part.

Or that she'd attack.

She'd been hurt at some time in her past, physically as well as emotionally, and would strike out like a wounded animal when caught off guard. "I've been healing."

"I see."

Worse than angry. She sounded hurt. His empathic gift picked up on the swell and ache of that emotion.

He had plenty to tell her, but he needed her to hear something first before he shared all the details about what had happened. One thought kept jamming his brain, pushing its way to his lips. "I missed you."

She stood there, racked with indecision for several seconds, then gave him a watery smile and lunged into his arms. "I missed you, too."

He caught her, hugging her to him, surprised at how his body trembled at the feel of her close again.

His definition of heaven.

One he fought guilt over enjoying since she didn't know he had no soul. Back in South America, those who knew his history had called him a demon. What others thought hadn't mattered . . . until he'd met Evalle.

Now he had every intention of fixing that problem.

Just as soon as he got his hands on that witch doctor who'd stolen his soul.

When Evalle lifted her head to look at him, he kissed the mouth he'd dreamed about during his fevered days. Her lips were soft and yielding, then demanding. All woman with a passionate side that kept him on his toes, whether she was kicking someone's butt or allowing him a rare embrace. He'd never call Evalle a tease. She didn't know how to play those games. Like right now. She kissed without restraint.

Her emotions sometimes overwhelmed her.

He overwhelmed her.

If she ever got past her fear of intimacy, one he suspected was caused by prior abuse, the sex with her would be phenomenal. He had no doubt.

But for now, he'd take having her in his arms.

Her heart thumped like wild jungle drums against his chest and she clutched his back.

She might not realize how big a step this was for her to come to him so openly, but he did.

When their lips finally parted, he dropped his forehead down on hers. "I've been worried about you."

She pulled back and brought her hands around to grip each side of his open-collared shirt. "Me? Why didn't you call or e-mail me again?"

"Again?" He covered her fingers with his and she let go of his shirt, yet allowed him to hold her hand. Nice.

"I *knew* that wasn't from you," she muttered, staring at his chest, thinking.

"I'm not following anything you're saying." He lifted one of her hands and kissed her knuckles, bringing a flash of surprise to her eyes, which twinkled with undisguised happiness.

She smiled. Such a simple thing, but her smiles were gifts to be cherished. He brushed his fingers over the damp hair that fell loose around her shoulders, but the weather had been dry and cool all day. "Why are you wet?"

Looking down at herself, she said, "What?" She had a thing for vintage clothes and wore a short-sleeved, beige army BDU—battle dress uniform—shirt with jeans and boots. "Oh. We just had another gang battle. This one was in Oakland Cemetery. I had to clean off . . . stuff."

"What gang battles?"

"Where have you been, Storm?" She lowered her hand from his and moved back, opening up space between them. Her face suffused with concern and confusion. With the change in subject and reminder that he'd been out of touch for three weeks, she withdrew emotionally.

He tried not to flinch at the abrupt change in her emotions, the loss of her warmth and happiness so near.

He should be glad for the uninhibited welcome he'd received and not expect more, but he wanted her body back against his. "I told you, I've been healing. I've only been conscious twenty-four hours."

"Why didn't you call me?"

"I don't have a phone yet. That's why I came to see you in person." And his guardian spirit had been none too happy about Storm going out while still recovering, but he had to know for sure that the danger that stalked him and now threatened Evalle had not harmed her.

He didn't know why the witch doctor would target Evalle, only that she did.

Now that the crazy bitch had tracked him to Atlanta,

had she discovered that he cared for Evalle and planned to use that against him?

If that were the case, why hadn't the witch doctor shown her face by now?

Didn't matter. He planned to find her first.

Evalle asked, "Have you been in a hospital?"

"No." He'd just as soon not discuss his healing any more than he had to, like explaining who had been tending to his wounds. Going back to Evalle's earlier comment, he asked, "What did you mean by my e-mailing you *again*?"

"The e-mail I got from you the night they let me out of VIPER prison."

"So they *did* lock you up?"

"Yes."

Storm had tried to tell her Tristan would screw her over. "Why didn't you tell Sen where Tristan and his bunch of renegade Alterants went? He could have caught them."

"Only Tristan and his sister are Alterants," she corrected. "The other two are Rías. I couldn't hand them over to win my freedom."

A growl climbed up Storm's throat.

Evalle moved her shoulders in a dismissive way. "And do you really think sending Sen after Tristan would have mattered? The last thing Sen would do is something to keep me *out* of prison. He was thrilled when I had to face the Tribunal empty-handed."

If Storm had been conscious, he'd have gone crazy trying to find Evalle when she was locked away. Blood would have flowed. "How'd you get out of prison?"

"Macha offered me a deal that she'd petition the Tribunal for Alterants to be a recognized race—"

"That's great."

"—if I can deliver evidence to support our origins and bring in Alterants to swear loyalty to Macha, specifically Tristan."

"You've got to be kidding."

"I wish I was." Evalle swallowed and winced, which drew his eyes to her neck.

"What the hell happened to your throat?" He lifted his finger to her raw skin. That move drew him close to her again, so close he'd have to be a stone to miss the flutter of excitement that sheared off of her.

His ego enjoyed the momentary stroke.

She waved a hand at her throat. "A Svart troll jumped me tonight and wrapped a chain around my neck."

The jaguar inside Storm woke and pushed at his skin, wanting to kill whatever had hurt this woman. He'd never before had the animal who shared his body notice a woman this way, not after what the witch doctor had done to him and his father. But his jaguar shared Storm's protective urge when it came to Evalle.

He ran his fingers gently over the skin on her neck and she shivered. "Did you kill the bastard?"

"Yes."

"Good." Though he'd have liked to hunt and dismember that troll himself. "What's a Svart?"

"Some kind of black-ops mercenary troll."

"You get extra points for killing those, like in a game?"

She laughed at his teasing and the sound woke his

heart with a jolt. Shoving a handful of hair over her shoulder, she said, "No, just extra bruises."

With her soft and pliable again, he wanted one more kiss. He lowered his head, touching his lips to hers and smiling over the way she leaned into the kiss and let him bunch her into his arms.

Another small step forward.

She made a throaty sound and the world disappeared around him. One day, he'd have all of her. But not right now on a public sidewalk. He slowed the embrace, kissing her lips lightly once more.

This time when she put her hands on his chest and pushed away, she did so reluctantly and with a smirk. "Enough distracting me."

"Oh, that's just a brief interruption. I would need a far more private place to fully distract you."

Her eyes flared with awareness.

She wasn't backing up and snapping at him, so he went fishing for more. "Speaking of which, it seems like you agreed to have dinner with me for helping you with Tristan."

She stabbed a hand at each of her hips, then quirked a saucy eyebrow at him. "I don't think *that* was the deal."

"I remember dinner being in there somewhere, but we can talk about it later." He'd planted the idea. "Back to this e-mail. I had no way to send one after Sen tried to kill me."

A flash of worry swirled around her when he mentioned his near-death. Storm indulged in a moment of pleasure. He'd spent a lot of the last twenty-four hours concerned over the reception he'd get after not being in touch for almost a month.

She had a grim set to her mouth. "So you didn't get your phone out of my tank bag."

"No. Thought your bike was warded."

She shook her head. "It is, at least against *most* beings, which means someone powerful got past it."

"Was anything else missing?"

"No. I looked for the clothes you left near the MARTA station, but they were gone . . . and so were you. What happened?"

I came close to spending my eternal life wandering in the hellish half-world where my father is stuck because we don't have our souls. But he couldn't share that yet with Evalle, a woman who spent her nights hunting demons and other powerful dark beings. At one time he'd thought if he told her the truth about having no soul, she'd see him only as a dangerous demon to protect humans against, but now he worried that she'd take it on herself to hunt the witch doctor. She might be terrified of intimacy, but she was fearless in battle.

Evalle waited silently. She deserved as much truth as he could share.

He hooked his thumbs in his jean pockets and tried to explain something most people would have a hard time comprehending without the benefit of his upbringing. But Evalle dealt with strange every day.

"You know I'm Ashaninka and Navajo. I have a guardian spirit from my Navajo side who watches over me—"

"Like Grady?"

"No, your Nightstalker friend is a soul that is stuck in this realm. A guardian spirit is one who chooses to watch over us. Some are passed down from family to family. Mine came to me when my father died."

"Is yours a man or a woman?"

"Woman. Her name is Kai, which means 'willow tree' in Navajo. We hold the willow tree in high regard."

"How *old* is she?"

Storm hid a smile at Evalle's suspicious tone, confirming that he would be wise to keep the details of his recovery to a minimum. "She was in her late thirties when she died and has been a guardian for many people over something like twelve hundred years."

"Oh, okay. So what did she do?"

"She watched over me while I was unconscious—" He stopped short of saying his guardian had located a human to help him.

Evalle chewed on one side of her lower lip. "I don't understand. Did Kai teleport you somewhere safe?"

"She can't do that. She cloaked and shielded my body with a field of protective energy—what you might call a smoke screen, but the smoke was invisible."

"Then what? Did this Kai save you with majik?"

"No, she can't do that either. But I'm healed now. About that e-mail from my cell phone—"

Evalle had that stubborn look, the one she got when she would not let go of a topic. "If she can't save you from dying, then what *did* your guardian spirit do that kept you alive?"

He could probably tolerate the low level of pain that

came with skewing the truth some, but not an outright lie. Leave it to Evalle to ask a question that left him no way to give anything except a straight answer. "Kai found a human who could help me."

Evalle clammed up, staring at him for a long time before she asked, "How did she know which human?"

Any attempt at maneuvering around her questions would only guarantee a worse reaction once she knew everything. "While I lay dying, I went to her in spirit form and told her I needed help and who she could trust not to kill me while I was vulnerable."

Disappointment in Evalle's eyes sank his heart.

Storm hurried to reassure her. "I sent her to you first, but she told me later that your spirit had been blocked from her."

Her face relaxed at that news. "No, you're right. I must have been in the VIPER holding cell under the mountain where no one could reach me. Who *did* help you?"

He debated on his answer, sure that the edge of anxiety wafting off Evalle now would only turn into roaring anger. "I want you to understand—"

"Just spit it out, Storm," she said, not a lick of patience in her words.

"Adrianna."

Realization hit Evalle first, followed close behind by fury. "You told your guardian to fetch that *Sterling witch*?"

He waited for the second part to hit Evalle, whose brilliant mind would process it right about now . . .

"And you spent *three weeks* with Adrianna? Alone?"

SIX

Evalle curled the fingers on one hand, seething.

The whole time she'd been sick with worry over Storm, he'd been with that Sterling witch.

Adrianna. A witch who practiced dark arts, oozed sexuality with every move, and had a voice like an erotic kitten.

She'd spent weeks with Storm. Alone.

And hadn't said a word to Evalle.

That . . . *witch!*

Tall and foreboding, Storm stood quiet as a night sentinel watching Evalle, and obviously waiting on the tempest to roll in. But he didn't run from it.

She refused to let him know how much it hurt to find out the whole time she'd been trying to convince herself he wasn't dead that Adrianna had been nursing him back to health.

Nursing all parts of his body.

"Evalle."

She answered him with a glare.

"Why are you angry?"

"I'm not."

Storm raised one eyebrow. That's right. She'd just tried to lie to a walking lie detector. She couldn't help it. Her heart burst with crazy relief that he was safe and still alive, but hearing about Adrianna felt like having a baseball bat slammed into her chest. And her heart. It blindsided her.

She'd never been in a relationship before—wasn't even sure she was in one now. What determined if you were in a relationship or not? She didn't know and was floundering trying to decide if she had any right to be hurt.

Maybe this wasn't *that* kind of relationship.

Not if Storm trusted Adrianna as much as he trusted her, because in the past he'd called Adrianna only a friend.

Storm sighed, a deep, husky sound. "There is nothing going on between me and Adrianna."

"Really? But she's on the short go-to list for your spirit emergency line?"

"She was the only person I could trust, other than *you*, who would not tell VIPER about me. I'm not ready for anyone to know I'm alive until I find out if Sen knew I was the jaguar he tried to kill."

Evalle considered not sharing her thoughts, but that smacked of pouting. "I'm pretty sure he knew it was you."

"Why do you say that?"

"Because . . ." She struggled to hold her emotions in tight, but Storm needed to know the truth. "Sen held me in limbo long enough for me to see you bleeding and that you weren't breathing before he teleported me to the Tribunal meeting that night."

Storm covered his eyes with his hand. "So you thought for sure that I'd died?"

"Yes . . . at first. But I refused to believe it."

He dropped his hand, eyes full of warmth after her admission. "I'm sorry he put you through that. I had no way to reach you until today or I would have."

"What about the Barbie Witch? Adrianna could have called or you could have used her phone."

His laugh sounded cynical. "She made it very clear that she agreed to help my guardian spirit, but she was not getting involved when it came to me, you and VIPER. She has her own issues and didn't go into them. She had no phone, but now I think that's probably a good thing. It would have been risky to call you since someone could have been listening in."

"Why would someone do that?"

"Why would someone send you a bogus e-mail from me?"

He had a point. And who *had* sent that e-mail?

She needed time to process everything, including the part about Adrianna. On the one hand, Evalle didn't care what it had taken to keep Storm alive and offered another silent thanks that he stood here before her. But on the other hand, she suffered bitter disappointment over another woman caring for him. Call it foolish, petty, whatever, that didn't change the hurt tunneling through her chest right now.

Storm tilted his head a tiny bit, studying her. "We're not discussing the e-mail anymore, are we?"

Don't make me talk about Adrianna again, please. That only made Evalle feel insecure, which pissed her off. Besides, she had to get to the Iron Casket so she didn't miss Tristan. Lifting her arm to make a show of checking the time, she said, "I won't say anything about you being alive until you tell me I can, Storm, but I have to go now to make a meeting on time."

Storm didn't move a muscle, but he vibrated with frustration. "That's it? I tell you the truth and you're angry?"

"I'm not angry." She turned to her bike.

"That's the second time you've lied."

She pulled her jacket on and lifted her helmet, pausing to look at him. She would have done anything to see him alive again and here he was. How he got here shouldn't matter. But it did. "You're right. And to be perfectly fair, I have no right to be angry. I *am* glad someone was there to take care of you." *Just wish it had been me.*

"Maybe I should take it as a compliment that you're angry." His eyes shone with a hint of humor that barely hid the tethered frustration. "I'm still expecting dinner."

She'd pulled her helmet on and could pretend she hadn't heard him, but that would be childish. Did she want to see him again? Absolutely. But she needed some time to get her emotions under control. "Let me get back to you on that."

"We need a way to communicate."

Just have your guardian spirit contact me since she chases down women for you. Evalle bit back that reply. That wasn't the truth and she knew it, but she'd never dealt with emotions like these and wasn't enjoying it one bit. Which was why she needed some space. "You have my cell phone and e-mail."

Storm stepped over to stand next to her bike. "Let's not use cell phones yet. I set up a new e-mail account." He gave her the address and the password.

"Why give me your password?"

"Because we're not going to actually send the e-mails."

"We don't *send* them? How hard *did* your head hit that wall?"

He smiled, but his eyes were sad. "I've missed your smart mouth, especially your lips."

When he said things like that and looked at her as if she were his favorite dessert, she wanted to kiss him again, which went to show how much this man jumbled her feelings. "You have thirty seconds to explain. I'll be late if I don't get moving."

"Go into the server and open a new e-mail. Write my name and the date in the subject line, then type your message. When you're done, save it as a draft. I'll find your messages in the draft and leave one for you the same way. That way no one can intercept our e-mails or trace them."

That sounded pretty cloak-and-dagger, but Storm had not been this careful prior to being injured, so he must have good reason to be so now. She'd lost a lot of sleep over his possible death. If this kept him safe, she'd do it.

That didn't mean she'd have dinner with him.

She had too much to sort through right now and no time to waste figuring out her screwed-up psyche. Cranking her motorcycle, she reached up to lower her face shield, but Storm stopped her with his hand on hers.

Then he leaned close and said, "Plan on dinner . . . at my place tomorrow night. I'll post the address in an e-mail draft."

She waited for him to step back, then she dropped her face shield and drove away, glancing at her rearview mirror.

The sidewalk was empty.

Storm had disappeared into the night again.

After pushing her bike through yellow lights the whole way to the Iron Casket, she parked in an open spot far enough from the front door to study the lay of the land.

The pair of behemoth bouncers guarding the entrance missed little. With the boss they had, their lives literally depended on their performance. Even now she'd bet they were making a mental note of how long it took her to peel out of her jacket.

Last time she'd been here, she'd come close to a throw-down with the owner, Deek D'Alimonte, over Kardos, a teenage male witch who had foolishly taken an interest in Deek's sister.

Committing suicide by torching yourself would be an easier death for a man than being caught sniffing around the sister of an immortal centaur.

Evalle had just barely managed to extricate herself and wisecracking Kardos from that tight spot. Deek hadn't forbidden her from coming back, but he wouldn't be happy to see her either. With a little luck, she'd slip through unnoticed.

She headed for the door. Tristan had picked a perfect

place to meet. Deek allowed no weapons, and no use of majik or powers, inside his club. Tristan didn't have to worry about being surrounded by VIPER agents or a battle with Evalle.

When she'd first transferred to the southeastern region of VIPER, she'd been warned about Deek. That he'd been in this area long before VIPER formed the Coalition and he'd refused to join it. He took no one's side but his own. Rather than face Deek as an enemy when VIPER was still in its early stages, they'd struck a deal. Deek agreed to be neutral territory if a summit meeting was ever needed. In return, he had full autonomy within his domain.

In other words, stay out or enter at your own risk.

Weapons could be found with a body search, so she left her spelled dagger hidden on her bike. When she reached the entrance, she handed cash for her cover charge to one of the Goth giants guarding the door and walked in.

Inside the two-level, glittery nightclub, which had a soaring open center, music rocked the walls with heavy bass and screaming guitars. Sweat and alcohol leaked from the pores of gyrating dancers. Deek had pulled out all the stops to turn a basic warehouse into floor-to-ceiling sparkly when he'd dated a Fae woman, but that had been before the ugly breakup.

No Fae allowed now, thus the reason for the tongue-in-cheek name Iron Casket, since Fae majik supposedly would not work around iron, and Deek would kill anyone who broke his rules.

Calling this crowd Goth would sound too homogenized

for the creative types that packed the dance floor, crowded the bar and filled dark pockets everywhere.

Waitstaff circled the room carrying casket-shaped trays filled with drinks in crystal glasses. Evalle waved off two before a familiar voice close behind her said, "Don't you ever dress for going out?"

"Some of us have to work," she said, turning to find Tristan, who had taken his wardrobe for tonight more seriously than she had. He wore a long-sleeved, button-down shirt in a saturated bloodred color, black dress pants and dark sunglasses. He'd wised up after a month in civilization, now hiding his Alterant-green eyes at night, even though his eyes weren't light sensitive and he didn't have natural night vision like hers. His blond hair had grown out, brushing his collar.

Women passing by gave him looks filled with erotic offers.

He returned their smiles, the rogue, telling Evalle, "Like you ever wear anything different for work or play? Oh, wait, that would require having a playful bone in your body, right?"

He could save his breath at trying so hard to get under her skin. Just by saying hello, Tristan could irritate her more than poison ivy on intimate body parts. "I might enjoy a night off and expand my wardrobe if I didn't have to spend my time tracking down losers like you. Where have you been? Why didn't you answer any of my telepathic calls until now?"

His gaze tracked past her, sweeping over the room. "We can't discuss this here. Follow me."

"No way."

He shot her a glance lacking patience. "I've got a private room upstairs so we can talk. You know I'm not going to pull anything in Deek's place."

No, she didn't know that, if he and Deek had become friends. Before asking him her next question, she tapped into her empathic sense for something that might help her determine his intent. Her empathic gift was still new to her, but she often picked up something useful. "You know Deek well?"

"I know *of* him. I hear he's dangerous to cross and has zero tolerance when it comes to using any powers or majik in this place. I don't know what he is, but just his reputation sounds deadly. *I'm* not crossing him."

Tristan's usual arrogance came through perfectly clear, but mixed in with it had been a healthy dose of respect when he mentioned Deek.

Most nonhumans feared Deek for good reason, and she doubted anything intimidated the centaur, but as long as you played by his rules in this club, Deek wouldn't touch you.

Break a rule and you were fair game.

Feeling better about going upstairs, Evalle gave Tristan a nod to lead the way. At the second level, he directed her to an alcove with a plush love-seat-size sofa, two cushy side chairs and a low glass coffee table. Sparkling translucent silver curtains pulled back with gold-and-silver cords framed each side of the opening.

The waiter who stepped out from a dark hallway had nickel-size, black earrings, a pin through his nose, a skull-patterned scarf that hung to his waist and gorgeous tats climbing one arm. He carried a tray with a mixed drink, bottled water and a bowl of fried calamari.

Once the waiter left, Evalle snagged the bottle of water and took a side chair, angling it so that she could see anyone approaching.

Tristan took up most of the sofa, spreading his arms. "You like calamari, right?"

"I can take it or leave it." Right now she wanted to take all of it. Her mouth watered. "Where're you getting money?"

"Eat, Evalle. Unless your life has changed drastically, you still run on fury and determination. I ate before I came here and the money is from a friend who's helping me."

No point in wasting the food. She dug in, practically moaning over the flavor. Deek prided himself on having the best of everything.

Tristan lifted his chin in the direction of the area outside their alcove. "I was told these rooms are soundproof even with the curtains open."

"I doubt anyone could hear us yelling in here with that music going on." But she had to give Deek credit for his design or whatever he did that made it possible to talk at a normal level in this pocket. She sat back, tapping her finger on the chair arm. "Okay, what gives? I know better than to think you contacted me only for my benefit. Not after leaving me to face the Tribunal empty-handed after I saved your butt."

"That was unfortunate—"

"Unfortunate? No, no." Evalle sat forward. "Getting a speeding ticket is unfortunate. Losing your wallet is unfortunate. Getting locked away forever in VIPER prison is more like being castrated with a dull knife and no morphine."

Tristan flinched hard at that. "Looks like you got yourself out of jail."

"No thanks to you."

Tristan ran his fingers through his hair and looked away. When he turned back to her, he actually appeared remorseful. "Later on, I thought about everything that happened that night and realized you might not have called in that bunch of military guys to kill us."

"You mean Isak Nyght's men? You should have realized the truth the minute I blocked for you so you could escape." Isak Nyght hunted Alterants and gave a standing shoot-to-kill order to his men, all former military.

Isak hadn't known she was an Alterant before that night, and she'd be on his shoot-on-sight list if Sen hadn't wiped the memories of Isak and his men after they'd seen her shield Tristan's group.

Isak was yet another complicated relationship she didn't have time to dwell on.

Forcing her attention back to the male complication du jour, she said, "Couldn't you have used a little logic? Why would I have brought in a bunch of black-ops boys with weapons who wanted to *kill* Alterants?"

Tristan held his hands out. "Look at it from my side. Sort of tough to reason all that out in a split second when someone's trying to kill me. I had the safety of three people in my hands, which included my sister. Tell me you'd have made any different decision if you'd been in my place, with you trying to haul us in to face a Tribunal and men pointing cannons at someone you care about."

Nothing would be gained by arguing the past. She picked at the calamari some more and said, "You said you had information on the traitor. What is it?"

"I can't tell you—"

She slapped the chair arm. "Don't even start that crap with me again."

"If you'd let me finish, I was saying *I* can't tell you because I don't know anything about the traitor, but I have someone who does."

"The friend who gave you money?"

"Yes."

"Where is he or she?"

"He, and that's why I'm here, because he said he can't get near you with Tzader, Quinn and everyone else so close."

"Tell him to call me."

"Nope. He won't risk talking on the phone or any other electronic format. He wants you to meet with him."

"Why?"

"Because he has a personal interest in helping the Beladors and said you'd understand as soon as you meet him."

She toyed with that, trying to decide what to do with this opportunity. "Why is he helping you?"

"He runs the equivalent of an underground network

that helps people like us, beings without any support or pantheon."

What choice did she have at this point other than to play along? She needed Tristan and he knew it. "It will have to be at night and I'll pick a place"

"It's *tonight* and I know the place. I'll take you there."

She made a chuffing sound of disbelief. "You really think I'm going to let you take me somewhere?"

"It's the only way he'll talk to you. He *wants* to talk to you specifically about Conlan O'Meary."

Crud. Could this be for real? Tristan shouldn't know about Conlan, so clearly this guy had some information. "Let's say I agree to do this. What do you get out of it?"

"Safe passage out of the country for me, Petrina, Webster and Aaron."

"Where'd you put your sister and those two Rías?"

"Somewhere safe."

"Webster and Aaron still able to control their beast?"

"Yep. Getting better all the time."

That brought up a question burning the inside of her brain that Tristan might be able to answer. "Speaking of Rías, what do you think makes them different from us . . . besides eye color?"

"Why?"

"Because we've had another one shift in Atlanta."

Tristan tapped his chin with a finger. "That fog return?"

"No. We've had gang wars breaking out and found a few trolls mixed in, but tonight was the first time a Rías appeared in one of the fights." She considered mentioning the Svarts, but changed her mind. Until Tristan gave her a reason to share more, he had all he needed to know for now. "But you met up with Webster and Aaron before the sentient fog was released. Where'd you find those two Rías?"

"Remember when you and I first met? And I was here with the Kujoo?"

She looked up in a mock show of trying to remember. "Let me think. You mean the very first time in Piedmont Park when you turned Nightstalkers into demented ghouls that attacked me?"

"*I* didn't change them. The Kujoo warlord did that."

"I don't see the difference since you *were* working with the warlord."

Tristan rolled his eyes. "Do you want to know how I met Webster and Aaron or not?" He waited for her noisy sigh before continuing. "When I got a chance to slip away from the warlord, I was down in the project housing late at night when Webster and Aaron tried to mug me. I didn't want to hurt them since they were human, but the demented ghouls had followed me and swarmed those two, then Webster and Aaron started shifting."

"So maybe it takes an unnatural source of hostility like the sentient fog or aggressive ghouls to cause the Rías to shift."

"Maybe."

That supported the theory she'd worked out with Quinn. She'd have to let him and Tzader know. "The Rías I know about had no control. They just shifted and killed immediately. What about Webster and Aaron?"

"They would have, but I shifted into my Alterant beast the minute they changed."

Evalle groaned. "VIPER would have gone crazy if they'd heard about that."

"Screw VIPER. I can control my beast and I have no doubt you can control yours. The minute I grabbed those two guys and made it clear that I was the dominant beast, they immediately changed back into their human forms, scared shitless."

She wasn't acknowledging or denying that she could control her beast since no one could know that she had fully shifted once. "So fear of something more powerful that forces back their aggression snaps them out of the change?"

"That's a possibility," Tristan said, more to himself than her. "I spent a couple of hours with Webster and Aaron, making them shift back and forth, then explained the danger of being exposed to VIPER agents. Once I believed they could control their shifting, I stuck them in the Maze of Death to hide them."

She remembered that place *beneath* the underground MARTA rail system all too well. "Weren't you worried a dangerous spirit in there would trigger their change?"

"Not where I put them. You met the passive spirits in the chamber where I'd left those two."

"I also met that crazy spirit with a pitchfork who stabbed you." But she lifted her hand, stalling any further talk on the Maze. "Back to my original question. How are Rías different from Alterants?"

"From what I've figured out, they have super strength

and some weak kinetics, but nothing like an Alterant's powers."

"I beg to differ. I fought one three weeks ago that slammed me with a kinetic punch that knocked me off my feet."

"Really? That's new. Maybe it's hit or miss on their powers, because I haven't met one like that."

She tucked that into her ongoing mental file on Rías. "What else can you tell me?"

"Like I said about you and me, I think Alterants can control their beasts from the first time they change, but the Rías seem to immediately turn into aggressive beasts on attack." Tristan paused. "I think the difference is our blood. We carry Belador blood, but maybe they don't."

Evalle considered everything he said, then argued, "But there were reports of *Alterants* who shifted and killed, several in the Southeast in the past year."

"I heard about those *reports*," Tristan echoed with a heavy dose of accusation. "Who says so? Macha and Brina? But *you* haven't witnessed an Alterant turning into a mindless beast, have you?"

"No." Much as she hated to feed Tristan's distrust of Macha and Brina, Evalle had to admit he had a valid point.

"And that's why I'm getting my group somewhere safe soon."

Evalle snapped her fingers, excited. "Wait. I haven't told you the good news. That's why I've been trying to find you. Macha is the one who got me out of prison. She petitioned the Tribunal for Alterants to be recognized as a viable race . . . *and*, wait for it, Macha has offered amnesty to all Alterants who come forward and swear loyalty to her. They'll be safe as long as they can keep their beasts under control."

Tristan listened with interest, unable to hide his surprise at that last declaration.

She beamed at her accomplishment. "See? You can stay."

He started shaking his head. "I can't give her or the Beladors that kind of trust, not after what they did to me."

Evalle tried not to lose her patience with him since he'd been locked away inside a spellbound enclosure in a South American jungle . . . twice. But he couldn't turn his back on a once-in-a-lifetime opportunity.

With Macha, this could mean a life-or-*death* opportunity.

"This is a limited offer with a short time span, Tristan."

He scoffed at her. "That's what I mean. So much for a sincere offer."

"It *is* sincere, but I haven't been able to find one Alterant in three weeks to bring forward as a show of good faith from our kind. And now an Alterant—or a Rías—has killed one of Dakkar's bounty hunters, so Dakkar's screaming for justice." She could see his disgust at her taking Macha's side in this, but fair was fair. "How can Macha stand before a Tribunal and support us when no Alterant besides me is willing to come forward?"

Tristan's gaze traveled everywhere but her face. He muttered, "She should have thought about that five years ago when she had Brina lock me up for no reason."

"I'm not discounting what she did to you, but things have changed and she's making you—and every other Alterant—an offer you aren't going to find anywhere else. She'll probably accept Webster and Aaron, too, once we show her their control."

"There is no way in hell I'm trusting *any* offer from Macha."

Evalle kept her voice calm and understanding. "You're the only person I've met who claims to have information on the origin of Alterants and what we all have in common."

"It's not just a claim and it's more about our origins in particular. Mine, yours and my sister's."

"Okay. Great. I need that information and your help now while we have this chance to become a recognized race. You may be willing to live with a target on your back forever, but other Alterants deserve the chance for freedom."

That must have struck a chord in Tristan. He leaned forward as if reconsidering his stance, then shook off some thought and sat back, arms crossed. "I'm not sharing anything unless you talk to my guy."

They were back to that. "If I agree to go with you tonight, then in return I want you to talk to Brina about Alterants."

"Not a chance."

"Why not?"

"I'm not meeting with Brina or Macha. The minute I come out of hiding, I'll lose any hope of getting back to my sister or leaving the country with my group."

"VIPER is everywhere, Tristan. There is no safe place where you won't be hunted."

His mouth set in a stubborn line. She was not going to get him to budge on that point. "If I can guarantee that you can walk away, would you consider speaking to the Tribunal?"

A muscle twitched in his cheek. "Can you guarantee that?"

"I have to talk to Tzader first. If he says he can do it, then you'll be safe. So what do you say?"

"Meet with my guy and I'll talk to Tzader. If he convinces me I can't be trapped, then I'll consider a meeting on neutral ground."

That was a step closer, but Evalle needed to end up with something tangible tonight. "Okay, but as a minimum I want what you have on Alterants before I leave tonight's meeting."

"Agreed."

Finally. She finished off the calamari and followed him outside. "Give me a minute to stop by my bike."

He turned around. "No. We're leaving straight from the club. It's the only way to be sure you won't have a weapon."

"I won't use my dagger on anyone . . . if I don't have to."

"No weapons. That was the one requirement this guy made from the first minute I met him, and I've stuck by it. I've been around him for three weeks. He's not a threat. Even if he was, between the two of us, he's no match."

"You want me to just trust you?"

"Says the woman who wants me to walk into Macha's lair."

"Never mind. Let's go." She still had the blades in her boots.

When Tristan reached a four-door Toyota, a rental car, Evalle noted how the license plate had mud over the numbers. She'd settled into the passenger seat when Tristan tossed a wad of cloth onto her lap and said, "Put that on."

She picked up the black bag. "You can't be serious."

"As a heart attack. I agreed not to let you know where I was taking you and that you wouldn't bring anyone with you."

"If that's the case, why don't you just teleport me, or can't you still do that?"

"I can, but my sister, Webster and Aaron are at a different location this guy's people are guarding. I can't teleport long distance two times in a row easily, so I'm conserving my power in case I ever need to get to my sister quickly."

That meant he could teleport away as soon as Evalle met this other guy and leave Evalle stranded. "I'm not comfortable with this, Tristan."

His sigh stretched into a growl. "Look, I didn't want to say this until you spoke to my guy, but you really need to talk to him for your own safety."

"Why?"

"Remember when we were underground in the Maze of Death with Kizira?"

"I tend to remember near-death experiences, so, yes."

"Did you tell anyone that Kizira said Quinn told her where to find you?"

"No."

That shocked Tristan. "Not even Quinn?"

"*He's* been gone for the past three weeks, *too*, and just got back tonight. I'd be discussing it with him right now if not for meeting you."

"What about Tzader?"

"No," she said louder. "I'm not throwing any suspicion on Quinn based on something that Medb witch said."

"This guy says Quinn did tell Kizira how to find you."

"How could *he* know?" Evalle fisted her fingers, unwilling to believe Quinn had betrayed her but needing the truth.

"He says Quinn is tied to the traitor."

"What?"

"End of discussion. Put the bag on your head and don't try to contact anyone telepathically. I'll be able to hear it."

Evalle lifted the sack and took a deep breath she let out slowly. Her pulse hit panic pace, but she couldn't back out this close to finding answers on the traitor.

And on Quinn.

SEVEN

Tzader hated being out of his body.

Felt creepy every time.

Purplish haze blurred his vision when he traveled in hologram. This beat not seeing Brina at all. His physical body couldn't pass through the warding at Treoir Castle. No immortal, except Brina or Macha, could enter without dying.

Brina's father had installed that little safety feature to protect his only daughter when he and his sons went to battle the Medb four years ago. None of the male Treoirs had returned alive and that had left Brina the lone survivor, stuck in Treoir Castle.

I shouldn't be immortal. Tzader loved his father, but the man had done his part to doom him and Brina, too. On the way to battle alongside the Treoir men, Tzader's father had asked Macha that if he died in battle, to make his only child immortal.

Then *his* dad had died that night, fighting beside Brina's.

Tzader's life would be a tragic comedy if he could find any humor in this screwed-up situation.

The distorted sensation of winding through a vortex of blurred colors calmed until he floated in a cloud-like haze. Entrance to the castle required Brina to offer invitation each time Tzader visited in holographic form.

He called to her telepathically. *Brina, I'm here.*

At one time, he'd have gotten an immediate answer. A breathless answer filled with anticipation.

Nothing. He shouldn't be surprised since he hadn't heard from her in weeks and their last meeting had ended poorly, but as the minutes stretched on, the delay bordered on insult.

You are welcome to enter, Tzader Burke.

He considered several smart replies and decided raising her hackles would not set the right tone for this meeting.

When the cloud dissipated, he stood in hologram form inside the great hall of Treoir Castle.

And there was Brina. She lounged on a sofa her da had carved from the trunk of a tree. It was intricately detailed with Celtic family emblems. Hair the color of a river on fire lay across her shoulders in a loose, tousled way that took him back to when he could touch her and run his hands through the fine strands.

The triangular Celtic Triquetra, mark of the Beladors, had been stitched in white on the cuffs of her radiant deep-green gown. This woman had taken his breath away when she'd worn baggy pants and a faded shirt for training as a warrior.

He'd waited four long years to touch her again and would wait an eternity if Macha had not forced a promise from him to allow Brina to move on with her life and marry.

According to Macha, Brina claimed she was ready to produce an heir.

Without Tzader.

He'd never suffered a wound so painful as how those words had gutted him.

Macha made it sound like a case of logic. The Beladors needed a Treoir heir to safeguard their future. Brina couldn't leave, and Tzader couldn't enter.

Tzader had been raised to understand that sacrifice was part of being a warrior, but he'd never expected to give up something so precious.

"You've a report?" Brina asked with a brisk efficiency that exaggerated her Irish lilt.

"Hello to you, too," he snapped back at her, leaving off *Your Highness* at the end. Why did she sound as though he were interrupting her day? She'd called this meeting after all.

"Very well. Hello, Tzader. I'm wantin' news on the traitor. Have you run down the rat yet?"

She'd had the same uncharacteristic waspish tone last time, part of the reason Tzader had given in to Macha's wishes. In that last meeting, Brina had been clear about both of them accepting their impossible situation.

Ready to move on. That's how she'd put it.

He admitted, "Nothing on the traitor yet."

"I expected to be hearin' we were closer to findin' O'Meary." She sat more upright, her fingers flitting around until they settled together in her lap.

Nervous? Was she as unhappy about ending their relationship as he was? Maybe reconsidering . . .

Her gaze had been as active as her hands until she glanced up and caught him studying her. That put a steel rod in her backbone and grit in her voice. "I still cannot believe he escaped from VIPER lockdown. 'Tis unheard of. Someone must have helped him."

"I agree." *And I accept the blame since the responsibility is all mine and I just hope—* Tzader paused mentally when a guard entered the room from the front hall.

Like all Treoir guards, this one wore an emerald-green and black vest with black pants and a Belador sword in a scabbard that hung against his back.

As Tzader started to admonish the guard for interrupting a meeting, Brina turned her head and . . . *smiled*? "I'll be with you in a minute, Allyn. This won't be takin' long."

The guard—*Allyn?*—nodded and retreated to the main hall.

She resumed her imperial pose where she perched on the sofa, and her personality flatlined again. "As you were sayin', Tzader?"

"We've had an unusual number of gang battles."

"Oh, please. If I were wantin' a crime report, I'd be askin' Macha for satellite television."

Don't snap at her. "This isn't about local human issues. We've found trolls involved in several of the attacks."

"I do read your briefings, so how is this news?"

"The trolls alone aren't news. But things changed tonight. We had a Rías shift and a Svart troll involved." He watched her face for any sign of concern, because Brina knew how dangerous the Svarts were.

She stilled, masking her thoughts until she finally asked softly, "Was anyone injured?"

In the past she would have wanted to know that *he* was okay first. Tzader shrugged. "The usual, but no casualties on our side. Evalle fought the Rías and the Svart."

Unease slipped through Brina's lack of expression before she contained it again. Lifting her chin and looking off at nothing in particular, she waved a casual hand. "Evalle would be best equipped for facin' somethin' so dangerous."

Where had the Brina he'd known gone?

That Brina would want to face him at eye level, not sit there lounging like the princess she'd never wanted to be.

His Brina would have been pacing the floor, rattling off questions to be assured that her warriors were all safe. Even Evalle. Brina would be demanding to know who did what and strategizing their next move.

Tzader added, "I had to authorize Quinn to use extreme force on the Rías or it would have killed Evalle."

"Understood. An' what of the Svart? Was Quinn able to retrieve information to shed light on these battles?"

"He didn't get a chance before the Svart died."

Brina nodded, speaking as much to herself as anyone else when she said, "Aye, a Svart will always take his own life before allowin' himself to be captured or interrogated."

"Evalle actually ended up killing him."

"*Before* Quinn could search his mind?" Brina sat up, fingers tense, gripping the cushions on each side of her. "What was she thinkin'?"

"She was trying to survive," Tzader said in a voice one bump louder than Brina's. "The Svart had a chain wrapped around her neck."

"What about her powers?"

"She was fighting the Rías, too. She did the best she could."

"Knowin' Evalle, she didn't *wait* for anyone to help an' just kicked the Svart's butt herself. You defend her no matter what she does."

"No, I don't."

Brina lifted both hands in a moment of frustration, then slapped them down on the cushion again. "Is that all?"

No, he wanted to yell that this was *not all*. That he missed her and expected her to miss him, but he'd made a deal with Macha that he would not encourage the relationship he and Brina had shared since their teens.

His honor forced him to hold up his end of the agreement. "I guess that is all . . . to do with my report."

"What else can I be doin' for you?" she asked in such a brisk tone that it grated his already shredded patience.

"Nothing. Your *Highness*. Not. A. Thing." Tzader ordered his essence to travel back to his body, which sat in a secure room at headquarters, halfway across the world.

"Come back in, Allyn," Brina called out, standing up.

"Yes, Your Highness." The man she'd chosen to be her new personal guard strode back into the room with solid confidence that matched his physical appearance. Her royal guards were all well trained and strong, and his uniform was no different from that of the others, except in the way it fit Allyn's spectacular body.

Aye, she'd chosen a fine-lookin' man for her purpose.

His gaze tracked over to the empty spot where Tzader's hologram had been. When Allyn drew close, he whispered, "How did it go?"

"About as I was expectin'." She kept her voice down and her senses alert for Macha, who tended to pop in unannounced.

Allyn asked, "Then you're pleased?"

Brina crossed her arms. "For now."

She'd tested the waters with this visit. The next time, she'd put the first step of her plan into action.

Tzader had best prepare himself for the battle of his life, because she had no intention of givin' up on the two of them.

EIGHT

I should have left a clue at the Iron Casket so the Beladors would have some way to find my body.

But what clue? Evalle kept trying to think what she might have done that Tristan wouldn't have noticed. She couldn't have even gone to the ladies' room in the Iron Casket before they left because Tristan would have followed her in to make sure she didn't leave a message somewhere for Tzader.

The car she rode in took another turn in the rutted road.

She swayed toward the console on her left, the motion giving her a moment of nausea because of the sack over her head. They bounced along until Tristan finally parked the car and turned off the engine.

"Can I take the spy bag off my head now?" she groused.

"Sure."

The driver's door had slammed shut by the time she'd shed the black bag and could see her surroundings. Tall grass and weeds crowded a white farmhouse with faded red shingles. The dirt road to this place must have been a half-mile long, ending at this spot hidden by woods on all sides. Tristan had brought her somewhere in rural Georgia or maybe even Alabama, because they'd driven over an hour from Atlanta.

But with all the turns Tristan had taken, she had no idea in what direction they'd ridden after leaving the Iron Casket.

She hadn't anticipated so long a drive. Tristan had better make this a quick meeting. She could get away with running late for her meeting with Tzader and Quinn, but what she couldn't do was show up at her bike after sunrise since she had none of her protective riding gear with her. Thanks to her strange Alterant DNA, she had a deadly reaction to the sun to go along with sensitive eyes. Tristan knew about that.

So what, exactly, had her neck muscles so tense right now?

The location?

Abandoned farmhouses weren't something to be concerned over, as a rule, unless you considered the wackos that broke into them sometimes to hide from the law. But those were generally human perpetrators. What was giving her a hinky feeling about this? Climbing out of the car, she stretched her legs and sniffed a toasty scent in the air. Woodstoves wouldn't be unusual out here.

Tristan strolled up the weed-infested gravel path to the front steps, past bushes that hadn't been trimmed in a long time.

A light glowed in a window on one side of the porch.

She took her time following Tristan, watching for any sign of nonhuman presence nearby. That she didn't sense any felt strangely wrong since she ran into Nightstalkers around every corner in Atlanta this time of night.

Make that morning.

Midnight had come and gone a half hour ago. Tzader and Quinn would wonder where she was if she ran really late meeting them, but she couldn't reach them without using telepathy.

Taking that risk this close to getting answers would be foolish.

At the front door, Tristan opened it and walked in.

A female voice came into Evalle's mind, whispering, *Trust those who've earned it and no others.*

Evalle stopped in mid-stride.

That voice. Who was talking to her? She felt no Belador power behind the voice, and it was the same female that had spoken to her at the most unexpected times in the past month. As soon as she got some time off, Evalle was going to ask her witch friend, Nicole, if she could help Evalle figure out who was communicating with her.

I don't need voices in my head right now. I'm out of my element as it is out here in the country. That should be enough to deal with, but unease of a different kind still snaked down her spine.

She didn't like anything about this setup, from the location to the house. Climbing three rickety steps, she entered a stuffy-smelling room where an old geezer sat in a ragged recliner that faced the door. Clear tubes ran from a nasal mask over his ears and down to a mobile tank next to his chair.

Taking care with his tubes, he unfolded to a tall, thin body with skin that gravity had pulled at for many years. His cheap brown suit hung on his bony frame. Wrinkled brown eyes watched while she finished her assessment, but she needed only seconds to figure out the most damning trait.

"You're a Belador?" she asked the old guy.

"Yes."

Tristan stopped between them and turned to her with a big grin, his arms opened wide in an "Am I good or what?" look.

She braced her feet apart, ready for battle, and pointed at Tristan. "This is the last time you screw me over."

"What're you talking about?" Sincerity rang through Tristan's voice.

"He's a *Belador*."

"So?"

"So you could have told me that. But you didn't, which makes me wonder why not and why this guy didn't want Tzader or Quinn involved." She shot Tristan a withering look. "Or maybe *this* is the traitor and you've brought me into a trap."

"What?" Tristan dropped his arms.

The man across the room spoke in a shaky voice. "I asked Tristan to not tell you I was Belador, Evalle."

"Why?" She kept both men in her field of vision, prepared to bust out the blades in her boots at the first wrong move.

The withered old man said, "Because you would have wanted to check me out with Tzader or someone else."

True. With Conlan O'Meary on the loose, no possible lead could be held back. She cut Tristan some slack for the moment and directed her questions at the Belador. "Who are you?"

"Sam Thomas. I once fought in battle beside other Beladors, just as you do."

"I take it you're not *with* the Beladors as a warrior now."

"I left."

"Nobody *quits*."

"You're right. That's why I left after a battle almost seven years ago. I'm sure they counted me as dead or forever missing since bodies are sometimes vaporized in battle."

How could he just walk away after having been accepted as a full Belador warrior? She'd give anything to have what he'd tossed aside. To not be shunned as a half-breed. And he'd sworn the same oath she had. She didn't hide her disgust when she said, "So you just deserted?"

Sam sighed heavily and the air came out with a rattle. "I didn't leave *during* a battle. No one was at risk when I disappeared and became another statistic. *You* would condemn me for wanting a life?"

She caught his point—that she of all people should understand wanting a normal life—and discounted that excuse for the crap it smelled like. "You want me to believe you walked away from the Beladors so you could play golf and spend time with the grandkids? Not buying that, Pops."

"Let's just say I'm supporting the tribe in my own way."

She let that go for now. "Where have you been since leaving the Beladors?"

"Around, but I'm not here to talk about past history."

I'm not either. "What do you want to talk to me about?"

The wrinkles on Sam's face rearranged into a crooked smile that ended with a grimace. "Can we sit a spell? Got a bad back."

She took the single chair facing him, which didn't match any of the other furniture. Not entirely true. Every piece in the room sported rips that belched stuffing. "What do you know about the traitor?"

Tristan settled onto a lumpy couch. He piped up, "Sam knows more than anyone at VIPER."

Evalle sent him a scathing look intended to say, *You don't have a speaking role.*

Tristan grumbled, "Whatever," and propped an elbow on the back of the couch to support his head.

Taking his time to speak, Sam said, "To begin with, the traitor will lead the Medb to Brina if you don't stop him."

"We *know* that, which is why we have everyone looking for him. But we may not be talking about the same person."

"Conlan O'Meary?"

So this guy did know something about Conlan. She asked, "Do you know where he is?"

"I have an idea."

She sat forward. "Where?"

"I'll tell you once you hear the rest of what I have to say."

If you keep talking as slow as molasses dripping in the winter, this will take what's left of my morning. "I'm listening."

"Do you know what happened before Conlan escaped?

"You mean the mind probe that Quinn did?"

"Yes. But Conlan is not necessarily guilty."

"Then why did he escape and run?"

Sam's knee jerked every so often as if it wanted to bounce. "That isn't the question you should be asking."

"I'm in no mood for a game. What's the right question?"

"How did Conlan get out of VIPER?"

She'd wondered that many times herself. Conlan hadn't been in just any holding cell. She'd asked Tzader how anyone could have found a way out of VIPER headquarters, which was tucked inside a mountain north of Atlanta.

According to Tzader, any escape from VIPER required inside help. She said, "We know Conlan couldn't have gotten out alone. Do you know who broke him out?"

"I know who could have."

She hated vague answers and didn't trust someone who wasn't part of their VIPER teams. "Why do you even care what goes on at VIPER after you walked away?"

"Because I have people to protect besides Tristan, Petrina, Webster and Aaron. I got tired of being restrained while expected to fight things that often defied death."

Ah, the real reason behind his desertion. Evalle had been in that situation at times, but she would never turn her back on the Beladors because of feeling stymied by rules. "We took an oath to do what's honorable *and* protect humans while we fight things that are tough to kill."

"True," Sam conceded. "But I think we may all be forced to fight against impossible odds soon. You may not respect my choices in life, but please believe me when I say I don't want to see the Beladors destroyed."

She didn't acknowledge one way or the other, but his words rang with sincerity, as if he needed her to believe that one thing. "I'm still listening."

"I'm in a better position now to help the Beladors, and Alterants, than I could have before, which is why I agreed to help Tristan. My people told me about him after the Rías were changing everywhere across the country. We have a network that has kept his group safe." Sam's knee finally started bouncing up and down in tiny jumps.

Nerves or a twitch?

Back to the heart of this, the traitor. She asked, "Okay, so who do you think might have broken Conlan out of lockup?"

"Vladimir Quinn."

"*Liar!*" She pointed at Tristan, who had a sick-gut look on his face. "You brought me here for *that*?"

Tristan said, "Just hear him out—"

"I'm not lying, Evalle." Sam tapped his fingers on his bouncing knee and his jaw moved as if talking stressed him. "Listen to me. I have reason to believe that Quinn is key to finding the traitor."

And what reason did she have to believe this stranger? "Quinn has been a loyal Belador warrior since signing on at eighteen. I trust him with my life. Why would he betray us now?"

Sam pulled his lips tight in a frown. "You're not going

to like hearing this, but if you want to protect Brina, you're going to have to start thinking with your head and not your heart. Everyone knows how close you, Tzader and Quinn are."

No argument there. She waited for him to continue.

"I have people in Atlanta. I received a report through them from a Nightstalker contact that stays in and around the Ritz Hotel. The ghoul snitch saw Kizira going into a room there."

Holding a calm, disinterested expression while her heart thumped wildly was no easy task for Evalle. She'd been working on schooling her features better and managed to act as if that news didn't send a chill up her spine. When she and Tristan had fought Kizira in the Maze of Death, Kizira had claimed she'd seen Quinn, in his room at the Ritz, and that Quinn had told Kizira she'd find Evalle with Tristan.

Evalle hadn't wanted to believe Kizira even when she'd shared details no one should've known about Quinn's room except Evalle and Tzader.

Quinn's elaborate security measures meant only Evalle and Tzader could find his location, which changed every day when he stayed in Atlanta. Even then, neither of them could get past the temporary barrier that Quinn's warded Triquetras provided.

But Evalle wasn't ready to jump on the Quinn-can't-be-trusted bandwagon. "So what? The Medb like the thread count of Ritz linens."

"Kizira visited a guest in the hotel. The room belonged to Vladimir Quinn."

Quinn never registered under his name. How would this Sam have found out that information?

Evalle opened her empathic senses as Sam spoke. She hadn't trained to develop her ability, but she'd become pretty good at figuring out what someone was feeling. Right now she could only discern one thing from Sam. Worry.

Possibly damning or not, depending on what worried him.

Where was Storm with his lie-detecting ability when she needed him?

She wanted to rail at Sam, but he'd tossed down the challenge that she wasn't objective. She could act detached. "Let's say there's a remote possibility that Quinn met with a Medb witch. For what reason?"

"That is a question Quinn has to answer, but I think I know why he would have helped Conlan."

"Why?"

"Did anyone tell you what Quinn found when he performed the probe?"

"No," she lied, but telling this guy anything Tzader had shared with her in confidence was out of the question. Quinn had found potentially damning evidence of Conlan being the traitor, but even Tzader called it inconclusive because the images Quinn had accessed were of the future.

And the future could always change.

"Quinn saw images in Conlan's mind of Conlan joining the Medb, then aiding them to breach Brina's castle and kill her."

Sam's information matched what Tzader had shared with her and VIPER. That gave credibility to Sam's claim of having people in Atlanta, even inside VIPER.

Or had he gotten his information from the traitor?

She pointed out, "What Quinn saw would explain why Conlan was put in temporary lockup, but he still shouldn't have run. Conlan hadn't even faced a Tribunal yet."

"I agree." Sam wheezed another breath. "Except for the last part. Conlan's father was convicted as a traitor years before. Conlan knew he'd never leave that cell until another person was found guilty of being the traitor, which could take years . . . and might never happen."

Just as no one would ever forget that Evalle was an Alterant. She understood carrying an invisible ball and chain.

But she faced her battle every day.

Conlan had run.

Tristan continued to watch the conversation volley between her and Sam, but he glanced over at her with an obvious question written across his face.

She lifted her shoulder in a silent shrug, letting Tristan know she hadn't decided yet, and asked, "Why would Quinn go against VIPER, and the Beladors, to free Conlan?"

"I've thought on that a long time. One reason I wouldn't let Tristan contact you until now."

Swinging his head to face her, Tristan chided, "Feel better about why I haven't been answering your telepathic calls?"

"Not a bit. I've been stuck trying to save *all* the

Alterants instead of just my closest buddies." She hoped that would remind Tristan that he he still had to make good on his part of this deal. He'd better not teleport away before she got what she needed from him, too. "Finish what you were saying, Sam."

"I've come down to one of two reasons Quinn would have helped Conlan escape—"

"If he did," she interjected.

"Understood. Either Quinn also believed Conlan would not get a fair trial and didn't want to be the reason the young man ended up in prison for the rest of his life . . ."

She could see that, but would Quinn have taken it upon himself to release Conlan without at least clueing in Tzader?

"Or," Sam continued, "Quinn is working with Kizira and released Conlan to draw attention away from the real traitor, who is still among the Beladors." Sam's frail chest lifted and dropped with his sigh. "I can see you don't want to believe me and are ready to go to Tzader, but I wouldn't do that if I were you."

Did this guy read minds? Of course, she had to tell Tzader. "Why not?"

"Because Quinn might or might not have had control over what he did . . . if he did help Conlan."

She made a derogatory noise. "I've never been one to accept the 'I didn't know what I was doing' defense."

"Even if someone is compelled, Evalle? Kizira might have been able to do that when she went to see Quinn in his hotel."

If that happened.

If Quinn did break out Conlan.

If, if, if.

Evalle rubbed the back of her neck. Quinn had one of the most powerful minds among the Beladors. Evalle had seen *him* overpower Kizira's mind two years ago, so she doubted Kizira had compelled Quinn. "So why would I not tell Tzader?"

"You would destroy your friends."

"What do you mean?"

"If you say anything to Tzader"—Sam paused, panting as if just living took an effort—"he'll have no choice but to have Quinn's mind probed to prove Quinn's innocence or confirm his guilt. If Quinn did help Conlan, even for a noble reason, a druid will find that memory. What do you think Macha would do?"

Horrible images flashed through Evalle's mind, all ending with Quinn dying in excruciating pain.

And Quinn would accept a death sentence before giving up Conlan if he truly believed Conlan to be innocent.

What other possible reason could there be for Quinn to break trust with the Beladors? But he had no reason to deceive her or Tzader. Did he?

Sam's assessment of the situation had merit.

Tzader's first duty might be to protect Brina, but Evalle had picked up on something more going on between Brina and Tzader beyond the Belador-Maistir-to-Warrior-Queen relationship.

He would never jeopardize Brina's safety, and he'd

hate himself for putting Quinn's neck on the chopping block.

But did Quinn really present a risk to Brina? Evalle needed more than Sam's word. "Is that all you have?"

Sam's hand shook where he held his knee still. "If Kizira did meet Quinn inside his hotel room, then that would explain how Kizira knew she'd find you with Tristan when you went underground with him in the Maze to retrieve the two Rías."

Evalle hadn't wanted to believe Kizira's claim that Quinn had given her information. She still wouldn't accept the word of a Medb witch and this unknown Belador over talking to Quinn first.

Loyalty meant standing up for those you cared about. Giving that person a chance to tell his side.

She asked Sam, "How do you know all of this?"

"I still have my resources within the Beladors—"

Just as she figured. "Spies."

"Friends. And since going off the radar, so to speak, I've developed *resources* within other factions."

"The Medb?"

He didn't respond, neither confirming nor denying.

Evalle had heard all she wanted to from this guy. Time for him to show all his cards. "Why are you telling me all of this when we don't know each other?"

Sam's eyes creased with admiration. "I've heard all about you, Alterant. How you've had to fight to stay free of imprisonment simply because you're not a full-blood Belador, yet you're the first one to step forward to protect humans and the Beladors. That you don't shift into your beast no matter what, even when your life is at stake. I'm telling you because you're the only Belador that I'm sure is not the traitor."

How could a stranger see more than many of whom she'd fought alongside? She shook off how that touched her deep inside and kept her business face in place. "We agree on that one thing. So what am I to do with this information?"

"Find the traitor. A war is coming with the Medb and the battle will be fought over Alterants."

"I thought they wanted to kill Brina and capture Treoir Castle."

"That's what I understand as well, but the Alterants will be the difference between success and failure."

"I don't understand."

"I'm helping Tristan and Petrina escape before the Medb find them. That's all I can do for these two Alterants. But you must find the others and keep them from the Medb. I will help you hide them."

"I have no idea where any other Alterants are or I'd be bringing them in to Macha."

Sam's liquid gaze slid over to Tristan. "Tell her what you've learned in the past few weeks."

Tristan stood and walked across the room to a fireplace with a hearth covered in cobwebs from lack of use. He leaned back against the mantel and crossed his arms. "Sam caught me walking in my sleep a few times, heading toward Atlanta. Petrina would do the same thing. It's as if something was making us go back, some inner animal urge to return to Atlanta."

"Good, because I need you to go back."

"Not going, Evalle."

"We had a deal."

He shook his head. "I said I'd give you information, but I did not say I'd return with you."

Sam cut in, "The point is that I think the Alterants are beginning to be drawn to Atlanta."

She ignored Tristan for a moment and asked Sam, "Why?"

"It could be you."

"Oh, sure. I'm a regular Alterant magnet." She hadn't found one in the past three weeks.

For once, Tristan didn't make a smart follow-up comment, but spoke in earnest. "Didn't you claim there's been an unusual number of Alterant shifts and attacks in the past year in the Southeast?"

"Yes, but Rías could have committed some, or all, of the unprovoked attacks blamed on Alterants. You said so yourself."

"True, but the point is, this hasn't been as prevalent in other parts of the country, right?" Tristan said, leading her to see Sam's point.

"Right, but . . . I don't buy this theory that they're coming because of me. Why me? Having outbreaks in the Southeast doesn't prove anything. And three weeks ago lots of beasts shifted all over the country because of the sentient fog."

Tristan argued, "Rías. Sam's talking about Alterants."

"Just give me facts . . . and tell me where you're getting these facts if you want me to believe you."

Sam's arms shook when he pushed against the chair arms as if to stand, but didn't when the effort was too great. "Believe me or not, but you don't have a lot of time. If the Medb get their hands on the Alterants, they'll be able to breach the castle and kill Brina. Find the other Alterants."

"You're just full of ideas, aren't you? What makes you think I can find Alterants when I haven't located any others since meeting Tristan and his sister? Fat lot of good that's done me." She glared at Tristan, who examined his hands as if critiquing a manicure. Turning back to Sam, she asked, "Any tips on how I can find these Alterants?"

"Yes, you can—"

The living room windows exploded into the house.

Evalle smelled the burnt-lime odor that screamed Medb. She jumped to her feet and vaulted over the back of her chair, landing sure-footed.

She reached toward her boot for her dagger.

Which was still on her motorcycle back at the Iron Casket.

Two warlocks in snug, black, ninja-type clothes jumped Tristan, who hit them with kinetic blasts. Barely fazed them.

Poor Sam had been snatched up and shoved against the wall by another warlock.

Evalle swung her hand in a horizontal arc from left to right. The kinetic slice had been intended to take out the knees of the warlock attacking Sam.

Her blast bounced off the Medb.

No way.

Evalle started toward Tristan, but two more warlocks leaped through the windows.

She had her own fight coming on.

Her and Tristan's kinetics were dulled in here for some reason. A quick stomp released the blades in her boots as the last two warlocks reached her. Twisting her body, she swung her feet, cutting the first warlock's neck. Purple blood spewed everywhere.

Tristan yelled in her mind. *Link with me and I'll teleport.*

She didn't hesitate, opening her mind to feel his power surge through her.

The second warlock coming after her had paused to shove the one with the slit throat out of his way.

Evalle stuck her arms out when the room started spinning. She experienced a moment of panic. That warlock could attack her in this vulnerable position, half in and half out of teleporting.

But he'd turned from her to face the window where the Medb priestess Kizira came floating through, landing next to Tristan. She clamped a hand on his shoulder and he screamed in pain.

Evalle jerked when the pain lashed through their bond. Her body vibrated with the teleporting disrupted.

Kizira yelled at the warlock nearest Evalle, *"Stop the Alterant!"*

All of a sudden, Evalle spun into full teleportation.

At the best of times Evalle hated traveling this way. She didn't feel Tristan's presence near her as when he'd teleported her in and out of the Maze of Death.

All at once, her body whipped back and forth like a jet gyrating out of control.

She lost the link to Tristan.

But her body still flip-flopped through space in a crazy spin. Alone.

Had he managed to send her flying before he disengaged from her? She couldn't do this on her own, and she'd been teleported enough times to know something had gone wrong.

Please don't send me into a solid wall or drop me in the middle of traffic or . . .

The calamari she'd eaten churned in her stomach. She flipped and rolled, turned upside down, then all at once . . . she slammed to a stop. The spinning ended. Hallelujah.

When she opened her eyes, she was down on all fours on soft ground. Grass? And the air smelled . . . ancient.

She didn't want to raise her head.

Please, not the Tribunal. How could Tristan do that to her? How would he even be capable of sending her to the realm of gods and goddesses? But then she heard music in another room. Loud, synthesized tunes pounded the walls around her. Nothing like the shrill silence of the Nether Realm where the Tribunal met.

Two massive boots stepped into her view.

She lifted her head to meet black eyes.

Definitely not a Tribunal. Deek D'Alimonte, which meant that reverberating sound shaking the floor had to be music blasting through the Iron Casket.

Hard to believe, but she'd landed somewhere worse

than facing a Tribunal. The gods and goddesses had laws to uphold.

Deek made his own laws.

VIPER never sent anyone into Deek's club for intel for one reason—they would not come to save the agent stupid enough to break any of Deek's rules. Not without declaring war.

She'd been dumped in the one place on earth no one would willingly teleport without an invitation.

Deek surveyed her with surprise. "Evalle Kincaid?"

She'd take it as a good sign that he hadn't fried her yet, but she couldn't answer him. Not while she kept her mouth clamped shut to keep from humiliating herself by getting sick.

He angled his head in a confused-dog look. "Didn't I warn you about causing problems in my club the last time we met?"

She nodded, hoping he'd allow her that for a yes.

"And you know my rule about anyone using majik or powers inside the Iron Casket."

She gave him another nod, but technically she hadn't committed either infraction. He never said anything about teleporting. She'd point that out if she could.

Just how powerful was a centaur in his human form? Sweat ran down Evalle's cheek and dripped off her chin.

His face tightened with fury, but his voice came out soft. Dangerously soft. "You dare to teleport here uninvited?"

She shook her head, hoping to convey that this had been an accident.

"VIPER would not question my right to discipline someone who breaks into my domain." He'd leaned down so far his breath fired across her face. "I will allow you *one* chance to use that shrew's mouth to explain why I should not rip your body to shreds and use the parts to decorate my dungeon."

That required opening her mouth.

He roared, *"Speak."* The walls trembled.

She threw up on Deek.

NINE

Pain crawled up Tristan's arms and around his neck, twisting and biting. Phantom snakes with spiked skin squirmed inside his body. He clenched his eyes tighter.

Had Evalle escaped? Alive and in one piece?

He'd sent her to the Iron Casket, he hoped. Hell, he had no idea what happened after he'd shoved that blast of power into the teleporting.

He might if he'd been *born* with the ability to teleport. Unlike this witch priestess who was born with that power, Tristan had gained his ability secondhand by drinking a concoction that included the blood of immortal Hindu warriors.

Fat lot of good that blood had done him. Immortality would have been more helpful than limited teleportation skills.

A saucy female voice said, "Tristan, we meet again."

The bane of his life. He forced his eyes open and gritted out one word. "Kizira."

She released her grip on his shoulder and her warning-flare-red blouse shimmered with the movement. Sheer sleeves ruffled along her arms, down to her wrists, where slender hands had fingernails painted to match. Jeans hugged her shapely legs stuffed into knee-high boots made of eel-skin . . . that undulated.

Some men would consider her dark green eyes and oval face surrounded by a mane of sunset-red hair attractive.

He'd like to stake that head on a pike.

"What do you want, Kizira?"

"I'll let you know when I think of something." She swung around, taking in the old guy.

Whoa. Tristan blinked his eyes. What was going on with Sam? His decaying image shifted and changed . . . a glamour? Sam pulled the tubes off his mask and tossed them aside. He lost a little height with the alteration to his new form, but this early-thirties body had a substantial, even robust appearance. And, he was *not* currently being held prisoner by the warlocks.

Tristan demanded, "Who is he?"

Kizira looked from Sam to Tristan. "Oh, that's right. You think he's Sam something or other. Meet Conlan O'Meary."

The pain slithering through Tristan's veins became inconsequential compared to the surge of fury over having been screwed. "You bastard."

Tristan opened his mind to call a warning to Evalle. *Sam is—*

The words in his head bounced back at him, beating his brain with the force of a gong slamming inside a giant church bell. He grabbed his head, yelling, "Stop!"

And the sound disappeared.

Tristan took shallow breaths to keep from passing out. Stars shot across his gaze.

Kizira warned, "If you try to reach Evalle again, or

anyone else telepathically, you will suffer until your ears bleed." Then she told Conlan, "Were you successful? Convincing?"

"Hard not to be when I'm compelled," Conlan said with an edge of irritation. "I don't need that to do my part. I came to you willingly, didn't I?"

"I didn't do anything to you. If you have an issue with being compelled, file your complaint with Queen Flaevynn. But take it from someone she compels on a regular basis, you'll end up being forced to do far worse than fool an Alterant." Kizira ordered her warlocks, "Leave no trail from here."

Tristan had nothing to offer in trade to protect his sister, Petrina, and two Rías friends, except himself, and Kizira already had him wrapped in invisible binding. He hoped his group would stick with his backup plan and leave immediately when he didn't call them with news in the next fifteen minutes as scheduled. He'd told Petrina to contact Evalle or Tzader if anything happened to him.

Tristan would accept his fate as long as those three were safe. "What do you want with me, Kizira?"

She moved across the room, pausing to eye him as a useless speck of a creature. "At the present moment, not a thing. You did better than I expected."

"What do you mean?"

"Thanks to you, Evalle will find the Alterants for us."

"No, she won't." Not once Petrina gave Evalle the letter he'd written. The first part explained what he knew about Alterants that Evalle could use with the Tribunal.

The last part warned her to stay as far away from the Medb as she could.

The Medb wanted Alterants, especially Evalle.

Now he had an idea why.

The Medb believed Evalle would locate more Alterants, including specific ones they clearly had plans for, and once that happened, the Medb would capture Evalle and the other Alterants.

Not if Tristan's contingency plan worked and Petrina traded his letter in exchange for asylum with the Beladors. Evalle would protect her and the two Rías. And the minute she read the letter, Evalle would realize that coming to save him would only give the Medb what they needed most to kill Brina and take Treoir.

He grinned at Kizira. "You'll never get your hands on Evalle."

"You're wrong, Tristan." Kizira leaned forward and whispered, "Evalle will lead us to the green-eyed Alterants."

"If you say so." He gave her a noncommittal look. "I'd think by now you'd realize that Alterants aren't as easy to catch as other nonhumans."

Kizira picked her head up and looked into his eyes. "That's why I've sent a team of Svart trolls to Atlanta to keep VIPER busy until I'm ready for them to bring Evalle back with our Alterants."

Svart trolls? What the hell were those? "You think a bunch of trolls can capture Evalle?"

"To be perfectly honest, not really. But she'll eventually come to us, because she's a sucker for a lost cause."

Tristan chuckled in spite of the pain that ripped through his chest. "Here's a tip, Kizira. Don't hold your breath waiting on Evalle, because I've made sure she won't come back for me."

Kizira levitated a couple of inches off the floor, smiling indulgently as one would at a naïve child. "Evalle will never see your letter. I took it when my warlocks delivered Petrina and those Rías to TÅµr Medb . . . right before I left to come here."

"No," Tristan roared, lunging against the invisible bonds that sliced his skin. "I'll kill you!"

TEN

I t's almost one thirty. Evalle's not with you?" Quinn slowly closed the door to his suite behind Tzader.

Why did Evalle have to be late this time? What could she still be doing this time of night . . . morning?

He'd waited long enough to confess his betrayal to her. Guilt, and the potential for losing a friend, were eating through the lining of his stomach.

"No, haven't heard a word from her," Tzader called over his shoulder. When he reached the living room, he went straight for a cushy side chair and sank into it. "Glad to have your help at the cemetery, but why didn't you let me know you were coming back?"

"I made up my mind at the last minute, as soon as I felt ready to return." *And I hadn't planned on seeing you until tomorrow, but that would only have delayed the inevitable.* "Should we be concerned about Evalle?"

"Any other time I might be, but with her on some errand for Macha I'm thinking she's just running late or I'd probably have heard something from her or the goddess."

Quinn detoured to his wet bar, pulling a Guinness from the refrigerator for Tzader and pouring Boodles on the rocks for himself. He handed the chilled brew to Tzader, who wasted no time cracking it open.

Where to start?

Quinn had gone over this conversation in his head a hundred times and it never improved. "I would prefer for Evalle to be present so I only have to say this once, but now that I think about it, talking with you first may be better."

That brought Tzader's head up, his brown eyes sharpening. "You still having issues from probing Conlan's mind?"

"No noticeable residual issues."

"Then, what's bothering you?"

"We do have a complication. When I went into the precognitive area of Conlan's mind and accessed the future . . . I ran into a problem."

Tzader leaned back, shaking his head. "You think I've forgotten how you bled from your eyes, nose and every other place blood could get out? Just glad you survived. Hate that you had to be the one to see Conlan joining up with the Medb. I know you had high expectations for him as a Belador warrior."

"We both did." Quinn swirled his drink, staring at the ice. "I condemned a good man to being hunted as a traitor."

"Not your fault, Quinn. You were doing your duty. And Conlan did more damage to himself by escaping from VIPER and running."

"We gave him no other option. He'd worked double time to prove he was not his traitorous father. Conlan came to the probe session willingly. Why would a traitor allow me, of all people, to search his mind?"

"I don't know, but nothing will change popular opinion right now."

Hearing resignation in that comment, Quinn asked, "What about you, Z? You thought Conlan was innocent at one time. Do you still think so?"

"Until I see hard evidence, I'm not willing to convict any person based on a vision of the future." Tzader twisted his neck, stretching it, then settled back against the chair. "You and I may be the only two who believe in that kid. Best way we can help him is by keeping our game faces on when we're around VIPER and Brina. Act as if Conlan's on the top of our most wanted list at all times. That way when we find the *real* traitor, they'll listen."

"I see your point."

Tzader's arm dangled off the side of the chair, beer loosely clasped in his fingertips. "Right now we have to come up with a plan for the Svart trolls and find out what they're after in Atlanta. I met with Sen and the other teams at headquarters—"

This was the part that Quinn had been dreading. He interrupted by raising his hand. "Stop. Before you go any further, there's something I need to tell you."

This time, the drink Tzader took clearly allowed him a pause to think. "Okay. Shoot."

"I did experience problems that lingered after the mind probe, but thought I'd heal like I had in the past."

"You didn't?"

"Yes and no. My mind has healed completely and I'm strong enough to handle a threat or a probe, maybe even stronger than before, but right after the probe while I was in my hotel room, I thought I was having hallucinations of Kizira being in my room."

That raised an eyebrow on Tzader's grim face. "What do you think caused that?"

"When I was in Conlan's mind and found the vision of the future where I saw him at a Medb meeting with Kizira, I got distracted and . . . dropped my shields."

"What?" Tzader put his beer down and sat forward, feet on the floor, hands on his knees.

Quinn circled the mustard-yellow sofa and sat down, placing his drink on the glass end table and propping an arm across cinnamon-red pillows. "The spirit of Conlan's dead father showed up, but he didn't interfere. At first, he asked me to protect his son, then later he taunted that we were all fools. When Kizira didn't see or hear him, I took that as a positive sign. But when she started talking about the attack on Brina and Treoir Castle, I was caught off guard and allowed my shields to fall. Kizira saw me when I did."

"To be caught *that* off guard is . . . unusual for you." Tzader spent a moment assessing Quinn. "What shook you?"

Quinn had argued with himself for hours over how much to tell Tzader, but he, Tzader and Evalle had always had each other's backs. He'd have to trust that Tzader would continue watching Evalle's when Quinn was no longer around. "I told you Kizira mentioned Evalle in that vision."

"Right."

"But I didn't say in what specific context her name was mentioned. I could claim having been in too much pain, but the truth is that I needed time to digest what I'd seen and heard. With Evalle's future on the line at the time with the Tribunal, I hesitated to repeat *everything* said about her."

Tzader propped his elbows on his knees and cupped his laced fingers under his chin, sorting through something mentally. "I took what you said to mean we had to keep an eye on Evalle because she was in danger."

"I know."

"That wasn't it?"

"To some degree, yes, but in the vision I observed Conlan telling Kizira that when the time came to take possession of Treoir, he would deliver Evalle to Kizira so that Evalle could destroy the inhabitants and breach the castle."

"No way. Evalle would never do that."

Lifting a hand to hold off Tzader's anger, Quinn said, "You'll get no argument from me, but with Conlan loose, VIPER, Macha and even Brina will have to give every possibility serious consideration, even that one."

"I won't let anything or anyone harm Brina." Tzader's conviction shook the air. "But neither will I give Sen the evidence he needs to bury Evalle in a VIPER prison or Macha to terminate her. We'll capture the traitor before anyone can get to Treoir. Besides, the Medb would have to find Treoir Island first."

"That's not the *entire* problem." Quinn looked Tzader in the eye when he told him the last bit. "When I was in my hotel room, I thought I hallucinated that Kizira was there and . . . we made love."

Tzader chuckled, sitting back. "That wasn't a hallucination, bro. That's called a fantasy." Then he sobered and heaved a sigh. "Trust me, I understand about wanting someone you can't have. You said you two met when you were really young. One time. Your mind and body will never forget her. That's all. Nothing to feel guilty about, and I *know* you're loyal to the Beladors."

Quinn allowed a smile, albeit sad. "I wish this was only about lust, but there's much more going on. When you arrived afterwards at my hotel room and woke me up, I didn't recall everything about Kizira immediately, but I kept having a feeling that something was wrong. That someone had been *inside* my hotel room."

"*I* couldn't get past your warded Triquetra until you moved it from the doorknob, and no one even knows how to figure out which hotel room you'll be in on any given day but me and Evalle." Tzader added quietly, "What are you saying, Quinn?"

"That Kizira *did* come to my hotel room and we did make love."

Rarely surprised by anything, Tzader squinted in disbelief. "Based on what proof?"

"I had scratches on my back from her nails." In the precise spot where she'd left them on his back years earlier.

"She's a witch. They have ways to make you *believe* something that's not real. She could have put a spell on you when she saw you in Conlan's mind."

"She did something to me during the probe, but not a spell. In that split second when I dropped my shields and she saw me, she slipped inside my mind."

Tzader muttered a particularly nasty curse, the impact of that not lost on him. "Okay, but that still doesn't mean she was in your room."

Quinn fished a strand of woven hair in the shape of a bracelet from his coat pocket. He'd have to share what he'd never told another soul. Holding up the bracelet, he said, "This is hard evidence. She made this when we were together back when we met thirteen years ago. It's my hair. She showed this to me at that time right before admitting she was Medb and telling me she had to return to TÅµr Medb. I warned her not to take it with her, that she'd regret keeping the bracelet. She put it on her wrist and said if she ever did regret her time with me, she'd give it back to me. Then she teleported away."

"How'd you end up with the bracelet?"

"Found it on my bathroom vanity right after you left my hotel room. I tried to call out to you telepathically, but my mind exploded with so much pain I passed out again. When I came to, I found out Evalle had been taken into custody."

Tzader said, "Figured when I didn't get an answer even on your cell phone that you'd gone into a deep sleep to heal. I could have used more in your e-mail than 'Leaving US. Contact you later.'"

"Sorry about that." Quinn had plenty of reasons to be disappointed in himself these days. "I sent you and Evalle the only words I could type. I was losing my ability to communicate verbally on the way to the airport. By the time I could speak again, I was deep in the mountains, on another continent."

"I understand."

He trusted Tzader but didn't specify what mountains or what continent because he'd given his oath many years ago not to tell where he went when he had to heal. "With Evalle out of VIPER prison and safe from Kizira—"

Tzader cut in, "If not for that bastard Tristan, Kizira wouldn't have had a shot at Evalle."

"That's not entirely true."

"Why not?"

"I'm the one who told Kizira she would find Evalle with Tristan. At least, I think that's what I told her. I spent much of the time I was gone dredging through my memories to determine how much damage I might have done before leaving." Quinn had spent long nights ferreting out pieces of information and even longer nights trying to come to terms with his guilt.

Tzader hadn't shown any reaction to that news, but the Belador Maistir seldom allowed his emotions to surface. "Go ahead and get it all out, Quinn."

"I convinced myself I *had* to leave immediately to keep from endangering you, Evalle, Brina and the Beladors. Looking back, I don't see myself in quite so altruistic a way." Quinn had been afraid of what he might do involuntarily if Kizira tried to control his mind, but escaping without a word still felt cowardly. "As I healed and my mind strengthened, I managed to piece together what I believe truly happened. Kizira *was* in the hotel room with me, we did make love and she did convince me to tell her that Evalle was with Tristan."

"I hear ya, Quinn, but know this. No real harm done as far as Evalle is concerned, because she outsmarted Kizira in the Maze of Death, but it does bother me that Kizira can get to you in a room you've warded. How'd that happen?"

"I think she was able to teleport into the room because she accessed my mind and found a way to move the Triquetras by using *my* kinetics."

"Can she still do that?"

"No, at least not the part about getting through my security. I had someone different ward new Triquetras and told him to ward them in a way that the blades can only be moved by my hand, no kinetics."

"Good."

"That protects me . . . but not everyone else."

"What do you mean?"

"Kizira is still inside my mental walls. I can feel where she's been and that the pathway is open." He wouldn't admit that a part of him enjoyed having a sense of her being near. What kind of person was he to feel that way about an enemy of the Beladors?

A fool.

Tzader asked, "Has she come back into your mind?"

"Not since that night. I would know immediately now if she tried." He'd expected her to try again but hadn't felt a thing in three weeks, maybe because of where he'd been while healing. "Doesn't matter. I'm still a security risk. That's why I stopped you from telling me anything about what was discussed at headquarters or with Brina."

"You said you'd know if Kizira entered your mind again?" Tzader continued, stuck on that for some reason.

"Yes."

"Then this isn't as bad as it sounds. Evalle will understand about what happened. You know she'd never hold that slip against you."

"No, she wouldn't. I do feel strong enough to keep Kizira from taking control of my mental abilities again, but that doesn't change the fact that she still may be able to slide inside unexpectedly. There's too much at risk to . . ." Quinn paused. "Allow her this level of access to the Beladors."

It took about ten seconds for Tzader to understand what Quinn meant. "You expect me to have you *executed*?"

"I expect you to do whatever is necessary for the safety of Brina, Evalle and the Beladors. My mind has been one of the most powerful weapons in our tribe since I learned how to control it. Now I fear that weapon might be used against everything I've spent my life protecting."

Contemplative would be a good way to describe Tzader, which Quinn had expected. He never anticipated Tzader's next words.

"We can use this to our advantage."

"Come on, Tzader. You're only delaying that which is inevitable."

"I'm not delaying a damn thing." Tzader could boom

his voice without raising it loud enough to be heard in the next room. "I. Will. Not. Kill. You."

I would never ask that of you, my friend. "You won't have to make that decision. I intend to turn myself in to VIPER, and the Tribunal will hand me over to Macha."

Tzader pushed to his feet, moving across the room, his brow creased with heavy thinking. He turned back and crossed his arms in a way that meant he would not be swayed from some decision. "I need you and your mind to fight what's coming. These Svart trolls are most likely a sign of the Medb stepping up their game, but I don't know how. You're right about one thing. Your mind *is* one of our most powerful Belador weapons. Brina can't afford to lose you. *I* can't afford to lose you, and neither can Evalle."

The desire to survive was a strange bedmate for honor when faced with duty.

Quinn had spent the past twenty-four hours getting prepared to face the Tribunal and Macha. He'd been sure everyone who mattered to him would be safer from the Medb with him out of the picture. Tzader made Quinn's sacrificial death sound as though he would be turning his back on everyone.

Enticing, but Quinn still had one deadly problem. "What about Kizira?"

"Can you vow to me that you will put Brina and the Beladors before Kizira, even if it means Kizira's death?"

The insult Quinn felt must have shown on his face, but Tzader owed him no apology for asking the blunt question. Quinn said, "Without hesitation after what Kizira did to me and Evalle."

Tzader nodded. "That's good enough for me. You aren't going to tell anyone what happened with Kizira, but you will tell me immediately if she makes any unexpected appearance in person or in your mind."

"I can do that. What if I'm wrong and—" Quinn couldn't imagine what might happen because he'd put his mind up against the powerful druids who had trained him and they believed Quinn to be stronger than before. He still woke at night with *what ifs* pounding his skull.

"I'll stop you before you can do any damage, Quinn."

Quinn would trust that vow only from Tzader, who, Quinn knew, would do whatever duty demanded, no matter the personal loss. "This changes everything . . . except for still having to confess my betrayal to Evalle."

"You can't do that."

"I have to, Tzader. I have been tormented for weeks with guilt."

"Hate it for you, bro, but she can't know about what happened with you and Kizira. No one can. Telling Evalle would put her at risk and implicate her down the road."

That put only Tzader in the position of losing everything he'd lived for his whole life if anyone found out what had happened between Quinn and Kizira.

Quinn could still turn himself in.

Tzader must have picked up on his thoughts. "This isn't really any different than the agreement you, I and Evalle made after the night we were caught by the Medb in Utah. We've all protected each other's confidences out of honor and friendship. Nothing's changed. Brina and the future of the Beladors will always come first, but you and Evalle are right behind them."

"I will do my best to assure that your trust is not misplaced."

"No chance of that." With the decision of Quinn's death apparently settled, Tzader drew a deep breath and changed subjects. "About the Svarts."

"You were going to tell me about a conversation with Sen."

"If you want to call Sen's rant a conversation. He's popping off about not having time to constantly come out to clean up our battle messes."

Quinn pointed out, "He tends to only complain about the ones involving Evalle."

"I know. That's why I'd like to get dickhead out of our hair if I can. We need a weapon that will kill something like a Svart without harming a human or drawing unwanted attention. Something that can be used at close range."

"There's only one person who would have something of that nature. Isak Nyght."

"Yeah, I thought about that, but I haven't figured out how to get one from him without Isak's bunch realizing these battles involve nonhumans."

"Nyght sells to the military. Any chance your government contacts could get the weapon?"

"How? They'd have to tell him they needed a weapon for nonhumans, which would expose our Beladors in the government since humans aren't supposed to know about us." Tzader ran his hand over his head, thinking.

"That's all we'd need to draw Isak's attention. He'd have been in the middle of these gang battles already if he'd known trolls were involved and had any idea of when the battles were going down, but the fights erupt with no warning. There's no way to approach Isak without alerting him to VIPER, and that would turn his sights on our people."

On his way to get Tzader another beer, Quinn had an idea how to acquire a Nyght weapon. A suggestion Tzader would not like. "There is one person who can ask Isak for a weapon without drawing his attention."

"Who?"

"Evalle."

"Oh, hell no."

"She knows him better than any of us, *and* he likes her."

"*That's* the problem." Tzader started pacing again. "Isak likes her a little too much."

Quinn pulled another Guinness from the small refrigerator. "She's a big girl who can take care of herself. And Isak would give her a weapon if he thought she needed it for protection."

Tzader stopped at the massive window, looking out at Atlanta twinkling against the night sky. He turned around, accepting the cold brew, and leaned against the windowsill. "He won't hurt her as long as he doesn't know she's an Alterant, but Isak and his men drew down on Evalle once already."

"When did *that* happen?" Quinn hadn't seen that in in any e-mail briefings.

"After I left your hotel room that night you were out of it. Isak and his men saw Tristan's green eyes and wanted to blast him and his group, but Evalle protected them."

"Of course."

"Then Sen showed up out of thin air, which didn't help."

"So Isak *realized* Evalle was an Alterant?" That changed everything. Quinn had missed a lot.

"I don't know if he knew for sure that night or not, but his entire team fired when Sen just appeared."

"Bad move. Did Sen vaporize them?"

Tzader chuckled, a dry, sarcastic sound. "Not even Sen is going to kill a human and face the Tribunal. He stopped the bullets with his hand."

"He teleports, vaporizes bodies, materializes whatever he wants out of thin air, wipes minds and probably hasn't even shown us all that he *can* do. What is that guy?"

Tzader lifted the bottle when he shrugged. "Wish I knew."

"So now Isak knows that Evalle associates with Alterants? Or does he know that she *is* one?"

"No on both accounts. Sen wiped the minds of all the Nyght men before he teleported Evalle away, so Isak and his men shouldn't remember anything."

"Sen probably regrets having wiped those minds with Evalle free again."

"Bet on it," Tzader said.

Quinn returned to their original topic of finding a weapon to kill trolls. "Then Evalle can still ask Isak for the weapon."

Tzader growled, but an agreement surfaced in the midst of the sound. "I guess she can do that—"

"If Isak's interested in her as a woman, she should be safe enough."

"I don't want to hear that. Bad enough that she's been in such a foul mood with Storm missing that she's become a one-woman demolition crew in battle."

Quinn kept his face neutral, but secretly smiled at Evalle's budding social life. He didn't want her harmed any more than Tzader did, but she needed a chance to have a real life. "What's the story on Storm?"

"We don't know, and Evalle hasn't told me anything other than Storm helped her when the Tribunal sent her to hunt down the missing Alterants."

"Oh?" Quinn lost his battle not to laugh at Tzader's flat don't-go-there gaze, which only pissed off Tzader that much more.

"What's so funny, Quinn? You okay with all these guys sniffing around her all of a sudden?"

"You are the epitome of the overprotective big brother. Let's just say that I think we'll know if anyone gets out of line." Quinn did admit, "I'd enjoy sending someone into the next world if they hurt her physically, or emotionally, but I'll place my money on Evalle dealing them as much pain as we would dish out if someone dared to harm her."

Tzader finally relented and smiled. "Yeah, guess I need to accept that she can't be protected from everything." His phone buzzed. Lifting the small cell phone from his pocket, he read the screen. "Damn. Got a battle going on in south Atlanta."

"Another cemetery? Let me get my key."

"It's a cemetery, but a small battle. They have a local troll in hand. Told them to call me when we had someone to interrogate. You stay here and talk to Evalle. Explain to her about getting the Nyght weapon." Tzader shoved the phone into his pocket, then snapped his fingers and stopped, giving Quinn a pained look. "One more thing."

"Yes?"

"On the way here, I got a call from one of our Beladors who'd been trading for intel with a Nightstalker. He picked up a tip that a woman was asking around about you early this evening. I'll break loose a couple of agents as soon as I can to see what they can find out."

Quinn had no idea who it could be. "Did you get a name?"

"Just a first name. Lanna."

"Bloody hell."

Tzader had started for the door and swung around, his gaze sharp with concern. "The Medb?"

"Worse. Family."

ELEVEN

Evalle's mouth tasted too disgusting to describe.

But she could not ask Deek for water. If she uttered a word, it could well be her last.

She'd sit here quietly on the nicely sodded floor of his office and not draw his attention. Again.

Deek stood bent over with his hands propped on his desk, intent on something he read. Gleaming black hair hung loose around his shoulders. When he took on human form, he did so in a breathtakingly gorgeous body. He'd ignored her for the last couple hours, which had probably been easier to do once he'd showered and changed into the chocolate-brown linen shirt and matching pants.

Had to smell better without the contents of her stomach slimed all over his pants and shoes. His men had washed the residue of her calamari upheaval off the office lawn.

She would never have guessed that Deek would floor his personal space with sod, but then she didn't spend a lot of time wondering about someone like Deek.

Better to avoid him mentally *and* in person.

Her wrists burned from where she'd struggled against the shackles anchoring her to the wall, but she'd stopped that once it became clear she breathed Deek's air for only one reason.

He'd said he'd give her a chance to explain why he shouldn't kill her. "A chance" probably meant one sentence. She doubted she could plead her case thoroughly in one sentence. But Deek must have some personal code of honor that prevented him from toasting her until she actually supplied him with a reason for being here.

The way she saw it, the longer she kept her mouth shut, the longer she stayed alive.

Her refusal to speak had brought on a bout of yelling.

He'd done so in four languages, one that sounded old enough to be biblical. He'd shifted into a centaur, then back to human form, clothes and all, shouting at her with every breath.

When he'd returned from showering, he'd calmly asked her one time to explain herself.

Nope. She'd kept her mouth shut and held on to her only hope of surviving. He hadn't said another word since then.

His silence bothered her far more than his yelling.

She *could* call Tzader or Quinn telepathically, but their lives would be at risk, too, the minute they walked in here. What could either of them do? Demand she be released when Deek had full authority here?

That would probably get her tortured slowly before he killed her. The thought of torture brought on another wave of worry over Tristan. Where was he? What was Kizira doing to him?

Evalle had to get out of here and find a way to help him.

A knock at the door broke into her thoughts and

Deek's formidable concentration. His black gaze shot to her first, then he looked at the door, and it opened on its own.

Now that he'd noticed her again it didn't matter if she made noise. She sat up, shifting her tired body.

A hot security guy with a smoking body—one of the many who worked for Deek—decked out in a black Iron Casket T-shirt and cargo pants strode in. "We can't budge it."

"Ridiculous." Deek hit the solid-marble desk with his fist. Sounded like Thor striking his hammer.

The security guard held up both hands. "Don't know what to tell you, boss. Must be warded or something. Won't roll, and four of us tried to lift it."

Not roll? They were trying to move her motorcycle?

Good luck with that, boys. They weren't human, but she hadn't picked up any superstrong energy, which meant they were probably just male witches.

Anger smoldered in Deek's vicious gaze for a moment, then his eyes thinned with an unholy smile. He told his man, "Leave us."

When the door closed, Deek stepped over to where Evalle peered up at him from her uncomfortable position. "Listen up, Alterant. I said I'd give you a chance to convince me not to kill you. I did *not* say you could stay here while you composed a novel. One sentence."

Where would he send her?

She'd heard rumors about Deek's basement—*dungeon* would be more accurate—and didn't want to find out if those hideous stories were true. The Beladors would eventually come looking for her, and when they did, they'd find her gold GSX-R sitting outside the Iron Casket. Her motorcycle would be easy to spot after daylight in the nightclub's empty parking lot.

But that didn't appear to concern Deek. And why should it, since VIPER was no issue for him?

"Well, Alterant?"

Trying not to offend him, Evalle lifted both shoulders in what she hoped conveyed her desire to discuss the situation, but that she needed more than one sentence to do that.

"You are trying my patience, which is unwise since I have none to begin with. You hold your tongue thinking to prolong your life?"

She smiled and nodded. *Now you're getting it, skippy.*

"I can assure you a very long life while you wait, one that will be filled with *interesting* activities."

She didn't care for the sound of that, which must have shown on her face. So much for practicing not exposing her emotions. She'd never make a decent poker player.

Deek grinned. A happy centaur in this situation could not mean good news.

He lifted an eyebrow, smirking. "Your motorcycle is no problem. I can destroy it, even with the warding, but not yet. For now I'll have it covered with a small storage building or a construction Dumpster with the middle cut out. No one will find it . . . ever."

That trumped her staying quiet.

"I see that we're finally communicating," he said.

Gloating is unattractive, Deek.

Better to take her best shot now and find out if she had to risk contacting Tzader and Quinn for help getting out of this situation. She drew in a deep breath so Deek couldn't assume she was done if she stopped to breathe. "I would never come into your building uninvited and I didn't this time because I had no idea where I was being teleported since someone else was doing it and I'm sorry I threw up on you but teleporting makes me sick and"—she was running out of air—"if you'll let me go I can promise it will never happen again—"

"Really?"

Evalle sucked in a quick breath. "Well, sure. I'm not stupid, Deek. No one breaks your rules in your house."

"Your time is up."

Just as well. She couldn't think of anything else to say. "The Beladors *will* come for me if I go missing. And there's a tracker who will find my bike."

Deek said, "I am not concerned about who comes for you. Don't try to convince me that VIPER will question my right to sanction anyone who breaches my domain, regardless of the reason."

True. Especially for an Alterant.

Sen would offer suggestions on how to torture her.

But Deek hadn't done anything to her yet, so she held out hope of negotiating. "Isn't there some way we can work this out, Deek? It *was* an accident."

He strolled back across his office, then turned, facing her as he leaned a hip against his desk. "Who sent you here?"

Now she'd get Tristan in trouble after he'd clearly

given her all his teleporting power to help her escape. "It's complicated."

"When you figure it out, let me know." Deek vanished.

The door opened and two of his security men came in.

Should she use her kinetics and risk getting toasted on the spot?

One guy reached down and unlocked the manacle on her left arm. She yelled, "Deek! Come back."

The other guard locked a metal collar around her neck.

"Oh, come on, Deek. You want to hear what I have to say."

Deek reappeared in front of her. He lifted his chin at the two security guys, who immediately withdrew from the room. When the door closed, Deek told her, "Speak."

"I was with another Alterant and we got ambushed by a Medb hunting party of warlocks. Someone started teleporting me, then a fight broke out, and the next thing I know I'm in here . . . uh, talking to you."

"You mean barfing on me."

"That was unintentional."

"So how do you plan to work this out, as you say?"

She had one hand still hooked to a steel anchor in the wall, but lifted her free hand in an open-palm gesture. "I've apologized. What else do you want?"

"You offered to make amends."

"Of course, just tell me what I can do." Hope fluttered in her chest.

"I'll have to think about it and let you know."

That sounded like they'd just made some sort of deal, but she'd missed the part with the details spelled out. "I don't understand."

"I will let you go and you will owe me a favor."

Oh, man. Now she understood why he hadn't killed her. "What kind of favor?"

Things had been rocking along nicely until she said that.

He spread his feet and crossed his arms, staring down at her as if she'd asked a stupid question. "The kind of favor that buys back your life today."

Good point. "Got it. Just wanting to be clear since we don't really have each other's cell number to talk about it later on."

"I will find you when I have something for you to do, Alterant."

The second manacle disappeared along with the metal collar as well as the steel anchor that had held her to the wall. She rubbed her wrists where they'd chafed. Did you thank someone who had threatened to kill you, chained you to a wall, then made you agree to an open-ended favor for the chance to continue breathing?

When the person doing all that was Deek D'Alimonte, then the answer was yes. "Thanks."

Evalle stood up and started for the door, but in two steps she was outside, heading toward her motorcycle.

Had Deek teleported her out here? She didn't have the urge to hurl. Maybe someone as old as Deek—and she had no idea how many centuries old that might be—

had luxury-level teleporting. She couldn't wait to dig out the bottle of water she'd stuffed in her tank bag and wash out her mouth.

Downing the balance of her water, she considered her next move.

Finding Tristan was going to take some time since he hadn't answered her telepathic calls. She doubted he was still at that farmhouse and had no idea how to find it again.

With a little over an hour before daylight, she had to touch base with Tzader and explain being late. After calling out to him with no answer, she tried Quinn, who answered.

Where have you been, Evalle?

She hated her hesitation, but a lot had happened over the past few weeks and she still didn't know exactly what had occurred between Quinn and Kizira, if anything. She answered, *That thing I had to do for Macha took longer than I expected . . . and I really can't talk about it. She got me out of VIPER prison and so . . .*

That sounded lame and not like her, because she shared everything with Tzader and Quinn.

Quinn said, *I understand completely. We were worried about you.*

I called to Tzader, but he didn't answer.

He's interrogating a troll from another gang battle. Tzader may have had Sen teleport them both to headquarters to lock down the troll, and couldn't communicate.

Sorry I missed our meeting, Quinn. I would have called one way or another, but I wasn't where I could do that.

Where are you now?

Around midtown, headed into Atlanta.

I'd still like to see you.

Had she picked up anxiety in Quinn's telepathic voice or was it just a case of her being overly suspicious about everything right now? *Sure. Where do you want to meet?*

He surprised her by suggesting a diner she ate at regularly near Five Points, a block away from Woodruff Park. Not Quinn's caliber of cuisine at all, but he knew she kept vampire hours due to her deadly reaction to the sun, and sunrise would come soon. Quinn had chosen somewhere close to her underground apartment to make it easy for her.

A good friend. The best.

She hated the way suspicion played fast with her heart.

By the time she parked her bike near the diner, her stomach had settled and now complained again about the lack of food. During normal business hours, the diner hosted an eclectic group of patrons that ranged from men in suits to casually dressed tourists. But the late nighters who stumbled in when Evalle normally ate here tended to dress on the scruffy side.

That made it easy to spot Quinn's blue-gray sport coat, black sweater and dark gray pants. Not that his clothes stood out in the chrome and Formica diner so much as did the man inside the window dressing. He could wear rags and still appear out of place sitting in a booth that was upholstered in purple plastic.

Sliding onto the seat across from him, she waited for the waitress, who came over to take Evalle's cheeseburger and fries order. Her idea of comfort food.

With no better way to open the conversation, she asked, "Are you okay? Z said you'd gone away to heal."

"Yes, I left rather abruptly, but it was unavoidable." Quinn's fingers tapped against a chipped ceramic mug of coffee. "Sorry I was unable to offer assistance when Sen came for you."

What had him so edgy? If he felt guilty over that, she could ease his worry. "You couldn't have stopped them from putting me in a cell."

He paused in tapping and opened his hand in a maybe/maybe-not motion.

"Seriously, Quinn. Macha was the only person who could get me out of that prison, and she did, so it all worked out." For now. But Evalle wouldn't burden him with her problems when he seemed to be just getting back on his feet. "Z said you were bad after the mind probe. I'm just glad you're okay. We missed you. Where were you?"

Quinn's lips tilted, a smile slow in coming. He'd always been the one to joke with her, always ready to lift her spirits. "I missed you as well. I would be happy to share where I've been, but it's a place hidden high in the mountains in another country that has been kept secret for more than eight hundred years. They've taken me in before when I needed their . . . gifts. I know I can trust you, but I gave my word to never share the location."

She wasn't insulted. In fact, *now* she felt better about

not being able to tell him where she'd been earlier. "Hey, no problem. I was just curious where someone with a mind like yours went for a tune-up." Her joke fell flat.

She couldn't put her finger on why things were weird between them when they'd always been comfortable in each other's company. Now would be the time and place to ask Quinn about Kizira, but Evalle couldn't make herself bring it up yet.

No reason to rush.

She picked at a loose thread on her jeans and couldn't figure out where to look. To get the conversation moving, she switched to a subject that should be easier. "Any word on the Svart trolls?"

"Yes. Tzader asked me to catch you up." Quinn paused as the waitress served Evalle, then he hit the high points with his usual precise way of speaking.

She noticed how his attention flitted between the coffee mug and the edge of the plastic menu he picked at with his thumbnail.

The imperturbable Quinn nervous?

No way. She opened her empathic senses just enough to get some read on him. The first feedback surprised her. Why would Quinn be feeling distressed? The next sensation she picked up hurt her heart.

Quinn was sad.

So not like him.

He finished his rundown on the Svarts by saying, "Sen has made it abundantly clear that he expects us to find a way to deal with the trolls without constantly calling him."

"As if we *want* to call him? What does he expect us to do?"

"Sen offered no remedy, but Tzader has an idea. He thinks if we could acquire a weapon that would kill trolls and other nonhumans in a way that doesn't harm humans or expose our activity to them, we wouldn't have to call on Sen so often. A weapon that could be used at close range."

"There's only one person who might have that."

Quinn lowered his voice even though the closest patron was some poor old homeless guy six booths away who had nodded off. "We know. Isak Nyght."

"The problem with that is keeping Isak out of our way the minute he catches wind of any nonhuman activity."

"Exactly." Quinn stopped fingering his coffee mug and studied her now. "We thought you could ask Isak."

Evalle had finished all she could eat and tossed the paper napkin on top of her plate, then shoved it away. "He'll be suspicious if I ask."

"Not if you tell him you want it for your own protection. Based upon his interest in you, I believe he would loan you a weapon."

Now she got it. "You want me to play the *girl card*? Are you serious?"

That got a smile out of Quinn. "You make it sound as though you aren't equipped for such a mission."

"Oh, sure. But that's like using a car built from scrap parts to chauffeur the governor around."

"You discount your appeal, Evalle."

"No, I'm a realist. I have no idea how to flirt and you know that."

"I don't think that will be necessary. Isak Nyght took an interest in you the first time he found you with a demon. Do you look any different now than you did then?"

"No." She'd even shared a meal with Isak wearing clothes ripped from battle, bruises on her arms and her hair askew. But that was the best a man could expect when he sent an armed team to snatch her off the street just to have dinner with him.

"Unless . . . you're concerned about exposing your identity to Isak. I won't agree to anything that puts you at that type of risk."

She waved that off with a flip of her hand. "Nah. We seem to be past his wanting me to take off my sunglasses. As long as I keep these on, he has no reason to suspect I'm an Alterant."

Quinn was right. Isak had taken an interest in her, one that might come back to bite her someday, but he'd made it clear in the past that she could come to him if she ever needed help with a threat. This should count. "I'll do it, but I'm surprised Tzader's going along with me seeing Isak."

"It took some convincing to persuade our overprotective friend." When she grinned, Quinn continued. "He balked when I suggested you as the best choice to approach Isak, but he finally agreed."

Should she feel proud that Quinn believed in her ability to gain a weapon they desperately needed, or suspicious of a secret ulterior motive because of what Kizira had said? *Why can't that witch stay out of my world? I trust Quinn. Period.*

Quinn must have taken her silence as concern. "If you'd prefer, I could accompany you."

She'd love to have Quinn or Tzader with her, but Isak had acted territorial around her in the past, so she'd be better off going alone. "Thanks, but I'd have to spend more time explaining you than getting the weapon."

"As you wish." Quinn eyed his watch, some elegant piece of Swiss craftsmanship. He'd lost that moment of cheerfulness and turned quiet again. "I don't want to rush you, but you have only a half hour to reach your apartment."

She had a five-minute drive, but Quinn could be just as overprotective as Tzader in his own way. Standing, she reached for her money, but Quinn tossed down more than enough for the meal and tip, saying, "I've got this one."

She generally balked at his picking up the tab, which would turn into good-natured bantering by the time they reached the sidewalk. But the air between them had cooled in the last minute, once again riddled with a strange discomfort. *Am I acting paranoid around Quinn or is he being overly careful around me?*

She still hadn't asked Quinn about Kizira.

When they walked outside, the air carried the crisp chill of early autumn. Great for wearing full riding gear. Quinn walked with her to where Evalle had parked her bike at the corner. When she stopped a few short feet away, they both seemed to hesitate to say good-bye.

Her chest would never stop aching if she didn't get this said. "I need to ask you something, Quinn."

"Sure. What about?"

"It's about back when the sentient fog was coming through Atlanta, before you left to go heal."

"Go on." Quinn had turned away from the streetlight with half of his face lost in a dark shadow. His posture stiffened.

Nobody liked to relive hellish memories, and that probe must have been pretty rough to send Quinn into hiding to repair his mind.

Her throat tightened against the words. She hated questioning her friend, but she couldn't take another day inside her head with this. "Did you . . . uh, run into Kizira anywhere during that time?"

"No."

His decisive answer gave her a rush of relief for a moment, but her empathic sense picked up something out of sync—that Quinn was uncomfortable. Why?

Maybe she hadn't been specific enough.

Better to get this done all at once, like ripping off a Band-Aid. She scratched her hair, knocking her ponytail loose in the back. "So there's no way you would have told Kizira that she could find me with Tristan that day?"

"No." He stared off into the darkness for a moment, then must have decided they were finished. "You should go before it gets any closer to daylight. I'll see you later." He turned and walked away.

She couldn't fault him for the cold tone or quick

retreat. She'd be insulted, too, if their roles had been reversed and he'd questioned her loyalty to him.

What she didn't understand was the wild whip of anxiety she'd picked up from Quinn as he left. It contradicted his stiff answers.

But he had answered her.

Maybe everything would make more sense once she caught up on sleep. She hadn't seen her bed in two days. Reaching for her helmet hooked on the mirror of her bike, she paused. Unease skittered over her skin. Someone approached from behind.

Evalle swung around, prepared to face a threat. And it was, but only to her heart. She crossed her arms. "Stalking me is dangerous, Storm."

Although she sort of liked that he'd come searching for her.

"Not as dangerous as the other things stalking the city tonight. You'd know if you'd been in the city since midnight."

Had he been looking for her since then? But that didn't explain his finding her here. "How did you know where I'd be right now?"

"I didn't. I was in this area for another reason."

Oh. So he hadn't come looking for her.

She kept her chin up and squashed her disappointment. She'd already made a fool of herself earlier by getting annoyed about Adrianna. "I did leave the city for a bit. Had some business to take care of. Why are you still out and about?"

"I had some time to burn."

He should be burning that time at home in bed. His eyes had a dark, hollow look. The urge to fuss over him snuck up on Evalle . . . and reminded her how Adrianna had spent weeks fussing over him as his nurse. She had to let that go. That discussion had been seven hours ago.

A long seven hours. Amazing how exhaustion took the edge off her hurt, and anyway, the hurt hadn't been Storm's fault. He shouldn't be blamed for her insecurities. "What have you been doing tonight?"

"Talking to Nightstalkers for one thing."

"About what?"

"The gang battles."

"Did you find out anything?"

"Few things. That's why I ended up tracking something to this spot."

He'd been using his ability to track nonhumans. The same way he'd found her in South America when no one else could. He'd defied Tribunal orders to come after her.

Her tired mind immediately tallied points in his favor for that—points to wipe out any lingering irritation over the whole Adrianna issue. "What were you tracking?"

"I picked up a Svart scent from the cemetery where you fought."

Why had he done that? "VIPER doesn't even know you're back yet and you don't owe them anything. You should be home resting and not risk being seen."

He closed the distance between them, never moving his flint-hard gaze from hers. His chest rose and fell sharply in time with the slow blink of his eyes. Muscles along his jaw tensed and flexed until he released a hiss of air and sighed. "I can't rest. Not when I'm worried about you."

She caught herself before she sighed, but her lips slipped into a smile. How was it when she thought she'd never let a man touch her skin, much less her heart, that Storm had found the route? A twisted and rutted path, and one that required the steel will of a man like Storm to navigate. She was touched by his concern but didn't want to encourage him to stay on his feet when he didn't appear fully recovered.

She said, "We both know I can take care of myself."

"From what I'm hearing, these Svarts are not to be underestimated. The one I tracked left the cemetery, then went to where I met you by your bike, then I caught a similar scent not far from here, in the area of your apartment. I picked up yet another Svart scent that led me here, then it vanished. I think these trolls might be looking for you."

"Me? Why?"

"I don't know. I just have a feeling I'm right."

She had yet to learn everything about Storm, and with his unusual heritage she respected his gift, but a Svart looking for her? "I can't come up with one reason why a Svart would be searching for me. Probably just a matter of them covering a lot of ground in the city that crossed with my movements."

"I knew you'd come up with some excuse instead of realizing you shouldn't be running around alone right now."

"I'll be fine."

"You don't have to fight every battle by yourself." He touched her hair, lightly running a finger down the side until his hand stopped on her shoulder.

She wished he'd pull her to him and kiss her again.

He asked, "Where have you been?"

"I can't tell you."

His hand slid off her shoulder to hang at his side. "Now who's keeping secrets?"

"It's not like that. I had something to do for the Beladors."

His face closed down, guarded again. "You take backup?"

"Not for this."

"It's not safe for you."

"Since when has it ever been safe in our world?" she asked with a grim smile. "I fight demons and trolls and whatever else shows up to threaten humans. That's my job."

"Svart trolls are more deadly than demons and local trolls. Plus there's been another gang battle since I saw you."

"How did you know about—" Evalle's heart frosted over at the realization that only one other VIPER agent would have told Storm anything. She kept her voice free of a jealous tinge, but just saying the witch's name caused her to grind her back teeth. "Did Adrianna tell you?"

Storm shook his head slowly. "I've gone home. She doesn't know where I live."

So where had Adrianna and Storm been when she was taking care of him if not at his apartment, house, hut . . . whatever? Evalle shielded her momentary relief at that small confession, until she realized *she* didn't know where he lived either.

But Storm had said he'd put that in the e-mail draft for her so she could come to dinner. Had he done that yet? Evalle pushed her tired mind back to business. "So where'd you get that information on the gang battles?"

"From your Nightstalker buddy."

"Grady?"

"Yes."

"I'm not surprised he knows about the Svarts." Evalle yawned. "I need to get going. Sunrise is coming."

"You've got eighteen minutes to make a mile on your street jet."

She gave him a wan smile. "That gives me sixteen more minutes of sleep if I leave right now."

"I can think of a better use for those sixteen minutes."

"Oh? How would *you* use them?" She smiled, enjoying a warm glow from his flirting.

"Proving how wrong you are about Adrianna."

Adrianna? Evalle lost the warm glow. She didn't want to listen while Storm painted the witch as someone only concerned with his health. Men would never see Adrianna the way women saw her.

Just when Evalle thought she'd put this unexpected jealousy to bed, the green-eyed devil reared its ugly head. "No."

TWELVE

Evalle pinned Storm with a look that should warn him his health could soon be in jeopardy again and said, "I'm not wasting my time or breath discussing Adrianna."

Storm put a hand on her arm and leaned down, nose to nose with her. "You are the most thickheaded female I've ever met."

"Not winning any points right now, Storm." She pulled on her arm, not enough to break his hold. Just to make a point. "Let go of me if you don't want to land on your butt on the other side of the street."

"Sixty seconds."

"For what?"

"To prove—"

She huffed. "I got it. Adrianna did you a favor. Nothing to discuss."

"You may be *trying* to believe that but you don't. I can't stand knowing every time you see Adrianna you're going to be hurt all over again."

See? Things like that made her heart wiggle. "If I'm hurt, it's my problem to deal with. I believe what you told me."

"But you're still bothered about Adrianna."

She hated to admit he'd hit that nail dead center, but

she couldn't deny the truth. Angling her chin in challenge, she said, "Okay, I'll give you sixty seconds—"

He had her in his arms, kissing her before she realized
he'd moved.

Her righteous anger over Adrianna, which had fes-
tered since last night, tumbled beneath the onslaught of
emotions crashing through her.

She had the backbone of a caterpillar when Storm
touched her. He held her close, secure in his arms.

She'd missed everything about him in the past few
weeks. Missed the way he took her in stride, accepting
her as she was. Missed his voice, which whispered across
her skin. And most definitely missed the way his mouth
felt against hers right now, teasing and nipping.

Heat zinged through her core, spinning tornadoes of
excitement everywhere and shocking her skin, coiling
deep inside until she murmured against his lips.

He smiled, never slowing the kiss that said so much.

Much more than sixty *hours* of talking could accomplish.

She tasted his sincerity, knew by the way his heart
slammed with each beat that she mattered to him.

Blood barreled through her own heart, forcing the
organ to feel alive after years of being an iceberg, frozen by terror. Another man had sent her into emotional
lockdown as a teen.

But Storm could stir a fever inside her with nothing
more than a look.

His hand cupped the back of her head, carefully and
gently. Probably still remembering how she'd reacted like

a trapped animal when he'd stepped too close to her in an underground subway tunnel. She'd shoved him thirty feet across the tracks. He'd landed against a concrete wall.

Nothing like Sen had done to Storm, but a hit that would have seriously hurt a human.

And would have sent any other man backpedaling to get as far away from a freak as possible.

Not Storm. He'd dusted himself off and had come right back, refusing to let her retreat from him. Looking at her with too much understanding as if he could see past her fears, all the way to the emotional wasteland where her personal demons crouched in the corners of her mind, laughing at her.

She'd tried to warn Storm away more than once, but he could be beyond stubborn at times.

He moved his long fingers lightly over her face and hair, forcing her to think about him and only him. The last three weeks melted away. She ran her hands up into his hair, then folded her arms around his neck. He kissed her with a hunger that sent shivers of excitement fingering along her spine.

She'd never expected to feel *that* with a man.

The female voice haunting her mind lately said, *To feel is to live. To live is to love.*

Evalle hoped the woman could hear *her* when she silently replied, *Go. Away.*

Storm paused. He swept his lips softly across hers and murmured something in a language she didn't understand. But she could feel the passion in his words.

He was telling her he cared.

Then his lips were gone and his breath coming hard as if he'd been battling for hours. He dropped a kiss on her forehead, then pulled back, raking a knuckle over her cheek.

Her eyes fluttered open to find him waiting patiently. He had something to tell her.

She pulled her hands back to his chest and conceded the challenge. "You win. I was an idiot."

Storm brushed his fingers over her hair and spoke in a deep whisper. "You're not an idiot. You're a woman who does everything with passion. Even being jealous."

"I wasn't . . ." The lie died in her throat. "Okay, I was jealous."

"I know, and that's why I need you to understand why you have no reason to ever be when it comes to me." His chest moved under her hand as he took in a deep breath. "My guardian spirit, Kai, stayed with me the whole time I was injured. She said she doubted that I would come back to this world."

Evalle's fingers clenched his shirt, unable to stop the knee-jerk reaction. What if he hadn't come back at all? She couldn't bear the thought.

He kissed her again, a quick touch, as if not quite finished with her, then continued. "I told Kai I was not ready to leave. That I had to come back. She said I would have to fight a fierce battle to return to the human world, and even then she didn't think I'd survive. But she believed that the will to live could be greater than the pull of death if my reason for fighting was powerful enough. She asked why I had to come back."

"What did you tell her?" The question slipped out of Evalle on a strained breath.

"I had to hold you one more time."

Evalle never, ever cried, but she came close when he said that. She dropped her head onto his chest, so glad that his guardian spirit had been with him. "Thank you for coming back."

"There was never a question of my returning. Not in my mind. I owe Adrianna a debt for her help that I plan to repay, but only as a friend. I'm not interested in seeing her again for any other reason."

"Okay." Evalle lifted her head. She still had some work to do on her lack of confidence as a woman, but she believed Storm.

His gaze searched beyond her. "I don't want you to go, but you're running out of dark, sweetheart. Horizon's getting lighter all the time."

Sweetheart? She reached up and placed her palm on his face, reminding herself that he had come back to her. Alive.

He turned to kiss her skin. "If you keep that up, I'm going to have to kiss you again," he teased, then wrapped his fingers around her wrists to pull her arms down.

She hissed at the contact.

He pulled her wrists up into the light. "What the hell happened to you this time?"

"It's a long story and I can't really talk about it."

"Why not?" Now *he* was angry.

Why couldn't they both end this on a happy note?

"Because I'm doing something for . . . my tribe and

I'm not supposed to say anything about it." She hoped Storm didn't read a lie in that because she'd been doing Macha's business when she went to see Tristan, so in a warped way that was technically for the Beladors. Pulling one hand free, she reached toward her bike to grab her helmet.

Indecision shot through Storm's gaze, but he didn't press her for more when he released her other wrist. He asked, "What are you doing tonight when you come back out after dark?"

Going to find Isak and ask for a weapon that can kill trolls. But telling Storm that would not go well and hesitating to answer wasn't helping.

Shaking his head, he muttered, "Still can't trust me, huh?"

"That's not true." She would tell him if not for having to then explain Isak and hearing Storm rant about her meeting a man whose goal in life was to kill all Alterants. "I just have to do something for Quinn and Tzader, then I'll be in touch."

"That sounds like VIPER business."

"It is."

"Then why can't you tell me what you're doing?"

"It's not that I don't trust you—"

"Right." Frustration fueled his glare. "Let me get this straight. You don't trust me enough to share what you're up to, and you question me on something when I tell you the truth, but just accept it when Quinn lies to you?"

"What *lie*?" She shoved her helmet back over the bike mirror.

Storm dropped his chin, staring at the sidewalk. "I shouldn't have said anything."

"Did you hear my conversation with Quinn?"

"Not intentionally. I was focused on tracking the Svart when I saw your bike and had just walked up when you two stopped to talk. I backed away but I can't help that I have exceptional hearing. Forget that I said anything. I know he's a good friend of yours."

"What. Lie."

He lifted a face teeming with regret. "When you asked him about seeing Kizira or if he'd told her that you could be found with Tristan back when you were in the Maze of Death, Quinn lied. On both accounts."

THIRTEEN

"Cathbad?"

He smiled at the sound of Flaevynn's voice fillin' his dungeon chamber, but kept his head bent over an ancient tome he was readin' for the third time.

This had to be the one.

"Do not ignore me, *druid*," she warned.

Liftin' his head, Cathbad searched his cell, his gaze runnin' over the wall of books, single bed and few amenities . . . but no Medb queen present. "Hello, Flaevynn. Why do ya no come to see me in person?"

"And risk you trapping me down there?" Her voice swirled around him. A tempting, seductive cadence that men succumbed to all the time. After more than six hundred years with this woman, Cathbad knew better. Would seem only fair to lure the witch into his dungeon an' lock her here for a few years since that was what she ha done to him. But he could no indulge in fantasies of payback until he got what he wanted of her.

He'd waited patiently for this moment when Flaevynn had to admit she needed him or face her death. He poked at her, sayin', "Why would I do somethin' so foolish as trap ya down here? Does no you nor me any good for us to no work together."

The lack of immediate response meant she probably

tapped one of those long, black fingernails against the arm of her throne and fumed over the fact that she ha run out of options, an' way out of time.

When she finally spoke again, her words were carefully chosen. "I will bring you back up into the tower *if* you swear to help me fulfill the curse . . . on *my* time frame."

He'd given up explainin' that the prophecy was no a curse, but to argue that point would only waste time an' breath. He'd taken to callin' it a curse just to quiet her yapping.

Acceptin' her offer without bein' clear on one point would be foolish. "Whether I agree to that or no, ya canna fulfill the curse without my help." He gave her a moment to swallow that medicine before adding, "But in a show of good faith, I will tell ya what ya need to know about the Alterants *if* ya lift the ward on the cell and free me. 'Tis somethin' only I know."

Silence hushed across the cool stone walls and floor for several long seconds before she said, "Agreed. Don't make me regret this or Kizira will pay."

"Understood." He had no doubt Flaevynn would sacrifice their only child for her own goals. She'd used Kizira to trap him down here an' believed he would forfeit his daughter just as quickly in pursuit of *his* goals.

How little Flaevynn knew of him, even after six centuries.

Power flushed through the dungeon as Flaevynn destroyed the ward that had prevented him from teleporting out before now.

He took his time, freshenin' up at his small sink and mirror, trimmin' his beard and smoothin' back his wavy, black hair. He smiled into the mirror at the handsome image that dinna look a day over thirty-five. Then he stepped to the center of the room and waved his hand up and down once in front of his body. His black robe disappeared, replaced by a fresh suit, the first he'd worn in two years.

Nice to have access to all of his powers again.

He'd been surprised when Flaevynn ha allowed Kizira to bring him robes to wear when he'd first been imprisoned, but realized later that Flaevynn ha done so to make a point. She wanted Kizira to see Cathbad brought low, provin' to Kizira that if Flaevynn could trap a powerful druid, she could do anythin'.

But she can no rush the curse timeline without my help.

"Cathbad!"

"I know ya miss me, woman, but be patient. I'm on my way."

Sharp lightnin' bolts shot about the room, forcin' him ta duck his head as he chuckled. She cared for no man beyond what swung between his legs and, in Cathbad's case, only for what he could do ta save her from dyin' accordin' ta the prophecy.

The Curse, as she called it.

Amused by the woman's temper, he took a moment to close the heavy book he'd been readin'. The swirlin' purple material coverin' the book had a raised silver image. Two snakes entwined in a vertical mirror image. Each asp ate its own tail . . . an ouroboros, which represented the cycle of life to death to life. The snakes circled a Medb sword.

Cathbad passed his hand over the cover, changing the exterior to a worn leather finish with the colorful image of a bard playin' a flute. The spell he'd used would alter the contents visually, shroudin' everythin' real in a glamour that hid the true information to all but him.

Druids were no known for keepin' written records, but bards scribbled stories all the time, and this one told a fascinatin' tale about beasts.

A tale that explained missin' pieces about the Alterants.

He chuckled again.

Ha the original Cathbad intended to keep this bard's tale secret or ha this been given to the bard to write down for a future Cathbad descendant wise enough to decipher the connection between this tale an' the prophecy?

It does no matter either way so long as I am the last Cathbad the Druid, the one ta find immortality.

He hummed as he tidied the cell. The time had come for the prophecy to be fulfilled, and no just because Flaevynn wanted it to be so.

He believed the original Cathbad the Druid must ha intended that the curse should come ta fruition now since the Alterants were bein' revealed. Hard ta know what the original Medb queen an' Cathbad the Druid ha planned, but he was sure the book he'd just bespelled held the key to unlockin' the curse.

When Flaevynn snooped through his chamber, an'

she would, she'd take one look at the bawdy poems and bypass that book as frivolous entertainment for a man left alone.

She would likely no figure out what he ha discerned from studyin' the words over and over for months. Odd poetry with cryptic messages, which supplied the missin' key to the curse, words struck as a pact between the original Cathbad the Druid and first Medb queen from which today's Medb Coven arose.

They'd been a wily pair, those two. Leavin' enough hints for each of the future queens of the Medb, such as Flaevynn, ta try outsmartin' the curse and gain immortality. But all the queens, except Flaevynn, ha been lulled into a false security by no knowin' their true birth dates and they'd died, leavin' the throne to their daughters as decreed in the curse.

But when Flaevynn discovered she'd been lied to about her birth date, she refused to uphold her vow and give the sacred words to Kizira on the day Kizira was accepted as a priestess. If Flaevynn ha, Kizira would become the next Medb queen upon Flaevynn's death.

If Flaevynn died, she wanted no other to rule after her.

But if she did no figure out how to reach the final step of the curse before her 666th birthday in less than two weeks, she would die.

And he would die one day later.

He sighed and rubbed his forehead. That ha been his one mistake. Flaevynn would no have learned her true birth date if no for usin' sex to catch him at a weak moment when all the blood in his brain went to the wee head between his legs.

But he would share no detail about the curse with Flaevynn a minute too soon . . . and only then if he could no find a way to take Treoir Castle from the Beladors without her help.

Smilin', Cathbad prepared to teleport and blinked once. When he opened his eyes, he found Flaevynn standin' with arms crossed near her waterfall built of precious stones.

Orange sparks shot from her purple gaze. Black hair coiled and moved down the back of a queen as beautiful as she was deadly. Dark purple lips snarled, "What took you so long?"

"Packin', cleanin' up behind the movers, fillin' out a forwardin' address card for—"

"Oh, shut up, would you?"

"Then no ask me a question." He took a deep breath, enjoying the fresh air of freedom in TÅµr Medb, the coven's tower hidden away on a dimension parallel to the human world. "Is Kizira no here?"

"She's on her way, but there's no reason to wait for her." Flaevynn floated away from the massive wall where water rolled down a dazzlin' array of diamonds, emeralds, rubies . . . every precious stone imaginable piled high an' catchin' the light of hundreds of candles flickerin' in her private quarters.

He asked, "What happened with the myst ya released?"

Flaevynn settled on her elaborate throne carved in

the shape of a gold dragon with its head curved over the top of hers, protective an' forbidding. Green dragon eyes glowed and shifted to face Cathbad when Flaeyvnn scowled. "That female Alterant with the Beladors destroyed the myst. Wiped it off the face of the earth."

That surprised him. "Evalle? How could she ha done so?"

"Kizira said the VIPER Tribunal gave her three gifts for hunting Tristan and his cohorts. Evalle used one of the gifts to destroy the myst forever."

"Ah. Quite the wise one." He tapped his chin.

"Don't be impressed. She got lucky, and luck will only take you so far."

He would disagree that it ha been mere luck, but appeasin' Flaevynn suited his purpose more at the moment than antagonizin' her. "You did no ha to release the fog so early."

Turnin' a furious gaze on him, she snarled, "It would have worked if that Alterant hadn't been given the power of *three* deities. The sentient fog was flush with violence, making Rías change, so Alterants would have, too. With a little more time, we'd have found all five green-eyed Alterants."

"'Tis no what I mean when I said you no ha to release it yet. Those Alterants will be drawn to the home of this Evalle."

"Why?" Flaevynn sat up, face alert with curiosity, remindin' him of the gorgeous creature he'd been enthralled by as a young fool.

But her eyes turned deep violet with smug knowledge.

He'd bet she already *knew* Alterants were bein' drawn to Evalle.

"I ha unwoven a twist in the . . . curse," he explained. "'Twas written that the green-eyed Alterants will be drawn ta the home of a female Alterant who stands alone with the Beladors. Some will join her an' some will fight her."

"I had an idea that might be the case."

This time, he pretended surprise. "Why would you be knowin' that?"

"Don't like it when someone else is a step ahead of you?" She laughed, and the sound echoed with the sharp caw of a crow. "We observed two Alterants who have fought the urge to go to Atlanta when they weren't conscious of their actions."

Cathbad gave an admirin' nod, maskin' his pleasure at confirmin' how little she really knew. *Time ta gain Flaevynn's respect so she'll keep her word an' work with me.*

"'Tis good, Flaevynn. This female Alterant Evalle is evolvin' faster than the other Alterants even though she may no realize it until her gifts are tested. When the other Alterants shift into beasts, they may challenge her at first before they end up followin' her . . . if she does no ha ta kill them. You may no want ta hear this, but we must be patient ta find all five."

Flaevynn smiled, her face aglow with arrogant pleasure. "While you sat around reading, *I* have been productive. Those two I mentioned that feel drawn to Atlanta? I captured those Alterants *and* Evalle."

He remained calm to keep his power from shakin'

the room. The fool ha captured the female Alterant? The magnet needed ta draw the other four? "Holdin' Evalle will no help us."

"I know that. Kizira set up a ruse to convince Evalle that she had to find the other Alterants before we did, then had our warlocks attack so that Evalle *thinks* she escaped. She is now back in Atlanta overseeing the hunt for the Alterants."

He had to give her credit. No a bad plan. "Well done, Flaevynn."

"Of course." She preened.

Since she'd had the female Alterant in hand, she should be able to answer another question for him. "What did this Evalle's aura look like?"

Flaevynn stared off for a moment, thinkin'. "Kizira mentioned it was bright gold. Said she thought that odd."

"No silver?"

"No. Why?"

"That means she's begun evolvin'."

"Into what?"

Oh, he would no tell her that yet. "I do no ha all that figured out yet, but will soon. If ya still ha the female Alterant in hand, I might ha been able ta study her. But for now 'tis best you leave her be so she will draw in the other four we need."

"We'll have her back soon. Once she finds *two* more green-eyed Alterants, we'll recapture Evalle with them."

He hid his smile. Just two more? Could Flaevynn

really have two of the five? He nodded. "Time's a wastin'. I need ta see these other two ya ha captured."

Movin' back to her waterfall, Flaevynn lifted her hands an' closed her eyes. She swayed in a trance in front of the wall of water she used for scrying. When she opened her eyes and said, "There you go," the image of a blond-haired man and a young woman with kinky, brown hair appeared, each in a separate room.

Cathbad studied them silently.

Flaevynn finally turned to him. "Well?"

"I applaud your ingenuity in capturin' them, but neither of those two is one of the five Alterants we need for the curse."

"What?" Malevolence twisted Flaevynn's face. She lifted a lethal black fingernail that sparkled with inlaid diamonds. "You lie."

"I ha no lied to ya. Pointin' a weapon at me is no a good way ta gain my aid." He let his tone tell her he would no tolerate threats now that he ha *his* powers again.

When she lowered her finger, he said, "But 'tis not all bad news. There is a use for these two once we ha the others. And you'll be needin' me when it's time ta recapture Evalle."

She warned, "I am not waiting any longer."

"Ya ha no choice, Flaevynn."

"You think not?" She tossed her head to one side, her wild black hair flutterin'. "I will not risk my future solely on these five Alterants."

"Now ya make no sense."

"I have another plan in motion. I may capture Treoir before Evalle finds the other Alterants."

He ha no thought her capable of doin' more than carryin' out harmless harebrained schemes, but he'd been gone for two years. She might surprise him. "And how would ya be capturin' Treoir any other way than by the curse?"

"I came up with a brilliant plan." That coy expression would be charmin' on another woman, but on Flaevynn it meant she merely rewrote the truth.

Disbelief rolled through Cathbad's voice. "By yourself?"

"Oh, all right. Kizira did help a bit. For all that she lacks in other ways, she is quite the strategist."

He agreed about Kizira's ability to plan, but disagreed with the rest of Flaevynn's assessment. Their daughter ha many strong qualities, her only flaw bein' her soft heart. "What plan did Kizira create?"

"*I'm* the one who came up with using Svart trolls to do my bidding, but I admit that she had a couple of good suggestions."

"You brought Svarts into this?" He hoped Kizira was no tryin' to play a shell game with Flaevynn. "What were you thinkin' ta bring in those nasty creatures?"

Flaevynn's glare could melt steel. "That the Svarts will be able to locate the Alterants first."

"At what cost?"

She balked at answering.

"Do no play with me, Flaevynn, if ya want me to tell ya all the curse."

"All right!" She spread her fingers, nails sharpenin'

into claws. "The Svarts want that human country for some reason."

"Which country?"

"Where the female Alterant lives."

"An' face the strongest VIPER division in the human world?" Cathbad put his hand to his forehead. "Do the Svarts realize the number of pantheons aligned with VIPER?"

"Yes, they do, and are frankly tired of having to constantly pass on lucrative opportunities because of VIPER. They realize once I take control of Treoir and we destroy the Beladors that there will be no more VIPER alliance. The only alliance will be between me and the Svarts." She struck a pose, head held high as if she already ruled the universe.

"An' ya think the Svarts will no turn on ya if someone offers 'em a better deal?"

"No. The Svarts want to move their entire operation to North America and bring in trolls from all over the human world to organize in one country. The Svarts have agreed to be my personal army once they take over that worthless strip of dirt and disband VIPER."

He dinna know if he should be in awe of Flaevynn's audacity or fearful of what she'd put into motion. Deals with Svarts could be deadly for everyone involved. "An' what of the five Alterants? Are ya sure enough of this plan ta no care if ya find them?"

"I'm not such a fool as to stake my life on *one* plan. I still expect the Svarts to deliver the Alterants to me once Evalle finds the other two . . . *four* now."

"Svarts are no easy ta kill, I'll grant ya that, but Alterants might be able ta win a battle against one."

Her lips curled into a smile flush with confidence. "Kizira actually came up with how to assure we had Svarts that could overpower an Alterant. She suggested I have a couple of them dipped into Loch Ryve, which I did."

Ah, Kizira, what are ya doin', child?

Flaevynn continued. "The two that were immersed into Loch Ryve are practically unkillable Svart trolls."

"Are ya mad? Those waters would turn a Svart into a demon troll. There'll be no controllin' 'em!"

Her words struck with the venom of a cobra. "They would not cross *me*."

"No on purpose, but Svarts fight ta the death and are no willin' to die for *anyone*." He shook his head, an angry sigh hissin' from his lips. "Now you've unleashed a troll that is capable of killin' Evalle *and* the other four Alterants, especially capable of harmin' her while she's still evolvin'. An' ya *do* need her ta gain Treoir. Even if a Svart does no kill her, the troll can cripple the Alterant an' prevent her from evolvin'. Ya may ha just cursed yourself."

FOURTEEN

Few things could be more dangerous than an eighteen-year-old female on the hunt for trouble, especially when you added hormones and powers.

How much stronger might Lanna's powers be than the last time Quinn had seen her?

He maneuvered past tourists bunching along Peachtree Street in downtown Atlanta. Sunshine and succulent smells from restaurants brought them out in hordes at lunchtime to window-shop and impede his progress.

Every minute counted until he found Lanna.

He vowed to never have children.

The same vow he made every time he got stuck tracking down Svetlanna Brasko. He'd called her Lanna since she'd been an adorable two-year-old who'd floated Cheerios in the air. He'd thought her precocious at eleven when she turned a mean-tempered mutt into a lapdog that performed tricks.

But when Lanna reached thirteen, Quinn became the go-to man for finding her. She'd taken it upon herself to help another young girl escape an abusive father in their small village. Yes, he admired the way Lanna stepped forward for others, but she was too impulsive for her own good and had almost died at the hands of a

Siberian warlock, the girl's father. Quinn dealt with the bastard, found a home for the girl and warned Lanna not to use her gifts until she trained. Those had been yet more wasted breaths.

The Braskos were a *gifted* side of his family tree, if you could call dysfunctional beings with the ability to wield majik gifted.

Lanna's mother struggled to handle Lanna alone, but her bloody Ruska Roma relatives—Gypsies originally from Russia—should have reined the girl in and taught her discipline by now.

Someone should have.

Quinn's conscience poked at him about how long it had been since he'd gone home to visit Lanna and her mother, who was his aunt. He loved them both, even if the brat did make him crazy sometimes, and watching over his father's only sibling and niece had fallen to Quinn when his father died.

Quinn had a duty to family, and right now that duty called for getting Lanna out of this country before VIPER discovered her presence. The minute Sen got involved, this would turn ugly.

Based upon the reports Tzader had shared, it sounded as though Lanna had been here only since last night.

Alone all night.

The thought terrified him even if she did have powers.

Who knew what she could do these days? He *should* know. Bad case of *out of sight, out of mind*. Not anymore. He'd have to take some time soon and deal with this. But who would train Lanna when not even her mother had a clue what the girl was?

Her mother had disappeared for a month almost nineteen years ago, then reappeared with no knowledge of where she'd been . . . or how she'd become pregnant.

A suspicious beginning to any child's life.

Quinn picked up his pace when Woodruff Park came into view, hoping the Nightstalker he'd traded for intel was right about her destination. The old ghoul had said he'd overheard a young woman with powers, of Lanna's description, asking for a public place where she could wait for her cousin to find her.

Somewhere with a lot of people, boys to be specific.

Quinn blew out a frustrated breath over that.

When he reached the stair-step fountain at the north end of the park, a gust of wind came out of nowhere, twisting along the streets and causing the water to splash hard as it cascaded over the tier of steps. He paused at the sudden change, looked around, then dismissed it as Atlanta's fickle weather, which had been dead calm beneath clear blue skies minutes ago.

Circling the area, he watched for a petite chess shark sitting on one side of a game board. Lanna might have come here looking for him, and boys, but she couldn't pass up a challenge and would have wormed her way into one of many chess matches going on across the eclectic venue.

Got her. She sat on a short concrete wall bordering the tree-studded lawn.

Blond curls ink-tipped in black fluttered in the breeze.

The last time he'd seen Lanna her hair had been half red and half purple.

She observed her opponent—a blond-haired boy around seventeen or eighteen intently studying the game board. He moved a black rook, capturing her silver pawn, then hit the egg timer on his left. She took her time looking over the board as though she didn't already have her next six moves planned.

But Lanna would choose someone she considered an equal with whom to play, so the boy must be pretty good.

Quinn noted the small brown suitcase nearby. It had seen better days, but hopefully held something other than the red shorts and skimpy blue top she wore. What had happened to the cherub face he recalled from their last encounter? When had she become a striking beauty? But she was safe and alive. The fist of worry in his chest relaxed as he strolled up to her.

She pushed her knight into risky territory, drew a long breath, hit the timer, then tilted her head back, eyes excited when her gaze lit on him.

Jumping up, she hugged him. "Hello, Cousin."

Quinn expected her to be taller, but she still topped out at barely five feet tall. He smiled in spite of everything, the sound of her Romanian accent reminiscent of his childhood. She might be eighteen, but she still hugged his neck the way she had at ten, and he'd missed that. When he released her, he asked, "What are you doing here, Lanna?"

The boy hadn't made a move to acknowledge Quinn's

presence, but the frayed edges of his misfitting clothes and the wariness in his tight shoulders spoke of time on the streets and someone who wouldn't engage easily.

Not with Quinn, anyhow.

Lanna lifted her shoulders. "I play chess." Then she plopped back down and glanced at her chess partner, saying, "This is Kell. Kell, this is my cousin—"

"Vlad," Quinn interjected, which caused her to cock her head at him, but she let it go. He used his first name when he didn't want his last name bandied about.

The kid mumbled a hello and turned his head halfway up for a second, but not enough to face Quinn.

"Let's go, Lanna," Quinn said.

"Game almost over."

That drew a questioning look from the boy.

Subtle had never worked with the girl. Might as well be blunt. "You can't stay in the States, Lanna."

"I thought this was free country." She looked at her opponent and asked him in her somewhat choppy English, "Is this not free country?"

The boy clearly didn't want to get involved, but said, "Yes."

She smiled at Quinn again and made another brilliant chess move—this time without paying attention to her hands or the game board. "I am adult. I choose where I go. I come to see you. Are you not glad to see me, Cousin?"

Hard to answer that honestly and spare her feelings. "It would have been helpful to have a bit of warning."

"I have no phone."

Out of patience, Quinn picked up her suitcase and said, "Tell your friend good-bye, Lanna. We need to talk."

She gave Quinn a put-upon glare and had enough left over to share with the top of the boy's head. Quinn stifled a chuckle at the boy's lack of attention. Her opponent appeared immune to her charms. She'd enjoyed harmless flirting ever since the first time a boy had called her pretty.

It was undoubtedly a blow to her ego for this one to be more interested in the game than in her.

After a dramatic and exaggerated sigh, Lanna told the boy, "Thank you for games. I concede this one, but you would lose queen in three more moves."

That brought his blond head up sharply. "Not a chance. I'd have put you in check in two."

Not one to accept defeat easily, she leaned forward, eyes flashing ire. "How long you have suffered hallucinations?"

Quinn interrupted with a stern "Lanna."

That silenced both of them. Quinn considered telling them both to show sportsmanship and end on a good note, but the young man spoke first.

"Thanks for playing. You're . . . good." He extended his hand, and after a slight hesitation Lanna took it, shaking.

"You are welcome. Thank you also."

When Lanna stood again, Quinn walked her several long strides away to stand near the corner of Five Points, next to the bronze statue of a woman releasing a phoenix. He eyed the foot traffic and kept his voice soft.

"It is imperative that you leave this country right away, Lanna. I cannot play tour guide." He'd had to explain his role as a Belador the last time he'd tracked her down in Canada and had been forced to tap local Belador resources to get her out of *that* country. "You *know* what I am and what I do."

"Yes. You are snake."

Quinn gritted his teeth, but kept his voice low. "No, I'm with a coalition called VIPER. You are not an ordinary human, Lanna, which means you cannot stay in this country unless you register with VIPER or have a sponsor."

"I will consider this."

"No." He said that word a lot with Lanna and knew the minuscule degree of influence it was likely to have. "There is no way I can sponsor you. That would require me to be in one place for six months. An unrealistic expectation."

"Tell them I am visitor. I will get visa."

"Your idea of a visa is one with no credit limit. Visitors still have to be cleared through VIPER, and I haven't the time for that now. I'm very busy. I have work to do."

She brightened. "I will help you."

"Yes, you can by going home immediately."

"Not possible."

"Why?"

"Because I am not well after flying. I have . . . what you call dizzy and sick? Closetphobia?"

"Claustrophobia? No, that's fear of being closed in. Are you talking about vertigo?"

"Yes. Sick everywhere. Flight attendant . . . she hide after first two hours."

"I'll get you motion-sickness medicine."

"A passenger give to me. Made me more sick. Medicine does not like my majik."

"Fine. I can have you teleported." But Sen would have to teleport her, and Quinn didn't want him to know she existed.

She put her hands up. "No, no. That is terrible. I almost die when Bernie's uncle teleport me. No, I am not leaving."

Quinn refused to accept that with all of his resources, both human and supernatural, he could not find a way to get one teenage girl out of this country.

Even if he *could* get her cleared through VIPER, he'd end up stuck with her here. Forever.

Or worse. VIPER might actually consider her powers of some use and . . . he'd be stuck with her here. *Forever.*

He hated to use fear, but he couldn't spend his time watching over her when Beladors needed help fighting Svart trolls. He'd have to be tough with her. "VIPER will find you any minute now. When they do, I'll have no choice but to allow our liaison with the agency to teleport you home."

Guilt plagued him when her cheeks lost their rosy hue and her eyes widened in trepidation, then lost focus, staring through him. She started trembling.

Lightning crackled overhead and thunder rumbled.

Wind raced through the park.

Bloody hell.

FIFTEEN

S top it, Lanna."

Lanna realized Quinn was shaking her shoulders. She blinked, looking up into his worried gaze. "What?"

"The storm," he hissed near her ear. "Are you doing that?"

Thunder rumbled overhead.

She gulped air, glancing up at dark clouds threatening to break open and flood the earth. Breathing deep, she tried to calm herself. Slowly, the sky quieted. Elements reacting to her was only one problem she had because of taking Grendal's potion. She did not drink by choice.

The cruel wizard had poured his potion down her throat to turn her into powerful puppet to do his bidding. No one, not even Grendal, had been prepared for bad reaction of her majik. Good thing. Explosion helped her escape wizard and Transylvania, but what had potion done to her majik?

Go home to Transylvania? She would not.

Could not.

She did not want to lie to her favorite cousin, but if Quinn knew truth, he would rush home with her to fix problem. And end up dead.

So technically, he was at fault for any dishonesty on

her part. She patted his arm. "I am sorry about bad weather. Was not intentional. You scare me with threat of teleporting."

He let go of her and shook his head, muttering, "You can affect the weather."

"Sometimes. It is accidental." She rubbed her head, which ached from little sleep. "You are master deal maker. What can I offer VIPER for me to stay? Not long. Only until I find teacher for majik."

"Regardless of my negotiation skills, there is nothing either of us can offer VIPER in exchange for their allowing you to remain in this country. I would have to go through weeks of meetings. I simply don't have the time right now."

His phone buzzed. He grumbled something and put his phone to his ear, but he looked at Lanna and said, "Do *not* leave."

"Finally we agree. I have no plan to leave."

He covered the mouthpiece with his hand. "I only meant don't leave while I'm on the phone. You *are* going home before anyone finds out you're here."

Her cousin would not win argument. Once he accepted this, he would talk to VIPER and fix everything. He must.

Quinn hid his mouth with his hand when he spoke into the phone, but Lanna heard the first part. "I had my mind closed to telepathy. I'm dealing with my family . . . problem. I spoke to Evalle. She's getting what we need tonight . . ."

His gaze lost focus and he stopped speaking.

She had seen him look that way when he spoke telepathically and must be holding phone in place as a pretense.

With Quinn busy, Lanna sent her gaze skipping over chess players still in tight battles. Most were much older than her . . . except that blond one. Kellman. The one she had spent almost an hour with, and still had yet to pay her any attention beyond her skill at chess.

A lock of blond hair fell across his forehead, like a slash of light against his tanned skin. Only thing out of place in his orderly appearance. In spite of clothes that did not fit, Kell had efficient, controlled look.

A serious boy. Much too serious for someone her age, and so intent on chess he missed important things.

Like me.

No man should miss Brasko woman standing so close. *We are like sun after dark winter, warm and bright.* How could he not notice sun?

She was not wallpaper flower to be ignored. She had been adored since very small and noticed by boys as soon as she had breasts, instead of socks, to fill bras.

But Kell paid her no more mind than he paid the wrinkled-up man who took her place as his chess partner.

Still, he was nice boy and she owed him. He had stepped up next to her when a smelly older man in shaggy clothes and greasy hair had bothered her. She had struggled to keep her anxiety from upsetting weather and could not use majik to get rid of smelly man.

Cousin had told her not to use majik on humans, and her powers had already failed her three times since taking potion, so she only used energy force in small amounts that would not put anyone at risk.

She could tell Kell had been afraid when he stepped in to help, because he swallowed hard as if he expected a fight. He still moved between her and the smelly man. Kell said she owed him a game. When the man left, Kell had been surprised when she sat down to play.

But had he looked at her while they played? No. Had he talked to her? Only to ask what color she wanted to play. Then nothing.

Same way he was ignoring her now.

Staring hard, she moved her lips in a silent chant to the wind and sent three leaves down from tree above Kell to fall across his face.

He looked up, then down, startled. His eyes reached out with question, then his gaze landed on Lanna.

She tilted her head to say hello again. To let him know she had not left the park. She winked at him.

Red flags brushed his cheeks. He jerked his gaze back to the game.

She had embarrassed him with wink? This boy who had been her champion with nasty man?

Quinn made a sound that came out part tired and part out of patience as he shoved his phone back into his pocket. His eyes were shadowed. He had been sick not long ago. Lanna could tell. Men in this city needed to have fun.

Quinn said, "Back to what we—"

She spoke at the same time. "Let us sit down, Cousin."

"Are you not well?"

Guilt pinched her over his instant concern. "Yes, just tired."

Snagging her suitcase on the way, she led him to the shade now that clouds were gone and sun was out. Dusting off a spot on concrete wall, she sat down not far from Kell.

With Quinn settled between her and Kell, she could see them both while she spoke to her cousin. "I did not mean to cause you trouble."

His eyebrows climbed in a show of disbelief, then he seemed to dismiss whatever he was going to say. "Then let me charter a private jet to get you home. It'll be more comfortable than commercial flying. You can sleep the whole way."

She shook her head. "That could be dangerous for others."

"Why?"

"When I was upset on way here, airplane had bumpy ride."

"What do you mean?"

"I think my majik shook airplane. Elements do not like when I get upset." A side effect of Grendal's potion.

Quinn leaned down, speaking in a tight voice. "You *rocked* a commercial flight? With storms?"

She hoped he saw how she felt bad about this. "The pilot said weather was clear. One hour later, I am dizzy. Very sick and plane started to bounce and shake. People stumbled around. Much screaming. I am sick everywhere, in bathroom, walking, at seat. I try to sleep, anything to fix problem. When I calm down, plane calmed down. Happened many times on way here. My fault. I do not want to hurt anyone."

"Oh, good goddess." Quinn put a hand on his forehead and closed his eyes.

She muttered, "Much praying on flight, too."

Quinn washed his hand over his face, looking more tired than before. "When did this start happening?"

She couldn't tell him about Grendal, but she had to make Quinn understand one thing. She could not return to Transylvania. "This is why I can not go home. My majik . . . has problems."

"What exactly do you mean?" he asked.

"Long time ago, you were right. You said I need teacher for majik." She held up her hand to stall what she knew he would say. "Not in Transylvania."

"Why not? They're your people."

"My majik caused small fire to explode and burn neighbor's barn. Village is afraid of me." All of that was true enough.

"Did someone threaten you?" her cousin asked in soft voice that would raise fear in demons.

"No, but they think I am dangerous." She shrugged. "I am sorry to burden you, Cousin, but I have nowhere else to go." *And you are the only one who can keep Grendal from taking me again if he finds me.* "Mama asks you please help me."

Quinn had a look that said this couldn't be worse timing.

Lanna hated to be trouble, but she would make it up to him. Her cousin had messed-up aura. He was unhappy. She would work hard to make his life better while she was here.

He finally said, "I'm not sure what I'm going to do. We're in the middle of something major right now. I don't know—"

He would not help her? She must have looked like she would cause storm again because her cousin hurried to say, "Don't get upset. I'll figure out something. Give me a minute."

He started typing on his phone, and she let out tight breath she was holding.

Just then, another Kell raced past her, sliding to stop beside first Kell. Boys looked exactly alike. Twins. But second Kell was free spirit. Full of energy. Excitement.

So not like his quiet chess-master brother.

What luck to find two attractive young men her first day.

The new brother said to Kell, "We've got to clear out of the shelter."

Kell asked, "Why? What's wrong, Kardos? Did you get into trouble?"

Kardos shook his head and jostled something in his hand. Dice? He rolled the cubes around and around. "Not this time. It's the gang wars going on. Child services is rounding up any underaged kids around the shelter."

That surprised Kell. "We *look* eighteen. They don't know we're seventeen."

"Doesn't matter. We'll get hauled in for public loitering if we don't have an ID."

"We have to tell Evalle."

Lanna thought about Quinn's call. Her cousin spoke of an Evalle. *Is that common female name in this country?*

Kardos argued, "She can't help us right now, not until after sunset."

Why would she not help Kell and Kardos until sunset?

Kardos kept jiggling dice in his hand, more like nervous action than anything else.

Kell made grumbling noise, then apologized to his opponent for not finishing game and stood up. He followed his brother to statue of woman with firebird. The boys spoke too soft for Lanna to hear.

Moving her lips with silent chant that Quinn would not see, she heard what Kardos whispered to his brother.

". . . too risky to hide in the places we know. There's a badass group of trolls in the city."

"What, like some weird kind?" Kell acted annoyed, but Lanna could tell he worked to hide his concern.

"Don't know what kind of trolls they are, but Jurba said—"

Kell growled at his brother, "We don't have the money for you to be gambling with Jurba, and he *is* a troll!"

"He's a local troll, not one of the out-of-towners."

"How does that make it okay?"

"Because I know him. We've shot craps a lot."

"Kardos!"

"Hey, I usually win, so no big deal. Back to our real problem." Kardos bunched his shoulders in a conspiratorial move. "Jurba warned me to watch out for any guy with a scar in the shape of a runic *S* on his arm. Says the glamour won't hide the scar. He drew the design for me. Here's the kicker. Good thing I found that out or I wouldn't have noticed a guy with that scar outside the shelter. He was handing out free food."

"At the shelter? Is he gone?"

"No, and he's studying everyone who goes into the shelter like he's looking for something or someone."

"That's because the damn local trolls use the place like a bunkhouse sometimes." Kell rubbed his neck, eyes filled with worry. "Then how are we going to get our money and other stuff hidden in the shelter's back wall?"

"I don't know, and Jurba said to avoid the trolls with the scar at all costs. He just got word that those trolls are taking local ones to some headquarters location and threatening the local trolls if they don't do what they're told."

"Where's the headquarters?"

Kardos threw his hands up in the air. "I don't know. Jurba knows, but I was in too big a hurry to find you to care. He's on his way to meet his buddies and grab a truck big enough for them and his girlfriend. They're getting out of the city."

Kell's face lost his nice tan, turned white when he raised his eyes to his brother. "If a *troll* has nowhere to hide, then we're SOL. The best thing we can do is stay right here where we're surrounded by people until dark."

Lanna did not know SOL, but she understood that these boys were in trouble and would lose their shelter soon. She knew what it was to hide dangerous things and the desperation of having no place safe.

That was how she ended up here.

Kell had helped her without even knowing her name.

Glancing around, Kell scowled and rubbed his neck. "We're screwed."

"No, we're not," Kardos argued. "Jurba said he'd take us with them."

Lanna felt better because this Jurba would help them. Wait. Jurba had information that might also help her. Would VIPER want to know about strange trolls? Enough to let her stay if she traded for learning troll location?

She turned to Quinn. "Cousin?"

"Yes, Lanna?" He stopped typing and lifted weary eyes.

"Does VIPER care about trolls in city?"

Her cousin went on alert, just as he had in Canada when they faced demons. "What made you ask that?"

"I hear things."

"You heard about trolls and you haven't been here a full day?" He eyed her with misgiving. "You made that up, didn't you?"

She would be offended by anyone else, but Cousin Quinn did know her well. "No. I hear about special troll with runic letter as scar on his skin."

He grabbed her arm. *"What?"*

She stiffened. Her heart pounded dangerously fast in her chest. Her cousin would not harm her, but still she did not like to be grabbed. She liked it not at all on that arm where she still had phantom pain even though her skin had healed. She tried to stay calm but her voice carried a warning when she told him, "Let. Go."

Quinn released her immediately. "I'm sorry, Lanna. Did I hurt you?"

"No, of course not." She had reacted to ugly memory, not her cousin, who was most honorable man she knew and would never harm a woman. "I told you. Plane ride made me uneasy."

"Okay, so what did you hear about those trolls?"

"That one is in city." She guessed at the distance, but if twins had no transportation of their own, they would most likely stay close by.

"Do you know where this troll is?" Quinn asked, all ears now that he appeared to believe her.

"Near shelter. Not far from here."

"I know of a shelter in this area," he muttered, his gaze spiked with suspicion. "From whom did you learn of this?"

Lanna had been watching Kell and Kardos, who spoke in angry tones. She jerked her gaze back to Quinn. "I do not know—"

"Don't lie to me, Lanna."

She kicked her foot out and back, thinking. "I will tell you, but you will promise they will not get in trouble, yes? You will not jail them."

"Why would I do that and who are *they*?"

Must be more careful around cousin. She had just told Quinn more than one was involved. "One who heard this about strange trolls found out because he plays crap game with local trolls."

"Where did you meet a nonhuman?"

"See? You are angry."

"No, I'm worried. That's different. You could have gotten hurt by them."

"I am not child now, Cousin." Not after what she had gone through to survive and escape to America. "I can handle teenage boys any day."

Quinn sat up and slowly swiveled his head until he looked directly at the twins. "Those two."

Her mouth sometimes moved faster than her mind. Bad flaw. "No."

"Yes. You tuned in to their conversation while I was on my phone." Quinn stood.

So did Lanna. "No, Cousin. They have troubles with shelter and children service."

"I'm only going to ask them questions. If I like the answers, they'll be fine."

"And if not?"

"They'll have bigger problems than child services."

When Quinn took a step toward the boys, Kell's head whipped up, alert. He grabbed Kardos's sleeve and started backing away.

But not before he noticed Lanna. Kell's eyes were two angry slits, his eyebrows tucked tight over his gaze.

With one look, he accused her of betrayal, though he had no idea what she had said or done.

She had not meant to cause him more problems and wanted a chance to explain, but now the boys were backing away. Fear mixed with their angry looks.

Kell had said best place for them was here in park until sunset. They would not stay if Quinn frightened them, and her cousin could be a most intimidating man.

Walking calmly toward the twins, Quinn called out. "I'd like to talk to you."

She had noticed small police station across street when she first arrived at park. Three men in uniforms walked from other side of street toward corner of park where the boys stood by statue.

Kardos looked over his shoulder at the same three men and told Kell, "Can't go that way. One of those cops . . . knows me. If he's heard about the underage roundup, he'll grab me and ask questions later."

Boys were caught between Quinn and men in uniforms.

Her fault.

Accusation flew from Kell's gaze. How could she fix this?

She could not draw deep on powers or Grendal would find her. Because of potion, he could feel her use her powers to call on elements . . . but *not* if the elements merely reacted to her anxiety. Closing her eyes, she did worst thing for her. She called up memory of what had happened to her with Grendal back in Romania.

Thunder boomed overhead.

Quinn swung back to her and shouted, "No, Lanna."

She opened her eyes and looked up at sky. Same place Quinn looked, where clouds had changed from puffy white to threatening gray.

In that instant, she glanced over at Kell and winked to let him know she would help him escape.

He blinked once, but did not waste opportunity she had given him. He latched onto Kardos, towing him away.

If those two knew where special trolls were, they

could help her, and she would help them again, too, but that would only happen if she found them again.

She focused on Kardos's hand and whispered short chant.

Dice fell from his fingers.

Kardos turned to go for the tumbling cubes, but Kell had tight grip on his brother, urging him to keep moving. The two rushed away into a small cluster of people walking around park.

When the sky quieted, Quinn dropped his head and looked at empty spot by statue where boys had been. His growl sounded rough with frustration, but her cousin would never harm someone who was not a threat.

He turned back to her. "You summoned that thunder on purpose."

Lanna did not agree or try to lie. Instead, she waved him off. "Go, Cousin. I understand. You are busy and can not play guide with me."

"You really think I'm going to leave you out here alone?"

She hoped not. "I am fine, Cousin."

He lifted handle of her rolling suitcase and tilted his head to point the way he wanted her to walk.

She followed, letting her steps take her by the dice that sat in piled leaves, where she scooped them up on her way by. She had located people by holding personal items and hoped it would work this time.

"Where are we going, Cousin?"

"To my hotel. I can't deal with this right now, but I'll be back tonight and you'll be safe if you stay out of view."

Quinn waved a taxi over. The driver took them to a nice Ritz Hotel where the doorman spoke fondly to her cousin. Everything about hotel bragged of much money, from porters to fancy doors.

She had just stepped from taxi behind Quinn when he paused and stared into distance again. This time only for few seconds. He dismissed whatever had stopped him, then scratched his head and gave Lanna a card from his pocket. He spoke low for her ears only. "The Belador Maistir called. I have to go. It's important."

Ah. He had communicated with his mind again.

Quinn handed her a plastic card. "Here's the room key. If you're hungry, order food. You can watch movies, too."

Taking the room key card, she hurried to speak before he started giving orders and demanding promises. "I understand. Thank you for room, Cousin. Do not worry if you find me asleep when you come back. I am very tired *and* hungry. I could sleep for two days after bumpy trip here."

His irritation softened. "I'm sure it was a difficult flight. If you need anything—"

"I will call from room. I can tell this hotel will be most helpful. Go, Cousin. Do not worry about me. No one will bother me."

Quinn spoke quietly, but in a rush. "I just checked in today, so no one other than the hotel staff knows I'm here. I don't like leaving you without the warding on the door—"

"That would not be good unless you can stay for half

hour to find out if my majik reacts to warding. Last time I—"

"Never mind. Double-lock the doors." He handed her a business card that displayed a phone number. Nothing else. "Call me immediately if you need me."

"Yes, yes. I know how to get help. Go and be careful." She lifted up on her tiptoes and kissed Quinn's cheek. "Do not let something happen to you. I would be lost without you."

He patted her head. "I'll be fine."

She told him good-bye and turned to walk away, knowing he would not leave until she was inside. Dangerous trolls were in Atlanta. The world was lucky to have men such as Quinn who protected humans from bloodthirsty creatures.

After reaching the suite and depositing her suitcase, she ordered food and felt much better, then left a note for Quinn. Before riding back down in the elevator, she experimented with cloaking herself. Last night she had disappeared completely, but now only the top half of her body vanished before she gave up. Majik was much trouble some days.

Once she found Kell and Kardos, she would get the location of the strange trolls' headquarters and give that to Quinn when he returned to the hotel.

Quinn would worry if he knew what she was up to, but she had fought a troll in Transylvania last year.

That one had no special marks, but a troll was a troll. She only needed help with evil wizards.

SIXTEEN

Asking Isak Nyght for a weapon that killed non-humans would open a door Evalle might never be able to shut. She grabbed a towel to dry her hair, needing to head out soon even if the meet point was close to her underground apartment in downtown Atlanta.

Isak had to know she wanted a weapon after she'd sent a text asking to borrow something. What else would she want to borrow from a man who created custom weapons just to kill beings with supernatural power?

Could she avoid telling him why? Not an easy task when she had yet to give Isak a straight answer about why she sometimes ran into nonhumans. At least he wouldn't remember that he'd discovered she was an Alterant three weeks ago.

Nope, she wasn't worried about Isak . . . as long as he didn't kiss her.

He'd kissed her only a couple times, unexpectedly. The man had a nice mouth, more than nice.

But then Storm had kissed her.

She stopped rubbing her hair and tossed the towel over a hook. Thinking of Storm and Isak at the same time gave her a headache.

No kissing tonight. She'd treat this as business. One goal—get the weapon. But she couldn't tell Isak about the trolls. That meant she had to play up her fear of something nonhuman.

She'd rather spend a day off with Sen than act afraid of anything.

Take one for the team. Tzader and Quinn sure as the devil couldn't pull off looking frightened of anything.

She finished dressing and went out to the kitchen, where her two-foot-tall gargoyle, Feenix, sat on the island counter playing with his pile of lug nuts. The leathery skin on his wide forehead wrinkled with how hard he concentrated to place the silver half-inch circles on top of each other with his pudgy hands, especially while having to reach around his potbelly.

"Whatcha doing, baby?" she asked on her way to snag a power drink from the fridge.

"Cathel."

Took her a minute of studying the wall and tower structure he'd built to understand he meant *castle*. "Fun. Did you see a castle on TV?"

"No-o." He answered her as if he expected her to know the right answer.

Where had he seen a castle? She'd found Feenix during a mission to locate and stop a mad sorcerer who'd been creating an army of vicious creatures that killed on command. Feenix had been left in a cell with a note marking him as a flawed creation to be used for food. The best she could tell, the poor little guy had failed as a killer. Easy to understand with all the other creatures towering over ten feet tall and Feenix so much smaller and with a sweet disposition.

Quinn would argue that Feenix *could* blow a hole in the wall with a blast of fire if something frightened him.

True, but he knew he was safe with her. "Who lives in the castle, baby?"

Feenix angled his head to look up at her. Bright orange eyes flashed with intelligence when he smiled. Two small fangs poked down on each side of his over-bite, glowing against his brownish-green skin covered in dark green scales. "Printheth."

"A princess, huh?" Oh, that's right! She'd watched *The Princess Bride* with him the other night. "That's a great castle. Is it for Princess Buttercup?"

"No-o." He shook his head and his batlike wings flapped gently. The chortling sound he made usually meant he was proud of something he'd figured out. "For Printheth Evalle."

Her heart thumped. She'd never celebrated a birthday or received a wrapped gift, but moments with Feenix had become as cherished as any package in shiny paper. "Thank you, baby."

He pointed at another lug nut. "Demon." Then he picked up that lug nut and tossed it into his mouth, chomping on the steel and clapping his hands.

"Attaboy." She smiled. "I'll be back in a while. Don't eat my pots and pans, okay?"

Feenix quieted and dropped a hand to his bent knee, which he patted slowly as if saying, *That again?* "Accthi-dent. Member?"

"Yes, I remember, but I wanted to make sure *you* didn't forget." It wasn't as though she did a lot of cooking, but she would like to keep the last two pots she had. She hadn't figured out if he had short-term memory loss sometimes or if he just did things out of pure mischief.

"'Kay. Go ride?"

"Not right now. Maybe later." Once she knew for sure the Svart trolls were gone. Before heading out on her motorcycle, she leaned over and kissed his forehead, careful not to get stuck by one of his horns.

The ride to meet Isak took no time since the meet point was only a mile from home.

His black Hummer sat alone on the top level of an expansive parking deck. The deck was not being fully utilized, and she'd chosen this location specifically because the upper floors would be empty in the early evening. After stowing her gear and adjusting her sunglasses, she turned to find Isak standing by the open passenger door of his truck.

Black dress pants and a cobalt-blue, button-down dress shirt did nothing to tone down the black-ops warrior beneath the civilized veneer. Short brown hair with gray flecks at his temples shouted former military, just as much as the hard jaw and intense blue gaze that scoped the area around her in a blink.

"How ya doin', Isak?"

"Not bad. Ready?"

"I hadn't planned on going anywhere."

"Thought you wanted to borrow something."

"I do, but I haven't told you what yet."

"Does it turn demons into shrapnel?"

She didn't want to explode the troll. "Maybe."

"Then I know what you want. Let's go."

"Are you going to put a sack over my head, Isak?"

"No." Mr. Serious didn't even crack a smile.

"Then why can't I just follow on my bike?"

"Because you'll be blindfolded."

Crap. She walked over and put a foot up on the running board, picking up the seductive scent of cologne. Humongous hands grabbed her around the waist and lifted her onto the seat before she could protest. Taking a breath to keep herself calm, she told him, "In case you haven't noticed, I'm five-ten, I'm wearing jeans and need no help getting into a truck."

He put his left hand on the back of her seat and leaned in, a glint of heat burning in his eyes. "I noticed. Every. Sweet. Inch. Especially the jeans. Buckle up . . . unless you want help with that, too."

Guess she'd find out how much of a gentleman he was, or he'd find out just how dangerous she could be.

Once he had the wide black cloth in place over her sunglasses, she prepared to be pelted with questions about why she wanted a special weapon. But when Isak cranked the engine, Garth Brooks crooned a country tune as the vehicle backed up, then headed forward.

Ten minutes into the ride, Isak hadn't said a word.

She tapped her fingers, picking up speed with each tap until a warm hand covered hers.

Every muscle jumped to alert.

He started brushing his thumb back and forth over her skin, the simple gesture reminding her that he was no threat to her. With that realization, tension that had locked the muscles in her shoulders all afternoon eased.

When the truck rolled to a stop a half hour later, Isak said, "You can remove the blindfold."

She uncovered her sunglasses to find his truck parked inside a huge warehouse. At the far end of the ginormous building, people stood beneath bright fluorescent lights at workstations. She assumed they were assembling weapons or some defensive devices that Isak manufactured.

Heavy-duty, twelve-foot-tall stainless-steel cabinets lined forty feet of one wall in the thirty-thousand-square-foot building with a ceiling that peaked at twenty feet. One section of the warehouse had been framed in as an office area that could provide six to eight average-size rooms.

But this was not the hangar she'd visited the night Isak had kidnapped her for an Italian meal. The hangar hadn't been as bright inside, and it had been more open, with fewer shelves and minimal office area. A place his teams—the Nyght Raiders—could congregate and plan.

This place was a production facility with bright lighting, tools on workstations and the smell of machine oil.

One young man in jeans and a flannel shirt ran a forklift, carrying loads from the rear of the building to the front. He moved stacks of crates, lifting them high in the air to place on neatly organized shelves running in rows just left of the overhead door behind Isak's Hummer.

The forklift driver's shaggy gray hair and rumpled clothes didn't match Isak's buff military look, but the guy's sharp gaze scanning everywhere as he worked and his taut posture spoke of alertness on a par with the other Nyght Raiders.

Two more vehicles were parked inside. With the right color scheme and a few decals, one could have been an armored security truck for money pickups. But who drove that sleek, do-me-red BMW Z8?

Not Isak, who filled the cockpit of this Hummer.

He'd have to wear that tiny car.

"You're looking for one of my Nyght weapons, right, Evalle?" Isak hadn't made a move to get out of the Hummer yet. He had his arms crossed and his attitude locked into quiet-curiosity mode.

"Yes. Hopefully, a smaller version of the one you used to destroy that demon when we first met." She'd been interrogating a Birrn demon until Isak blasted it with one of his superweapons. The demon imploded before she could get intel she'd desperately needed. Granted, when Isak showed up the Birrn had appeared close to chowing down on her. Small detail.

"What're you trying to kill?"

She could only dodge him so long without having to share something. If she said the weapon was for another demon, she'd get the wrong weapon. "I need something that would stop a troll without drawing the attention of . . . citizens."

The drone of the forklift motor running back and forth filled the pause before Isak said, "Trolls."

She nodded, but that hadn't been a question.

"When did you see a troll?"

Answering that honestly opened the door to more questions. "I'd rather not say."

"But you're not protecting the troll."

"No. I want to protect myself *from* the troll." There. She'd played the girl card in spite of how vulnerable that made her sound. She could kick a troll's butt any day.

Isak shifted his body, muscles bunching when he propped an elbow on the driver's door. "Tell me where to find this troll and I'll handle it."

She stopped herself a second before snarling that she didn't need a man protecting her. What had made Quinn believe she could do this? Unclenching her jaw, she spoke with an even tone. "I don't know where the troll is right now."

"I can put a detail on you."

Isak could be a persistent son of a gun, but he wasn't going to get the answer he wanted. "I'm not interested in having bodyguards follow me around. If you don't want to loan me a weapon, then just say so and I'll figure out something else."

Isak gave it a couple beats, then said, "Wait for me to open your door."

That wasn't a yes, not yet.

He allowed her to step down unaided.

Just as her boot touched the concrete floor, the door to the office area opened and a slim woman of average height walked out. She could be late forties or early fifties, too attractive to pin down. Beautiful brunette hair in a short, swooshy style fanned around her tanned face. She wore knee-length white pants and an aqua-blue shirt with a flared collar. Cinnamon lips smiled when she noticed Isak.

He put a hand to Evalle's back, gently urging her toward the office and this woman.

The forklift's tires squealed with a sharp turn.

Evalle glanced at the machine . . . then at the driver, who was heading straight for the three of them.

The driver's head began stretching into a grotesque shape, his mouth widening with fangs. Brown eyes.

Seconds slowed down with each heartbeat that thudded in her chest at this living nightmare unfolding.

A Rías.

As the forklift careened toward them, Isak grabbed Evalle, then lunged for the other woman, shoving them both toward the office.

Evalle kept her balance and spun around in time to see the driver alter his direction toward her and the woman.

She didn't doubt that every person in this building was armed, but not one of those technicians two hundred feet away would get here in time, and the handgun Isak had just drawn would only anger the beast further.

No one could stop that Rías in the next five seconds.

Except Evalle. If she didn't use her kinetics, this woman would die, and possibly Isak as well.

No time to worry about consequences.

Evalle slapped a kinetic shot at Isak's hand, knocking the weapon away. She ignored his furious shout and threw up a wall of kinetic energy to block the forklift from plowing into her and the brunette at full speed.

The forklift hit the invisible energy and bounced backward with the front end lifting into the air.

What had been a human driver only a moment ago had now fully shifted into a Rías, which dove off the forklift as the machine tilted over on its side.

The beast lunged to attack.

Evalle called her dagger up from her boot, spinning it in her hand as she surged forward to meet the threat. She pulled her arm back, aiming to drive the dagger into his chest, but the Rías moved like a spear of lightning, diving for her feet.

He knocked her legs out from under her.

She flipped, landing on her back, and jumped up.

The Rías came at her again.

She hit the beast with a kinetic blast, but he swatted it back at her, knocking her glasses off. The sudden light blinded her.

Out of instinct, she kinetically exploded all the overhead lights, confusing the Rías long enough for her to spin around and boot him hard in the chest. He flew backward twenty-five feet, slamming against the wall and falling to the floor . . . where he started shifting back into a human.

It all happened in a matter of seconds.

The sound of weapons being racked echoed behind her.

Evalle shouted, "Don't shoot! He's a human." She turned, looking for her sunglasses.

Red dots lit up her chest.

Her sunglasses were hooked over the long barrel of a Nyght demon blaster Isak pointed at her heart. "So your eyes *are* green. Alterant green."

"I can explain, Isak."

"What makes you think I care?"

SEVENTEEN

D *on't shoot*, Isak."

Evalle hadn't said that. She'd *thought* it, but the shouted order had come from the brunette dusting off her white pants.

No hysterics. No glazed look of deep shock.

The brunette ordered another man to throw on the backup security lighting in the warehouse. Her heels clicked all the way over to where the unconscious Rías had now shifted back into the human forklift driver.

"Don't get near that thing," Isak snapped at the brunette, who ignored him with a wave of her hand that caused silver bracelets to jangle.

Evalle would like to get a better look at this woman beyond what she could see in her peripheral vision, but Isak still had his weapon pointed at her chest.

He'd picked up a night-vision monocular somewhere, looking even more deadly than usual—like a cyborg on a death mission. He said, "So what was this trip about, Evalle? Thought you could come here and kill all of us?"

She shook her head, suffering unexpected pain at the look of disappointment on his face and even more at his words. She'd had a strange relationship with Isak so far, but she'd always considered him a friend. "No. I don't harm humans."

"That's a hard sale when I know what an Alterant is capable of. What'd you do to make our forklift guy turn into a beast?"

He thinks I'm the reason that Rías shifted? "What makes you think I can make someone change into another form?"

"I have no idea what *something* like you can do. I don't make a habit of letting Alterants live long enough for someone to study them."

She flinched at the insult, then moved straight from terror of dying to seriously pissed off.

But now was not an advisable time to let her temper rip. Isak hadn't shot her. Yet.

This called for diplomacy.

She sucked at that, but gave it a try. "I know you don't like Alterants, Isak—"

"I like 'em just fine . . . well-done."

The brunette clicked across the concrete floor until she stepped up beside Evalle.

Men armed for combat formed a perimeter of firepower.

Isak's finger trembled as if it took all his willpower to not shoot. Muscles flexed in his jaw, his neck, his forearm, straining against his need to act.

Even though the brunette's head barely reached Evalle's shoulder, she spoke with unquestioned authority. "I mean it, Isak. Don't shoot her."

"She's an Alterant, Kit."

So that was the woman's name. It fit her.

"She saved my life."

"Alterants are killers."

Evalle shook her head. "I have *never* harmed or killed a human. I have protected thousands."

Halogen lights started coming on overhead, slowly brightening the warehouse.

Out of reflex, Evalle reached toward the sunglasses.

Weapon controls clicked in succession all around her.

Kit ordered, "Stand. Down. Now!"

Who is this woman? Evalle felt her sunglasses being tapped against her arm, and Kit said, "Here, sugar. Put these on."

Evalle took the glasses and slipped them over her eyes, shocked to see all the weapons at ease.

All except Isak's.

When Kit said, "Isak?" it was as though the little woman hit a pressure release valve.

He ground out a curse that could ignite the air, lowered his weapon to his side and took a step toward Kit.

Evalle jumped in front of the brunette. "Don't take it out on her."

Isak's jaw shifted out and back with unrestrained fury. "Get out of the way, Evalle."

"Not until you promise not to—"

"Not to what? Do you really think I'd hurt a woman?" Isak's rage went up another notch at that implication.

Evalle hurried to calm him. "No, of course not, but I don't want you to . . . to fire her."

Feminine laughter erupted behind Evalle, then Kit stepped up beside her. "Thank you, sugar, but *I* run this place."

"Oh." Evalle lifted her shoulders at Isak, who was still ramping up his death glare.

He shifted his steely glint to Kit. "You almost died because of her kind."

Technically, the beast that had just attacked Kit had been a Rías, but Evalle would save that clarification for later.

"You're wrong," Kit argued. "Jasper, the other one, does not have bright green eyes like, uh . . . Evalle, was it?"

Evalle nodded mutely, keeping her attention on the biggest threat in the room. Isak.

Kit continued. "Thought Alterants had neon-green eyes."

Nothing swayed Isak. "I am *not* letting beasts, with or without green eyes, walk free to kill humans."

Kit stepped up to Isak with her hands on her hips, looking just as intimidating as Isak in that moment. "You're not killing this one, son."

Son?

"You don't know what they're capable of, Kit."

"Considering how she stopped that forklift with kinetic energy, if Evalle was going to attack anyone, she would have done so already." Kit turned to Evalle and smiled. "Of course, if you make a threatening move at this point, every man here, including Isak, will use any means to stop you. Now that we have all that clear, thank you for saving my life." She extended her hand. "Everyone calls me Kit."

Isak ground out a disgusted sound and stepped past

Evalle without another word, on his way over to where the forklift driver was still on the floor.

When Evalle's brain spun into gear, she stuck her hand out for a brisk shake with Kit. "Thanks for saving my hide, too. Please don't kill that Rías."

"What's a Rías?"

"The man who shifted into a beast is not an Alterant, but a Rías." Evalle couldn't believe she was having this conversation with a human. She didn't want to think about how many VIPER rules she was breaking at the moment. "I'd like a chance to talk to him."

Kit turned to where Isak stood with a cluster of his men and called over, "Have them take Jasper to the holding cell."

Isak peered over his shoulder, clearly not happy with Evalle or Kit. When he swung back to his men, he murmured orders. One of the men walked over to a cabinet, where he pulled out some space-age-looking handcuffs and leg cuffs.

Isak's men had Jasper trussed up in less than a minute, then carried the poor guy out of sight.

Evalle would like to see this cell that Isak and Kit obviously believed could restrain a nonhuman.

Yet another part of this secret operation.

Evalle gave Kit a smile of relief. "Thank you."

"You're welcome, but you do understand that just because I stopped Isak from blowing you to pieces right now doesn't mean you're in the clear . . . or free to leave."

And here I'd mistaken Isak as the greater threat in the room. Should I call in Tzader or Quinn?

No. That would only draw them to the one group of humans capable of killing them.

Evalle had to handle this on her own and hope she walked out of here alive, but what would Macha and VIPER do when they found out she'd been made as an Alterant by humans?

EIGHTEEN

"Any word from Evalle?" Tzader wiped blood from his hands and face with a rag now soaked with the smell of death.

Quinn grimaced as he cleaned his own hands. "Not yet."

Tzader handed the rag back to Horace Keefer, wishing he could get rid of the troll problem as easily. He asked Horace, "Did you hear back from Trey?"

"Yep. The boy said he'd be here soon with ten of ours and has sent more Beladors to the other teams. That oughta stop a Svart. One at a time."

"We can only hope. Once Trey arrives, take our injured to headquarters. Tell Sen I'll talk to him as soon as I can." As Horace strolled off, Tzader scanned the blood-swathed ground of yet another cemetery and shook his head. "At least we don't have to call Sen in to clean this up since Adrianna's on site." Tzader paused. "I'm glad you were here to pull some intel from that troll."

"For what good it did." Quinn's self-inflicted disgust was as evident as it was unfair.

"No one else would have stopped that troll. You saved human lives and our team."

"I didn't manage to retrieve much useful information, only that jumbled mess."

"You found out more trolls are coming. That's something we needed to know, Quinn."

"But this one kept thinking about *demon*, then *Svart*? What could that mean?"

"I don't know. Maybe he meant they were bringing in demons, too."

"We would have had our first chance for some real intel if I could have breached his shields and held control for one minute. One. Minute."

"Next time." Tzader sent telepathic messages to the Beladors on-site, ordering them to scour the cemetery for any more humans present. Fortunately, this had been a small skirmish, except for the damned Svart troll. Adrianna had put the three human gang members caught up in the fray to sleep with a spell that would leave them thinking they'd dreamed the entire battle.

Those humans would be dropped in the respective neighborhoods for each of their gangs.

Tzader turned back to Quinn. The man had the sick-gut look of someone who'd been sucker punched. Just to distract him from the dead troll, Tzader asked, "You get your family problem dealt with?"

"Yes."

"She headed home?"

"No." Quinn's attention had definitely shifted from the troll. Frustration simmered in his gaze. "Found her downtown. She can't go home yet."

"Think anyone has seen her yet?"

"No one with VIPER that I know of, but now that the Nightstalkers know, it won't be a secret for long."

Quinn's expression dropped another notch on the grim scale.

"Ah, hell."

"That pretty much sums it up. She's hidden in my hotel suite for now. I'll deal with her as soon as I get back."

Quinn looked beat, but the man had been forced to destroy two minds today. He held himself accountable and to such a high standard, nothing would offer consolation except a chance to redeem himself in his own mind.

Tzader didn't want to push Quinn further, but they weren't gaining ground on this Svart problem, and what he had in mind might help Quinn if it didn't destroy him. "Are you sure your mind is strong?"

Quinn's head came up. "Yes."

"And you think you still have an open path to Kizira?"

Slower to answer this time, Quinn still said, "Yes."

"If she came into your mind, could you control her invasion long enough to mine her thoughts for information?"

When Quinn didn't answer right away, Tzader added, "The better question might be could you *do that* to Kizira?"

"Yes, I'd have no qualms about extracting what we need. I assume you want to determine if the Medb are behind these attacks?"

"That and anything else you can dig up." Tzader doubted it would be that simple for Quinn, whose integrity prevented him from entering a mind involuntarily unless the person represented a dangerous threat, but Kizira had taken advantage of Quinn while he had no ability to resist.

And she'd used sex to do it.

Tzader had a feeling some of Quinn's guilt came from *not* regretting that part of her visit.

Maybe if Quinn could gain information on the Svarts, it would ease some of his remorse over what happened with Kizira, and hopefully help the Beladors stop whatever the Svarts were planning.

If Kizira did not overpower his mind again.

Tzader had to trust that Quinn knew his limits.

Quinn checked his watch, then took stock of the VIPER agents. "Can you afford to be without me for a while?"

"I think we're good. VIPER has teams running all night, and we have more Beladors arriving from the West Coast, since this seems to be isolated to the Southeast, Atlanta in particular. I'll be back as soon as I can, too."

"Where are you going?"

"Brina wants *another* meeting." Tzader lifted his hand in a don't-ask motion. He'd heard her telepathic call just as the battle started. She had something to discuss with him as soon as he could return to Treoir.

"Should I remain until you make it back here?" Quinn offered.

"No. Trey should be here soon. So far we haven't had more than one Svart troll at each battle. If ten Beladors can't stop a troll, we're in big trouble. Trey can find either of us if he needs us." Tzader was a powerful telepath, but Trey McCree had legendary telepathic ability. "Right now we both need to grab some rest or we're going to put our Beladors and other VIPER agents at risk."

"Understood." Quinn nodded and walked away.

Trey arrived, looking as if he'd just climbed out of bed, his normal state of grooming. He gave Tzader a nod, accepting control of the teams for the night.

Striding quickly to his 1970 Hemi 'Cuda, Tzader climbed in and locked the doors. A warding had been worked into the vehicle's frame back when he and his dad had stripped the engine down to the camshaft, then rebuilt the entire car from the ground up. His body would be safe inside here.

Slowing his breathing, he called upon his ability to change into holographic form.

He locked his jaw against the chill that covered his skin when he left his body so he could travel to the hidden island few Beladors knew how to find. A select few that he trusted to protect Treoir should anything happen to him unexpectedly.

Until then, he'd be on the front line keeping Brina safe.

When he drew close enough to feel the pull of Treoir Island, Tzader called telepathically to Brina, letting her know he was ready to enter.

A minute passed.

What was the problem?

In no mood to be kept waiting, he called out again. *Brina, are you there or not?*

I'll be only a minute, Tzader.

It wasn't like she had to open a door. *Brina? Are you all right?*

Yes . . . just hang on.

So now his visits were being downgraded to the level of a phone call? Now wasn't the time to get cranky, but sleep hadn't been peaceful or lengthy for him over the past few weeks. He rubbed his face and eyes to push off the irritation riding his shoulders.

You are welcome to enter, Tzader Burke.

The room came into focus just as Brina walked in from the hallway that led to her private quarters.

Had she been lying down? Was she not well?

Asking those questions could be misconstrued as encouraging a relationship with her, which would break his vow to Macha. In fact, he'd agreed to convince Brina he was no longer interested in . . . them.

Treoir needed an heir. Now.

He couldn't think about that, about her having a child with another man, and behave with any civility. So he blanked his mind of everything except dealing with the Svart problem.

"My thanks to you for returnin' so soon, Tzader."

That sounded damned formal, but he had no reason to criticize her. He had to let it go and be just as businesslike about this. "Not a problem. To update you, we're in the process of getting a Nyght weapon. Something that will kill the trolls without putting so many of our people at risk."

"Excellent."

She sounded pleased. Maybe this meeting would go better than the last. He added, "We think the Medb may be behind this Svart problem. Quinn's searching for intel to determine if they are and, if so, why."

No point in sharing *how* Quinn intended to gain that intel.

"That is most encouragin' news." Brina's light voice held a pleasure Tzader hadn't heard in a while.

The unexpected sound eased the stiff muscles in his neck.

She settled on her sofa. "I'll be makin' this quick, but I need to tell you about the situation with Evalle."

"What do you mean?"

"Macha is at a Tribunal meetin' to pacify Dakkar."

"The bounty hunter? What's his problem with Evalle?"

"An Alterant shifted an' killed one of his hunters. He's expectin' to be compensated."

Tzader's muscles wound back up with that news. How far would Macha negotiate in Evalle's favor when Evalle hadn't been able to deliver a single Alterant over the past three weeks since making a deal with the goddess? "What kind of compensation?"

"I have no word yet, but I expect that we'll be hearin' word by tomorrow."

"Why are you telling me this?"

Brina's fingers tensed where she clutched the cushion she sat on. "I assumed you'd be wantin' that information in case . . ."

"In case Evalle just disappears again."

"I did not say that," Brina countered in a tight voice.

"But that's why you're telling me. I thought Evalle's deal with Macha meant Evalle wouldn't get yanked into Tribunal meetings anymore to answer for someone else's transgressions."

Brina sat up straighter, just as in the past when she'd get her back up over something. "I mention this only so you'll not be surprised."

"What I *know* is that Evalle shouldn't be held responsible, especially when I bet no one has determined if it was even an Alterant that killed the bounty hunter. Could have been a Rías since not everyone knows the difference." Tzader struggled to keep from raising his voice. Yelling at Brina wouldn't help Evalle or him right now.

Macha might like the friction climbing between Brina and him these last two meetings, since the goddess expected him to break off their relationship, but *he* didn't. For the first time in his life, Tzader questioned whether he could put honor first and walk away from Brina.

Just as he questioned whether Brina truly wanted him out of her life.

With Macha away at the Tribunal, he didn't see the harm in getting some straight answers from Brina. What could be dishonorable about asking her straight up if she still loved him?

Tzader shook off his anger and smiled at her. "Do you—"

The male Belador guard Tzader had seen during his earlier visit came walking up the hallway, and Tzader lost his train of thought. That hallway led to Brina's private quarters.

What was that guy's name? Allyn?

The top three buttons on the guard's jacket were unbuttoned.

What the devil?

Brina snapped her fingers. "Tzader? Hello. Are you payin' me no mind?"

"I heard you," he muttered, watching as the beefy guard carried something concealed in his closed hand and offered it to Brina.

Allyn said, "I believe this is what you were searching for."

She held her hand out to receive what looked like a tiny coil of gold chain. Her eyes lit up. "My mother's necklace! You found it. Where?"

"On the floor next to . . . your bed."

Tzader cleared his throat, hoping the sound came across as deadly as the intent behind it. Why had Brina sent a guard to search for her necklace *in* her bedroom? She normally cleaned her own room, preferring to keep her room private and allowing only Tzader in there.

Or had at one time.

Brina angled her head at Tzader. "Have you not met Allyn? He's my new *personal* guard."

"No, I haven't." Tzader had known *all* of her guards up until four years ago when he'd stopped entering the castle in his physical form. Since then, Macha had approved the inside guards, and Tzader rarely saw any of them inside the castle since their job was to prevent anyone from getting through the front door.

Allyn smiled briefly at her, then shifted his expression to professional when he faced Tzader. He had the thick neck of a young man who pumped iron. "Nice to meet you, Mr. Burke."

Mr.? Tzader's *father* was Mr. Burke. This guy might be five or six years younger, maybe midtwenties?

Thirty sure as hell wasn't old. Tzader corrected him, "It's Maistir."

That set-down registered in the guard's face for only a second, then his demeanor shut down to stoic again. "Maistir."

That was the extent of Tzader's acknowledgment of the other man. If he said any more, he'd give away the surge of fury at seeing the guy stand too close to Brina. Saying the wrong thing right now would get Tzader in deep trouble with Macha and knock the wheels off this conversation with Brina.

Allyn turned to Brina. "I'll wait outside, Bri—uh, Your Highness."

"Absolutely not, Allyn. I want you . . . *here*." She gave him an extra look as he stepped past the giant stone fireplace and circled the sofa to stand behind her. Once he took that position, Brina faced Tzader again. "As I was sayin', I'm only the messenger on this Dakkar issue an' merely wantin' to keep you informed. Now, about these Svart trolls, I wish to know who they're workin' for as soon as you find out."

Giving a quick nod of acknowledgment, Tzader had to swallow the lump in his throat to get any words out with reality crashing in on him with double fists. Macha had not been twisting the truth after all when she'd said Brina was ready for someone else. That she had accepted the futility of her and Tzader's impossible situation.

He hadn't believed Brina a month back when she'd told him they had no future.

Tzader would respect her wishes and—

The guard leaned forward and put a hand on Brina's shoulder, clearly to comfort her.

Tzader roared, *"Take your hand off of her!"*

Guess his control wasn't as good as he'd thought.

She reached up and placed her hand over Allyn's, preventing him from moving his.

The guard's face showed no emotion, but his eyes held a warning when he stared at Tzader and said in a low, threatening voice, "It's inappropriate to raise your voice around the queen. I won't have her upset."

You won't have . . .

Who did this guard think he was talking to?

But Tzader's power, because he was present only as a hologram, did not extend to inside the castle.

Tzader took in the way Brina's head tilted back as she looked up at Allyn with adoring eyes she'd once had only for Tzader. At that moment, Tzader finally accepted what he'd been denying since seeing the guard walk into the room.

Brina wasn't just ready to move on.

She *had* moved on.

All this time, Tzader hadn't wanted to believe Macha when she'd claimed Brina wanted him to walk away and forget about her.

Asking him to cut off both of his arms would have been easier.

But the truth stared him in the face.

He had to leave before he did or said something really stupid, or dangerous.

Brina lowered her chin, her cool gaze unwavering.

Tzader squeezed the words from his clenched throat. "My apologies, Your *Highness*. Unless you send for me, I will forward any future reports via e-mail until I've located the traitor, to prevent imposing on your time. Excuse me as I take my leave."

She opened her mouth to speak, but he'd already started the hologram transfer back to his body in North America.

Within a few minutes, he'd be whole again.

Except for the spot where his heart used to be.

"This was a mistake of astronomical proportions." Allyn spoke softly, but his face was hard.

When Brina drew a breath and released his hand, Allyn's fingers slipped from her shoulder. She needed a moment. Couldn't be lettin' her bottled-up tears fall. Not now. Tzader had left as if he couldn't wait to get out of the room.

But that had been the point, had it not?

She had no time to coddle her misery. "It will be all right, Allyn."

"You actually believe that, Your Highness?" Her guard expelled a long stream of breath born of disbelief and paced across the room. He stopped, turning to face her. "Tzader is not one to be easily fooled and neither is Macha. Do you really think he'll walk away from you this easily?"

"I would have said no until just now. I have never seen him so put out with me."

"That was far more than put out." Allyn looked up at the tall ceiling for a long moment, as if someone would help him, then back down at her. "You have no idea what a man like Tzader will do for the woman he loves, do you? This is a dangerous game you play, Your Highness."

"Aye, you're right, but this is no game." She forced iron into her backbone, prepared to do whatever it took to see this through. "This is war an' I swear to you that I intend to win it, an' soon."

Macha had given Brina a deadline to produce an heir in twelve months, of which two were almost gone.

My fault for bringin' up the topic of an heir, foolishly thinkin' Macha would find a way for me an' Tzader to be together. Instead, Macha had turned the tables on Brina by demanding she perform her duty as the Belador warrior queen and get busy producin' an heir, which meant releasing Tzader of his vow of love and Brina choosing another man.

Did Macha believe men were as interchangeable as her hair color that shifted with her moods?

The goddess had painted Brina as the one with no honor for refusin' to let Tzader go. As if Brina didn't feel guilty enough? She could not expect a man like Tzader to wait forever. He'd never be able to cross the protective ward on the castle and Macha couldn't break the warding. Or so she claimed.

The goddess had manipulated a deal where Brina now

had to convince Tzader that she no longer cared for him, which Brina would do. Her word was her bond.

But Macha had made a tactical error.

The goddess had allowed a loophole by agreein' to reconsider their situation if, once Brina convinced Tzader they were done, he still came back for her. Dealin' with gods and goddesses was much like handlin' a greased eel. Just when you thought you had a grip on the situation, it slipped away. That's why Brina had pressed Macha for a specific time frame in which Tzader had to walk away and come back. If . . . no, *when* Tzader came back in time, Brina had another chance with him.

She got her deadline.

Brina had until she married another man.

Macha clearly believed she'd settled the situation, but Brina had been reared a warrior's daughter who did not give up easily.

For that reason, she had taken matters into her own hands. She'd start the clock tickin' now by sendin' Macha to see Tzader so that the goddess could determine immediately whether he believed his relationship with Brina was over.

Then Brina would move to the next step in her plan to get him back.

Unless she'd misjudged the depth of Tzader's love for her.

Allyn took a step toward her, arms crossed as he moved. For the three years that he'd been part of her guard, he always had a positive word for her when he checked in on her first thing in the mornin' and again at the end of each day. The grim shape of his mouth indicated that he'd resigned himself to his role of royal boyfriend.

Good thing, since she could make no change in her game plan now that she'd introduced Allyn as the new man in her life.

He said, "I will gladly do my part, Your Highness, to convince one and all that you are mine. But what if this does not work? Have you considered the consequences?"

Brina flapped a hand at him. "Do not worry. I'll make good on my part as well, an' you'll have your year to travel away from Treoir even if I have to ship your cold body 'round the world in a casket," she teased, wantin' to lighten his somber mood.

"That's not what I meant."

She frowned at Allyn's suddenly serious tone. What was she missin' in this conversation? "Speak your mind."

"What will happen if, once everyone is convinced of our relationship, Tzader walks away rather than interferes?"

The look on Allyn's face said he had considered the possibility of failure and Brina losin' her bid for Tzader. If that happened, Macha would demand a wedding. Allyn and Brina would be honor bound to marry.

That could not happen.

"It won't be comin' to that, Allyn."

He shrugged. "You may not be able to stop what you've set into motion today. Only time will tell, but there's no going back at this point. Not without breaking your word to Macha." His dark blue eyes met hers with an intensity that surprised her. He added, "As I said, I will stand by you until the end. No matter what."

Brina listened to his tone more than his words, tryin' to decide what else he was not sayin'.

But he was right about one thing.

She could not go back now that she'd started this campaign without risk of losin' time and ground she could ill afford to give up. Allyn appeared unconcerned about that, but a warrior such as he would not allow fear or any similar emotion to show on his face. Still, he had to believe she would never put him in a corner where he'd be forced to marry her.

But as she thought about Tzader's exchange with Allyn . . . what had Tzader seen in Allyn's eyes that caused his rigid control to snap?

Allyn's face eased back into his blank, polite-guard look. "If you have no further need of me at the moment, I'd like to check our perimeter patrols."

"Of course." Brina shook herself mentally, dismissin' her ridiculous thoughts as Allyn strode away. He had no true interest in her. She'd chosen him based upon appearance and loyalty. No, he was merely a young man ready for female company, which was why Brina had refused to allow his participation in her plan without his receivin' compensation. Allyn had claimed he deserved no extra consideration for doin' his duty, but Brina would not ask so much of him without a well-deserved reward. She'd agreed to give him a year of travel. Some-thin' she knew he'd secretly longed for since childhood.

Aye, that would provide him the chance to find a

woman for himself. She laughed at her unexpected vanity in imaginin' the guard's desire. Just went to prove what a grand performance they had given today.

Allyn might need to take care in the future and not be too convincing, but she couldn't fault him. Not when she'd made it clear that she would do whatever it took to win Tzader.

But doubt poked at her in spite of her resolve.

Would Tzader fight to keep her or, after what he'd seen today, would he walk away?

NINETEEN

". . . preventing my bounty hunter from performing his duty, which in turn has cost me not just the bounty but a client—"

Tired of Dakkar's nonstop drivel on how he'd been wronged and was due justice, Macha shifted her simmering anger toward the Slavic god Varpulis, the entity called in as arbitrator over this Tribunal meeting. Varpulis wore only bright yellow shorts and ran in place. Skinny, pale and no muscle.

A god of wind or some such.

She'd had enough. "Dakkar is not a member of the Coalition and, therefore, is owed no compensation for any loss not committed as an act of intentional aggression by a member of my pantheon."

"I may not be a member, but the Coalition calls upon me when they have a need that requires my resources." Dakkar paused, his face reflecting undisturbed emotions. He had the chiseled lines, blunt nose and smooth, nut-brown skin of a man born under the rule of Genghis Khan. He'd been addressing Varpulis as if Dakkar actually cared about the Tribunal arbitrator's opinion in this discussion.

And this certainly ranked no higher than a discussion.

Macha appeared here only out of respect to the other gods and goddesses who supported the Coalition, but she would not tolerate another minute listening to Dakkar's ridiculous grievances.

As if he really cared about losing a bounty hunter? To Dakkar, that was merely a cost of doing business in his field.

His kohl-black eyes shifted from Varpulis to her. "As I understand it, Goddess, you have filed a charter for Alterants to be accepted as a recognized race . . . though it appears an unwise move on your part."

She'd grind the little peon into the dirt. "You are not much of a judge of what is unwise if you dare to criticize any choice I make. If you have nothing new to add, I suggest we dismiss this meeting and stop wasting the time of deities." She'd come up against this mage more than once over the decades and had no intention of repeating a mistake she'd made the last time they'd met.

Undeterred, Dakkar pressed on. "I don't repeat what's known to merely hear myself speak. I bring up the charter you've filed for a specific reason. You have offered sanctuary to Alterants. They are not hunted as the dangerous beasts they are known to be, now that you've opened the charter, which would indicate a certain level of responsibility."

Macha answered carefully. "Only for those who come forth and swear their loyalty to me. Make your point while we're still in this millennium, Dakkar."

"My point is simple. An eye for an eye."

He wants Evalle? "I am not handing over my Alterant."

Dakkar held his arms out, palms up in a gesture of we're-at-an-impasse. "You refuse to compensate me. I'm penalized every time one of my people has to enter the southeastern region of North America. I am offered nothing in return. Not even a beast."

She ignored the poke about Evalle being only a beast, something that could be handed off as easily as cattle. "If Evalle had committed this crime, she would be forfeited, but she did not."

His body radiated confidence and passivity, but his fingertips straightened, then curved, flexing with contained anger. "Then I want an agreement based upon precedent."

"Of what nature?" Varpulis asked, not even winded by his running.

"That if one of my bounty hunters *accidentally* kills an Alterant, *any* Alterant, there will be no retaliation and no recompense expected."

The miserable cur wants blanket amnesty for all of the future, for one killing?

He had to be crazy to think she'd agree to that. "I will not tolerate anyone attacking or killing a being who has been accepted into my pantheon and is under my protection."

Dakkar's eyes thinned with impending battle. "I feel the same way about my bounty hunters. I think it only fair that you either finalize the charter and accept responsibility for all the Alterants or withdraw your charter until you are ready to make that commitment."

"If I withdraw the charter, it will not be due to a

bounty hunter's losing one of his mutts." Now she understood what this was all about. Dakkar was merely establishing his position in the eyes of the Tribunal, setting the stage for what he really wanted. An Alterant.

Offering him anything else at this point would be a wasted effort, but she would flush him out. "What will compensate you, Dakkar?"

"A decision on this before the next full moon."

"Done." Varpulis sped up until he turned into a blur. Dakkar's sly smile widened into a predator's grin.

Macha understood why. He knew she'd have to go against a Tribunal to change that decision. With the Medb threat hanging over her warriors and Brina, this was not the time to start a war on all fronts.

He gambled that he would walk away with an Alterant. And damn his miserable hide, he just might.

Evalle had better come through on her promise to bring in Alterants. And on time.

TWENTY

How could someone so small be so scary? Evalle followed Kit, the diminutive package of energy who, it appeared, ran Nyght Industries as she'd claimed.

Isak's mother.

Kit directed Evalle to follow as she headed for a group of men who'd been assembling weapons before the Rías attack. She made short work of dictating who would take what shift to guard the cell containing Jasper.

Evalle recognized some of these men. She'd seen them carrying special weapons on black-ops maneuvers with Isak Nyght when he hunted nonhumans.

Men born with sharp eyes who lived on a diet of adrenaline and grit.

Not a one of them said a word to Kit other than a respectful "Yes, ma'am."

Oddly, Kit's high-handedness didn't put Evalle off the way other people's had when they'd tried to force her to jump through hoops. Kit gave orders to keep chaos from turning into insanity, not as a power play. Evalle could respect that and go along to get along, for now.

Turning toward the area in the gargantuan warehouse that had been sectioned off into offices, Kit said over her shoulder, "How does my son know you, Evalle?"

"Uh . . ." What could she say to Isak's mother without knowing what he'd told Kit? "He didn't tell you?"

Kit didn't answer her. She opened the door to the offices and passed through an interim sitting area furnished with blue leather chairs and a sofa. A hallway to more offices spilled off to the left.

Evalle kept step right behind Kit, who finally entered a windowless room painted in soft beige colors. The plain cherrywood desk suited Kit's bullet-point style. Files and paper sat on one side, neatly organized. A picture of her and Isak was perched on an eye-level shelf of the matching credenza behind the desk. Kit's all-in-one computer monitor had been mounted on an adjustable metal arm, ready to slide into any position for the woman who clearly demanded respect and compliance even from inanimate objects.

She dropped into a high-back leather office chair that consumed her body, then she pointed at the armchair facing her desk. Not a request. "Don't answer my questions with a question. How do you know Isak?"

Had there been an *or else* at the end of that?

Evalle saw no way around giving this woman a version of the truth. "I met Isak by accident when we both found a demon at the same time."

Leaned back with elbows propped on her chair arms, Kit folded her hands together in a thoughtful pose. "What happened?"

"Isak used his blaster and turned the demon into chips."

"Were you trying to kill the demon, too?"

Tricky question. "I needed intel first. I was questioning the demon to find out who had sent him to Atlanta and how he was involved with a human that had been killed by another demon."

"You must have seen Isak more than once for him to bring you to the warehouse." Kit could probably play poker with the pros in Las Vegas. She had an unreadable face.

"We've crossed paths a few times."

That drew an indulgent twist of Kit's lips. "Isak called to tell me he was bringing a friend here. That's enough alone to pique my curiosity since Isak hasn't exactly been social since losing his best friend since high school to an Alterant. Then you show up . . . and he finds out the truth about you."

Things had been going pretty good until Kit reminded Evalle of Isak's loss.

She needed to convince Kit that she presented no threat to humans. "Just so we're clear, I did not come here to harm anyone or to sabotage your operation."

"I can accept that."

That sounded promising. Almost too easy.

Then Kit asked, "What are you to Isak?"

"We're friends." Evalle said that before she'd thought about it, but they *were* friends, at least from her point of view. She doubted Isak would agree at the moment. Worse than angry, he'd been disappointed when he found out he'd been associating with an Alterant, as if her being dangerous wasn't nearly as bad as her lying to him about her identity.

Questions buzzed silently through the room until Kit

snagged one from the air. "How long ago did you two meet?"

"Couple months back, not long." Evalle preferred questions about the demon, the forklift-driver Rías in Kit's lockup or the weapon Evalle had come here hoping to borrow.

Evalle would disappoint a string of men today. First Isak, now Tzader and Quinn, who had put their faith in her returning with a weapon for the team.

The door between the office and the warehouse opened and closed behind her on a soft hush of air, but she didn't hear footsteps. No doubt one of the men had stuck his head in, realized Kit had a meeting in progress and withdrew just as quietly.

"What kind of friend of Isak's are you?" Kit asked with enough steel in her voice that Evalle caught the protective warning.

How do I answer that? I haven't had so many friends that I've had to break them down into categories. I thought you were either a friend or not.

Evalle gave Kit the best answer she could. "The kind who has eaten dinner with Isak and who told him about how to see the Rías in a dangerous fog that covered parts of the country a few weeks ago. I fought a Rías on my way through Atlanta and was forced to kill it to protect a human, then I ran into Isak and gave him a tip about the fog camouflaging the shifted beasts."

"Dinner?" Kit mused aloud. "You went on a date with Isak?"

Of course Kit picked up on *that* and not Evalle's point

about helping her son. Evalle had never been on a date and doubted what Isak had done that night qualified as such. "Not exactly."

"How exactly?"

Evalle wouldn't win any points with Isak's mom by saying he'd sent a team to kidnap her, but that's what had happened.

"We had dinner at the hangar," Isak said, entering Kit's office.

Had he been standing in the other room behind Evalle all this time? She angled her head up so she could assess his mood when he stopped next to her chair.

He glanced down at her with ice-blue eyes that could drop the temperature ten degrees before he looked away to address his mother. "She missed a meeting. I sent the men on a 'snatch and grab.'"

Kit's poker face fell away with a scowl. "You kidnapped her for dinner?"

Isak moved one stiff shoulder in a half shrug. "I had to interrogate her . . . it."

He *what*? *It*? Evalle had originally thought he'd hauled her into his hangar for a browbeating, but that had been before he'd acted like the perfect gentleman and served her a mouthwatering Italian dinner *he'd* prepared.

Then he'd kissed her.

She turned all the way to face him. "*Interrogation?* Really? That's not how I remember it, Isak."

"I'm not speaking to you, *Alterant*." He crossed his arms, eyes staring straight ahead, refusing to look at her.

"Well, I'm talking to you, buster." Evalle stood up with her hands balled at her sides and stepped in front of him, turning her back on Kit.

That should have forced Isak to face her, but he stared over her shoulder.

She would not tolerate his attitude. "Okay, the secret is out. I *am* an Alterant and there's no twelve-step program to cure it. But I've also put my life on the line many times to protect humans. You can be mad at me for not telling you the truth, but you can*not* stand there and judge me for things I haven't done."

His jaw muscle clenched, but he made no sign of listening to her.

She wanted to pound on his chest to make him see her again like he had before. As a woman. But he only saw a beast, so she stuck to facts. "I'm sorry you lost your friend to an Alterant, but I didn't do that." She nodded when his eyes finally shot to hers. "I can understand how you feel about losing someone who's important to you. That was one reason I tried to avoid you, but you wouldn't stay away from me."

That square jaw of his moved when he ground his teeth. Blue eyes turned thunderstorm gray, but he didn't say a word.

She unballed her fingers, dragging as much calm from her next breath as she could before she spoke.

"*You* may not think of me as a friend anymore, but I still see you that way. I meant it when I said I didn't come here to cause you any problems, only to get a weapon to use against the trolls."

"What trolls?" Kit asked. "Why are you fighting trolls and demons?"

Evalle took a step to the side and turned so that she could keep both opponents in view when she spoke to Kit. VIPER might fry her over saying any more than she already had, but Kit and Isak knew about nonhumans. Continuing to lie to them would only turn their operation into a more dangerous enemy of the Coalition. Maybe, with a little luck, Evalle could show Kit and Isak the value of nonhumans.

"I'm part of an international coalition of unusual beings that protects humans from supernatural predators . . . like trolls."

Isak made a nasty scoffing sound.

"It's true," Evalle argued. She looked to Kit. "I've been doing this since I was eighteen, and the group I'm a member of is sworn to uphold a vow of honor under penalty of death. That includes protecting humans."

Kit tapped her fingers against each other. "This isn't the first time you've fought trolls, right?"

"No."

"What's different now? Why do you need a Nyght weapon?"

Evalle had been right to tell Kit the truth about what she did. The woman was too sharp to play games with and had been fair so far. "There's a special group of trolls called Svarts that are far more dangerous than regular ones. They're out of Switzerland. We're trying to figure out what they're doing here and protect humans without exposing ourselves."

"Why do you hide from humans?"

Had that been a trick question? The woman had to know how dangerous it would be to expose nonhumans to their world. Evalle said, "If humans knew about us, then they'd have to know about the nonhuman predators, which would create mass chaos. At that point, the good guys would be hunted along with the deadly ones, and you would end up with no one capable of protecting humans."

Isak interjected, "We've been doing a pretty damned good job."

Evalle rounded on him. "You have no idea of all the things out there. That Rías in your lockup is just one of many, and humans like your forklift driver don't even know they *can* turn into a beast. At least with Alterants we have bright green eyes, but there's no indication of a human who can shift into a Rías."

"We can produce plenty of weapons to take those *things* down."

Evalle ignored the dark way he'd said "things," determined to get her point across. "You don't understand. The Svart trolls are only one of the problems we face every day. The Svarts are a deadly black-ops group with different powers and abilities, plus they can glamour themselves so that you can't tell one from a human. I fought a Svart last night that was so dangerous it almost killed me."

Concern flickered in Isak's gaze for a second, then he shut it down, but that tiny moment of emotion warmed Evalle's heart. Gave her hope that he might stop hating her someday.

She swung her gaze to Kit, who had a warm, feminine

version of Isak's blue eyes when Kit studied her son, but that same gaze turned back into all-business when Kit looked at Evalle. Kit asked in a pointed tone, "Who will be responsible for this weapon?"

That got a rise out of Isak, stoking his anger back to full force. "There's no way in hell I'm giving *it* a weapon—"

A snarl crawled up Evalle's throat at being called *it* again, but Kit stood with the speed of a bullet and spoke first.

"Has Evalle *ever* presented a danger to humans that you know of, Isak?"

Evalle held her breath. Could this mean what she thought? That she might really get out of this alive *and* walk away with a weapon?

One look at Isak diminished that hope.

A ball of fury wrapped in corded muscle fumed at her. His words rolled out like thunder. "That's not the point, Kit."

Evalle frowned at him. "You keep calling your mother Kit. That's not right."

Isak broke off the tense glaring match with Kit and stared at Evalle as if she'd spoken another language. "What'd you say?"

Kit chuckled softly. "He's been calling me that since before he got his driver's license."

Heat brushed Evalle's cheeks. She muttered around the foot she'd stuck in her mouth. "Oh, well, that just didn't sound right to me."

"Didn't you tell me you never knew your parents?"

Isak ground out, still not willing to let go of his righteous anger.

"Yes."

"Then how would *you* know what was right or not?"

Evalle lifted her shoulders, cutting her eyes to Kit, judging his mother's reaction—amused?—before she answered him. "It's what I've seen on television and read in books. I thought calling her mom, mother, ma or something equivalent was a term of endearment and respect. I haven't heard anyone call their parent by a first name."

Kit walked around her desk, chuckling over something that entertained only her. "I listen to my instincts, and mine are telling me I can believe you, Evalle." Kit extended her hand again. "Good to meet you. We'll loan you a weapon—"

Isak growled loud as a grizzly awakened in winter hibernation, but he couldn't dampen Evalle's growing enthusiasm over the way this had turned out.

Kit finished shaking her hand, then continued. "As long as you are entirely responsible for it."

Like I wouldn't be anyhow? "No problem. I assure you—"

"I'm not done," Kit said. "I also expect you to report regularly to Isak about nonhuman activity in the city."

Evalle nodded, letting Kit know she was still on board. She didn't want to rock the tentative truce.

"And . . . " Kit added.

"Yes?" Evalle said in too bright a voice, but Kit could still refuse the weapon or try to lock Evalle in a cell.

That would be a mistake.

Kit eyed both of them. "You come to dinner at my house soon, very soon."

"*What?*" Isak and Evalle both shouted at the same time.

"What word did either of you not understand?" Kit asked in a brisk voice similar to the one she'd used to issue orders in the warehouse.

Isak just turned around and stalked out of the room without a sound except for slamming the door, making what he thought about spending another second in Evalle's company pretty clear.

Which was fine. Dinner with Isak fell a ways down her priority list with Svart trolls invading the city and Tristan captured by the Medb.

Smiling at Kit, Evalle said, "Thank you for the weapon. I promise you won't be sorry about loaning it to me."

Kit smiled back, a confident take-no-prisoners smile. "I'm not the least concerned about the weapon, because we can disarm it remotely if need be."

Crud. That could be a problem if Isak decided to flip the off switch without notifying her, but Evalle would just have to take that gamble. "That's good to know."

As she moved closer to Evalle, Kit's pleasant voice turned deadly soft. "I have only one concern, and that's Isak. There's nothing that can protect anyone from me if something happened to him. I would unleash everything within my power, and trust me, I'm not someone you or any other nonhuman wants to go up against."

Evalle chilled at the obvious threat, but not one she'd have to be concerned about. Based upon his loud exit, Isak wouldn't come within a mile of her again. Even if she had to follow through on the strange dinner invitation, Isak would bail out just as he'd done a moment ago. She assured Kit, "I understand and would never harm Isak."

"That's what I expect." Kit turned toward her desk.

Rather than dwell on that any longer, Evalle moved the conversation to another concern. "What about the Rías in your holding cell? What are you going to do with him?"

Pausing next to her chair, Kit asked, "Why?"

"Please don't kill him. Once he understands how to control the shifting, he won't be a threat. He is trainable."

"Really? Who would do this training?"

Tristan could do it if Evalle knew where he was or if—when—she found him again. Another problem she had to figure out sooner than soon, plus things were going to deteriorate between her and Macha real quick if Tristan didn't show. "I know someone who can do it, but he's not available at the moment."

"When *will* he be available?"

Do I look like a crystal ball? "I don't know yet, but if—"

"Let's make this simple, Evalle. I'll give you a week to bring this trainer to me. After that, I'll hand the forklift driver over to Isak. I can't run a halfway house for non-humans and be fair to my son."

"You would just kill that man even though he hasn't hurt anyone?"

"Yet. He hasn't harmed anyone *yet*. Based on the reports we got from across the country a few weeks ago, others like him have murdered families. If you want to help this one, bring in the trainer," Kit said, nicely side-stepping a direct answer about the man's fate. "Or if you can't find the trainer in time, you can discuss the forklift driver's fate with Isak."

Oh, yeah. That'd be as productive as building a snowball factory in hell. Evalle couldn't do anything about the poor man right now, but Kit didn't strike her as the kind of person who would starve or torment a defenseless being. With her list of priorities growing by the minute, Evalle focused on getting the weapon and making it back to Atlanta. Alive.

Would one of Kit's men be willing to drive an Alterant back to the city? "Since I can't tell anyone how to find me—"

Holding up a hand to stall Evalle, Kit lifted a two-way radio from where it had been in a charging cradle on the bookcase behind her and spoke into the receiver. "Lambert, pull out a BXZ-12 for Isak and tell him to meet Evalle at the Hummer. Thanks."

She wants Isak to drive me home?

When Kit looked up again, she said, "That should give you two ample opportunity to discuss the forklift driver. And, just so we're clear, I expect Isak to come back without a scratch on him. Take care of my weapon."

Right. Mustn't harm Isak, the Alterant-hating human who would have the troll-killing weapon in his possession and Evalle at his mercy in the Hummer.

TWENTY-ONE

Twenty minutes into the ride back to Atlanta, Evalle tired of Isak's stony silence . . . and the stupid blindfold over her sunglasses. "Kit said I only had to wear this until we reached the interstate. I can tell we're not on secondary roads any longer."

The blindfold loosened and fell away from her face. Isak flipped the cloth over his shoulder onto the rear seat of the Hummer next to a fat viola case that shielded the weapon.

She cut her gaze at the silent hunk driving and tested the waters with a simple yes-or-no question.

"You ever going to talk to me again?"

The hardheaded man wove his way through the interchange onto the northbound interstate in downtown and stared ahead at the traffic, ignoring her just as he'd been doing since she'd climbed into the Hummer. At the warehouse, he'd stood by her door, making no move to help her to the passenger seat.

Or to show any concern about her being buckled up.

Not that she'd needed his help, which meant she had to have the most contrary emotions to feel hurt over the way he'd ignored her this time. She hadn't considered what Isak meant to her before today because of their bizarre friendship, but she already missed what they'd had.

Riding with someone who hated you sucked.

She'd had good reasons for not telling him the truth, but somewhere inside her cluttered heart she admitted that he deserved an apology. "I'm sorry, Isak."

Still no reply.

"What's it gonna take to fix this?"

Not a word from the driver's seat.

She could appreciate his reason for being angry. Still, he of all people should understand why someone like her had to protect her identity. Especially to shield it from one of the few humans capable of killing her in a one-on-one battle.

She tried a different tack. "I like Kit."

"Stay away from her."

Four whole words spoken in a command, but she'd take that over brooding silence. Keeping her voice light, she pointed out, "Did you miss that Kit *ordered* me to see her again? You may be able to ignore her, but she scares the stuffing out of me."

Had his lips twitched?

Maybe she'd hit on the right topic. She kept going. "I saw the way those men jumped to attention. And who wouldn't when a human woman is fearless in front of nonhumans? Easy to see why your men all respect her."

She could swear Isak's jaw softened.

What else could she say to keep the stubborn man talking? She'd been making progress with the truth, but he'd been right about one thing. She had no parental experience to draw upon. "I can't imagine growing up with a mother, especially one like Kit. You're lucky to have her."

She hadn't intended to be quite so honest, but the longing in her voice had been as real and true as her words.

It still took Isak a moment to respond. His words came slowly when he did speak, as if he didn't want to allow this conversation to keep rolling and pick up speed toward actually communicating again. "I know."

Two words, both filled with admiration and love.

She'd never envied a human anything other than the ability to walk in the sun, but she coveted what Isak had—a parent who cared deeply for him. Someone he'd known since birth.

She let him drive silently while she considered how else she could widen the tiny opening he'd allowed. Killing demons was a whole lot easier than dealing with cranky men. She could ask him about the weapon Kit had loaned her, but Isak's man Lambert had gone through the operation of the weapon with her—because Isak wouldn't. To be honest, a monkey could hit a moving target with that custom superblaster.

The Nyght family built impressive kill toys.

"She likes you."

Evalle jerked around at the unexpected words from Isak. "Really?"

"She likes the forklift driver, too."

In other words, don't go taking what he'd said about Kit's liking her to heart. "I see."

"No, you don't. Kit's hard as nails on the outside with

a gooey center. Worst person I ever saw for taking on the broken refuse. Thinks she can save everyone."

Now Evalle understood why he'd decided to speak to her. He wanted to make it clear how low she ranked on the scale of life in his world. Not worth saving.

All her good intentions toward Isak dissolved with that ice pick to the heart. The muscles in her neck clenched at the need to yell at him that she was not some homeless animal. She hated being treated like a dangerous creature who had no control over killing others, but more than that?

She hated being pitied.

She was *not* a loser and did *not* need him, Kit or anyone else saving her.

Isak scratched his head, then grumbled something under his breath and elbowed the door panel hard enough to crack it. That wasn't going to improve his mood.

Evalle's resolve not to snap at Isak crumbled under his whip of anger. The man couldn't ride for a few more minutes in peace? Was sitting inside a vehicle with her so abhorrent?

He clearly had something he wanted to say and might as well say it now.

"*What, Isak?* Think of some new insult? By all means, don't waste your chance to get back at me for being born. Go ahead and tell me whatever you're grumbling about, because you won't get another opportunity." Not if she had anything to say about it. What did she need with him as a friend?

A friend who insulted her.

"Yeah, I've got something else to say," he admitted glumly. "Kit would be pissed with me if she heard what I just said. That forklift driver's a good guy and a brilliant combat engineer life kicked in the nuts. She wouldn't consider you or him as broken or refuse . . . and neither do I."

Evalle's thoughts stumbled all over themselves at the unexpected admission. Why would Isak tell her the truth when he had plenty of reasons for being ticked off at her?

Anyone else would use that opening to vent.

She knew why Isak hadn't. He had a personal code of honor. The same one that had stilled his trigger finger when he'd discovered her identity as an Alterant and his heart had screamed at him to shoot, that she deserved to die.

That all Alterants had to pay for the death of his friend.

She'd feel the same in his shoes if someone had killed Tzader or Quinn. But just like her two best friends, Isak was a man of honor.

This friend business could be so messy and complicated some days. Just like the situation with Quinn and that he'd lied to her about what he'd told Kizira. What was she going to do about Quinn? Should she give him another chance to explain? Storm had confirmed at least a part of what Sam Thomas had tried to tell Evalle. Her chest ached from feeling betrayed by someone she'd lay her life down for, and the pain would not subside until she found out if he was truly guilty or not.

But Kit had given Evalle the benefit of the doubt—a second chance. Could she do any less for Quinn? And what about Isak? He could have killed Evalle and Kit wouldn't have said a word, but he hadn't.

So she shouldn't give up on trying to keep Isak as a friend.

Once Isak pulled inside the parking garage and parked next to her motorcycle, Evalle took her time unbuckling her seat belt to give him long enough to come around to her side.

She wanted to grin, but didn't. The gentleman in him *had* to open her door.

Taking in a deep breath, she schooled her face to be calm and prepared to take one more shot at parting under better terms. She had an idea—one that might backfire on her, but she'd gambled her safety on worse odds.

When he opened her door, he moved back, stopping between her and her bike.

She climbed out and took a slow step toward him, watching to see if he'd flinch or back away.

Like a wall of determination, he didn't budge.

She closed the space between them to inches, then lifted her hands slowly and gripped the lapels of his shirt. When he didn't shove her away, she pulled herself up on her toes and kissed him lightly on the lips.

He didn't lower his head or kiss her back, but he wasn't entirely indifferent either. She'd opened her empathic senses and picked up a flush of heat coming off him. The kind of heat she'd recently figured out meant interest from a man.

Easing back down, she released his shirt and said, "I am your friend."

He didn't respond. Just stood there like an Isak statue.

Turning around to the Hummer, she retrieved the modified viola case that held the compact weapon and slung the strap over her shoulder. She'd settled the case across her back when energy stirred through the air.

Something strong and tense.

Spinning around slowly, she searched the dark parking deck for a hint of what that could have been, listening for a sound. Human . . . or other?

"Evalle?" Isak said in an even tone.

That drew her full attention. "Yes?"

"Don't ever do that again."

Well, crud. She'd never figure out men. This one just used up all his good deals and the last dregs of her patience. "You can bank on me not ever kissing *you* again."

He stepped up to her, crowding her comfort zone. Did he think she'd back away? Not a chance.

His big hand came up slowly to her cheek. "That's not what I meant."

There weren't enough hours in a day to figure out how a man's brain worked. "What *did* you mean?"

"Don't ever just . . ." He leaned closer, whispering, "Peck me and call it a kiss." His lips touched hers, warm and simmering with heat.

She barely had a chance to catch her breath before he took it away with his kiss. Nothing like the last time he'd kissed her, which had been gentle and sweet. This was a bold kiss, one she wouldn't soon forget. He slipped his hands around her neck and back, drawing her in closer with each pass of his lips over hers.

Her skin tingled with excitement, a warm feeling that reached her toes and started back up her body. She'd just gotten her bearings when the kiss ended as abruptly as it had started.

She licked her lips, trying to figure out how she felt about *that* kiss. That very sensual kiss, which had started out as only a let's-stay-friends kiss. At least on her part.

When he pulled back, dark satisfaction ringed his harsh eyes. He touched her chin with one finger and said, "Just a warning for the next time I see you."

What exactly was he warning her about? "Does this mean we have a truce?"

"Truce." With that, he dropped his hand and walked around, climbing into the Hummer.

Another wave of energy swept past her, much fiercer this time.

She opened her empathic senses all the way, searching quickly to figure out what was hovering nearby.

The energy retreated, but she picked up a cold rage so chilling her skin pebbled in reaction.

Isak cranked his engine and looked her way, waiting until she waved him off before he backed up and left.

The minute the Hummer disappeared, Evalle lingered to see if the energy continued to pulse, but nothing followed that last quick rush. Who, or what, had been watching her and Isak?

Another Rías?

She lifted the strap off her shoulder, bringing the viola case around to sit on her bike seat where she could access the weapon inside.

A deep male voice that belonged to her favorite Nightstalker rumbled with Southern undertones. "Don't tell me you done gone and started violin lessons. I ain't listenin' to no screechin', so don't come 'round here to practice."

Evalle looked over her shoulder to find the translucent image of Grady in his usual red-and-black-plaid, short-sleeved shirt and wrinkled trousers a size too big for his tall, bony frame. He hadn't aged beyond sixty-eight, the age he'd been when he'd died well over a decade ago. "I didn't ask you to listen to me play, old man, and this case is for a viola, not for a violin."

"Why don't you git a gee-tar?"

She heaved a sigh and stood the case against the back wheel of her bike. "What're you doing here?"

"Watchin' your pitiful excuse for a love life."

That meant Grady had been here long enough to witness her kissing Isak. "Can we move this along? Why are you here and not over by the hospital?"

When he'd failed to give her a name the first time she'd met him, Evalle had started calling him Grady due to finding him always around Grady Hospital.

He got that ornery-old-cuss look. "Gotta shake if you wanna know what I know."

She hadn't shaken hands with him since she'd made

the mistake of doing it too long one night out of sympathy when she should only have been shaking for intel. The result had allowed Grady to take human form with no help at times and hold that form longer than he should.

"What happened to taking human form any time you want, Grady?"

"I never said *any* time." He bunched his lips and squinted one eye in a stare meant to let her know she'd aggravated him.

She grinned, refusing to make this easy. The wily old dog could outmaneuver the best of VIPER agents. Shaking too quickly would cost her more next time.

Grady gave up on his mean look and turned pouty. "I can still do it some on my own, but I had to use up my solid form to come here."

"Why? What was going on here?"

"Nuh-uh. You know the rules."

Now she shoved an ornery look at him. "All right, but this needs to be quick."

"Like Ironman said, 'Waitin' on you now.'"

She'd ask him where he'd seen that movie, but she didn't have the time to waste on chitchat.

When his filmy hand connected with Evalle's, heat flushed through her hand and arm with the power she generated.

Grady's form turned opaque, as if someone had poured cocoa-brown pigment into his body. Even the faded colors on his shirt sharpened. His face muscles relaxed into an unguarded smile that always gave her a warm feeling in her chest.

"Start talking, old man. What were you doing here?"

Grady stretched his arms as if just waking up, then wiped his wrinkled mouth in a patent sign that he wanted a drink, but she had nothing to offer him this time and he knew it. He said, "You don't want to know about the Svart trolls first?"

"What have you got on them?" He'd more than earn this handshake if he had information on Svarts.

"They're stirrin' up all this gang mess."

"We *know* that."

"Bet you don't know how many are here."

She'd heard Horace tell everyone last night that the Svarts often worked in teams of two or four, so she expected more than one. "How many?"

"Eight came into the city and—"

"Eight? *Crap!*"

"Save all that exasperation for the bad news." Grady licked his lips and scratched his grizzly beard. "There's more comin'."

"Why? What do they want?" Evalle had the best snoop in the underworld of Atlanta standing in front of her. Grady always had more pertinent information than any other Nightstalker she could name.

"Don't know. But those Svarts are plannin' for more trolls like the local ones to arrive as soon as the Svarts finish somethin'. Sounds sort of like a troll convention in the makin' with Svarts runnin' the show."

She chewed on that mentally. "What could be worth their facing off with VIPER, especially this division?"

"Somethin' they been promised once they finish their job would be my bet."

"What do you mean?"

"Our world—the unnatural one—don't work like human-world logic. If the Svarts are here now, it's to do somethin' for a powerful group. And if they're plannin' on callin' in all kind of trolls soon, that makes me think whoever they got a deal with has the Svarts believin' VIPER ain't gonna be able to protect this country soon."

Unimaginable. But she'd seen enough in her five short years, since becoming a Belador warrior at eighteen, to know that anything in her world was possible. "Svarts are pretty powerful, but I don't see where eight are a force to match with VIPER. I'm not wishing more trolls of any kind to deal with, but if the Svarts intend to bring in more, why aren't all those extra trolls here now?"

"My guess would be that the Svarts are waitin' to call in the rest after someone *else* clears the way."

She tapped her forehead, drawing together all the bits and pieces she'd gleaned and adding those to Grady's information. "I'm confused. If the Svarts believe they're capable of taking down the North American division of VIPER, which I hope can't happen, why would they wait on anyone else to pave the way?"

"You ain't listenin'. Svarts do *exactly* what they contract for. If they're holdin' off callin' in more trolls, it's probably because the folks the Svarts made a deal with are the ones that are gonna take down VIPER, not the Svarts."

Pieces of the puzzle started flying at her, demanding to be put into place. "Who could possibly think—"

"You ain't lookin' at the big picture."

That wrenched her attention back to him. "How much bigger should I think beyond seeing this world destroyed by a bunch of trolls led by seriously dangerous ones?"

Grady gave her an indulgent look and switched into his all-knowing—and much better educated—teacher tone, which popped up at the most unexpected times, hinting at a past that contradicted his homeless persona. "What's the backbone of VIPER, the strongest force within the coalition?"

"The Beladors."

"Right, so it stands to reason that whoever made a deal with these ugly cannibals may have a plan to take down the *Bel-a-dors*," he stressed as if he spoke to a slow student. "If that is the case, then maybe the Svart only have to accomplish whatever their mission is, then wait for their client to destroy the Beladors, which would gut VIPER. Once that happens, the Svart can call in their other buddies and turn Atlanta into Troll Central. Then the whole US of A."

Could he be right? Could this be about the Beladors? And, if so, that would make the Svart client . . . "The Medb could be behind this."

"That's what I'm thinking."

She flexed her fingers in and out, ready to get moving. Grady had put together a lot of information. "Did you figure out all that on your own?"

He scratched his neck, jumping back into his street persona. "Naw."

"Got anything else to tell me?"

"Only that those things are huntin' you."

Just like Storm had told her when he'd followed a Svart's trail to her bike this morning while she met with Quinn. "So that's why you came to find me."

"Had to since you ain't got sense enough to stay outta trouble." He cut his eyes at her with intent. "Next time, you best have a bottle if you want to trade."

Grady knew some places to hunt for her, but he wouldn't have known to locate her bike in this deserted parking deck. "How did you find me?"

"That Injun tracker came lookin' for me by the hospital."

"Storm? What did he want?"

"Said he was worried about you. Somethin' about the Svarts and some other woman he had to keep you away from."

"Adrianna?" Evalle's fingers curled into a fist instinctively.

"Naw. Wasn't her. Some witch doctor."

Ah! The woman Evalle had agreed to help Storm find in exchange for his helping her hunt Tristan weeks ago. And Evalle still had to make good on her part of that deal.

Grady tsked at her.

"What?"

"That Injun told me about the Svarts huntin' for you. Said you were in danger but you didn't want his help. What's wrong with you?"

She didn't have enough hours in the day to do justice to that question. Making a hand motion to move this along, she said, "I'll catch up with Storm and find out what he knows. But don't tell anyone you saw him, okay?"

"I *know* that. I told him I wouldn't say nothin'."

"Just tell me what Storm told you about the Svarts." She had a tough time following Grady sometimes.

Did attention deficit transfer to ghoul form?

"Said he'd been trackin' them things around town and smelled a Svart not far from Oakland Cemetery that had a tainted odor . . . like a demon."

"A demon? Two different kinds of Svarts?" She could use some good news anytime now.

"Maybe. Or might just be he stank."

"We need Storm to find these things before this gets any worse. Maybe that's what I sensed earlier when I got out of Isak's Hummer. I felt a wave of energy over there."

Grady looked around, peering in the direction she'd pointed. "Naw, that wasn't a Svart 'cause that Injun slipped into the dark over yonder right before you showed up with Rambo."

What? Her mouth turned cotton dry. "Grady . . . do you think Storm—"

"Saw you smoochin' Rambo? Yep."

Evalle slapped a hand over her eyes. This was catastrophic. "What was he doing here?"

"I done told you. That Injun's a tracker. I talked him into findin' you for me." Grady looked around at the empty parking deck, mumbling. "Should be thankin' me, but you got a bottle or french fries? No."

"Grady, please."

Evalle had to find Storm, but how?

Wait a minute. As she lowered her hand, Evalle's heart started thumping at one possibility, a slim one. Storm had said he'd put his address in the e-mail draft he'd set up for them to communicate. Without that, the chances of finding him were less than locating one specific grain of sand in an hourglass.

She just had to get to a computer and access the e-mail with his address . . . before Storm changed the password.

TWENTY-TWO

Quinn stepped off the elevator onto the floor for his hotel room, debating on going to the suite or not. He didn't want to deal with Lanna right now, especially when he'd have to explain why he needed to leave again. But neither could he go to the second suite he'd taken without checking to see if Lanna was still safe.

If the gods had any respect for a man's sanity, Lanna would be asleep.

When Quinn entered the suite he'd sent her to, he found the minibar had been raided of everything except alcohol. Lanna's suitcase had exploded in the living area, clothes tossed right and left. At the door to the bedroom, he found a note that read, *Cousin, please do not wake me before midnight unless important.*

Quinn put his hand on the knob, prepared to open the door until he read the last line, *And cover eyes if you come in room. I did not pack nightgown and do not want embarrass us both.*

He jerked his hand back as though he'd reached for a snake.

There was no way he would go inside there short of the fire alarm going off. Not with his cousin naked.

Crossing the minefield of clothes all over the room, he found a hotel notepad and wrote her a message to call him as soon as she woke up, that he was close by. With a second look at the chaos in the room, he dragged a chair from the dining table into the walkway and put the note on the seat where she couldn't miss it. Then he retrieved the warded Triquetra from where he'd hidden the triangular stylized throwing blade beneath a small table in the foyer. He slipped the hand-size flat metal piece inside his suit jacket.

On his way to the elevator, he fingered the room key card for the second suite he'd taken on the top floor.

A room where he could confront Kizira without any chance of Lanna being around.

He used the silent ride up to check for any areas in his mind that felt weak before he undertook this gamble. All systems were go, just as when he'd left the mountain retreat with the druids.

Tzader and the Beladors needed him to turn the tables on the Medb, especially on Kizira.

Reaching the new suite, Quinn found everything in place, right down to the suitcase identical to the one in his room where Lanna slept. He'd made all the arrangements on his way back to the hotel. Clothes and personal items had been purchased and packed into the suitcase, then delivered here.

Kizira had to believe this was his only room.

And Lanna couldn't know Quinn had another suite or the teenage busybody would find a way to stick her nose in where it would get them both killed.

He made quick work of unpacking and placing personal items in appropriate locations, but he didn't hang his warded Triquetra on the hotel-room doorknob. He doubted Kizira had come through the front door the last time anyway.

Didn't matter. He intended to be ready for her this time.

Now if he could just toughen his heart.

She'd held a piece of that stubborn organ for years, but had never given him reason to think she'd take advantage of their connection to harm him or the Beladors.

Call him foolish for believing she cared for him.

Call him an idiot for having fallen in love with her thirteen years ago.

He'd had no idea that she was Medb when they'd first met and he'd saved her life, then she'd saved his. They spent two weeks hiding out, running from a threat, or so he'd thought. He'd figured out later that she'd been evading Medb warlocks sent to return a priestess-in-training to Queen Flaevynn of TÅµr Medb.

That had been then, before either of them had seen so much Belador and Medb blood flow beneath the bridge of hatred.

Ready to do his job, Quinn headed for the shower, more than ready to wash away battle crud from the last gang attack. When he stepped into the hot steam, he steeled himself for his next move and lowered his mental shields.

He envisioned Kizira inside his mind, in that private area that no one had ever entered until she'd rushed past his mental shields during Conlan's mind probe. He could have lived with that, but not with what she did later, coming into his room and using her powers to soothe his crushing migraine . . . to seduce him, and to use his weakness to gain information to harm his friends.

Be fair. It wasn't as though he'd required much seducing. When it came to Kizira, he rarely went a day without thinking of her and missing what they'd shared.

Quinn? Can you hear me? This is Kizira.

There she was. He soaped his skin, fighting the ripple of unease that raced along his spine at how easily she'd entered his mind.

Answering too quickly would be a mistake.

He'd have to act wary and not answer right away to convince her that she'd surprised him. He shampooed his hair, buying a few moments. Guilt gnawed at his resolve to do this, warning that what he intended to do—what he had to do—would carry a price he'd pay daily for the rest of his life.

Quinn? Please. I've been waiting to talk to you about . . . our last visit.

He crushed the bar of soap, forcing his breath to slow down and focus on her as a threat. Think about how she'd breached his mental privacy. Time to harden his heart and see Kizira as he should have all along— a priestess of the queen who ruled the most dangerous enemy of the Beladors.

Grasping a towel to dry off, Quinn walked out to the living room and answered, *What would we possibly discuss, Kizira?*

Please, Quinn.

Why are you asking when you clearly didn't need permission to enter my hotel room last time?

I'm asking this time.

He had to take care that he made her work for every inch she gained or she'd sense the trap. *I found the bracelet of my hair you left in my hotel room.*

She said nothing to that, but then how could she?

The bracelet had been a clear message of finally admitting her regret over having ever met him. He just couldn't understand why she'd wanted to make love with him three weeks back.

No, not make love. That had been a straight-up shagging.

He would not confuse that one time with what had happened between them in Chechnya years ago.

No one could take that from him.

Her voice came to him, a soft plea pushing her words. *I don't think you understand why I left the bracelet, Quinn.*

He wrapped the towel around his lower half, tucking the ends, and allowed a healthy dose of frustration to boil through his reply. *If we must have this conversation, we might as well have it now. You may enter my hotel room.*

Light glowed between him and the wide window.

Tiny sparkles glittered in the air until Kizira took form, every gorgeous inch of her covered in a Mediterranean-blue gown. A river of hair the color of hot embers rushed around her shoulders. She'd actually toned down how brightly she could glow. He'd seen it darker, almost black sometimes. But this color suited her best. Gave her a fiery appeal.

She tested a smile. "Hello, Quinn."

His body held a party downstairs that kinetics

couldn't stop from pressing against the towel, but that actually worked in his favor to help sell his plan. Sounding angry took little effort when he spoke. "You're here. Make it quick."

Her gaze traced his body, pausing at the towel. "Are you going to deny you're happy to see me?"

"We both know that a penis is easily influenced by the simplest suggestion, such as a woman stroking it . . . even when the man it belongs to has no control over his mind or actions."

She raised hurt eyes to him. "I came to tell you I'm sorry."

"You think saying I'm sorry will work? I got the message you left on my bathroom vanity just fine. Why are you here?"

Shock stole over her face. "No, you don't understand." Kizira walked forward, hands clenched. "I left the bracelet to tell you that I regretted what I had to do that night."

He didn't understand, which must have shown in his confused expression.

Taking another step closer that put her an arm's reach away, she said, "I will *never* regret having met you in Chechnya or the time we spent together. I would never have given up that bracelet if there had been any other way to leave you a message."

"Explain," he said with no small amount of suspicion.

"I wanted you to know that it killed me to take advantage of you when your mind was in ruins from a probe, and I'm glad I could ease your pain, but I'm not happy about interrogating you then. I was terrified you wouldn't recover from the damage you suffered."

Could that be true? She *had* eased the hideous explosion of pain in his head . . . but she'd also withdrawn information about Evalle. Momentarily caught between his duty and his heart, he asked, "Then why did you use me to find Evalle, Kizira?"

"I had no choice." Her eyes were damp, overflowing with pain. "Flaevynn compelled me to find Evalle immediately. Her compulsion demanded that I find her no matter how I did it. Flaevynn's compulsion works in strange ways sometimes. To fulfill her order to locate Evalle, I subconsciously tapped into a way to gain that information based on my relationship with you."

He made a disgusted sound that caused her to rush her words.

"But I've kept information about *you* shielded from Flaeyvnn. I've never shared a word about . . . us. And won't as long as she doesn't know to compel me to tell her specifically about you."

To have been born with such a formidable mind, Quinn cursed how soft his damned heart could be when it came to this woman. She hadn't wanted to return to the Medb when he'd met her in Chechnya, and to the day he died he'd believe that she had left him back then only to protect him.

But he had a duty to the Beladors, and his connection with Kizira put Brina and the entire Belador tribe at risk. He couldn't afford to make the mistake of folding to his emotions.

Kizira's coming here now could be nothing more than another stab at entrapping him.

Cooling his tone, he said, "Then it seems as though I should believe Flaevynn has compelled you to come here today, correct? Since you obviously have no autonomy when it comes to using your body to get what you want."

She blinked back tears, too strong to cry. "I came on my own today. I've been compelled to do a task, but it does not include seeing you, or having sex with *anyone*. I came here only to apologize for doing something I couldn't stop, but—" She lifted her chin, fire churning her gaze to the same blazing emeralds that passion had once brought out. "Know this. I don't regret making love with you thirteen years ago or three weeks ago and won't let you taint something you enjoyed just as much as I did."

She had that right.

He bloody wanted her now.

Just as much as he wanted to believe her when she said she'd been compelled.

That was the danger of playing this game. Someone would get burned and he couldn't afford for it to be him this time. Not with so much at stake.

He knew of only one hope for getting past the shields around her mind without her catching him. He'd have to overrun her senses until she couldn't think. Take her to the edge of climax and hold her there, separating her mind from her body.

She waited for him to acknowledge that he'd enjoyed their coupling as much as she had.

Refusing to allow the anxiety riding her gaze to deter

him, he answered with cold determination. "Fine. We'll call the shagging a draw. That make you feel better?"

She winced. "So that's it? You aren't willing to forgive me? Or is it that you don't believe me?"

He looked away, searching for the anger he'd carried for weeks. How could the pain in her voice slide past his resolve and feed the guilty knot in his chest? Swinging his gaze back to her, he admitted, "I don't know what to believe most days."

Hope unfolded in her gaze, delicate as a rose opening to sunshine.

Did she speak the truth?

He cursed the stars above for putting him on the opposite side of a war from her.

"I am sorry, Quinn. I would never use you against your own people if I had a choice." She floated just above the floor, moving toward him until he could feel the heat coming off of her.

He reached out and ran two fingers along her cheek. Her smile trembled. He swallowed, strangling on the urge to wrap her in his arms and keep her safe from everything, including himself.

"What is it, Quinn?"

"Foolish thoughts."

Her sensuous lips curved with a smile. "Tell me."

"Just wondering if we'll ever see the day we aren't enemies."

"You're not my enemy."

He started to correct her, but she'd realize how wrong

she was soon enough once he gained the information he needed.

Hadn't that been the point of calling her in? To seduce her so he could mine her memories?

She unfolded her hands as if she intended to lift her arms and wrap them around his neck, but hesitated.

He'd been an arrogant fool to think he could do this. Sweat dampened his upper lip. He would gain the information some other way, but not by using her.

She put her hand lightly against his chest and he stifled a moan. His skin yearned to feel her hands everywhere. Her fingers toyed with the dusting of blond hair on his chest. He grasped her hand to stop her from tormenting him.

He was supposed to be doing the tormenting.

Cupping her wrist to his lips, he kissed her skin.

She moaned as if his mouth had been somewhere far more intimate.

Her eyes were closed and her mouth slightly parted, waiting.

Reason fled with another slip of his control, leaving only the hunger that pushed him into dangerous waters. Releasing her wrist, he pulled her to him. He touched skin, lots of soft skin exposed by the backless gown.

He kissed her, savoring the taste he craved more than his next breath.

She clutched his damp hair and hugged him closer. Her lips burned against his with fierce determination, urging him to take as much as he wanted. More.

Nothing should taste this sweet. He devoured her mouth, tangling her tongue with his.

Hair finer than spun silk brushed over his hands, reminding him of times past. Her on top. A curtain of lava-red hair cascading over his chest and shoulders.

He held her with one arm, lifting a hand to cup her breast and brush a finger across her nipple. She gasped hard and tensed.

His conscience warned he had to stop now or go for broke.

Grabbing Kizira's upper arms gently, Quinn pushed her away. "You should go."

Her eyes blinked with confusion. "You want me to go? Why? Because you don't trust yourself around me?"

"I accept your apology. You should go before we do something else you'd regret."

"I would *not* regret making love with you, Quinn."

"We're on opposite sides of a dangerous conflict. We can't do this."

"Yes, we can. Don't waste our time. I might get called back to TÅµr Medb at any moment and I don't know when I can slip away again. If you accept my apology, then accept me."

He had a duty to the Beladors, but he saw no honor in stealing from Kizira's mind when he had no idea what Flaevynn might do to Kizira if she found out how he'd gained the information. "I am a danger to you."

"Because you want to search my mind for information?"

Dear goddess, *she knew*. What had he done to give himself away?

"Stop beating yourself mentally," she told him in a calm voice that showed no hint of worry, or anger. "I came here knowing you probably hated me for what I did, but I could not live with the guilt and hoped you'd allow me to explain. I didn't expect you to just welcome me back in. I knew you'd need a reason to allow me to come into your room again and assumed it would be to gain information on the Medb."

"You *expected* me to take advantage of you." He shouldn't take offense since he *had* baited her into his suite for an ulterior purpose, but that didn't wipe away the film of shame sliding across his senses.

"No." She shook her head. "You are the most honorable man I know, which is why you're trying to push me away. You can't go through with what you want to do, but I deserve to have my mind breached after what I did to you."

He frowned, trying to follow her. "What are you saying, Kizira?"

"That I will make you this agreement. If you can withdraw the information you need, I won't hold it against you, but I don't think you can pull anything from my mind because of the way Flaevynn compels me."

"You would *allow* me to enter your mind?" he asked with no small dose of disbelief.

"No, I'm not able to open my mind to you voluntarily. What I'm saying is that I will not feel betrayed if you can figure your way past my shields."

"Don't doubt that I can gain access now that you and I have a connection."

"I have a healthy respect for the strength of your mind, Quinn, but you underestimate the power of Flaevynn's compulsion that forces me to protect my thoughts. As long as I'm cognizant of everything around me, I won't drop my shields. And even if you could bring yourself to harm me—which you can't—the compulsion would force me to stop you before you rendered me unconscious."

"What about Flaevynn? She'll wonder how I got my intel."

"If you and I are both successful, that won't matter."

"I don't understand."

She sighed. "As I said, I can't share anything voluntarily, so you'll just have to trust me that I know what I'm doing."

"It's not a matter of trust so much as fear over what she'd do to you."

"I will be fine. Do you really think you can bypass my shields?"

He nodded. "Assuming I'm the kind of bastard who would use you, there is a way to push you to lose all conscious thought so I could enter your mind." He'd have to take her to the knife's edge of orgasm and hold her there while he dove past her defenses.

She tilted her head and gazed off while she considered his words. When her eyes lifted to his again, her lips curved in a knowing smile. "Ah . . . I hadn't considered that. I'm not sure what would happen, but finding out could be enjoyable as long as you eventually finish what you start."

This wasn't how he'd imagined their meeting going. Not for her to offer him access to what she knew of the Medb operation.

A jolt of suspicion woke the tactical side of his mind and saddened him, but he had to ask, "Why would you do this, Kizira?"

She wrapped her arms around his neck and looked up when she said, "I did not choose to be a Medb. I have no choice in my life beyond executing Flaevynn's orders and to be used as a tool for our coven, but I will not let her destroy you . . . or what we've shared."

He forced his hands to stay at his sides. If he started touching her again, he'd never stop. "But you *are* a Medb and I'm a Belador. Any help you offer me will be used against the Medb to its fullest extent. What then?"

"I do not make this offer lightly, but if you trust me at all, then believe that I am working toward the day when the Medb and the Beladors can live in peace. I want us to be together, to end this insanity between your tribe and my coven, but I can't do it alone. I need your help. With everything in motion at this point, I can't promise that we won't meet on a battlefield or that I won't be compelled to do something that will make you hate me, but I don't want to do it and I don't want to be your enemy."

She put her face against his chest, hugging him hard. "Search for what you want, but don't deny me this one stolen moment of pleasure when I have so few in my world."

He raised his hand and held it in the air, his body and mind arguing over sending her away or pulling her to him. In the end, he lowered his fingers to brush along the length of her hair. "I can't use you that way, *Phoedra*." *Divine one.*

He felt her heartbeat quicken against his skin at the Russian endearment.

She whispered, "I haven't heard that since our time in Chechnya. What I wouldn't give to go back there and live forever." She pushed away from him, her eyes pleading. "This may be the only chance you'll have at getting past the compulsion obstacles in my mind. It won't be easy, but I grant you my permission to do with all of me as you please. No, I beg you to do this and help us both."

Reaching out, she grasped the edge of the towel and tugged it loose. She ran her fingers over his abdomen, then lower, stroking.

He sucked in a sharp breath and caught her wrist, facing a decision that could change the course of his and Kizira's lives.

The future of the Medb and the Beladors might rest upon his next action.

Her lips moved with one silent word. *Please.*

May the gods forgive him. He lifted her into his arms and headed for the midnight-dark bedroom. Lowering her gently to the bed, he sat next to her and leaned over her body to drink in every inch. His heart thundered in his chest. Depending on what he learned, this might be the last time they had alone.

He ran his hand over her face. "You are even more beautiful than you were the first time I met you. I have never met another I wanted as I want you."

Tiny lights sparkled and flickered around her in a soft starburst of glittering light. He eased the sheer material off of her shoulders, baring skin that had been moon-kissed.

Her sigh came out soft as an angel's music.

"My lovely *Phoedra*," he murmured.

"Me . . . or my body?" She sounded small and insecure, so unlike the fierce priestess she'd always been.

He knew what she asked.

Anyone else saw only a Medb witch.

He saw the woman inside. "I see *you*, Kizira."

That must have been enough for her. The muscles in her neck and shoulders relaxed. She sat up and kissed him, her mouth raiding his lips.

His hand shook when he reached for her gown. One tug and the diaphanous material fell away, turning into tinkling sparkles of color that drifted apart.

How long had he wanted to see this body again, to hold her in his arms? He suffered equal parts of longing for the woman who gave life to his heart and guilt due to wanting his enemy.

But this beautiful creature had never been *his* enemy.

She lifted her fingers to his face. "I am yours. I have always been yours."

Quinn lowered his head, kissing her full mouth, taking all that she would give him. He grazed a finger over one of her breasts.

She shivered, warning, "You best be ready to break through my shields, Quinn, and prepared for anything you find. I need you to help me."

Was she only saying these things to make breaching her mental shields easier on him . . . or to trick him? He'd know as soon as he entered her mind.

Quinn kissed her other breast, drawing her nipple into his mouth.

She whimpered.

Sparkling bolts of light shot through the air.

When he moved his hand down her abdomen and lower, she lifted into his touch. His fingers knew this woman, remembered teasing her into a sexual fever long ago. He reveled in her response, holding her at bay every time she danced closer to climax.

When she bowed off the bed, he removed his hand and mouth, watching as she trembled, waiting for him.

This time he returned with vicious precision and drove her hard to the edge of release.

It took all the discipline he possessed to ignore his need to have her and instead delve into her mind.

His fingers held her body prisoner as he fought his way past mental barriers that would protect a king's treasures.

Sweat poured down his face. He was struggling to hold her at the pinnacle and focus on searching when his body screamed to join with hers.

She'd warned him about her shields.

Both of them had thought that would be his only obstacle.

By the gods, Quinn hadn't considered that he could observe Kizira's response from inside her mind. That alone almost sidetracked him with her inching closer to release.

Her emotions lay open to him, and no man who cared for a woman could ignore seeing his woman when she climaxed.

She cried out, pleading with him.

That was the moment her shields weakened.

Prepared for anything, he forced himself to drive deep into her mind just as his fingers pushed her over the cliff and she came apart in his hands.

TWENTY-THREE

No woman was worth this much aggravation.

Storm circled the living room of the house he'd rented in Midtown, just on the outer edge of downtown Atlanta. A quiet place for eleven o'clock at night. He liked this older neighborhood and had considered staying, but not anymore.

If he did, someone would die.

But he couldn't leave until he found that damn Ashaninka witch doctor.

To find out anything new, he had to speak with Kai. But to speak to her, Storm had to calm down enough to cross from one world to another.

And that wasn't going to happen unless he could close his eyes without seeing Evalle kissing the guy who had already tried to kill her once. Had she forgotten that Isak Nyght had taken a shot at her the night Sen teleported her to the Tribunal meeting?

Evidently so.

Evalle also overlooked Tristan's betrayal and his constantly letting her down at the worst times. *So why am I surprised she has no qualms about kissing someone who tried to shoot her?*

Storm scrubbed a hand over his face, shoving his mind away from everything that antagonized his jaguar.

His skin felt too tight already without riling the animal. As a Skinwalker, the full moon didn't force him to shift.

The control was his . . . mostly.

But one woman kept him on tenterhooks so much that his jaguar stayed on the edge of wanting to break out.

Taking a couple of deep breaths, he stared at one of the fat, white candles sitting along his mantel and focused his mind. Battles were won through control.

He could win the one raging inside him.

When he felt ready to try again, he stepped over to the Navajo-design rugs in front of his hearth and sat down with his legs crossed. This time when he closed his eyes and took a deep breath, he pushed his mind past the current world to the meadow in another dimension where he'd find his guardian spirit.

Seconds ticked past while his breathing slowed to almost nonexistent.

Once he was in the deep trance, Storm said, "I humbly request the presence of Kai."

"I am here, Storm," a pleasant female voice called to him.

No longer bound to earth, he opened his eyes to the peaceful setting of green-leafed trees surrounding her quiet meadow.

She smiled as she sat down across from Storm. "How does your healing progress?"

"I'll be fine." Physically.

"What troubles you?"

A woman. Not just any woman, but a raven-haired,

motorcycle-riding hellion who had been turning him inside out since he met her. But he hadn't asked to meet with Kai to discuss Evalle. "I have had no more dreams of the witch doctor whose name we will not speak. I fear she will arrive unannounced and catch me unprepared, and thus put others at risk."

"You will know when she is near, but in my heart I feel you will not find happiness once you face her."

"I will if I make her return my father's soul, and mine."

"What if you cannot regain what you have lost?"

Never get his soul back? "I won't entertain that possibility." He couldn't consider failure when his father had no one else but Storm to save him.

"If you do not kill her, she will take that which you most desire."

"She already has."

"That was then. This is now."

He'd heard this warning before, back when Kai had told him the witch doctor hunted Evalle, which paralleled his visions. Irritation over Isak Nyght would not interfere with his commitment to Evalle's safety. "I won't allow the witch doctor to harm Evalle, but to protect her I need to know where I can find the witch doctor or . . . when she'll find me."

Kai sighed deeply, her hands folded in her lap. "You risk much for this Evalle."

"Maybe so, but it's mine to risk," he said in a polite voice, since he couldn't fault Kai for pointing out that he might not be thinking clearly when it came to Evalle.

"Evalle has angered you."

Anger didn't come close to what he'd been feeling for the past hour. "Why would you say that?"

"Your aura was calm and happy during past visits when you mentioned Evalle, but it is now in chaos."

An accurate description of his insides at the moment. Chaotic and acidic. "That's a normal state around Evalle."

Kai smiled, eyes shining with the humor of an indulgent aunt. "Perhaps this is good for you."

"You think her driving me crazy is good?" he asked, forgetting to keep his tone even and undemanding.

"Yes." Kai smiled again, eyes light with humor. "She is the reason you fought to stay alive. She causes your aura to brighten even as she creates chaos. You have been consumed too long with finding the witch doctor and saving your father. You have had no thought for your own happiness."

She had a point.

He'd been pretty grim before he met Evalle. After only one day teamed up with her, Storm had decided he liked the prickly woman. She might know how to kill demons and stomp the butts of most men, human or otherwise, but she had an untamed innocence when it came to anything sexual.

Watching her open up to his slow advances had given him back something he'd lost—the ability to care about another person in the world of the living.

Kai watched him with eyes that saw more than he cared to share sometimes. "Or do you find the Adrianna who cared for you more interesting?"

"No." He answered too quickly before realizing his guardian teased him. He could rarely dodge Kai when it came to revealing the truth. "I admit that Evalle does make me happy, but not right this minute."

"How has she offended you?"

She kissed another man. When he said that in his head, it didn't sound as bad as what he'd watched. Especially since he had no claim on Evalle and might have to leave if the witch doctor slipped through his fingers. That didn't stop him from wanting to rip off Isak's head for touching Evalle. "The issue with Evalle is something I can handle. I'm more concerned over finding the witch doctor and need your help to do that."

Kai nodded, then shut her eyes and lifted her hands, pressing her palms together in front of her chest. She whispered a soft chant for several minutes, then became silent, swaying slightly left, then right, until she lowered her hands. When her normally soft brown eyes opened, they were milky orbs. He always found it odd to hear the shallow voice of an old woman coming from Kai's young form.

"The witch doctor's energy circles closer to you each day. She will find the one she seeks before the next new moon. Beware of her words, for you will lose if they entangle you."

Storm tamped down his impatience in spite of his pulse's thrumming at the hope of nearing the end of his search. The witch doctor would be here by the new moon at the end of this month.

But did that mean she'd find him first? Or Evalle? He asked, "Is there any chance she'll be here sooner?"

Kai weaved back and forth, her smooth forehead tensing, then relaxing. "Not before sunrise three days from now."

Good. That would give him time to work off the frustration tightening his insides before he spoke to Evalle again, without worrying about the witch doctor getting to her first. In his present state of mind, he might say something to Evalle he'd later regret.

Right now he wanted Kai to explain about her warning to beware of the witch doctor's words that could entangle him.

Kai's eyes cleared. She stared through him as if watching something else and warned, "You must return to your world. Someone approaches."

"Wait." Something pulled Storm backward as Kai faded along with the meadow. He closed his eyes, trying to catch up to the swift change in his body.

The sound of knocking on his front door shook him from his groggy state.

He cupped his head and pushed to his feet, trying to get fully back in his body. He opened the door.

Evalle stood before him, rigid as a general, but Storm always picked up on her emotions, with his empathic ability quicker than any other person he'd ever been around.

He understood the guilty feeling, which she'd brought on herself, but not the irritation vibrating beneath her nerves.

She had no reason to be angry with him.

When she didn't speak first, he said, "Yes?"

Huffing out a breath meant to make sure he caught her irritation, she said, "I found your place. You had a typo in the e-mail draft."

She deserved kudos for locating him since he'd changed his address in the e-mail draft to the house across the street and hidden his sport utility in the detached garage. He'd considered deleting the e-mail and should have, but he had an exterior camera facing the front yard and house across the street. He'd wanted to see if she'd even try to talk to him. Bonehead move since he wasn't ready to see her yet and should have figured on her stubborn tenacity.

He said, "You found me."

"Can we talk?"

"About?"

Her eyes darted past him to the door to the floor, then back to him. She picked silently at possible answers and finally said, "About you coming to the parking deck . . . with Grady."

"Grady should have been able to tell you all you needed to know." *Like the fact that I was standing in the shadows when you let soldier boy try to swallow your tongue.*

She growled her next breath and kicked her chin up, back into attitude mode. "Well, I want to hear what you have to say."

"About what?" Yes, he was being obstinate, but that beat being lame enough to say the kiss bothered him.

"The . . . " she said, dragging out the word. "When we . . . uh, tracking the Svarts."

He'd thought for sure she would have said *the kiss*.

He'd been a fool, thinking there was more going on between them than just working together.

Evalle crossed her arms, her fingers digging into her forearms. "Would you be willing to track—"

"No." He'd tracked for her many times and would do it again, but not right now. Bad enough that she blew off his warning that the damn Svarts might be hunting her. He had no desire to lead her to a freakin' troll who might kill her.

The idea of her getting hurt just amped up his pissed-off state.

His muscles tightened and flexed. His jaguar wanted out.

He clearly shouldn't be around her right now, not until he could get his head screwed back on straight. That would probably happen by tomorrow, once he found a place to let his jaguar run off some energy tonight. Maybe kill a troll and satisfy the blood lust pumping through his veins.

Evalle uncrossed her arms. "What's wrong with you?"

You. "Nothing."

"Is it because you saw me with Isak?"

"Who?" He had to be careful not to answer with a lie or the pain would be unbearable, but now it seemed lame to say anything about the kiss.

"The guy with the black-ops group."

"Oh, the one who took aim at you a mere three weeks ago when he saw you defending other Alterants and tried to kill you? That one?" Sarcasm boiled through his voice. "Why would I care if I saw you with him?"

"Well, crap, I knew you saw that. I can explain."

He held up his hand. "Don't want to hear it. Not after the grief you gave me over Adrianna, and I sure as hell didn't kiss *her*. It's your life, you can spend it with all the losers you want."

"He's not a loser."

"Then what is he if he kills Alterants?"

"And I don't think he would have shot at me that night in Decatur if Sen hadn't shown up."

That really pissed off Storm. "But. He. Did," Storm reminded her. "What were you doing with Isak anyhow? If he finds out you're an Alterant, again, he'll shoot you, *again*, and this time he may not miss."

"I went to borrow a weapon from him, and no, he won't shoot me." She had put her fists on her hips and cocked that adorable chin in fighter mode. "For your information, he found out about my being an Alterant right before he dropped me off in the parking deck and he's okay with it."

What?

She wasn't done blasting him. "I didn't know you were standing there when I kissed him, but I wasn't doing anything wrong, and it was just a kiss." Once she got on a roll, she didn't slow down. "At least *he* will help me find the Svarts if I ask, so if you don't want to, that's fine by me."

She was going back to him? "Fine!"

"Fine!" She swung around and barreled down his front steps.

He slammed the door, jarring the plate glass in the

front window. Skin rippled along his back with the impending change. He fisted his hands and fought for control to keep from bursting out of his human form and shifting into a jaguar. Not with his control in tatters. The jaguar could turn into a mindless animal, bent on whatever urge he wanted to satisfy.

Storm would never shift unless he had full control.

Not around Evalle.

Why hadn't he just checked the peephole on the door—or the damn camera—and ignored her knock?

Or better yet, why hadn't he just pulled her inside and kissed her until she couldn't think about another man?

He didn't want her to see Isak or any other male. That was so unlike Evalle to begin with. She didn't go seeking out men.

Storm stopped his stomping back and forth.

She said she'd borrowed a weapon from Nyght, which hadn't sounded like a romantic interlude. She *had* come to find Storm and even figured out where he lived in spite of the mistyped address.

She might want help hunting Svarts, but that hadn't been her main reason for coming to his house.

If Evalle really went to see Isak only for a weapon, then seeking me out to talk was a first.

What an idiot he'd been to miss that fact.

He wanted to kick the daylights out of someone's butt, namely his own. What had happened to the calm he always held around her? He wanted to rewind that conversation and try it again.

She wouldn't listen to him right now.

Let her walk off her own anger, then he'd go track her down and . . . tell her what? To stay away from Isak?

And it's not like I have anything to offer her, not as long as that witch doctor has my soul.

He had to get over this obsession with Evalle.

If she wants Isak, who am I to stop her?

Storm shook his head at himself. As if he could even pretend to be that noble. He wanted Evalle regardless of how many obstacles kept getting thrown in his path.

But what about that kiss with Isak? She'd acted like it had meant nothing. But what else would any woman say when faced with irrational jealousy?

He headed to the shower to clear his head. It was time to make up his mind and either stake a claim or let her go. Once he insured the witch doctor no longer presented a threat to Evalle, he'd be able to make that decision.

She'd had enough pain in her life and he wouldn't stand in the way of her happiness.

TWENTY-FOUR

Why had she ever thought she meant something to Storm?

Evalle pounded her way through inky darkness to the sidewalk in front of his house. She'd parked her bike along the curb two houses down and had made it half-way there when she stopped under a streetlight.

Her heart punched her chest with painful beats.

Why did Storm have to be so hardheaded? She'd meant to fit an apology in there somewhere, but things got all jumbled up. She slapped a hand over her fore-head.

That hadn't been the way she'd worked things out in her mind on the ride over.

Storm was supposed to open the door and tell her he didn't like seeing her kissing Isak. Then she'd say she hadn't meant for that to get out of control. She'd only kissed Isak as a thank-you, not the way she kissed Storm.

Then Storm would have smiled and forgiven her, say-ing he knew nothing was going on. He'd always been so understanding. What happened? Why hadn't he pulled her into his arms and soothed her and fixed everything with one of his unforgettable kisses?

That whole yelling part had never been in the script.

She fisted her hands and shook them in the air as

she walked three steps back and forth. Go back and try again? No. That seemed too much like groveling.

Yes, she had kissed Isak.

Storm did have reason to be angry.

But not *that* angry.

Why couldn't she get a computer program that would explain men? She could find out how to write music, how to rebuild her motorcycle engine or how to perform brain surgery somewhere on the Net.

Seemed like someone would have posted *Men 101*.

Or, in her case, *Men for Dummies*.

Her feet started moving back toward Storm's house, which didn't mean she intended to see him again so much as she needed to move around and think.

Standing still had never worked for her.

She'd reached his driveway when she realized someone was following her. Glancing around, she sized up the dumpy little guy with thinning hair, accountant glasses and a misfitting dark suit who trudged along in front of the house next to Storm's.

But energy from someone or something had shimmered across her skin, alerting her of a nonhuman close by.

Nightstalker?

Across the street a craggy, white-haired woman pushed a grocery cart over the uneven sidewalk. She moved along in the world of a bag lady, in no hurry to get anywhere since she had nowhere to go and no one waiting on her.

Evalle had felt like that most of her adult life until Feenix. Until Storm.

The lights were still on in his front room, where a sheer curtain covered a large picture window. If she sat on his front steps and waited a bit, would he eventually come out and sit down, maybe talk to her?

While I'm at it, I might as well hang a sign around my neck that says Pathetic Party. She would not humiliate herself by sitting there waiting. No, she would not lower—

A growl from behind reached her ears.

She swung around.

The human across the street still meandered along.

But the little business guy dropped his glamour and changed to a huge troll. He had to go over ten feet tall, had demon-yellow eyes and that strange runic *S* scar on his arm.

A Svart troll or a demon? Or door number three? Both.

She stomped her feet to release the blades in her boots.

Had he followed her here? Looked like Storm had been right when he speculated about the Svarts hunting her.

Evalle started to circle around the troll to keep the entire area in view, but a second growl rumbled right behind her as two clawed hands grabbed her arms. Where had the second one been hiding? She headbutted backward, forcing the attacker to lose his grip.

The Svart in front of her charged forward.

No time to worry about that human woman seeing anything. Evalle tossed a kinetic blast at the demon Svart, knocking him back a couple of steps. Swinging halfway around, she threw a blast at the second Svart coming at her, satisfied when he skidded twenty feet on his backside.

That was more like it.

Three massive fingers clamped around her throat and lifted her off the ground by her neck. How had the first one moved that quickly? She kicked her boots wildly but the Svart's long arm held her deadly blades away from him. He walked forward, squeezing the breath out of her.

She swung her arms, backhanding him with her kinetics, but he blocked her hits. That shouldn't be possible.

Stars danced in her vision. Her head felt as though blood would explode out the top any minute. Her neck muscles compressed until she couldn't breathe.

She called up her dagger kinetically to her hand, gripped it and swung over her shoulder, stabbing his forearm. He howled. His fingers released her neck.

She sucked hard. Air barely squeezed through.

Had he crushed her windpipe?

Now would be a good time for Isak's weapon if she hadn't dropped it off with Trey and the VIPER team.

Holding her throat, she stumbled back away from the troll. He yanked her dagger out of his arm and flung it at her.

She tried to push up a kinetic field to block the hit, but was a second too slow.

The blade struck her deep in the shoulder. She opened her mouth but the scream of pain stayed in her head.

Glass exploded close by.

She stumbled from the hit of the dagger, falling back in slow motion, and landed on the sidewalk.

An enraged black jaguar roared, charging the troll.

No, Storm. He'll kill you. But she couldn't even whisper the words. She clutched her throat and begged for air.

The troll met Storm halfway, lifting arms to slash his sharp claws through the jaguar's gleaming black coat.

Storm dodged at the last moment, his jaguar form whipping around the back of the troll before the giant could turn. The jaguar leaped up and sank sharp teeth into the troll's neck, ripping apart skin, muscle and bone. The troll's head flopped forward with his mouth open in a scream and eyes bulging. The jaguar snarled and ripped the head entirely off, slinging it away and jumping off as the troll went down.

The second troll grabbed Evalle by her arms and started dragging her away. His claws dug into her forearms, ripping flesh open.

New pain slashed through her shoulder. She cried out in her head, unable to gasp for air.

Dark folded in on her. The sound of rage roared past her, then her arms were free as a hideous scream ended in silence.

Someone shouted her name. She wanted to sink into sleep, get away from the agonizing pain stabbing her everywhere. She couldn't get air, suffocating.

"Evalle, open your eyes. Open. Your. Eyes."

She blinked twice, looking up at Storm. He had her in his arms, running with her.

Every bounce sent agony racing through her body.

Felt as though a fist squeezed her lungs. She ached with the need to draw a breath. Strangling for air, she reached up with her good arm and gripped his neck. Blinding white pain flashed behind her eyes.

"Stay with me," he ordered, pausing long enough to kick a door open. He walked into a room and lowered her gently onto something soft, a sofa, then knelt next to her.

She grabbed her throat, shaking with the need to breathe. Tears streamed down her face from the pain.

He took her hand away from her throat and held it in his. "Draw on your Alterant like Tristan taught you."

What? She couldn't think.

He must have read the word on her lips. "Listen to me. Call up your Alterant. Heal your throat now. You're turning blue!"

She gripped his hand and turned her energy inward, calling the beast. But she couldn't shift or the Tribunal . . .

If she died, would it matter?

Exhaustion pulled at her, offering her sleep if she'd just close her eyes.

"Come on, Evalle, you can do this!" Storm yelled at her, pushing her past the agony. "I won't let you die." He started chanting words she didn't know in a strange voice.

She fought through her panic and tried again to draw on her beast. Cartilage along her forearms popped up, breaking through the skin.

Storm kept chanting and the air around her swirled with strange faces. Native faces. Phantom hands touched her face and arms.

Evalle gritted her teeth and tightened all her muscles, eyes tearing at the pain in her shoulder and throat . . .

Her beast clawed inside her, threatening to break free, but she held her control and channeled the beast's power to her throat. Her airway began to expand.

Then she finally drew a breath, gasped, and drew another.

"That's it, sweetheart. Don't stop." Storm's hoarse voice sounded ragged with worry.

She kept wheezing with gasps of air. Her chest ached, but no longer as much as her shoulder. She looked to the right where her dagger had plunged deep inside her, cutting bone and slicing muscle. That had been the point in having a dagger that worked on nonhumans, but she hadn't considered the damage it might one day do to her.

Storm stroked her damp brow. "Ready to fix your shoulder?"

She fought down nausea at the idea of his pulling that dagger out.

He put his fingers on the handle. "Look at me, sweetheart."

When she faced him and nodded, he drew out the blade in one quick move. She arched at the agony of nerves being ripped again. Blood gushed over her arm. Stars swarmed in front of her eyes.

Storm snatched up a pillow and covered the gash, pressing down on it.

She felt herself falling, knew she was starting to black out.

His voice boomed at her. "Wake up, Evalle! Close the damn wound."

She opened her eyes to the battle face of a warrior.

Storm was trying to save her life and she wasn't helping. Clenching her jaw, she reached inside again, forcing her beast to the surface. Energy rushed up from her center and spread through all of her limbs, threatening to bring on the change.

She stopped the force just like Tristan had taught her when they were in the jungle weeks ago.

Time crawled by with each beat of her heart until Storm lifted the pillow and inspected her shoulder. He smiled at her. "The wound isn't completely healed, but it's closed up. The bone and muscle are redeveloping. You did it."

He sat back, looking weary as if he'd fought a hundred trolls, and wiped the sweat from his forehead with the back of his hand.

"Storm?" Her voice sounded thin and distant.

He leaned forward quickly, his hand going to her cheek, eyes dark with concern. "Are you hurt somewhere else?"

She licked her lips. "No. I'm . . . sorry." There, she'd said it in case she didn't get another chance.

He dropped his forehead down to hers. "I am, too, sweetheart." Then he stood up.

That's when she realized he was naked, but she only got to look for a second before he lifted her into his arms again and carried her to another room, somewhere dark. He put her on a huge bed and said, "Stay here a minute while I secure the house."

She didn't care if she moved for the next week. Her muscles were limp, her throat ached, her lungs burned and her shoulder felt as though someone had driven a hot poker through it. Her body was not done healing.

Storm disappeared for several minutes, then returned to the room with a towel wrapped around his waist. He'd put that on for her. She'd seen him naked once before, and the man had no problem walking around without clothes.

She closed her eyes.

He came back to check on her again with water this time. Easing her up to a sitting position, he put the straw to her lips. "Sip this."

She got a few sips down and paid for it when she started coughing. When he laid her back down, he kissed her forehead and said, "I'll be back in a minute. You're safe in here."

Those words barely registered as her eyes drifted shut.

Evalle came awake with a start, pushing up to a sitting position on a bed. In a dark room.

Storm's bed. Now she remembered.

She stood up and checked her balance. Everything worked, a little achy but stable.

A door across the room opened with glaring light before the click of a switch doused it. Storm came into view wearing jeans and T-shirt this time. "How're you feeling?"

"Like I've been dragged back from the jaws of death."

"That pretty much covers what happened. You danced too close to the edge that time."

"How long was I out?"

"Fifteen, maybe twenty minutes."

The last time she'd healed, in the jungle when Tristan had taught her how, it had taken much longer to reach this point of recovery. What had happened when Storm chanted? Had his majik done something to help her tap her Alterant powers?

She had pretty good recall of the battle and how she'd ended up in here, with the exception of a few blurry moments. The only thing she couldn't determine was where they should pick up after arguing, then fighting trolls, then her apologizing.

But hadn't he said he was sorry, too, or had she just imagined that?

The safest conversation would be for her to stick with the troll issue. "What about outside? There was at least one human when the fight broke out."

"I handled it."

"How?"

He stared at her, taking his time to answer. "With some of my Ashaninka gifts. A spell."

As in something a witch could do? Might be why he seemed hesitant to go into detail. Storm didn't like shifting into his jaguar, but he'd done it again. For her.

She didn't want to push him for more. "Good thing you could do something. At least we don't have to call Sen." She looked around, but nothing in the dark room would help her find the right words yet, so she stuck with trolls. "What was that thing? A demon or a troll?"

"Both. How's your arm?"

She rolled her sore shoulder. "Got a few aches but nothing I can't manage. I'm good to go after those trolls."

"Those trolls almost killed you."

"We have a weapon for them now."

"Where was it when you got attacked?"

"I took it to Trey. We only have one and he's running teams all night across the city, covering as many cemeteries as he can. He needs the weapon in case something big breaks out."

Storm made a disgusted sound. "You're heading back out to fight these things, knowing they can overpower you?"

"If there hadn't been two—"

"Yeah, and the second one was dragging you off. I can't figure out if they were trying to kidnap you or kill you, but either way it's *stupid* to go back out there."

"I. Didn't. Ask. Your. Opinion," she snapped at him, poking her finger into his chest with each word.

He grabbed her hand and held it in his grip for two seconds, then pulled her fingers up to his mouth and kissed her skinned knuckles.

"Storm . . ." Her heart did a fast tap dance in her chest.

He muttered, "You're driving me batshit crazy." Then he reached for her, pulling her close to kiss her.

One touch of his lips and her body came alive.

She lifted her arms around his neck, happy to be in the one place that made her feel safe and cared for.

His arms wrapped her up, hauling her closer. His mouth gave as much as he demanded, telling her without words just how afraid he'd been for her.

She couldn't remember when she'd gone from fearing his touch to craving it, but she did.

He lifted his head, took one look and kissed her again, then cupped her head against his chest. His heart raced wildly against her face.

She stood there like that for several moments while he held her and she breathed in his freshly showered scent.

He said, "I've seen you hurt before, but never so close to dying. Scared the shit out of me."

Smiling was probably the wrong reaction, but men like Storm didn't frighten easily and rarely admitted to it.

Did this mean he was no longer mad at her for kissing Isak? "Are we good now?"

His chest moved with a heavy sigh. "We're good."

"I owe you an apology."

"For what?"

"First for getting so jacked up over Adrianna, but I can't promise I won't hurt her if I ever find her hands on you."

He kissed her forehead, answer enough for Evalle, so she added, "And second because I was holding you to a double standard. You didn't kiss Adrianna." Evalle paused. "Right?"

"Never."

"I did kiss Isak, but I intended it only as a thank-you and didn't mean for it to get out of control."

Storm growled under his breath and his eyes warned retribution when he saw Isak.

She put her hand on his cheek. "I don't kiss you the

same way. He's a friend. You're . . . special." She stumbled around mentally, trying to figure out what to say, and realized she was avoiding the truth. "I care about you."

Storm's gaze darkened with a primal look of male possession, reinforced by the way his arms tightened around her.

She hated to push the point, but she needed to know he wouldn't go after Isak, and Storm had to answer honestly or suffer pain. He'd better not try lying and hurt himself. "You're not going to have an issue with Isak, right?"

"Not as long as he keeps his hands off you."

She couldn't expect any more than that right now.

Easing back out of his arms, she moved her healing shoulder around and couldn't believe how good it felt in so short a time. When she'd first met him, Storm had agreed to never use his majik on her without permission. "Did you do something about my pain?"

He crossed his arms. "Yes, and I don't want to hear a damned word about it."

Fair enough. She put her hands on his crossed arms and kissed him. "Thank you."

Nice to see that she could surprise him for once.

Stepping back, she reached up to fix her ponytail that had gone askew in the fight, and admitted, "It was wrong of me to ask you to track the trolls, and that wasn't why I came here anyhow."

"If you're hell-bent to find them, I might as well help."

"Really? What about VIPER?"

"I found out a few things when I talked to Grady and a couple of other Nightstalkers. Sen was the one who collected my clothes and took my phone out of your tank bag that night after the showdown with Isak, so he must have sent the e-mail you got after they released you from lockdown."

Figures that slimeball Sen would screw with her that way. "How did Sen not see your body if he went back that soon to my bike? He would have looked for you."

"Either Kai was still shielding . . . or my body had been moved by then."

Evalle started to ask how a guardian spirit had moved his body, but she knew the answer. Adrianna had helped Kai. But if that Sterling witch hadn't helped, Storm wouldn't be here now. Evalle understood, but it would be a while before she could face Adrianna and her smug knowledge of having been alone with Storm for so long.

Something else Storm had said struck her. "Grady knew about Sen getting your phone and clothes? He should have told me."

"He didn't know until I asked him to find out for me."

"Oh. Well, what about Sen, then? What are you going to do about him?"

"He's acting like I'm alive and just telling people I left VIPER, so I'm going to play along with it. I'll just have to watch my back."

"I'll help you watch it."

He put his fingers under her chin and ran his thumb over her lips. "We're going to have that dinner here soon."

"Doesn't look like it'll be tonight."

"Tomorrow, and if not, the day after."

She'd love to stay here and find out what he had in

mind, but Trey needed to know about this Svart attack. When Storm dropped his hand, she shifted gears, ready to work. "I tried to reach Tzader and Quinn on the way here, but they were both grabbing a couple hours rest. The last time I talked to Trey—"

Evalle, where are you? Quinn said in her mind. She held up a finger for Storm and whispered, "Quinn." Then she answered telepathically, *I'm in Midtown.*

Did you get the weapon?

Yes, I gave it to Trey. What's wrong?

The trolls are gathering up nonhumans for the Svarts to eat. When they feed on power, it increases theirs. We've got to find where they're holding the prisoners.

She wondered where the intel had come from, but didn't need to know right now. *Any idea how many they've captured?*

Six that I know of. One is a teenager, a female cousin of mine.

She'd heard snippets about Quinn's extensive family but thought they were all in Russia. *I'm sorry, Quinn. We'll get her back.*

There's more. My cousin said she's with twin boys who know you.

Kellman and Kardos?

She didn't say, but I saw her with two blond boys in Woodruff Park. One was playing chess and they both knew about the trolls.

Sounds like a pair of male witches I know, just innocent teens. Well, not all that innocent, but they didn't deserve to be troll dinner.

Tzader and I will round up the teams. Meet us at the street sign for Underground.

On my way.

He had to be talking about Kellman and Kardos. Those boys had no one to watch out for them except her and Grady. Evalle grabbed Storm's arm. "We have to go. The Svart trolls are gathering up nonhumans to eat as fuel. That could be why they were trying to drag me off."

He put his hand over hers. "What else is wrong?"

How did he read her so easily? "They have Quinn's cousin and two teenage male witches I know."

"The homeless twins?"

"Pretty sure it's them."

Storm cursed softly. "Grady believes more Svarts are coming. If they're here already, VIPER could be out-numbered."

Storm was right. The Svarts had already beaten her twice in combat, and Tzader would not allow Beladors to link with the chance of Svarts killing many Beladors with one blow. The Nyght weapon she'd borrowed to take out one troll at a time would not stop an army of trolls.

Isak had more weapons, but would calling him for support turn out to be a benefit or lead to bloodshed on all sides? She hadn't had a chance to inform VIPER about exposing her Alterant identity to Isak.

And only someone with a homicide fetish would put Isak and Storm in the same zip code anytime soon.

TWENTY-FIVE

Fear fingered along Quinn's neck. He'd lived his life alone for one reason—to protect those he would put in jeopardy with his line of work. All these years, he'd thought Kizira safe as long as she stayed away from him, but she had some bloody plan to see the Medb and Beladors at peace.

And Lanna shouldn't even be in the middle of this mess.

Both women were in danger, and not being able to protect either one right now was driving him mad.

He quickened his pace through the intersection of Five Points in the heart of downtown Altanta, wanting to break into Belador speed to cover the last quarter mile to reach the meet point, the sign for Underground Atlanta.

Every second counted.

The boys must have gone to Underground thinking it safe to stay in the crowded iconic venue that drew tourists and locals to shopping and entertainment beneath the streets of downtown Atlanta. Wise move if they hadn't trusted a troll to help them, according to Lanna.

Quinn hadn't heard from her in the past twenty minutes. Tzader and the team would find the Svart troll nest. But would they be in time?

"Quinn!" Evalle shouted at him as she rushed out of the bottom floor of a three-level parking deck on his left. Storm followed close behind.

That explained why Evalle had been in Midtown, but not why she had blood all over her. Did all the women in his life have to be one step away from death? "What happened to you?"

She lifted her hands. "I'm fine. Got jumped by Svarts."

That did nothing to calm Quinn's already sheared nerves. He unleashed on Storm the minute he walked up. "Where the devil were you when she was attacked?"

"Me?" Storm snarled. "You and Tzader are the ones sending her out alone."

Evalle stepped between them. "Whoa, you two. This isn't Storm's fault, Quinn. He's the only reason I'm alive right now, but we don't have time to waste and I'm healed."

"Mostly," Storm grumbled.

"And," Evalle added, "Storm came to help us find the kids."

Quinn raked his hand through his hair. "Sorry, chap. It's been a long day and doesn't appear to be improving anytime soon. Good to have you back."

Storm nodded, stepping up next to Evalle in a possessive stance.

Interesting, if Quinn had the time to waste thinking about it, which he didn't. When they turned back toward the meet point, he said, "I got another text from Lanna—"

"His cousin," Evalle said for Storm, then asked Quinn, "What exactly happened?"

"She was supposed to be in my hotel suite, but she slipped out and went looking for the two boys you think are witches and got trapped by a local troll called Jurba."

"Has to be Kellman and Kardos. How does she know them and why did she go looking for them?"

"Lanna's a meddler. She met the boys in the park and overheard them talking about a dangerous troll with the Svart marking on his arm hanging around their shelter. I think she went out to help them or maybe to dig up more information on the Svarts and got caught with the boys here at Underground."

Evalle said, "If not for getting caught, I like her already."

"Trust me, you speak too soon. I love the brat, but some days I want to strangle her."

"But what was she thinking to go snooping on Svarts?"

Quinn pinched the bridge of his nose, then dropped his hand. "My fault. I told her she had to go back to Transylvania immediately or VIPER would get involved, and she really does not want to go home. I'm guessing she planned to find intel or something she could trade with VIPER so she could stay here."

Storm spoke up. "What's the plan?"

"Tzader has to leave skeleton teams in each of the metropolitan quadrants to handle the gang battles, but we should have around forty VIPER agents."

Evalle argued, "That may not be enough."

"Why?"

"My Nightstalker says more Svarts are coming, but he doesn't know when."

Storm added, "And one of the two that attacked

Evalle tonight was something worse, some kind of demon Svart."

"Good goddess." Quinn slowed as he neared a group of VIPER agents made up mostly of Beladors. He swung around to inform Tzader, but waited as the Maistir sent out teams of four.

When he saw Quinn, Tzader lifted his chin in acknowledgment. Then glanced at Evalle and did a double take.

If Quinn had to guess, the murderous look crossing Tzader's face probably matched Quinn's when he'd first seen her, covered in blood. Speaking telepathically to Tzader, Quinn quickly explained Evalle's condition and Storm's intervention.

Evalle pointed at her clothes and said to Tzader, "Pay no attention to the blood."

"Quinn just told me." Tzader gave Storm an assessing glance and nodded at him. "Thanks."

Storm answered with a nod.

Quinn started to tell Evalle what he'd learned, but waited as Trey handed the viola case with the Nyght weapon to Tzader, then took over giving orders. Once he, Quinn, Evalle and Storm stood together, Quinn said, "I've learned the Svarts are under contract to the Medb."

Quinn caught the flash of suspicion in Evalle's gaze, but she didn't ask where he'd gained that information. Instead, she said, "Why are the Svarts here?"

Not telling her the truth about Kizira would eventually eat a hole in his gut, but Quinn would not involve Evalle. "The Svarts are gathering an army for a massive attack on humans to draw the bulk of VIPER assets out in the open at one time. They plan to destroy the South-eastern coalition, then take over North America."

"Is that possible?" Storm asked Quinn.

"We don't know. There's no intel on the Svart population, and we don't know exactly how the Medb play into this. And the information came in pieces, so we may not have it all figured out exactly right."

Evalle started to say something, then turned to Tzader as if he'd spoken to her mind to mind. Quinn would thank him later for keeping him off the spot about where he got the intel. Tzader moved them back to the current problem. "Did you tell them about the truck, Quinn?"

"Was just going to. The last text I got from Lanna said this Jurba troll was transporting them by truck somewhere. She's caused the truck to have a flat tire, and she thinks she's leaving a majik trail, but can't say for sure. She said there are a couple of other unconscious people with them."

Evalle's eyes sparked with admiration when she looked over at Storm. "Then it's a good thing we've got a tracker."

Quinn addressed Storm. "Those kids are being used as cattle. What do you need from us to pick up their trail?"

When Storm didn't answer at first, Quinn questioned if the tracker hesitated to deal with Svarts again.

Storm finally said, "I only need the freedom to use all my abilities."

Evalle's face fell. "No."

"Yes. That's the quickest way to track them."

"I can't ask you to do that," she said so softly Quinn almost didn't hear her.

Storm touched her chin. "You don't have to ask me." Then he faced Tzader and Quinn. "I don't like to advertise it, but I'm a Skinwalker. I can shift into a jaguar. My coat's black. I'll blend into the night, but I'm still a big animal that may draw unwanted attention."

Tzader just said, "Damn."

Quinn hadn't seen that one coming either, but he didn't waste time thinking about it. "We can't take you inside Underground as a jaguar, but I'm thinking since the kids are in a truck, the troll left here by a loading dock. We'll enter by the road the delivery trucks take to the docks and start there. If Storm picks up the scent, we'll follow."

"I'm riding my bike," Evalle clarified.

"I wish you'd go with them," Storm said.

"Not a chance. I can go places a bigger vehicle can't."

Tzader ended all discussion. "I'll walk Storm down to the delivery area with me. Quinn, we need a pace car on rocket fuel sitting here ready to go in five minutes."

"You'll have it." Quinn took the Nyght weapon from Tzader.

Tzader told Evalle, "Go get your bike."

Before she stepped away, Storm snagged her arm and said, "Do *not* face off with another Svart alone."

She bristled. "Who do you—"

He gave her a quick kiss, shutting her down, then walked off with Tzader, who glanced back, looking confused.

Evalle's cheeks were a rosy shade Quinn had never seen.

She took one look at him and snapped, "Don't say a word," then strode off in the direction of the parking deck.

Women. Quinn had tangled with more than his limit today. He rubbed his head and called telepathically to his Belador driver. While Quinn had rushed here on foot, he'd sent his driver to call up his Aston Martin Virage from where it sat parked in valet at the hotel. At Quinn's word, the car arrived outside Underground within minutes.

When Tzader called Quinn telepathically to confirm that Storm had picked up a scent and they'd left Underground, Quinn peeled out and caught up to the pair on Piedmont Avenue.

He pulled over long enough for Tzader to jump in and toss a handful of clothes onto the backseat just as the biggest jaguar Quinn had ever seen ran ahead, jumping over homeless people sleeping in doorways. In spite of his size, the sleek, black animal blended with the night like a racing shadow.

Evalle streaked past Quinn on her wicked motorcycle and stayed ahead, keeping pace with the jaguar.

Tzader said, "Trey's got choppers picking up some of the teams. The rest are spread out over a mile behind us, following directions I'm sending."

Quinn's grip on the wheel tightened with every mile that Storm covered. He had to get Lanna back. The jaguar led them away from the corporate jungle of glass towers in the center of downtown to the fringe, where tattered buildings with bar-covered windows intermingled with pockets of redevelopment.

Then Storm stopped. His sides heaved in and out with deep breaths, but Quinn doubted he'd paused due to lack of stamina.

Quinn pulled the Aston Martin into the parking lot of a closed medical office and got out. "What's wrong, Evalle?"

She'd parked and had her helmet off. "I don't know. Give him a minute."

Striding over with Tzader beside him, Quinn stopped next to Evalle. She watched Storm move back and forth, then squatted down and asked the coal-black animal, "Does the scent end here?"

Storm lifted his jaguar head and nodded.

Tzader said, "I bet this is where they stopped to change the damn tire."

Storm confirmed that with another nod.

Quinn asked Evalle, "Is there any way you know to reach those two boys?"

"No, but I know someone else who might help us."

The jaguar roared at her.

Sentient blades hanging at Tzader's hips came to life, snarling and snapping. "Evalle?"

"Storm's not going to do anything." She stood up and walked up to the giant beast and leaned down, stroking his ebony fur. "You agreed as long as he behaved himself."

Tzader warned, "Evalle, don't stand so close."

"He won't hurt me," she said with conviction, and damn if that jaguar didn't reach up and lick her chin.

Quinn sighed. "You scare the shit out of us sometimes."

He swore the bloody jaguar smiled at him until Evalle said, "We need Isak Nyght's help."

TWENTY-SIX

Evalle held the throttle of her Gixxer steady and hoped she wouldn't be late. The truck with the teens had parked eight minutes ago, just after the stroke of midnight.

One call to Isak and in less than fifteen minutes he'd performed the impossible, locating the truck. Storm had shifted back into his human body and put on his clothes by the time Isak had called Evalle two minutes ago with news that she was only three miles from where the truck was parked.

Storm's arms banded her waist as he snugged up close to her on the back of the bike.

She'd blame the cold air beating his exposed arms and face for the movement, but he never shivered. She had a strong sense that he wanted to remind her of their agreement that he would not touch Isak as long as Isak kept his hands off her.

As if she'd risk more bloodshed tonight.

She'd never been in this situation—between two men. She had no skills for handling either one of them, but they'd both be sorely disappointed if they didn't work together to help save nonhumans from Svarts using them as food.

Except Isak didn't save nonhumans. He hunted them.

Tzader came into her mind. *Just heard from a Belador named Vince who's with the captives inside the old Sears Building on North Avenue, so Isak was right about the truck being there.*

Can he get out?

Said it's too dangerous. Four prisoners teamed up against one Svart and tried to make a break for it. The Svart over-powered them and decapitated one. I told Vince to sit tight and feed us information on how to get to them.

Why didn't he contact you sooner? Not that she wanted to give the guy a hard time, but what took him so long?

Said he was unconscious until now. Lanna had his phone. Said the Svart took it away from her. Vince is one of the six nonhumans a troll named Jurba is using to negotiate with the Svarts to trade for his girlfriend. Two of the six are the twin male witches and one is Lanna.

How many more captives?

Vince counted eighteen so far, including Jurba's six.

Stinking trolls. Evalle turned onto North Avenue, a block away. *Are the Svarts feeding yet?*

Not yet. Vince said there are five Svarts guarding them, but he believes more are out in the city, and he heard one of them say they were waiting on the lieutenant. I told Vince we're close and to call out to me if any of the Svarts act like they're going to feed before we reach him.

Lanna and the twins were still safe—for the moment.

Leaning her bike low around the last corner, Evalle straightened and slowed when the backside of the gargantuan warehouse once known as the Sears Building came into view.

She parked along the curb.

Headlights off, Quinn pulled his Aston Martin up behind her as Storm climbed off her bike. Within seconds, VIPER agents appeared from where they'd parked within a quarter-mile stretch of the older, mixed-residential-and-business neighborhood.

For the benefit of agents not telepathically capable like the Beladors, Tzader issued spoken orders. "Break up into teams of four with a Belador leader in every team so we can keep in contact telepathically. We have a Belador captive inside who will lead us to their location once we're in there."

Evalle asked, "What floor did Vince say they're on?"

"Basement, but like the other floors in that place it covers as much area as a football field. We have to be careful not to kill a human. With this building in the middle of a major rehabilitation right now, the Svarts have very likely glamoured themselves to look like security for the developers."

Adrianna stepped up and Evalle tensed. She hadn't seen the witch until now. When Adrianna ignored her and moved closer to listen, Evalle glanced over at Storm for a moment, assessing him, then back at Tzader.

Evalle suffered a wave of jealousy she had no doubt Storm would pick up on, so she pulled back from the circle of agents crowded around the sidewalk. She could hear just fine without having to stand so near the Sterling witch.

Storm swung around to look at her, then his sharp gaze shot past her shoulder and turned murderous.

In one step, he reached Evalle and yanked her around behind him.

Was he crazy?

She shoved his arm aside and glared her opinion of his ridiculous action, then forced her way around beside him, ready to face whatever threat he was trying to protect her from.

Beladors picked up on intruders approaching first and dispersed, then all the VIPER agents followed suit, lining up in a show of force to each side of her and Storm.

Across the street, deadly-looking men seeped out of the darkness as if their bodies formed from the obsidian shadows. Five, no, eight of them. Hard faces beneath black-smudged eyes and cheeks, but none more hardened than that of their leader, Isak Nyght. Every black-ops soldier aimed a demon blaster at the VIPER team.

Evalle now understood Storm's action because she wanted to step in front of every agent here who had trusted her to contact Isak Nyght. So much for her and Isak's truce.

TWENTY-SEVEN

"What have you done, Roogre?" Kizira demanded of the eight-foot-tall Svart troll commander, as she entered her personal solar in TÅµr Medb. Home of the Medb, for now.

Roogre answered by eyeing her as he would a buzzing insect.

She found that amusing since *he* had the greenish-brown skin of a bug and stood out as a dirty smudge amid silk cushions and sparkling glass art. Thick arms bulged with so much heavy muscle beneath the goatskin vest that she doubted the hideous troll could cross his arms. If he had a neck it wouldn't improve a face that could make a mother wish she'd sewn her womb shut. Purple-inked designs scrolled around eyes as black as his soul, covering his entire face and slick head.

Kizira may have erred in dealing with a being demons would be wise to fear. "You said your trolls could go a week without feeding."

"True." His tenor voice threw the image of that body off-kilter. Roogre sniffed, causing his bulbous nose to flare and the lips across his wide mouth to lift, revealing sharp teeth.

"Why are your trolls gathering up nonhumans?"

"I said they *could* go a week, not that they would."

He'd intentionally misled her, and his murdering trolls might ruin everything.

Kizira had spent long nights figuring a way to slide around Flaevynn's compulsion spell so Kizira could orchestrate her own plan. She'd gambled much with Roogre, and even more with the man she'd just left, but she'd truly doubted that Qu . . . *he* could get past her mental shields. From the look on his face when he'd rushed out of the hotel room, he must have been successful.

Perhaps too successful.

She stalked across the room enclosed by peach, rose and yellow flowers blooming from vines that climbed a silver trellis. One day, she would grow real flowers in earth.

That would not happen if this step of her plan failed.

Or if Flaevynn found out why Kizira had convinced her to bring in Svart trolls.

Kizira swung around, giving Roogre her sharp censure. "Your trolls have drawn the full attention of VIPER in Atlanta sooner than expected."

"True."

"You have broken your word."

"Not true."

"How do you see that?"

"We agreed the mission would be completed by the end of the week. You chose no specific hour or day to draw VIPER out in the open. My trolls are on task."

Technically correct, but still a lie by omission.

She'd agreed to those terms, but the battle strategy

he'd laid out to her afterward had projected a timeline that suited her needs for capturing Alterants. Not feeding his trolls.

Humans wouldn't notice missing nonhumans, but VIPER would.

What else had Roogre done that he'd failed to discuss with her first?

She could either stand here and waste time arguing what would change nothing or accept that few plans ever went as intended. "The turmoil going on in Atlanta at this minute forces us to expedite the timeline."

"So we execute the second phase, the one you and I discussed . . . alone?"

The quelling look she gave him only raised an evil smile to his lips. He said, "Don't glare at me, witch. You said tell no one and I've told no one."

Miserable, untrustworthy trolls. She didn't want him to even whisper about their secret meeting while inside the walls of TÅμr Medb. She'd reply in a way that would dilute what he said in case the walls had ears, but once this was done, and he had the section of earth he desired, she'd never deal with such filth again.

"Everything I do is to benefit the queen. If you wish to be handed North America—by the queen—when this is done, do not say another word except to answer my questions. Understand?"

"Understood." Roogre's amused demeanor hid the temperament of a hungry cobra. He fingered the sword honed of a blue metal that hung alongside stubby legs in brown leather pants. Razor claws at the end of his fingers, matching those on his three-toed feet, curled with a hint of threat.

But inside TÅµr Medb, only Cathbad and Flaevynn were more powerful than Kizira. This Svart might be a danger to her outside the tower, but not in her home, where her power increased. "It's time to send in both of your demonic trolls."

"One is dead."

"Not possible," she whispered, shocked. "Where? How?"

"Killed in a skirmish with a Belador in Atlanta."

"Why did you risk sending one out?"

All amusement fled from Roogre's face. "To find those who killed two of my trolls. Before you speak too quickly, I told you I would exact payment immediately for any troll lost while under my command."

"You also said your trolls were practically indestructible against Beladors since they would avoid linking around a Svart."

"True."

"Obviously not." Then it dawned on her. "What specific Belador killed your trolls?"

"The Alterant Evalle Kincaid."

Kizira kept her temper under control or the air would explode with lightning. "Your trolls were to *capture* Alterants, not fight them, and none were to touch Evalle yet."

"My troll intervened to stop her from killing another Alterant and had no idea of her identity when he did."

That didn't sound like Evalle. Sure that Roogre held

back information he didn't want to share, Kizira asked, "Was she killing an Alterant or a Rías?"

"My soldiers don't have time to qualify a beast while it's changing if you want these things captured instead of killed. We'll bring you all the Alterants and Rías we find, then you can give me any you don't keep and I'll dispose of them for you."

She hid her disgust at his offhanded reference to eating the leftovers, so to speak. "How can you be so sure Evalle killed your troll if you don't communicate by telepathy?"

Roogre held up a six-inch-wide gold medallion hanging from a chain around his neck. He'd told her once that the runic *S* cut out of the center was used as the template for marking his trolls. "My blood is mixed with the acid that burns this emblem into the forearms of those under my command. With the exception of my Lieutenant in the field who can speak to me through my mind, my trolls can't communicate telepathically, but I receive a visual message from them upon death. The last heartbeat of a Svart troll sends an image to me of the one who killed him."

By the gods, she wanted to slash Roogre to pieces. "Then you sent one of the demonic trolls to kill Evalle and *she* won that battle, too?"

"No. A four-legged, black demon cat beheaded my troll, and he will pay with his life."

She didn't care how many demons Roogre destroyed, but Alterants were another issue. "You can't kill *any* Alterants."

"Why? You're ready to implement the second phase

immediately and said yourself that if it is successful, those five Alterants will no longer be necessary."

How had she allowed him to speak so openly again? The queen believed the Svart commander's only goal was Flaevynn's order for his trolls to capture Alterants in Atlanta.

Giving him death-threat glares did nothing. Again, she had to cover for the words he'd spoken out loud. "The second phase is only to support Queen Flaevynn's goal of seeing Treoir fall."

Humor flitted across Roogre's gaze, letting her know he understood—as well as she did—the dangerous game she played. "Don't worry. The demonic troll I sent to Atlanta was the weaker of the two. The second one still hidden is far more invincible after having been dipped twice in Loch Ryve. I await only your word to take my strongest team to . . . ?"

As if she'd tell him one second too soon or speak the location out loud? She gave up trying to cover his constant slips, which were by no means accidental, but Flaevynn had not come bursting in yet, so all still appeared safe at this point. Kizira had one chance to get a step ahead of the queen.

Time to take the plunge into dangerous waters.

Kizira said, "I'll send you and your team now, but I want your word to wait twenty minutes once you arrive before doing anything. That will give you time to get your trolls in place."

"I don't need twenty minutes."

"I do because I want to be present, but I must speak to Queen Flaevynn first."

"To assure her of impending victory?"

Why couldn't Flaevynn compel Kizira to turn miserable trolls into a pile of flaming cow dung? Kizira needed the extra time to direct Flaevynn's attention to her scrying wall to watch the Svart and VIPER battles in Atlanta. That should keep the queen busy while Kizira slipped away.

No matter. Kizira had to be on-site for one reason—to protect Qu . . . *him* from being ripped to pieces by Svart trolls.

Touching Roogre would probably give her nightmares, but she was ready to teleport him and his men to their next destination. By the time Roogre knew where he was going, the only person he could share that with would be his Lieutenant, who would say nothing to endanger Roogre and his fellow trolls.

But before she sent him on his way, she asked, "How many Svarts will remain in Atlanta?"

"My Lieutenant and enough to handle fifty Beladors, but we face only a handful at a time, just as I told you would happen. Attacking in the cemeteries gave our opponent specific target areas, too many to defend. With no idea where we'll strike next, they've spread their resources thin across the city."

"Hold out your forearm." When he turned the runic *S* scar up for her to see, she said, "Call up the list in your mind of who will go. When I touch you, they'll all teleport at once."

"I'm ready."

She placed her palm on the raised skin of his scar, which heated immediately. Kizira waved her free hand between them, but just before Roogre disappeared his eyes widened. She started to call him back to find out why, then realized it had to be due to his seeing where she'd sent him.

She looked at her hand, trying to decide if peeling off a layer of skin would clean away the troll's contamination.

"Looking for me, Kizira?"

Kizira froze at the caustic edge in Flaevynn's voice, but that rarely changed. Kizira forced a smile on her face and dropped her hand as she turned to find the Medb queen at the arched entrance to her solar. "Yes, Your Highness. Things are moving along sooner than anticipated with the plan in Atlanta. Perhaps you'd like to view it on your—"

"But Roogre is not following my directions, now is he?"

Flaevynn must have heard them, but how much?

Never show a weakness to a vicious queen. "I admonished Roogre about not executing as agreed upon."

"Really? Perhaps not the plan *I* agreed upon, but another version. Yours maybe?"

Kizira had climbed too deep into this game to play it halfway. "I often speak on your behalf, but I assure you Roogre knows who contracted him."

Flaevynn disappeared and reappeared right in front of Kizira. The queen's image flared with light and power meant to intimidate, a successful effort at present. Flaevynn purred in a dangerously soft voice, "You of all people should know what I do to someone who betrays me."

Kizira's pulse shot off the charts. She couldn't stop her

thoughts from racing wildly. Several images of torture came to mind unbidden.

Curbing her anxiety to manage a subservient voice, Kizira said, "I have been your loyal servant since taking my priestess training twelve years ago. I've done all that you've asked."

"Yes, you have, but you are also of my and Cathbad's blood, though I try to forget. He constantly tells me how intelligent you are and that you have a value. I never realized until now just how cunning you could be."

"Thank you, Your Highness," Kizira answered, though she couldn't see Flaevynn intentionally handing her a compliment.

Kizira believed she might be in the clear, until Flaevynn smiled. "I glimpsed Roogre's mind as you teleported him. I know where you sent him and his team, and what they will do when they arrive. You dare to steal what is rightfully mine?"

The blood drained from Kizira's head so quickly that she weaved with dizziness. She panicked and didn't have to pretend to beg. "I'm doing it for you—"

Flaevynn screeched.

Kizira went spinning head over heels in a blur. When she hit the floor and looked around, she sat in the same room Cathbad had endured for two years in the dungeon. "Noooo!"

Kizira would never leave here.

Flaevynn would win.

Quinn would die.

TWENTY-EIGHT

Evalle would kill for a sword to cut through the aggression thickening the night air. She took two steps, moving out in front of the VIPER team now facing off with Isak and his men, who had lined up side by side across the street.

Storm moved up beside her and growled softly.

Tzader yelled at her telepathically. *Get back so we can throw up a united kinetic wall.*

She answered, *Please keep everyone back and give me a chance to talk to him.*

If one finger twitches a trigger, they'll all die.

I understand. Then she called over to Isak, "I only asked for help *finding* the trolls. What are you doing here?"

After a tense couple of seconds, Isak swung his weapon across his chest in an at-ease gesture before walking across the narrow side street. His men still held their weapons at ready. When he stopped in front of her, he cut brutal eyes at Storm, who sent back an equally vicious look.

Then Isak took in the blood on her shirt. His face shifted with cold anger icing his blue eyes. "Who did that?"

"Trolls, but I'm fine, and we've got to get inside that building before they hurt anyone else. I appreciate the help in finding the Svarts, but why are you here?"

"You know what I do. You really surprised to see me?"

She ignored his question since he hadn't really answered hers. "*We* can handle this."

Isak's gaze swept over the men and women standing behind Evalle and Storm. "Everyone here nonhumans like . . . you?" he asked Evalle.

Storm answered, "All of us."

She wanted to kick Storm, who Isak now eyed with even more menace. She said, "Thought we had a truce. Please leave so we can do what we came to do, Isak, or people will die."

"People or nonhumans?"

"They're people to me."

He drew two slow breaths, then said, "I'll stay out here as *your* backup."

He made it perfectly clear who he intended to protect.

Storm threw off a whip of dark energy that made it clear what he thought of Isak's declaration.

But Isak hadn't touched her, so Storm had to keep his word. Turning to Tzader and the team, Evalle said, "Okay, everyone. Isak Nyght loaned us the weapon Quinn's carrying that kills trolls. He and his team will stay out here and back *us* up."

Storm smiled.

She lifted a testy eyebrow in caution and his smile only broadened.

Tzader said, "How will they know who they can and can't shoot?"

Isak called back, "You got any more of your kind showing up here?"

"No."

"We've scanned all of you. Any other nonhuman who interferes will be neutralized."

Quinn came into Evalle's mind. *Do you trust him?*

What could she say to that? Sometimes you had to go with your gut feeling. Isak hadn't shot at them when he could have without a word first. She told Quinn, *I have to trust Isak at this point.*

Isak asked Evalle, "Sure you can handle these trolls?"

"With this many agents, yes." She hoped.

She'd asked herself that same question over and over after having almost died at the hands of Svarts on two occasions so far. The Beladors couldn't risk linking around this many Svarts, but this VIPER team had plenty of power besides Beladors. As long as they stuck together, they should be fine.

Isak unclipped his demon blaster from the elastic dummy cord clipped to his chest and handed it to her. He put his finger on a lever just ahead of the trigger. "Not that you need it, but push this up for less force—to stun something—and down to kill."

"What about you?"

"I'm *always* armed."

Before she or Isak could converse further, Tzader spoke out loud to the team. "Just got word from our man on the inside that the other Svarts the trolls were waiting on have arrived. We've got to go in now."

Before turning to join the team, Evalle told Isak, "Thank you."

He nodded at her and gave Storm one last threatening look that the arrogant Skinwalker countered with a taunting smile Evalle could only describe as possessive.

And she'd thought men were more trouble when they were just trying to kill her.

She kicked into Belador speed to reach the front of the team with Tzader and Quinn. She shouldn't have been surprised to see Storm match her step for step. One day he'd have to tell her everything he could do.

Just before Tzader entered the building, his power as Maistir rushed into Evalle's mind, meaning he spoke to all of his warriors. *Vince just learned that the Svarts have a group of humans locked in the end of the building near Glen Iris Drive. He and the other nonhumans are at the opposite end. We have to split up and be careful around the humans.*

Evalle's stomach flipped. That cut their power in half.

But no way would anyone on this team go along with bringing Isak and his men inside.

TWENTY-NINE

Even if her cousin and his snake people could find her in this building the size of a small city, Svarts might kill him. Lanna had really thought she could overpower the trolls, but these Svarts were nothing like anything she'd met before.

She tapped her fingers on the concrete and wrinkled her nose at the musty smell of age clinging to the basement. Angling her head over at Kellman, who sat next to her and the pole they were both chained to, she whispered, "Jurba has not left with girlfriend. Why?"

"Don't know. Maybe he's cutting another deal."

"I do not think so. Jurba is shaking and female troll looks afraid." When Kell had nothing to say about that, Lanna pointed out something else. "The Svarts did not talk so much until that one with gold band around arm showed up. They call him 'Lieutenant.' I think he is boss they were waiting on." *To start feeding.*

Kell must have heard something in her voice in spite of her trying not to sound afraid. He turned to her and lifted his free hand to her face, gently touching her cheek. "How's your eye?"

He had nice touch. She could still see through the swollen lid. "I am fine. And angry my majik fail me."

Kell gave her a small smile. It warmed her heart as

much as his words did when he said, "It didn't fail you. You caused the truck tire to go flat. That bought us some time."

She had used a spell that called sharp objects to truck tires. Something finally struck hard enough to cut tire. Making spell work from inside of truck had not been easy. It had taken a while to do. She could have done more and quicker, but that would have meant drawing hard on elements, which would have caught Grendal's attention.

Once Jurba drove the truck again, he did not drive long enough for her to flatten a second tire.

She could not believe she escaped Romania for this. "My majik should have hurt Svart bad. Not make him crazy."

Kell's fingers grazed her cheek again, giving her chills that had nothing to do with the cold basement. He said, "I just wish the bastard hadn't realized who sent the cement block flying at him."

"I can heal from bruise, but troll took phone I borrowed from unconscious man."

"Jurba would have gotten it if he hadn't been too stupid to search for phones. These Svarts don't seem to make those kinds of mistakes. I've never seen trolls that hard to take down."

"Me either. Now we must give cousin time to find us. He will not come alone." She couldn't tell Kell about the snake people . . . VIPER, but she did relax a little, surprised at how talking to this boy made her feel better. Of the two boys, she would have thought the joking Kardos would be the one to lift her spirits.

"I'm sorry you got caught with us," Kell said.

"My fault." She could not blame the boys when she chose to follow them. With the power she possessed, she could get them out of here if not for fear of Grendal. She could not risk tapping that level of her power unless she had no other option. Even if she could break her chain, could she break all the chains fast enough to save everyone? "I will think of better plan."

"No!"

She held her breath at Kell's outburst and shifted her gaze to the Svarts, who had all stopped talking to look at Kell and her. She didn't breathe until they resumed talking. Without taking her eyes off the Svarts, she said, "Do not shout."

"I know."

"Then why did you?"

When Kell said nothing, she shifted her attention to him, but he just shrugged and looked away.

What did that mean?

She understood Kardos, who flirted even to hide fear in this place and had no control over his mouth. But Kell did not act without thought.

A shrill scream sent chills crawling up Lanna's spine. She jerked her head up to see a Svart grab Jurba, who was howling in terror. The Svart ripped Jurba in half.

Dead-troll stench hit Lanna. She covered her nose, the hideous smell making her eyes tear up.

Jurba's girlfriend kept screaming as if her heart had been clawed from her chest.

The troll ripped off one of Jurba's arms and hit the

girl troll with it, spraying blood all over her and knocking her out.

So much blood. The memory of that night in Romania rushed in at her.

Lanna started breathing faster. She had to calm down and hold control of her power, but her heart pounded harder until she could hear it in her ears. Noises and smells blurred into a hideous cloud around her.

"Lanna?"

Her body shook with tremors.

"Stop whatever you're doing," Kell ordered. "Now."

Her vision cleared. She jerked her head up and blinked. Kell was staring at her.

What had she just done?

Kardos leaned forward, shock on his face. "Did you do that?"

She looked around. Hundreds of chairs that had been neatly stacked to the side were now toppled in piles. Loose debris from the cracked ceiling had scattered across the floor. Two support beams were bent.

She might have killed all of them. "I am sorry."

Man she borrowed phone from who had been unconscious in the truck now stared at her, but the trolls looked around, confused, then zeroed in on the captives.

All except the Svart who had torn Jurba apart. That troll squatted over Jurba's body with his back turned to everyone like a dog attacking his first meal in days.

Then the troll called Lieutenant stared straight at her. His look said she had just moved to the top of his menu.

Cloaking herself right now, even if it worked again,

would be of no use with her still chained to the pole. And she would not leave Kellman, Kardos or the others to these trolls.

Kardos whispered in a jittery voice, "Just what are you, babe?"

She admitted, "I do not know some days."

Her cousin must show up soon or she would be forced to try something. And once she was out of here, she would not let Quinn out of her sight until they talked about how to fix her powers.

The Lieutenant barked something at his men, then started toward Lanna.

Time had just run out.

Kellman leaned forward to talk across Lanna to Kardos. "Got any spells that work inside?"

Lanna said, "Do not anger them more. They will hurt you."

Ignoring her, Kardos assessed the Lieutenant, shaking his head. "Nothing that will touch this bunch. Mine are better outdoors, but we can try the Halloween one I did last year."

Could they not hear her? "Do not be stupid."

Kell gave her a withering look and muttered, "Says the person who followed two witches into a troll trap after I *tried* to send you away."

Kell was only angry because he worried for her, so she teased him, "Good thing for you I have not time to turn you into bug."

Kardos piped up, "You mean a frog, princess?"

His brother said, "Shut up, Kardos."

"More like toad, in your brother's case," she muttered, then said to both of them, "I can not stop Svart if you interfere. Be quiet or you get me killed."

Kellman shook his head. "Don't."

"Listen to me. I must give my cousin time to find us. Trust me. I can do this and no one gets hurt." Except maybe her.

In spite of the skeptical look in his eyes, Kell said, "You're sure?"

"Yes. Be ready and do what I say."

Lanna took a deep breath and whispered the chant for her cloaking. What she was about to do would lead Grendal to her. Mattered not. She had to help the others. But how long until he found her once she drew hard on the earth's power?

She whispered a second chant and forced energy into the chain holding her and Kell. When the links snapped, she grabbed his arm and watched him vanish.

Kardos sputtered, eyes rounded with shock.

The Lieutenant stopped mid-stride, staring at where she had sat seconds ago. He roared with fury, then looked up and down, turning in a circle.

"Do not let go of me," she hissed, dragging Kell with one hand, using her other to grab the chain holding Kardos and the man who had been unconscious in the truck. Pushing her power into the chain, she watched it fall apart.

The man whose phone she'd used jumped up and ordered, "Get out of here while you can. Beladors are coming."

Was he Belador? Had to be. He meant for her and Kell to leave because they were invisible. But she would not leave Kardos, and neither would Kell.

Svarts charged across the room.

The Lieutenant swung around to attack the Belador man yelling at her. This crazy man lifted hands and shoved at the air, which stopped the Svart. Kinetic power.

His kinetics slowed the Svarts, but he was losing ground.

Lanna ran down the line of captives, breaking chain after chain. Prisoners jumped up and ran in all directions.

The Svarts beat back Belador man's kinetics, forcing him into corner.

She started toward him. Her cloaking failed.

"Grab her now!" the Lieutenant yelled, pointing at Lanna.

Kell and Kardos rushed over to each side of Lanna, ready to fight with her.

She felt light-headed from tapping her powers, but she needed them again to put strong force behind the spell she had in mind. Raising her arms, she began chanting Russian words.

The boys picked up the singsong words as she repeated them and joined the chant.

Lightning crackled, shooting across the room, popping against every surface.

Svarts froze, looking around until their leader shoved past the group, not worried about the bad weather inside.

His face twisted with rage.

Anything more violent that Lanna could call up might kill everyone inside. She looked into the Svart's eyes and prepared to die. She said to Kell, "I have new plan. You and Kardos dive away when I say."

That might give the boys a chance to survive.

"No." Kell squeezed her fingers, then released her as the Svarts created a wall enclosing them, moving cautiously toward her after that lightning display.

Power exploded into the room.

The Svarts wheeled around as one unit and chaos erupted.

Lanna sagged with relief. "I told you cousin would come."

"Evalle's here, too," Kellman said absently. "And she'll want us to stay out of their way."

Sounded good to Lanna, who had lowered her arms when the Lieutenant had turned his back to face the incoming threat.

He swung around and moved fast as a lightning strike, grabbing Lanna by the throat.

THIRTY

Beladors and VIPER agents scattered across the basement, attacking in teams of two, but not linking. Too high a risk that a Svart might rip off a head and kill all the linked Beladors with one strike. Evalle held the Nyght weapon, ready to blast a troll the minute a team had one beaten back. The weapon used a laser-delivered technology that entered the body and raced through the blood system, exploding internal organs. But it moved from one living thing to the next if two or more beings were connected, killing everyone that touched the target.

A Belador shouted telepathically and she wheeled to find a Svart pushed back by four Beladors shoving a kinetic wall at it. She squeezed the trigger and the Svart turned rigid and shook as if he'd been hit by high-voltage current.

She searched the room quickly for Kellman and Kardos but couldn't see past the battling trolls and agents to find them or a young girl fitting Lanna's description. Fourteen captives had raced out, screaming that the trolls were feeding.

Evalle couldn't be too late for the boys or Lanna.

Quinn had been told to search any troll mind he could, but from the strain on his face he wasn't having much luck.

One troll tossed aside two VIPER agents he had by the throats and howled, turning until he spotted Quinn.

Then Quinn grabbed his own head.

The minute the troll dove for Quinn, Evalle blasted the nasty creature to pieces.

Screw intel.

Shaking his head, Quinn staggered but gave her a thumbs-up that he was good for the moment.

Three trolls still engaged agents in the middle of chairs and other furniture that were piled haphazardly. Evalle pushed into the center of the carnage.

A clawed hand reached out from a battle and grabbed her, digging into her sore shoulder when he shoved Evalle to her knees. She clenched against the new pain and fought to turn the weapon on him.

Storm snarled, tackling the Svart and yanking his attention away from Evalle. She jumped up and took aim, but couldn't kill the Svart while he was entangled with Storm.

"Eeevallle!"

That was Kellman's voice.

Quinn rushed away from the fighting and called to Evalle, *One of them grabbed Lanna. Don't kill her when you shoot.*

Evalle flipped the lever on the weapon to the lower strength and spun in the direction of Kellman's voice. The teenager stood with a finger pointed at the Svart holding a young woman. Lanna. Kellman and Kardos chanted something that had the Svart slapping his face with his free hand. The Svart must not want to eat Lanna or he'd have done so, but the girl was turning blue from lack of air.

Evalle took the shot, hoping the level of stun wouldn't harm Lanna.

The troll jerked and lit up as if he'd been electrocuted by enough power to run Times Square. But he did drop the girl.

Lanna fell to the floor in a limp pile.

Kellman reached Lanna first, then Quinn and Kardos knelt beside her. Quinn called to Evalle, *She's alive.*

With them secure for the moment, Evalle turned to find Storm. He had bloody slashes across his chest and arms from claws where he still fought the Svart. The troll and Storm crashed through a pile of chairs, falling to the floor.

She yelled at Storm, "Get ready."

He didn't have time to ask for what when she lifted a hand and slammed a kinetic hit at the Svart. That caused the troll to jerk his head around to her and lift up in preparation to attack.

Flipping the lever back to deep-fry, she yelled at Storm, "Move. Now!"

The troll leaped at her, but hallelujah, Storm rolled to his left.

She blasted the troll in midair, spewing green ooze all over the place. Smelled like raw sewage in summer heat.

Storm jumped to his feet and headed toward the other two Svarts still battling.

Evalle said, "Hold up."

Storm turned back. "Why?"

"Don't jump in unless they can't break away so I can get a kill shot."

Tzader fought a Svart alongside Reece "Casper" Jordan, another VIPER agent who was not Belador. She told Tzader telepathically, *I need you to slam the troll with your kinetics to break away, then you and Casper hit the floor when I say go.*

Tzader said, *I told Casper. We'll go on the count of three.*

When Evalle yelled, "One, two, three," Tzader hit the Svart with a kinetic shot that barely knocked the troll back a step. Tzader and Casper dove for the floor, completely vulnerable. Evalle blasted the Svart, then finished off the last one the same way.

Tzader moved toward her. He walked with a limp, but he'd heal quickly. Evalle asked, "What about the humans?"

"All safe. There was just one Svart watching them, and Trey got him with the other weapon."

Casper swaggered up to her, wiping troll goo off his face. That cowboy only knew one way to walk. "Some fine shootin' there, Evalle. That cleaned house."

Not completely. Evalle had only stunned the one who'd grabbed Lanna. She was about to mention that when Adrianna came strolling up, not a drop of stinking troll goo anywhere on her tight-fitting, black jumpsuit. How did she manage to always look so put together, even at a smackdown?

Adrianna told Tzader, "Trey's with the humans. I put them to sleep with a spell, but it won't last long. There's more here than I can clean up. I can give them a memory that they dreamed this like I did the gangers today, but that's not going to work this time because they've got injuries that need treating. They'll end up at the hospital, all with the same 'dream.'" She held up her fingers and made quote marks in the air when she said the word *dream*. "They need their memories wiped, and transport to medical care, and I can't do that."

Was it petty of her to be thrilled about hearing something Adrianna couldn't do? Probably. *Too bad*. Evalle smiled.

Tzader said, "Got to call in Sen."

So much for enjoying the moment.

Sen would have to do more than just clean up the mess and wipe minds. He'd have to put this building back in shape, right down to repairing any structural damage, so the humans would never know what happened here.

Tzader sent Casper to assess agent injuries while he contacted Sen.

Evalle walked over to the teenagers just as a flush of power whipped through the air. She ignored Sen's arrival and searched for the boys. She let out a sigh of relief when she spotted them sitting next to the girl with interesting hair. Blond at the roots, but the curls ended in black tips. Lanna had a stunned look on her attractive face. "So you're Lanna."

Lanna lifted her face to Evalle. "Yes. You are Evalle."

Kellman took his eyes off Lanna long enough to smile up at Evalle. "Good to see you."

"Glad you and Kardos are safe." Evalle would have said more but Kardos pulled Lanna's hair back off her face and Kellman glared at his brother.

Kellman? Now, *that* was amusing.

Lucky for both of them that overprotective Quinn hadn't noticed either action.

The Svart Evalle had stunned let out a groan.

Storm walked up next to her and stood over the troll. "He's not dead?"

Evalle shook her head. "He had Lanna in his hands, so I had to drop the power on the weapon to stun." She lifted the weapon. "But I can fix that if he doesn't behave."

"Wait." Quinn snapped to his feet and looked down at the troll, who had a gold armband with odd carvings.

Lanna said, "They call that one Lieutenant. He is leader."

Quinn said, "I couldn't get into the mind of the other ones, but . . ."

Everyone fell silent as Quinn stared at the troll and it started trembling. The Svart must have mental shields up even when unconscious.

When Tzader walked up to them, Evalle held up a finger and pointed at Quinn. Tzader nodded and spoke to her telepathically. *Sen's here and he's going to be here for a while to clean up, plus I told him other trolls are expected to come back here to feed. Once Quinn is finished, Sen will take this Svart to VIPER lockdown.*

She hadn't thought past this battle, but Tzader was right. *I'm sure Isak will let us keep the weapon Trey has for a little longer. Trey should be able to pick off Svarts as they show up. I'll stick around to back him up, but I need to get these two boys out of here. I don't want them out on the streets until I know it's relatively safe again.*

Tzader turned around, facing the way they came in. *Ah, hell.*

Evalle turned to find Isak striding across the room.

Sen could have torched Isak with his glare and probably would have if Isak had not been human.

Isak ignored Sen, clueless about the power Sen wielded.

When Sen's glare shifted to Evalle, Tzader sighed and said to her, *I'll back you up when we go in to explain Isak and the weapons.*

Isak eyed the room as he stepped over troll body parts scattered around. When he reached Evalle, he paused. "Nice job."

She couldn't help but smile at him. "Thanks for the weapon."

Storm stepped up next to her with his arms crossed and a scowl planted on his face.

She ignored him and tried to return the weapon to Isak.

Isak said, "Keep it for now." His attention went to the three teenagers. "Are they—"

"Yes." That's when she realized she had an answer to her problem. "I need you to do me a favor, Isak."

He didn't say a word, but the grin he gave Storm might start a new battle. "Sure, darlin'. Whatever you want."

Oh, this was too easy. "Would you take those twins to your warehouse until I can come pick them up? I'll bring your weapons back when I do."

When Isak looked at her in horror, Storm broke out a grin.

Crap. She went for the kill. "Please."

"I'll take them to Kit." Then Isak added, "We'll be expecting you for that dinner you agreed to."

Storm's dark eyes slashed at Evalle, full of questions.

She didn't have time to answer any of them.

As if that weren't complicated enough, she caught Sen's gaze, which had latched onto Storm. Evalle caught Storm's attention and nodded toward Sen.

Storm ignored the evil glare. "I'll talk to VIPER tomorrow. Sen can stew until then."

She didn't think it would be that simple, but they could talk about that later. "Sorry Sen found out about you being here before you were ready."

"Not a problem. I wouldn't have stayed out of the picture much longer."

By now more Beladors were arriving and crowding the area. Tzader ordered everyone away from Quinn, who had dropped to his knees beside the Svart, concentrating. When he didn't appear to be in distress, Evalle moved the boys and Lanna away.

After a brief argument, Evalle convinced the twins to go with Isak and promised to come get them as soon as she could. Lanna kissed both Kardos and Kellman on their cheeks before they left with Isak, then eased over closer to Quinn but didn't bother him.

With Isak gone, Sen returned to working through issues with Tzader.

"Bloody hell!" Quinn shouted.

Evalle swung around to Quinn "Are you hurt?"

"No. We've been played. This was all a diversion."

Tzader said, "What do you mean?"

"There's a team of Svarts being teleported to Treoir. They're going after the castle—and Brina—and they have another demon Svart. Worse than the one that attacked Evalle."

Tzader rarely looked shocked. "That's not possible. How could they know where to . . ." Then something clearly transpired between him and Quinn that Evalle would love to have heard.

She saw the looks on both their faces. For the first time since she'd known these two men, they were at odds with one another.

Tzader shouted for Sen, who had been standing way across the room, but appeared instantly next to Tzader.

Sen growled, "What?"

"I'm taking all the Beladors I can with me to Treoir and need you to teleport us now."

"Why?"

Tzader swung a vicious look at Sen that warned him not to waste time. "Our warrior queen is in mortal danger."

Evalle had never seen Sen show understanding for anyone, especially her, but his whole demeanor changed to compliant. Did Sen know how much Brina meant to Tzader beyond being their warrior queen? Would he even care?

Evalle rolled her eyes at the ridiculous thought.

Sen said, "The fastest way to send you is as a group. Line up your Beladors so that they touch each other in some way, even if they just grab each other's clothing. When you're ready, open your mind to Treoir. I'll be the only person besides you who will know the path to your destination."

Tzader's voice boomed in Evalle's mind as he sent a telepathic message to all the Beladors, dictating which ones would travel with him and who would stay to aid Sen. He wanted everyone ready to go in sixty seconds.

Trey handed Casper his weapon and joined Tzader's group.

Quinn snagged Lanna and pulled her aside. "I'm glad you're safe, but I want you out of here."

"No, I *must* stay with you," Lanna said in a panicked voice that surprised Evalle. "I helped. You would not have known where Svarts held everyone if I had not been here. Do not leave me."

Quinn leaned down, putting his hand on her shoulder and patience into his voice. "We'll talk about all this when I get back. You'll be fine until then. I have a car arriving in five minutes to pick you up outside. Go directly to the suite and stay there this time. Understand?"

Lanna said, "Yes," but her eyes said she felt abandoned.

Evalle's empathic ability kicked in at that point, and she felt . . . not abandonment, but . . . fear. Hard-core terror. The Svarts were dead, so what scared the girl? But Evalle could do nothing at that point. She certainly owed the girl her gratitude for the boys' being alive, but Evalle would have to address that when she returned from Treoir.

"Is everyone ready?" Sen asked Tzader, who was snapping orders to get into position.

"Yes. Locate the Svarts on Treoir. Put us between the trolls and Brina, but closer to the trolls if possible."

Evalle hooked the strap of the weapon over her head so that it hung across her chest. Fingers crossed in hopes she wouldn't humiliate herself by throwing up, she stepped up to the packed circle of fifty Beladors.

Something touched her boot.

She looked down, but nothing was there.

As Tzader said, "Ready," two arms snaked around Evalle's waist and pulled her back against a rock-hard chest. She snapped, "Just grab my shirt, for crying out loud."

She tensed but had no time to swing around and shove the guy away as everything swirled into a blur of teleporting.

Warm air rushed along her neck when a deep voice said, "Don't worry, I've got you."

"Storm? You can't come with us."

"I'm not letting you face another demon Svart alone."

She relaxed in his arms, exhilarating in a selfish moment of feeling happy since she couldn't change what was already in motion. He kissed her neck and warmed her in his arms, but every good thing in her life usually came with a cost.

No one should be traveling to Treoir except Beladors.

She prepared herself for Tzader's reaction when he realized she'd brought an outsider into the sacred home of Belador power.

Tzader's words to Sen hit her. *Put us between the trolls and Brina.* What if the trolls had already entered the castle? Sending Tzader through the warding would kill him.

THIRTY-ONE

When the teleporting ended, Evalle opened her eyes quickly and finally took a breath. Not inside Treoir Castle. Tzader hadn't been killed.

She gawked at the glittering castle, which rose from a mist surrounding the curtain wall like a floating moat. She marveled at the grayish-pink twilight, neither sunlight nor the darkness she'd left in Atlanta. Lush green land sprawled for a half mile in any direction from the castle, flowing to forests with giant trees that reminded her of the redwoods in California. Sen had dropped them in knee-high, silky grass growing at the edge of a forest directly across a wide stretch of land from the castle entrance.

How far away were the purple-and-blue mountains in the distance beyond the castle? Hundreds of miles?

When Storm pulled his arms away, Evalle took a step back and almost fell over Lanna, who had a hand on her boot. Evalle hissed, "What're you doing here?"

Lanna looked up with wide eyes. "Please do not tell Cousin. I could not stay back there without him."

Quinn walked up and snarled through clenched teeth. *"Lanna?"*

Evalle couldn't recall Quinn ever losing his temper so easily and didn't know what Lanna's problem was, but she took pity on Lanna when Quinn's face contorted with barely controlled rage. Hoping to ease the tension, Evalle said, "We'll find a place for Lanna to wait, Quinn. She'll be okay."

"No, she won't," he snapped at Evalle. "She's going to get our people killed if she doesn't get herself killed first."

Lanna dropped her head. "I am sorry."

The hurt in Lanna's voice pulled on Evalle's heart-strings. Lanna had powers, but she was deathly afraid of being left behind for some reason.

Tzader walked up, took one look at Storm and another at Lanna. "What the hell, Evalle?"

"*I* didn't do *all* this."

Before Tzader said another word, a light began swirling in the middle of the Beladors, pushing them out in a circle. Everyone quieted.

When the light vanished, a cluster of Belador swords materialized, stabbed into the ground, ready to be drawn.

Tzader immediately turned his attention to the battle, telling everyone, "Your warrior queen has sent us swords that are more powerful here than in any other place. Take up your sword and prepare to face the enemy." Tzader told Quinn, "Send Lanna to stay in the castle with Brina until we return to Atlanta."

"Done."

When Lanna started to protest, Evalle put her hand on the girl's shoulder. "That's the safest place for you to be, because we won't let the Svarts anywhere near the castle."

Tzader told Evalle, "*You* take her there."

"Me? Why do I have to take her?"

"Are you questioning me?" Tzader asked in full Maistir mode and out of patience.

Good grief. What had she been thinking to speak so freely with Tzader in this situation? "Absolutely not, Maistir. My apologies."

He nodded. "Brina will give you a sword when you get there. Protect the entrance to the castle."

Evalle had a chance to fight with the tribe on Treoir and she'd been relegated to babysitter and front-door guard. The Beladors would stop the trolls before reaching that point, leaving her out of the battle, but the last thing she wanted was to give Tzader any more reason to be disappointed in her.

She handed off her Nyght weapon to Trey.

Tzader finished issuing orders and turned to Storm. "You can't shift here without Brina's explicit permission, and I don't have time to take you to her to discuss your presence on Treoir, but there's a sword for you, too."

Storm asked Tzader, "What happens if I shift without permission?"

"You'll burst into flames."

Storm lifted a sword, then turned back as if he intended to stay by Evalle's side.

She shook her head, silently pleading with him not to make things any worse for her by refusing to follow Tzader's orders. Storm held her gaze a moment, then left with the team he'd been assigned to, disappearing into the woods.

Ready to follow Tzader's orders to a T, Evalle asked Lanna, "How fast can you move?"

"Fast."

She took the girl's hand and ran toward the castle with her Belador speed. No one had to hold back powers here, but Evalle slowed to a human pace when she noticed the girl used majik to hover above the ground every few steps to keep up.

Halfway to the castle, howling screeches erupted behind her in the forest. Her tribe had found the Svarts. But how many? Sounded like a lot more than eight in those woods.

When Evalle reached the castle steps, she released Lanna's hand and stopped to peer up at the towering structure that was both fairy tale and dark fantasy. Blue, purple and black stones made up the outside with a Belador Triquetra carved into every blue stone. Two massive wood-and-iron doors fifteen feet tall and just as wide, together, opened into the castle.

Brina appeared in the opening, but stopped short of crossing the threshold. She frowned at Evalle. "Why aren't you with Tzader?"

Evalle grabbed a mute Lanna by the arm and towed her up the steps until they reached the first landing. "He told me to guard the entrance and bring Lanna here."

"Who is she an' what would she be doin' *here*?"

"Quinn's cousin and—"

Brina studied harder on Lanna. "You are *not* Belador."

"No. I am Romanian."

Evalle continued up the last two steps to the wide,

gray slab at the top landing. "She traveled with us by accident."

"Storm traveled same way," Lanna pointed out, clearly looking for safety in numbers.

What had Quinn called her? Brat. That fit. Evalle turned to Brina. "That was also an accident. We were in the middle of a VIPER op when Quinn entered the mind of a Svart troll and found out they were coming for you. Tzader had Sen teleport us so neither Storm nor Lanna knows how to find Treoir."

Brina nodded. "The royal guard just reported encounterin' Svart trolls. We've already lost two of our own."

Evalle's empathic ability came to life, picking up the anguish rolling off Brina, who had to be even more frustrated than Evalle about not joining the battle.

When the sound of howls erupted from the forest again, Brina asked, "Where is the other one who came with you?"

"Storm is fighting with the Beladors."

"Those Svarts found out how to get here," Brina said under her breath. "I will not sanction those two who traveled with you if Tzader feels they pose no security issue."

"Thank you." Evalle wondered who told the Svarts how to get to Treoir . . . or who teleported them here, but that was up to Tzader and Brina to figure out. She said to Brina, "Quinn respectfully requests that you keep Lanna inside the castle while we deal with Svarts."

Brina asked Lanna, "Are you immortal?"

"No. Why?"

"Because you would *die* if you tried to cross the

warding into this castle if you were. Come in." The minute Lanna entered, Brina told her, "Go over and stand with Allyn and the guards."

Evalle leaned to look past Brina and saw a wall of guards who would surround Brina and protect her to the end if anything got past the doors. After it had gone through Evalle.

A screaming howl like a devil on a killing spree spun Evalle around.

Stomping out of the woods and onto the field came the largest Svart Evalle had seen so far. Had to be twelve feet tall. He wore a rough-cut, brown leather vest and matching pants that stopped at his knees.

Brina said, "Even from here I can see the yellow eyes of a demon. How can a troll be so powerful?"

The demon troll swatted Beladors aside like flies.

A shining Belador sword appeared before Evalle.

She snatched it out of the air, ready to defend this castle. Adrenaline pumped through her, firing up the Alterant beast inside with the urge to fight. Cartilage snapped, lifting a ridge of skin along the top of her forearms. All Beladors could shift their bodies to battle form, but she had to be careful to stop at this point or her Alterant beast would break free.

She'd force her beast to remain caged, but something told Evalle she could not face another demonic troll in this human body and walk away alive. But shifting fully into beast form would break her oath to Macha and dictate Evalle's immediate death.

The battle between Beladors and Svart trolls filtered

out of the forest into the open field. Working together in a place where the Belador power only strengthened, warriors appeared to be gaining on the Svarts.

All except the demonic troll. He picked up speed as he headed toward the castle.

Brina beat her fist against the doorframe. "I hate bein' stuck in here like a glass treasure."

Evalle doubted the sword she held was going to stop that particular Svart. She called out to Trey, *We need the Nyght weapon at the castle.*

Trey answered, *The weapon doesn't work here.*

Ah, crap. *Are you killing Svarts with swords?*

Yes, but not the demonic troll. Nothing kills him. He's crushed two Beladors.

Yellow eyes glowed bright as lightbulbs in the demon Svart as his face came into better view with each thundering step. A female Belador warrior attacked him. He slowed to lift her off the ground and rip her body in half.

Brina shouted, "That vermin is killin' my people! Tzader has to—"

"Don't call him, Brina."

"Why not? He *is* Maistir."

Evalle understood more than Brina realized. The warrior queen thought since Tzader was immortal—something Evalle couldn't admit knowing—that he could handle the troll and survive, but Brina was wrong.

Keeping her eyes on the approaching threat, Evalle pointed out, "You don't want Tzader to link with the Beladors and risk this thing killing everyone with one blow."

"Of course not. That would be mass murder."

Evalle gave Brina a sobering truth, careful not to point out Tzader's immortality. "Even Tzader can't survive if that thing bites off his head."

Brina's fists gripped so hard her knuckles turned white. She said, "We need Macha, but I do not think I can reach her."

"Where is she?"

"At the Tribunal meeting, the one place she cannot hear my call."

That's right. Evalle would have to face Macha soon, and without Tristan, but that wasn't her top concern right this minute.

Brina ran her fingers through her hair, thinking out loud. "The only way to be sendin' a message to her right now is through Sen, but I cannot take him away from Atlanta until we send Beladors back. When Tzader arrived, he told me Sen was dealin' with the last of the Svarts there." She took a breath and said, "I'm guessin' we've about four or five minutes before that troll reaches us."

The unknown female voice that popped into Evalle's mind at the most bizarre times chose that moment to speak again. *Believing is the hardest thing to learn, but believing in yourself should be the easiest to do.*

Evalle shouted inside her mind, *If you're so smart, why don't you tell me who you are?*

She ignored the distraction, focusing instead on the one thing she *could* do. She told Brina, "I can stop that Svart if you'll help me."

"Name it."

Evalle swallowed. "Give me permission to shift fully into my Alterant beast state. Once I kill this Svart, I'll shift back into my human form." When Brina didn't reply, Evalle said, "I can do this . . . if it won't get you in trouble with the Tribunal."

"They have no say over what happens outside the realm of Earth, an' Treoir is not of that world, but I do not think that is a good idea."

"In that case, if you aren't going to give me permission, then take Lanna an' hide somewhere that troll can't find you. I'll hold him off as long as I can."

"Evalle, come with us or he'll kill you."

"I'm a warrior. My duty is to defend Treoir at all costs. You asked me to trust you in the past," Evalle said, her heart slamming her chest as the demon got closer. "I'm asking you to trust me and allow me to shift. If you do, order the Beladors to stay back or Tzader and Quinn will interfere."

No Belador could act against Brina's orders while here on Treoir, even if they wanted to. Storm might try, since he was not of the tribe. Evalle could only hope that Tzader would be able to stop Storm so he didn't die trying to help her.

In the next heartbeat, Brina said, "Evalle Kincaid, I give you permission to shift into your Alterant form. But know that if you do not shift back, Macha will destroy you."

"I understand. Now, please, move to the safest place you can with Lanna . . . in case I don't stop him."

THIRTY-TWO

Evalle drew on the power she held deep inside, calling up her beast. She walked down the steps of Treoir Castle as the change came over her. Power surged from her core, flooding her limbs until bones cracked and altered with her shape. Her clothes shredded away from muscles that bulged and twisted into grotesque shapes.

Her feet burst out of her boots, toes curling with claws.

Pain ricocheted through her head as jawbones popped and cracked, widening to accept the double row of jagged fangs. Scales covered her torso, and coarse black hair hung from her arms and legs.

Even when she reached ten feet in height, the demon troll still towered over her, but Evalle didn't care. She'd either prove her value to the Beladors here and now or die trying.

She flipped the sword over in her hand, holding the blade like a throwing dagger in her thick fingers now that her hands had outgrown the weapon. One strong strike could end this quickly. She threw the sword at the troll's chest.

He shocked her with his agility, spinning around as the sword flew past him and stuck into the ground.

She fisted her hands and threw kinetic blasts at him.

He staggered back a step, howled and kept coming.

She charged him, hoping her momentum would balance out the difference in size. Head down, she slammed him in the middle. He went backward, but her eyes crossed from the power of the hit. Falling forward on top of him, she scrambled off and whipped onto her feet, ready.

The blasted troll was just as quick.

He lunged and swung a fist at her, opening his fingers at the last moment to swipe three sharp claws across her chest. She growled at the slash of agony burning her skin and drove her fist into the troll's jaw.

She kicked him in the crotch.

That should have taken him to his knees, but didn't.

He battled her slug for slug, back and forth, draining her stamina.

She shoved away, backing up several steps as if she retreated.

His eyes glowed a putrid yellow with black diamond centers when he smiled.

You haven't beaten me yet. But he would if this didn't end soon. Blood dripped from the side of her mouth and more flowed from the gouge on her chest. She lifted a hand and waved him forward, taunting him to come at her.

And he did.

She waited until the last possible second, hoping she still possessed reflexes quick enough to dodge. His mouth opened in a snarl, claws reaching for more blood.

She dove down, taking his feet out from under him. Fear of being pinned under his weight gave her a burst of speed to push herself through his legs.

He hit the ground, dropping like a ten-story building.

She shoved up to her feet, swaying, then dove onto his back.

She grabbed his head and twisted.

His neck didn't break. Ah, crap.

He growled, teeth snapping. In a fast move, he bent his arms, pushing himself up off the ground and flipping backward to land with her beneath him.

His brutal weight hit hard on top of her. Ribs cracked. Hers. Excruciating pain blinded her.

She didn't have the strength to draw on her beast to heal.

Power barreled through her.

Tzader and Quinn were linking with her. *No, it's too dangerous.*

New energy pulsed in Evalle's veins, aiding her to keep fighting. But no matter how hard they fed their energy into the link, Tzader and Quinn couldn't send enough power to fuel the body of her beast.

The troll rolled off her and pushed up on his knees. He reached for her throat.

She slammed a fist into his head and then flipped away.

He growled and grabbed a fist of her hair, yanking her back until she could see the fangs in his open mouth.

Reaching her hand out, she used kinetics to call back

the sword that had missed hitting the troll. The cool metal handle slammed into her hand as the troll's jaws came down for her throat. She slashed across his throat.

Green blood spewed over her.

Eyes bulging, the troll hung there suspended for a second until Evalle shoved him to the side where his body twitched and jerked.

The giant finally stopped moving.

Her ribs screamed in pain, but she got to her knees, then her feet, weaving where she stood. As Tzader and Quinn unlinked with her, Evalle's body trembled from the brutal attack. She ached everywhere, except in her heart, where happiness exploded over having protected their warrior queen.

The silence drew Evalle's eyes to the field between her and the forest where Beladors stood among dead trolls and the bodies of fallen Belador warriors.

With the exception of Tzader and Quinn, who had seen her once before in her beast state, mouths gaped open on every other Belador.

Storm was in the grasp of two warriors, as if they'd had to hold him back at one time, but not now. The shock in his eyes tore her insides apart worse than her cracked ribs.

Tears flooded her eyes, but she squeezed them shut, refusing to show her hurt. What had she expected? That they would see past the hideous monster she'd shifted into . . . to the woman who fought to be accepted?

A roar went up among the Beladors, but Evalle had already turned toward the castle.

She found no joy in the cheering, which was nothing more than the cry of victory over an enemy defeated.

The horror in their faces would live in the back of her mind. She'd thought nothing could be worse than being an outcast.

Now the Beladors would see her as something much worse.

A monster.

She lumbered across the soft grass toward the castle, forcing her beast back into her body. By the time she reached the steps, she had her head down to keep the glare of even the minimal light from blinding her.

Lanna stood on the top landing with a robe in one hand and sunglasses in the other, which she stuck under Evalle's nose. "Brina said give this to you."

Brina had to be the reason that troll goo no longer covered Evalle. Sliding the glasses onto her face, Evalle pulled on the dark blue velvet robe trimmed in gold.

"Evalle," Brina called from the doorway.

"Yes." Evalle could barely get the word out past her raw throat. She met Brina's gaze, surprised to see admiration in her warrior queen's eyes.

"I am as proud of you as any warrior I've ever had."

Tears threatened again, but Evalle swallowed them back. "Thank you."

Tzader ran up the steps beside her. "How badly are you hurt, Evalle?"

"Not bad," she lied, feeling the trickle of warm blood running down her chest.

He put his hand on her shoulder. "You saved a lot of

lives, but to protect Brina is . . ." He looked away. "We'll talk later."

Evalle nodded and accepted Tzader's hug, flinching at the pain in her ribs.

Tzader turned on Brina, demanding, "How could you stop me from going to her?"

Evalle held up her hand. "I asked Brina to keep all of you back. If I couldn't kill that troll, then you would have died trying to help me. You're too important to the Beladors to sacrifice yourself, and you're the one who taught me duty comes first."

He scowled at her.

Quinn showed up next, just as ragged and bleeding around the edges as Tzader. He shook his head, saying to Evalle, "I don't know who took more bloody years off my life today, you or Lanna. You two are turning me into an old man."

Lanna hugged Quinn. "You are unharmed, Cousin?"

"I'm fine."

Tzader said to Brina, "I *know* Evalle's hurt worse than she's admitting. I could feel it when we linked and I smell the blood. She needs to heal."

Before Brina said anything, Evalle took a gamble and said to Brina, "I've learned how to heal myself. I can do it once I go home."

Brina looked over at Tzader, who said nothing, which made it appear as though he knew about her ability to heal when he didn't. Evalle would tell him and Quinn about it as soon as she got a chance, but for now Brina seemed to take his silence as approval that Evalle's healing did not involve shifting into her beast. She told Evalle, "I'll be sendin' you back to Atlanta as soon as you are ready."

Quinn added, "You can take Lanna with you, Evalle."

"That's fine." Then Evalle realized she couldn't go. She told Brina, "I can't leave until I talk to Macha. I haven't brought her an Alterant yet, and she gave me a deadline to do so by the time she finished meeting with Dakkar."

Brina held up her finger and looked off into the distance, her eyes unfocused. "She's on her way."

The air brightened and crackled with the introduction of power, then Macha appeared next to Brina. The goddess took one look at the group on the castle landing and said, "What's going on?"

Brina quickly explained what had transpired.

As Macha stared out over the field, her face morphed from appearing imposed upon to deeply concerned. Her hair floated and moved, changing from a deep auburn color to golden-streaked until the locks settled down when her gaze returned to Evalle. "Have you brought me Tristan?"

"No, Goddess."

"Any other Alterants?"

"No."

Tzader cleared his throat as though to speak, but Macha turned one raised eyebrow on him, and that silenced everyone. Then she said to Evalle, "Is it true you shifted into your beast?"

Evalle considered trying to explain, but that had been a yes-or-no question, intended for her to acknowledge what she'd done, because Brina must have told Macha telepathically when she called for the goddess. "Yes, I did."

"Your deadline has arrived for delivering Tristan to me."

"I understand. That's why I waited to see you." And accept whatever penalty Macha imposed. She'd given Evalle and other Alterants a golden opportunity, only to be disappointed.

Macha surveyed the carnage once more, then glanced back at Evalle. "I understand I have you to thank for defeating a demonic Svart troll."

Not sure how to reply to that, Evalle just kept quiet.

"Had that troll harmed Brina, bringing me all the Alterants in the world would not have made up for it. I will allow you more time to complete your task."

Relief was too simple a word for what Evalle felt. The deep breath she took sent pain streaking through her chest from where her ribs had been broken. She hissed and gritted her teeth.

Brina noticed and announced, "I was preparin' to send Evalle back to Atlanta."

Acknowledging her comment with a tilt of her head, Macha said, "Go ahead." She took in Tzader next and stated, "We have outsiders in Treoir."

"If you'll allow me to complete what I have to do out here first, I'll give you a full report about that and the Svart trolls before I leave."

"Do you require my assistance out there?"

Tzader looked over his shoulder, then back at the goddess. "No. Thank you, Goddess. We have this handled."

"Have Brina call me when you're ready to talk." Macha turned to Brina. "Is the castle secure?"

"All is fine now."

Macha vanished.

Evalle would normally wait to return with the team, but she couldn't face Storm. He hadn't come near her since she'd shifted back to her human form. Why would he?

What man would want anything to do with a hideous monster? Storm would never look at her again as a woman after seeing her beast today.

She could suffer any wound except seeing the revulsion he wouldn't be able to hide. But she couldn't leave without asking Tzader, "Will Macha do anything to Storm?"

"No, I'll explain that he helped us. Just go heal yourself." He added, "I need you back to full speed before you return. Take the time you need to *completely* heal."

When Tzader hesitated as though he had something else to say about Storm, Evalle's stomach dropped at the worry coming off Tzader. He had seen her shame before she turned away and would try to fix that, but as Maistir he had enough burden on his shoulders today.

Her smile lacked any power when she told him, "I'll be fine."

"Where do you wish to be sent, Evalle?" Brina asked.

"I need to get back to my motorcycle."

Quinn released a sigh full of frustration. "You're in no shape to ride that thing. I had a car sent for Lanna before we left the building. Take that home and pick up your bike tomorrow. No one can steal your Gixxer or harm it. But give me a minute with Lanna, then you two can go."

Numb to her soul, Evalle didn't argue. She couldn't find the energy to care about anything right now.

She missed Storm already. The desire to turn around and search for him was so strong she shook from it. But she might see more than shock this time. She might see disgust and couldn't face that.

He'd never touch her again.

Quinn pulled Lanna aside, speaking to her in a hushed tone.

Tzader stood next to Evalle, staring at Brina, who moved closer to the very inside edge of the threshold. He'd told Evalle that Brina was duty bound to stay inside the castle to protect the Belador power.

The Belador warrior queen looked miserable, and Tzader not much better. Brina whispered to him, "I feared for your life."

Tzader took a step toward Brina as if her words drew him, but he paused when someone in uniform appeared behind her. A guard. The young man's face tightened with fierce determination over something.

Tzader spoke to the guard. "Where were you, Allyn?"

"Covering her back in case a troll found another way inside the castle. She was *never* out of my sight."

Evalle believed only the three of them were privy to whatever played between Brina, the guard and Tzader.

Cool disdain swept across Tzader's features. He took a step back.

Brina's face fell beneath an onslaught of emotion.

"Tzader?" Her pleading voice sounded like the young woman she should be and not a warrior queen who carried the weight of so many lives on her shoulders.

The harsh line of Tzader's grim mouth softened with tenderness when he said, "I will always stand between you and danger." He turned and walked away.

Lanna grasped Evalle's hand, tugging down to get her attention. "We will go now."

Confused over what had just happened between Tzader and Brina, Evalle just nodded at Lanna and said, "We're ready, Brina."

Caught watching Tzader, Brina shook herself and blinked at Evalle. "What?"

"To go back to Atlanta. You were going to send us."

Brina drew in a shaky breath, then seemed to remember who she was and squared her shoulders. This time, her voice came out crisp and confident. "Envision exactly where you intend to arrive, and if you close your eyes, Evalle, the goin' will not make you so sick."

Why hadn't anyone told me that before? Or would that only work when Brina teleported her?

Evalle nodded and closed her eyes.

She still suffered the sensation of being out of control and swirling around, but she didn't throw up when she and Lanna reached the parking lot behind the old Sears Building. Light seeped along the eastern horizon, but she had enough time for a speed-limit drive home.

Casper appeared out of the dark shadows and strolled up to her with the Nyght weapon hanging in the crook of his arm. He surveyed her clothing and cocked an eyebrow. "Everything okay, Evalle?"

Nothing would ever be okay again, but Casper had been talking about Treoir. "We stopped the Svarts. How about here?"

"Before all of you hauled ass out of here, Quinn told me the Lieutenant troll knew of eleven more in the city. I got 'em all but one," Casper said, sounding like someone who could spin a six-shooter and drop it in his holster. "Sen took care of the last one. He's about done here."

"I don't want to see Sen."

Casper grinned. "Don't blame you, but it's going to be a bit airy riding home unless you've got on something under that robe. Not that I wouldn't enjoy the view when you rode off."

She smiled a little, hoping Casper still wanted to joke with her once he heard about Evalle the Monster. "Quinn sent a car that's supposed to be here somewhere."

"That'd be the sleek black ride sittin' over yonder." Casper waved at someone behind her.

When Evalle shifted around, a black limousine pulled up. The driver jumped out and said, "Miss Lanna?"

Lanna took on the air of a princess. "That is me. There are two of us."

"Absolutely." The chauffeur opened her door, then led Evalle to the other side, where she slid onto the luxurious leather seat next to Lanna.

As soon as the driver climbed in, Lanna said, "Evalle will give you her address."

Evalle had just sat down. "What?"

"Cousin said he must help Tzader and I must go with you to apartment."

Evalle had never allowed anyone inside her underground apartment except Tzader and Quinn, but this girl had done her share to save lives tonight, the twins being two of those. Evalle gave the driver an address *near* her apartment and dropped her head back against the cool leather seat.

When the chauffeur closed the privacy window to the passenger area and drove off, Evalle mumbled, "Thought Quinn wanted you to go to the hotel."

"He said I am safe with you and I am to tell you important thing about when you change into your other self."

Turning her head to Lanna, Evalle said, "I don't want to be rude to you, but the last thing I want to talk about is what happened back in Treoir."

"You are wrong. You must know this."

THIRTY-THREE

I should ha expected Kizira ta put her own plan into play since she shares the blood of both of us. Cathbad stood alongside Flaevynn in front of her scryin' wall, where rare gems glistened and sparkled beneath a shower of cascading water.

He could no fulfill his own plans as long as Kizira remained in the dungeon. Pointing at the images on the wall—the aftermath of the battle between the Beladors and the Svarts on Treoir—Cathbad said, "You're fortunate the female Alterant defeated the demonic troll."

"I never doubted that Evalle would survive a battle with the troll we dipped in Loch Ryve. I'm *fortunate* to have caught Kizira's betrayal now before she could ruin everything."

"Ach, Flaevynn. You're wrong. Kizira did ya a favor."

"How do you possibly see this as such?"

"Kizira told me she intended to gain the location of Treoir an' test the defenses with trolls. She ha planned it as a surprise for ya."

"You really want me to believe that?"

No, but he ha never won a battle from the point of defense. "I do. You compel her. Do ya really think she can get around that?"

Flaevynn shifted her gaze to him, eyes tense with undisclosed thoughts. "Not really."

"Course no. Ya need Kizira. She brought ya Tristan an' his sister. Kizira will deliver the other five Alterants, an' in time." Cathbad would ensure that she did.

Flaevynn floated across her chamber. In her wake, flames surged on hundreds of candles around the room, then died back to normal heights as her energy moved with her. "I can't abide a traitor."

"If that be the case, why does she live?"

Spinning around in a swirl of brilliant colors, Flaevynn cocked her head at him. "You would condemn your precious child to death?"

"No. I but question if ya truly believe she betrayed ya since she still lives."

He'd struck his mark. Flaevynn scowled at him.

Now that he'd stirred doubt, he added, "Ya need the girl to do your biddin', less ya want ta go out there yourself."

She sent him a look that suggested he'd been birthed by a rock.

He gifted her with the smile that ha once put him in her bed. "You an' I can no leave until the day the Alterants win Treoir for us. Until then, we need Kizira."

She smoothed a hand over her hair. Long, black fingernails adorned with diamonds sparked with tiny bolts of energy. "I'll release her *if* you share what you know about the Alterants."

He loved a good victory, especially since he'd been anxious to start pushing Alterants to the next level.

Waitin' until now ha played perfectly into his hands. He would share something, but no everythin'. "'Tis a fair request ya make. First ya must know that the other four *will* seek out Evalle."

"When?"

"That is the part that I will now share with ya. 'Tis said once the female Alterant has the gold aura and shifts into her beast—as she did today—the other four Alterants will seek her out. When that happens, Tristan an' his sister will become important, so do no lose them."

"I don't plan to lose any captive, but what would it matter since Tristan is not one of the five?"

"Open your scryin' wall to the arena an' teleport Tristan there."

Flaevynn considered his request with suspicion but floated over to her wall. When she waved her hands, the massive pit in the tower known as the arena came into view, an' Tristan appeared inside, lookin' around in surprise. He shouted, "Where's my sister, Kizira?"

Blank walls echoed his question back at him.

"Well?" Flaevynn said to Cathbad.

"Ya still have our wyverns we altered with Noirre majik?"

"Of course, and they are *mine*, not ours."

What man ever owned anythin' in a marriage? Cathbad let that go. "Call up the one known as Morvack."

"Why the wimpy one? Some have grown far larger than that one."

"Morvack is fine for what I have in mind. Just do it,

Flaevynn, an' allow Tristan to use his kinetic powers in the arena."

She shrugged and twirled the fingers on one hand. An iron door slid up, and one of the winged creatures Cathbad had begun acquirin' more than three centuries ago came snarlin' into the room. Unlike most dragons, wyvern had only hindquarters at one end of a black, snakelike body, but four massive orange-and-black wings with razor claws at the tip of each vertebra. The tail whipped back and forth, split at the end into two sharp, red spikes loaded with deadly Noirre venom.

Tristan took one look at the wyvern and began ta shift into a beast, growin' taller and thicker with twistin' bones and muscles. His head widened and stretched with jaws that snarled open, a black maw with jagged teeth. Saliva ran from his lips when he roared.

The wyvern flared its wings like an angry vulture, and fire shot from its snout. The black, undulating body twisted and arced back, liftin' a head with black eyes and red diamonds for pupils. Flames shot past the wyvern's two deadly fangs. Its head flared wide as a cobra's and struck with the same speed.

Tristan blocked the strike with his kinetics, then slammed his fist at Morvack, lookin' surprised his power worked, but he did no more than knock the beast sideways. The wyvern flew at Tristan, drivin' the Alterant to the floor and stompin' on his chest.

Flaevynn hissed at Cathbad. "I thought you said we needed Tristan. Why are we letting Morvack kill him?"

"Just watch."

Morvack an' Tristan battled across the arena. Tristan finally knocked the wyvern off its legs an' pinned him with kinetics, then jumped on the wyvern's neck. The wicked tail whipped 'round to stab Tristan's chest, but he grabbed the tail, an' used his power to hold the creature in place. He stomped the wyvern's head 'til it exploded.

Fire danced up the Alterant's leg, singeing his hair.

Tristan roared, his rage echoing around the arena.

Flaevynn sighed and doused Tristan with a wash of water. "That was a waste of a wyvern."

"'Tis no finished yet."

Tristan's back arched. He jerked 'round, moaning, an' fell off the dead beast, rollin' into the middle of the chamber. The Alterant's body began changin' again, elongating as the scales and hair gave way to a smooth gray-blue skin covered with new translucent scales the size of Cathbad's hand. Tristan's neck stretched an' his head shrank, but in proportion to a body that took on a lion's shape with front an' hind legs, all the paws tipped with sharp claws. Wings sprouted from each side of the body, then stretched and widened. Blue and black feathers covered the tops of the wings, but they remained smooth underneath. Predator green eyes shone from within a head shaped like an eagle's, right down to the hooked beak.

When the evolution finished, Flaevynn whispered, "He looks like a . . . dragon, but more regal."

Cathbad chuckled. "'Tis a gryphon."

"I didn't know any still existed."

"No for a long time an' these will soon be ours."

"Mine."

Women. Cathbad let it go. "All Alterants can finish evolvin' ta this state if they battle a wyvern . . . or a gryphon. But we must capture the five Alterants we need ta breach Treoir and finish their evolution here."

Flaevynn eyed Cathbad with irritation. "We only have four more wyverns. We have no choice but to use one with Evalle. Then what will we do about the other four Alterants?"

'Twas just like Flaevynn ta think in terms of *we* when she did no care for the task. Cathbad said, "We need no waste a wyvern on Evalle."

It took Flaevynn a moment, but she caught up to his thinking. She scoffed at him. "If you think to use Tristan as a sacrificial lamb for Evalle to kill so she can reach gryphon state, you'll be disappointed. She won't fight Tristan or his sister. Evalle is nauseating when it comes to caring for others, especially those she calls friends."

Cathbad would no tell Flaevynn exactly what he ha in mind or the alternative. He'd let her think she knew all there was ta know about the evolution. "I am no concerned. Evalle *will* fight Tristan in the arena, an' one will die. I promise you that." This much he knew to be true. "But ya must be able ta bring Evalle back ta us."

"If that's all you need, not a problem. Evalle has this misplaced sense of honor that will force her to come looking for Tristan and his sister. I'll compel Kizira to lay a trail for Evalle that leads to TÅμr Medb."

THIRTY-FOUR

"For the millionth time, I am not going there." Evalle slapped her hand down on the island counter in her kitchen. Why wouldn't Lanna let her enjoy a quiet Sunday night after all she'd been through? "Storm doesn't want to see me. Besides, I have a job to do."

If she knew where to start looking for Tristan, she'd leave now, but the Medb had Tristan . . . if Kizira's warlocks hadn't killed him after he'd teleported Evalle away from the farmhouse. It was going to take some time to find out where he was.

If he still lived.

She hoped so and would start searching tomorrow. If Tzader caught her out walking the streets tonight there'd be hell to pay.

Lanna had showered and changed to a bubble-gum pink sweater and jeans after having swung by the hotel to retrieve her small suitcase. The clothes gave her the appearance of an innocent teenager, but she called herself a sorceress.

Could she actually *be* a sorceress?

Picking up a lug nut, Lanna tossed it to Feenix, who snagged the treat with his tongue, then danced around chortling. Lanna said, "Tzader said you take time off. That was order. I know. I heard."

"That doesn't mean I have to go out to dinner."

"What do I tell Quinn? He does not like you unhappy."

"And that's the only reason he gave you that message for me." Evalle had a moment of excitement when Lanna had first delivered Quinn's message, then reality had set in. Quinn and Tzader had witnessed the looks of shock—and horror—on faces when she shifted into a beast.

Of all people, they would know how deeply that reaction cut her and, of course, want to do what they could to soothe her.

"You call my cousin liar?" Lanna could arrange her face into a seriously mean look for a teen.

"Of course not, it's just that—"

"Oh. Now you have gift to see future?"

"No." Sarcastic little snot.

"You say you like Storm. How can you *know* he does not still like you?"

Evalle shoved a handful of damp hair over her shoulder. Why had she spilled her guts to Lanna on the way home this morning? Because she'd never felt so alone and she'd had no one to talk to but Lanna.

"Cousin said—"

"I know, Lanna. The Belador warriors are proud of me, and Storm wasn't given the chance to speak to me before I left." Evalle would not put Storm on the spot to see her again just to prove Lanna wrong. She'd seen his face. He would still treat her as a friend, but she'd started thinking of him as more than a friend. Much more.

Someone she didn't want to lose.

"Do you not want Storm?"

Just cut me to the bone. "This discussion is over." Besides, Evalle had to focus on finding Tristan and his group. She owed him for helping her escape. She would not leave him to the murdering Medb.

But she would not have Storm's help tracking Tristan this time.

She already missed Storm ranting at her about how Tristan could not be depended upon.

Lanna played patty-cake with Feenix, whose wings fluttered as he hovered in front of Lanna where his hands could reach to hit hers. "I saw way Storm hold you when we teleport. His eyes only for you. Why you let Adrianna win?"

Feeling that strike right through her heart, Evalle opened her mouth to snarl at the brat, hoping to shut her up, then Lanna added, "She is nothing next to you."

Lanna's words cheered Evalle's bruised heart, but that didn't make the words true. "You saw Adrianna at the building. She's beautiful. I will *never* look anything like that woman or say the right things to a man or ooze sexuality the way it drips off her. I can't do it. And now Storm's seen me as a monster."

Lanna cocked her head to the side, black-tipped curls bouncing. "If Storm wanted someone else, he would not look at you as if you are his world. Clothes, makeup and hair . . . same as swords and daggers. Me? I am most excellent with female weapons. I would not let go of man like Storm and leave spoils to Adrianna . . . or any *other* women."

The thought of any other woman touching Storm hurt Evalle's heart. She crossed her arms, refusing to engage any longer with this pint-size spawn of Dr. Phil.

Lanna gave her a sly glance. "If you want to keep women away from your man, you must prepare for battle. Do you not tell me Storm will look for you at night until you show?"

"I'm not going." Evalle couldn't let Lanna talk her into humiliating herself.

"You would let this man wait forever?"

Would Storm wait forever? Hope quivered inside her, but Evalle shut the door on wishful thinking. "He'll realize in a couple days I'm not coming."

"So you agree he waits for you tonight?"

How had Lanna cornered her this way? "Maybe, but that was before—"

"You are not coward when you fight trolls and demons. You risk your life for strangers, but not your heart for man you want?" Lanna stopped smiling and patted Feenix on top of his head. "Storm would fight for you. He fought for your queen . . . for you. He does not deserve same?"

That struck home deeper than everything else Lanna had said.

Storm had come through for Evalle time and again. He'd taught her that a man could touch her without harm. He'd awakened her heart, and she feared the frightened organ would never beat again if he walked away from her forever.

But Lanna was right.

Evalle owed it to Storm to show up and give him a chance to say what he thought. If he wanted only to continue as friends, she'd honor that . . . from a distance. If he wanted nothing else to do with her, she'd accept that even though it would rip her heart in half. "I'll go."

Lanna's eyes lit up with excitement until Evalle said, "Quinn's driver refused to leave, so he can take you to the hotel, then drop me at my bike."

"No. You go nowhere like that. Take Cousin's car to see Storm so you dress nice."

Evalle looked down at her jeans and T-shirt and back up at Lanna. "I don't have dressy clothes."

"Good thing for you I stop at hotel for suitcase."

Evalle now feared what Lanna had in mind, but she feared losing Storm more.

The next thirty minutes became a battle of wills with Lanna determined to put Evalle in a dress with heels. Seriously?

When Lanna declared Evalle ready to leave the apartment, Evalle took one last look in the mirror and decided she'd never be Adrianna.

Lanna fussed at her over how late it was getting to be and how Quinn would be back at the hotel suite by now, playing Evalle's guilty nerves to get her moving.

Quinn's driver dropped Lanna at the hotel first. Before getting out, Lanna leaned over and hugged Evalle, whispering, "Remember. You are like Brasko woman. Too sexy to ignore."

Evalle hugged the brat and waited until Lanna was safely inside the hotel before leaving. Quinn might be in residence, but it was after eleven at night out here on the streets.

When the car pulled up in front of Storm's house, she experienced a moment of cold feet. Two icebergs.

She started second-guessing the blue sweater she'd allowed to be *sparkled*, as Lanna put it. The dress never happened. No way those tiny things that Lanna had offered to share would have fit her, and in the end Lanna admitted that Storm would want Evalle to look like herself, but with sparkles. She'd agreed to the glittery sweater, black jeans and her favorite boots, which felt dressed up compared to her normal look.

Lanna's shoes wouldn't have fit or been worth a dime for fighting even if they had.

Evalle fussed at her hair again, which fell around her shoulders, soft against her collarbone and neck.

Thanking the driver, she dismissed him. If this didn't go well, she'd call telepathically to Quinn or Tzader for a ride. Tzader had sent her a text that everyone had returned home from Treoir. He'd ended the message by reminding her about taking the time to heal.

Since he'd heard Evalle tell Brina that she could heal her physical injuries from the battle, had he been alluding to emotional wounds?

If this didn't go well tonight, she doubted a lifetime would heal this wound.

Regardless of tonight's outcome, she had to start making some decisions about her personal life. She might not be ready for the intimacy she'd seen in Storm's eyes the last time he held her, but she had to take a step forward at some point soon—if he gave her the chance.

Crossing the veranda to Storm's front door, she glanced at his boarded-up picture window. The one he'd crashed through in jaguar form to reach her before Svart trolls killed her.

He deserved a woman worthy of a man like him.

Not a beast.

Taking a deep breath of determination, Evalle knocked on his door and held that breath until it opened.

He stood backlit by firelight flickering deep inside his living room. He'd changed to jeans and a black pullover that only deepened the color of his skin. Freshly washed hair hung around his proud Native American face. He smelled of the night, a dark sensuality. She tried to memorize everything about him in case she never saw him again.

Storm's face went from blank to confused. He stared at her from head to toe.

The brittle silence answered her questions.

She'd been an idiot to come here thinking he'd forgotten what he'd seen twelve hours ago. Longer than that since she'd procrastinated till almost midnight.

He hadn't said a word and she couldn't bear up any longer under his intense scrutiny, but she wouldn't make this difficult for him. "I can see by your silence that you've changed your mind about dinner."

She turned and took a step away.

"Do I get a chance to talk?"

How could she deny him? Besides, she doubted he could say anything that would hurt worse than losing him would. Evalle shifted back around. "Guess that would only be fair."

"I'm angry."

"I know."

"First you kiss Isak."

"I know." But she'd told him that kissing Isak was not the same as kissing Storm. Completely different. When Storm kissed her, the world disappeared. She had nothing else to say to explain what had happened with Isak.

"I did as you wanted at Treoir and went with the team when I wanted to stay with you."

"I know."

"Then I had to watch you fight that demonic troll."

"I know." *You had to watch me turn into a monster.*

"Is 'I know' all you're going to say?"

She'd been wrong. She couldn't go through this and not lose control of her emotions. "No. Yes. I can't do this."

She turned around again to leave and his hands settled on her shoulders. If another man had touched her right now, she'd have hurt him, but with her heart cracking she didn't have the strength to fight. And she'd never harm Storm.

She drew in a raw breath and said, "I have to go."

"No." He wrapped his arms around her as if he

thought she'd go running off. "I've been sitting here for hours getting angrier by the moment."

"I can't help what I am," she whispered.

He made a noise she took as underscoring his aggravation with her. He said, "I *thought* I was angry when I saw Isak kiss you, but that was nothing compared to when you left Treoir without speaking to me first."

"I couldn't face you." There. She'd admitted she was a coward after all.

"Now I realize you left without speaking to me because you thought I wouldn't want you after seeing what you'd shifted into. That didn't matter to me."

Tears threatened to ruin Lanna's hard work on Evalle's mascara. She choked out, "Stop being nice, Storm. I saw the shock on your face when I was in beast form. I don't blame you."

He cursed. "When are you ever going to trust me? I was shocked that you killed the demonic troll. I went insane when Tzader had Beladors pin me down and came close to shifting. Do you have any idea what I was going through watching you almost die, *again*, at the hands of a troll and I couldn't get to you?"

She took his words into her heart and dared to hope. "You really aren't repulsed by what I turned into?"

He swung her around in his arms and brought her close, nose to nose. "You are the most beautiful woman between earth and heaven to me in any form. I don't care what you can turn into . . . as long as you end up in my arms."

A tear slipped out and ran down her face. He'd called

her beautiful. Lanna would probably take credit for that, which Evalle had no problem with. To be thought of as beautiful by Storm, if only for one night, was like all her wishes coming true at once.

He lifted her chin and used his thumb to wipe away her tear. His sexy voice smoked over her. "Know what happens now?"

She smiled, shaking her head.

"My favorite part, where we kiss and make up." Then he kissed her without restraint.

She'd come to realize how carefully Storm handled her, but tonight he opened the gates to his desire, holding her with fierce possession.

Was she ready for everything his kiss offered?

Would she disappoint him if he overwhelmed her?

What if—

He lifted his head and smiled at her. "Stop worrying and start trusting that I'll never hurt you and never ask more than you can give. Can you do that tonight?"

"Yes." She relaxed, willing to trust herself alone with Storm, and looked forward to spending time with him that didn't involve trolls, demons, or teleporting.

That could wait until she convinced him to help her track down Tristan.

Building a unique world with rich details often requires using unusual names and terms. These are sometimes fictional as well as being drawn from actual mythology.

Below is a list of pronunciations.

Asháninka	[ash – AH – neen – kah]
Batuk	[bah – TOOK]
Belador	[BELL – ah – door]
Birnn demon	[beern demon]
Cú Chulainn	[KOO – ku – lin]
Ekkbar	[ECK – bar]
Evalle	[EE – vahl]
Flaevynn	[FLAY – vin]
Gixxer	[JICKS – er]
Kizira	[kuh – ZEER – ah]
Kujoo	[KOO – joe]
Loch Ryve	[lock reeve]
Medb	[MAEVE or MAVE]
Nhivoli	[neh-VO – lee]
Nihar	[NEE – har]
Noirre	[nwar – EH or nwar – A]
Treoir	[TRAY – or]
Tzader	[ZA – der]
Vyan	[VIE – an . . . first part rhymes with BYE]

Turn the page
for a sneak peek of

RISE OF
THE GRYPHON

BOOK 4 IN THE BELADOR SERIES

BY SHERRILYN KENYON
AND DIANNA LOVE

Coming soon from Piatkus

Dependable intel made the difference in either walking away alive from a dangerous situation ... or not.

Evalle Kincaid stared down the rocky slope at bad intel.

She'd dug up one slim lead in forty-eight hours of racing to find Tristan, an Alterant like her, right down to his glowing green eyes. Except he hadn't been gifted with her natural night vision, an ability she'd needed while hiking up this mountain in the middle of the night.

She muttered, "That's no coven meeting."

"No," Storm agreed, his breath puffing white clouds against the chilly October air. He saw just fine, too, with preternatural night vision. "Looks more like a midnight festival for all things strange and dangerous." Coal-black hair grazed his shoulders and blended into his black leather jacket. Soft hair she loved caressing. The coppery skin and sharp angles on his cheeks had been handed down through a mix of Ashaninka and Navajo genes, along with his Skinwalker ability to shift into a deadly black jaguar.

Evalle leaned forward where they hunkered down behind an outcropping of boulders, and searched the area fifty yards away where moonlight cascaded across a valley. At least twenty people—nonhumans—had gathered, and more were coming. "You see any female in that bunch that *might* be a witch?"

Storm shook his head. "Only male human forms so far. Not even sure what some of those things are that have both animal and human parts."

One creature with an eight-foot-long orange lizard body, two sets of human arms, and a vulture's head skulked through the crowd, which parted like the Red Sea in front of him. Most of the beings meandered around a thirty-foot-wide circle created by torches stuck in the ground. A ceremonial circle?

Storm asked, "Think the goddess'll extend your deadline?"

"Again? Not a chance. I was amazed when Macha gave me four more days." That had been two days ago and Evalle had been given that reprieve from losing her freedom *only* because she'd defeated a demon Svart troll before it killed everything in its path.

Opportunities like that didn't come along every day.

Good thing or she'd stay in perpetual traction.

But gaining a couple extra days of freedom from Macha had balanced out getting beaten to a pulp by the Svart. Macha was goddess over all the Beladors, a race of powerful Celtic warriors who protected humans who didn't even know preternatural creatures existed. She'd offered sanctuary in her pantheon to all Alterants who swore fealty to her.

With a catch. Evalle first had to deliver the origin of Alterants, who were part Belador and part unknown. Since Alterants changed from human form into beasts that could kill even powerful beings, Macha wanted that *unknown* part cleared up before giving carte blanche freedom to Alterants.

And Tristan had that information.

But more than that, he'd helped Evalle escape a deadly enemy last week and gotten captured while doing it. She didn't want to think about the hideous ways he might be suffering. Freeing him was her first priority.

All she had to do was find a witch called Imogenia who was rumored to have information on Alterants, Tristan in particular, and the location of TÅµr Medb, home of the Medb Coven of deadly Noirre majik practitioners . . . where Tristan was being held captive.

A sick ball of regret rolled around in Evalle's stomach. She'd left Atlanta two hours ago with Storm to hike up the side of Oakey Mountain in North Georgia. She wouldn't have gambled the time spent coming here if she hadn't trusted the source.

"Damned ghouls," Storm grumbled as if lifting her thoughts, his deep voice ending in a growl. He didn't read minds, but he was a powerful empath.

"Don't blame him. Grady can only repeat what he hears." Evalle shifted on the cold ground to find a comfortable position. She knew Grady's limitations. He was a Nightstalker—just another homeless person who'd died ten years ago on the streets of Atlanta. Now he was her best source of intel. Usually.

"When we do find Tristan, I want ten minutes with him *alone* before you hand him over to Macha." A muscle played in Storm's jaw, the only sign of his frustration.

"I need him *alive*," she reminded Storm, though

she knew he didn't mean to kill Tristan, but those two couldn't stand in the same zip code without the threat of blood being shed. "I need *every* Alterant I can find. As it is, Macha is insulted that none have come forward to accept her offer. I have no idea where I'm going to come up with one other than Tristan."

She released a long breath, disgusted. She'd been so sure this would be the break she needed.

"Grady said *this* was the place?"

"Yes. Imogenia had a meeting in the valley north of Oakey Mountain at the hour between Tuesday and Wednesday."

"How specific was he on this information she has about the Medb?"

"That's where Grady got vague. He said while he was eavesdropping, he started losing his corporeal form, which caused him to miss parts of her conversation. He did get that she mentioned something about Alterants and was going to deliver it to the Medb, plus she mentioned Tristan's name specifically."

"Maybe she's here looking for *more* information she can sell to the Medb."

Evalle considered that possibility. "I just hope she shows up and if she does know anything about other Alterants that I can convince her to trade with me instead of the Medb."

"Think you have enough to outbid them?"

"I don't know. Somebody in Imogenia's Carretta coven wants to take over by using Imogenia as a blood sacrifice. A dark witch should be willing to sell her mother's soul to get that name." She checked the valley again. Something about the gathering sent bony fingers of anxiety clawing up her spine. What was going on? Evalle opened and closed her fisted hands, grumbling, "When we first showed up, I knew this location didn't look like somewhere witches would meet, not in an area this exposed."

"True, but I had hopes."

"You're really wanting that ten minutes with Tristan, huh?" Evalle teased.

He shifted around, using a finger to turn her chin to him. "You've been running on no sleep, little food, and frustration for the past two days straight trying to find *one* lead on Tristan. This is *it*, and digging up this tip was tough. I want to get that witch's information *tonight* and find Tristan as much as you do."

"Really? But—" She caught herself. *Why am I questioning him?* Storm couldn't lie without enduring pain, a downside of the gift he possessed that allowed him to discern immediately if someone *else* lied.

He chuckled darkly. "Don't misunderstand me. I still don't give a rat's ass about Tristan. He can rot in hell for all the times he's let you down, but if there's a chance that Imogenia does have *any* information on Alterants, we can't leave until we know for sure she's not here."

"Agreed." Between the frigid air and being immobile, she was losing feeling in her legs and butt. "Being still would be easier if it wasn't so freakin' cold up here."

"This isn't cold. You'd like it if you were doing something fun like camping or hiking."

"No way," she grumbled. "Anyone who'd hike up a mountain in the winter for fun would go to hell for a picnic."

"It's not even winter yet." He tugged her around onto

her knees and snaked an arm inside her jacket, pulling her to him.

She snuggled up close, welcoming the heat that surged off his powerful body. The man was a natural furnace and smelled like the outdoors and . . . male. Very male. He cupped her face and kissed her as if he had every right to do so.

As far as she was concerned, he did.

His lips played with hers, teasing, inviting her to do things her body wanted to go all in on. Her heart kept yammering at her to take that leap with Storm. Make a decision.

But her mind had not climbed on board with her heart yet.

He had more patience than a man should need. And to be honest, she was sick of letting her past rule her future. But she had good reason to hesitate, even though she knew Storm would be an amazing lover. Her worry stemmed from fear of losing control, which might end with her killing him.

A very realistic fear for an Alterant like her.

His fingers curled around her neck, softly massaging her tight muscles as he kissed her ear and chin. "Stop stressing over the small stuff, sweetheart."

His endearment spawned a silky swirl of heat in her stomach, as if he'd planted it there with his kiss.

When he pulled away, he dropped his forehead against hers, his deep voice rumbling against her skin. "I miss having you wrapped against me in front of my fireplace. I want you back, and rested. I'm getting damned tired of sharing you to help a renegade Alterant, but I'll do this to get Macha off your back. And when we find

Tristan *this* time, he *is* coming in to meet with Macha, even if I have to drag his miserable carcass all the way there."

That sounded more like the Storm who'd clashed with Tristan since their first encounter. To be fair, Storm only told the truth . . . if you looked at Tristan's past actions in strictly black-and-white terms.

But her job often required dealing with the gray areas in between.

Such as right now, when everything about this situation had taken an unexpected turn. From the looks of that group below, this had trouble written all over it with blood for ink. She'd asked Storm to come only to use his exceptional tracking skills to follow Imogenia once the coven meeting ended, not to put his life at risk to help someone he barely tolerated.

How was it right for her to always accept the comfort and support he offered when she couldn't even meet this man halfway to the bedroom?

A place *any* woman would rush to for someone as considerate, attractive and sexual as Storm. Raw masculinity that women ogled everywhere they went.

Like I'm doing right now. Mind back on business.

She broke the contact, twisting around to scan the growing crowd in the valley. He did too, but not before a light stroke of his fingers across her shoulder.

If Imogenia did show up, Evalle would not let the witch walk away without telling her how to find Tristan.

Storm tensed, leaning forward. "*That's* got to be her."

Evalle searched the odd mix of figures milling around for someone who matched the description and zeroed in when she found her. Torchlight reflected off a gold mask that adorned the face of a medium-height woman with white hair. Not silver, not blond, but white curls that fell past her shoulders. "At least the description I was given appears to be sound. But what has she got chained that's standing next to her?"

"I'm thinking demon with its head covered and the metal collar, but I don't understand why a witch would need to chain something if she has it under her control?"

Evalle fingered the top of her boot where she kept her dagger, the one with a spell on the blade she'd used more than once to kill a demon. "Does seem odd since he—it—whatever, looks puny. He can't be six feet tall, and a skinny sucker the way his clothes hang off his body. Think he's a sacrifice?"

"No." Storm rocked back on his heels, the movement hidden from the gathering below by the rocks they hid behind. "I need to stretch." In one fluid move, he was on his feet, offering her a hand that she took. He walked backward, drawing her into dark shadows created by a stand of pine trees. "This changes the plan from observe and track."

"Why? We can still wait for her to leave and follow her."

"That was when we thought this was a group of witches getting together. Imogenia has been impossible to find up to this point and—" He paused, nodding toward the bright pocket of torchlight and the strange group below them. "That's not a meeting of her coven, people she'd trust. With that many dangerous beings in one place, she probably has a way to disappear once she leaves so that no one can track her. Maybe not even me."

That was saying something. Storm had tracked Evalle to South America when no one could find her. With the exception of someone who'd teleported, he could follow a majik trail across the globe.

Evalle assessed the scene again. "And you don't think this is some sort of sacrificial ceremony?"

"No."

"Then what's your guess?"

"Don't need to guess. I *know* what's going on." Storm leaned forward against a tree, stretching his calves.

"You do?" She would have been glad to hear his decisive answer if not for her empathic sense picking up on a sudden shift in Storm's calm demeanor to one of tense anticipation, as if he expected trouble. "Why didn't you say so earlier?"

"Because I didn't figure it out until just now. Take a look."

She flicked another quick glance down the slope and did a double take. Two males with humanlike bodies had entered the circle of torches. One had skin that was a putrid shade of green. He wore nothing but a sheath of gray material wrapped as a groin cover and he sported a tail that dragged the ground. His shorter opponent's camo-green vest and brown pants were pulled tight over a squat bodybuilder physique bulging with muscles. He was the most human-looking of the two with his scraggly brown hair, except for the two short horns sticking out the top of his head.

Well, that and red glowing eyes she could see from this distance.

"Demons," Storm said, without any question, and she agreed.

The two demons circled each other, bodies hunched forward, arms raised, ready for attack.

She shoved her hands in the pockets of her jacket. "What are they doing?"

"Fighting."

"Why?"

"It's a Beast Club."

Her face must have shown her confusion when she looked at Storm to see if he was serious.

He explained, "Think illegal fight club, but with non-humans."

Now it all started to fit. People were crowded around the ring, already shouting like she'd seen on television when humans wrestled or boxed. "I've never heard of a Beast Club. How do you know what it is?"

"They had them in South America. The only way you found out was by being a sponsor . . . or a fighter."

She wanted to ask more about when he'd lived there, but not right this minute.

The hurling scream of something in mortal pain echoed across the mountains.

Evalle snapped around in time to see the green-skinned demon rip the head off the one in camo, silencing his opponent. She hadn't expected the big guy to lose—at least not so quickly.

Rubbing her neck muscles, she struggled to come up with a new plan. "I have to inform VIPER."

"You contact them and they're going to order you to sit tight and wait for them to raid this. If by some small chance that valley is owned by a person with diplomatic immunity from VIPER operations, the owner is technically within his or her rights to host the fight. By the time VIPER finishes busting up the party, your witch will be gone."

As an agent with VIPER, a coalition of powerful beings who protected the world from supernatural predators, Evalle would be in trouble if this did turn out to be an illegal operation and VIPER found out she knew about it, but failed to report it.

Caught between her responsibilities to VIPER, her promise to bring Tristan in to Macha, and her commitment to the Beladors, Evalle knew her duty to the Beladors and Macha came first, which meant saving her own hide came last, as usual.

But that still didn't solve her problem of talking to the witch if they couldn't track her. "Crap. What's the possibility of getting to Imogenia now?"

"Pretty good, actually. If she's got a fighter entered, she can't leave until her demon, or whatever it is, fights."

"Then we need to get to her soon, but how?"

"That part's easy. We just walk in."

She didn't like the I-already-have-a-plan-in-mind sound of that. "They aren't going to notice a couple of uninvited people?"

"You don't need a formal invitation to a Beast fight like that one. All you have to do is"—he paused, locking his hands behind his head and twisting, stretching his shoulders and chest—"show up with a fighter and you're in."

Grace be to Macha. She figured out what he was proposing. "No. I watched you almost die once. I'm not going through that again."

He dropped his arms and stepped close, pulling her against his chest, and whispered into her ear. "I don't know why there's a Beast Club in North America, but now that I do and that witch is involved, I know better than to risk leaving here and you hunting for her later without .me. I'm going down there to find Imogenia *now*. You can be my sponsor or you can wait up here."